MATERIAL NATION

Material Nation

A CONSUMER'S HISTORY OF MODERN ITALY

EMANUELA SCARPELLINI

Translated by Daphne Hughes and Andrew Newton

OXFORD
UNIVERSITY PRESS

OXFORD
UNIVERSITY PRESS

Great Clarendon Street, Oxford OX2 6DP

Oxford University Press is a department of the University of Oxford.
It furthers the University's objective of excellence in research, scholarship,
and education by publishing worldwide in

Oxford New York

Auckland Cape Town Dar es Salaam Hong Kong Karachi
Kuala Lumpur Madrid Melbourne Mexico City Nairobi
New Delhi Shanghai Taipei Toronto

With offices in

Argentina Austria Brazil Chile Czech Republic France Greece
Guatemala Hungary Italy Japan Poland Portugal Singapore
South Korea Switzerland Thailand Turkey Ukraine Vietnam

Oxford is a registered trade mark of Oxford University Press
in the UK and in certain other countries

Published in the United States
by Oxford University Press Inc., New York

Published by Oxford University Press by arrangement with Marco Vivegani Agenzia Litteraria
First published in Italian as *L'Italia dei consumi: dalla belle époque al nuovo millennio*

This edition first published 2011

British Library Cataloguing in Publication Data

Data available

Library of Congress Cataloging in Publication Data

Data available

Typeset by SPI Publisher Services, Pondicherry, India
Printed in Great Britain
on acid-free paper by
MPG Books Group, Bodmin and King's Lynn

ISBN 978–0–19–958957–9

3 5 7 9 10 8 6 4

This book is dedicated to my parents,
Irma and Alberto, with deep affection

Preface

In a classic anthropology text Peter Worsley tells us about the cargo cult. The native Melanesian population, watching the steamships of the white colonists laden with consumer goods (rice, flour, tobacco, radio sets), constructed a famous myth. Those big ships had actually been sent by their ancestors, but had been treacherously seized by the whites who had then forced the natives to serve them and remain poverty stricken. But the day would come when the ancestral spirits would return with the cargo, restoring justice and giving rise to an era of abundance and happiness. Everybody would be showered with riches. The dead would rise again and the whites would be punished by being drowned in the deluge or reduced to servitude.[1]

This myth has been used by scholars to explain the effects of culture contamination and the spread of messianic beliefs, but we can also read it in another way: consumer goods have appeared to the eyes of outsiders as the most conspicuous—even most desirable—sign of modern western civilization.

It may seem strange that such an obvious aspect, and one which we now consider so pervasive in our society, should have received relatively little attention from historians; or at least not been considered as a separate category worth including as part of the narrative of modern history, which is the very proposal this book will put forward. I will talk about consumption as a central element in the Italian nation's affairs from the earliest times of the unification, through Fascism (when it entered into the Italianization policy of the regime) and even in the Republican decades following the Second World War. The thesis put forward here is that it has always played an important role and that this importance has grown even greater with time, becoming a matter of public debate. The material culture linked to consumption has proved capable of giving structure to society, marking the boundaries of class, gender, generation, and regional differences. It has been reflected in the world of art and literature; it has been an integral part of economic

[1] P. Worsley, *La tromba suonerà. I culti millenaristici della Melanesia* (1957), Turin: Einaudi (1961).

production processes, as well as the commercial world. Finally, it has inspired government policies. It is therefore a cultural construct that has enables us to observe the evolution of Italy from an unusual angle, and to discover previously unknown and possibly surprising character-istics.

Writing a history of consumption that unravels parallel to the great narratives of cultural, economic, and social history presents many problems, beginning with the simplest but most basic one: how to define consumption. It could be restricted to the uses of certain goods or could fan out to include practically everything. I have decided to concentrate chiefly on material goods, and to some extent on non-material items and services as long as they are actually at the heart of everyday life. The other important choice was to avoid limiting our attention to the last stage, that is to say to the moments of acquiring and 'disposing of' the goods, but to try to reconstruct the complete cycle, which starts well before in the social and cultural sphere, materializes in the field of economic production and finds its way to the commercial world (indeed, market dynamics and sales places will be given promi-nence in my reconstruction). All this has a telling impact on the political level. Another argument put forward in this book is that consumption is always omnipresent in government policies, though with a weight and emphasis that varies according to the time. For this reason I have viewed the evidence through an interdisciplinary lens, in an attempt to recreate the multiplicity of facets in consumer practice. Such a task of synthesis in a young, largely unexplored area may appear to be ambi-tious (if not a little foolhardy), but in this case it arises from a need that has matured after several years of study in the field, together with the appearance of some significant publications in Italy and elsewhere: that is the need for an overall frame of reference in which pieces of original research can be inserted. Whatever the final result, if it succeeds in attracting the attention of scholars and readers to this branch of study, it will have completely accomplished its aim.

To return to mythology, the story of our Melanesians is a reminder to us of other things as well, starting with the importance of the geograph-ical dimension. Italy has always been among a restricted group of countries rich in goods and assets (it was among the top ten in 1860). One could object that the level of development and affluence does not automatically reflect the level of consumption. This is undeniable, but it is certainly an important indicator, as the inhabitants of Papua New Guinea (descendents of the cargo worshippers) well know. Their per capita income is ten times smaller than that of present-day Italians and they live in a country where over 40 per cent of the population exists on less than a dollar a day. In their eyes the distance separating the whites loaded with goods and the natives watching from the beach has not changed that much. And facts confirm this impression, the gap between rich and poor countries having progressively widened with time.[2] The premise is necessary in order to make one point clear: this book discusses the great changes that have come about for Italian consumers over more than a century, but it must never be forgotten that such transformations have taken place in a very precise geographical and cultural area with its own dynamics of development, not necessarily shared by the rest of the world. In particular the Italian experience cannot be understood outside first the European context and then the Euro-American one. This takes us back to a second element, which is the strongly transnational character of the consumer world: goods change places, technology circulates, sales places and models become international, people (the consumers) move around. Even if the focus in this book is on Italy, consuming often means travelling in a greater dimension, perhaps without being aware of it (to paraphrase John Donne, no country is an island, entire of itself; every country is a piece of the continent, a part of the main).

One last point concerns periodization.[3] The question is this: can we talk about an actual consumer revolution that is so widespread and has made such an impact that it can be compared to the industrial one? If so, when did it take place? The first suggestion would be to place it in the late 19th, and early 20th centuries, when the effects of the industrial revolution were self-evident: mass production, the creation of huge markets, modern transport, the spread of new sales structures like department stores, and so on. Other scholars, especially in northern Europe, are convinced that the birth of a modern awareness among consumers goes back further—to the 17th-century Netherlands or at least 18th-century England (with the spread of 'colonial' products such

---

[2] P. Bairoch, '*International Industrialization Levels from 1750 to 1980*', The Journal of European Economic History, 11, 2, autumn (1982), tables 2, 10 (pp. 275, 296).

[3] P. N. Stearns, *Stages of consumerism: recent work on the issue of periodization*, The Journal of Modern History, 69, 1, March 1997, 102–17; P. Capuzzo, *Culture del consumo*, Bologna: il Mulino (2006). 7–8.

as tea, coffee, tobacco, cocoa, and sugar giving rise to new forms of socializing)—and that it is not just a question of material culture: a new hedonistic sensibility is seen to have emerged in England and Germany with Protestantism (reflecting what had happened with the spirit of capitalism according to Max Weber). Another theory claims that it is not possible to talk of a consumer revolution until the 1950s and '60s. Was that not the first time that all levels of society—even the poorest—were earning enough to buy material goods, when there was an explosion of advertising, commercial centres multiplied, and consumption took on a central (possibly irreplaceable) role in social life and the formation of individual identity? Who can be said to be right?

There is no easy answer. A great deal more research may be needed before we can fully understand the dynamics of the phenomenon (especially where Italy is concerned). Perhaps it depends on what we mean by 'consumer' revolution. If we want to adopt a really long-term view it will be necessary to go even further back in time, probably to the Renaissance. Not only does the 17–18th century bracket have little sense for Italy, left as she was outside the mainstream of the great European commercial currents and early stages of the Industrial Revolution, whereas the birth of certain consumer practices and a new cultural evaluation of material luxuries had probably begun already in the Renaissance courts. Alternatively we could select a relatively shorter perspective capable of catching each change and viewing it in relation to the different spheres of society, economics, and politics (perhaps parallel to the processes that have led to the formation of the unified state). That last is the choice I have made, since it seems to stress not so much a unique, unrepeatable moment when consumption exploded once and for all, but a meaningful series of stages between the end of the 19th and beginning of the 21st century. Like a unifying thread, consumption has accompanied all the nation's experiences, helping to create an identity and give a common language to the Italian people.

This book has benefited from so many conversations with friends and colleagues in Italy and elsewhere that to acknowledge them all would be impossible, but I must write a few lines. My first thanks go to Enrico Decleva who has always supported and encouraged this project and given precious advice, especially in the final draft.

This work stems from research over many years in which I have been aided by illustrious institutions. The first, chronologically, was the

Rockefeller Archive Center at Sleepy Hollow, NY where I found material on the birth of supermarkets in Italy. Stanford University and the Departments of History and of French and Italian in particular invited me to teach and study on several occasions; I am especially grateful to Norman N. Naimark, Amir Weiner, and Jeffrey T. Schnapp for their unfailingly generous support. I shall not forget, either, the time I was allowed to spend with Bing Overseas Studies at Stanford in Florence. In 2005 and 2008 the Hagley Center for the History of Business, Technology and Society awarded me a research grant to consult their copious archives; special thanks to Philip Scranton and above all Roger Horowitz who made a fundamental contribution to the research by his skills and generous help. In 2006 I attained the Fulbright Chair at the BMW Center for German and European Studies, at Georgetown University, Washington, D.C. That too was a seminal experience which enabled me to gather materials and exchange notes with important scholars, first among them Richard F. Kuisel. I thank Victoria de Gratia for our stimulating conversations. I must also gratefully acknowledge a host of Italian institutions: state archives, Chamber of Commerce archives, university and public libraries, collections of audio-visual and photographic materials (like the Alinari in Florence), and others besides. To all, my heartfelt thanks.

Last but not least, I thank Paolo for his unstinting and affectionate support.

E. S.

Contents

List of Tables   xv

Part I. Liberal Italy

1. Italian Society from Unification to the Belle Époque   3
   Country of a thousand faces   3
   Peasants   8
   Industrial workers   14
   Middle classes   25
   Aristocracy   35
2. The State and Public Consumption   47
3. The World of Production   56
4. Commercial Spaces   67
   Markets and shops   71
   Department stores: a European model?   75

Part II. Fascism

5. The Regime   83
   Autarchy, gender, race   85
   Emigration   90
   Fascist consumption policy   92
   Collective consumption   98
6. Daily Life during Fascism   105
   Home   106
   Transport   114
   Popular department stores   117

Part III. The Economic Miracle

7. Society during the Golden Age of Capitalism   125
   The consumer revolution   125
   Immigrants   135
   Women (and men)   145
   Young people   165
8. Politics, Culture, and Welfare State   176
9. Advertising and Production   191
10. Large-scale Distribution and 'American' Supermarkets   209
    Supermarkets   209

Part IV. The Affluent Society

11. Impact of the Consumer Society   225
    From the 1970s to the new millennium: light and shade   225
    Politics and consumerism   242
    New products   244
    The limits and costs of consumption   250
12. Contemporary Everyday Life   255
    Fashion and the body   255
    Private and public space   259
    The new commercial places   263

Notes   271
Index   333

List of Tables

Table 1   Consumption per inhabitant for some types
           of food, 1861–1985   5

Table 2   Private Consumption supply, selected years (%)   60

Table 3   Public and private consumption, 1861–1985   93

Table 4   Average annual consumer prices for some
           products and services, 1861–1985   110

Table 5   Domestic private consumption by groups of
           commodities, 1861–1985   132

Table 6   Cultural and tourism consumption, 1861–1985   160

Table 7   Traditional commerce and large-scale distribution,
           1956–2006   211

Table 8   Consumption in Italy and Great Britain, years
           1900 and 2000   228

Table 9   Average Italian monthly family expenditure,
           1986–2005   236

Table 10   Consumption in Europe, 1995 and 2005 (%)   238

PART I

Liberal Italy

1

Italian Society from Unification to the Belle Époque

Country of a thousand faces

It is futile to argue whether today's colossal industrial enterprises are a good or a bad thing: they merely indicate the state of industry at the present time. Generated outside Italy, they came on that society like enormous monsters, threatening to swallow up national industries. Any attempts at defend with antiquated little firms was like going out to fight with blunderbusses and pitchforks against repeating rifles [. . .]. In this non-belligerent war fought with weapons consisting of sales catalogue figures, the Bocconi brothers have always been in the front line, advancing year after year since 1865—when their House was founded—acquiring a province here, firming up a conquest there, foraging further and further forward.

To understand the essence of Bocconi House you must go up to the third floor of what used to be the *Hotel Confortable*. It is like entering an enormous government department. For almost 300 yards a long corridor snakes between the four walls of the building and as you proceed you see nothing but glass doors of offices full of clerks driven by the relentless, frenetic pace of their work. Departmental sections with department heads, division heads, section heads, general accountants, branch accountants, large-scale delivery agents, general inspectors, managers, sub-managers—in all a staff of over 300 [. . .]. As for the sumptuous Milanese emporium *Aux Villes d'Italie* that took over from the *Hotel Confortable*, who hasn't heard of it? Does anyone come to Milan without visiting this shop, unparalleled as it is in Italy and without compare outside of Paris? Who has not spent a pleasant hour browsing on the ground floor, the mezzanines and first floor, admiring the orderliness, good taste, wealth and abundance of the merchandise on display? Who has not seen the splendid neo-Gothic hall that is the envy of the Parisian *Magasins*? And the marvellous range of goods, from 8-lira to 400-lira dress, from humble tea towel to splendid Flanders table cloth, from 80-cent mats to d'Aubusson carpets costing thousands, from 5-cent box of matches to furniture for an entire bedroom. What variety in every area![1]

If the years from 1870 to 1913 have been called the age of the 'great transformation', referring to changes wrought by the industrial revolution, a first glance at Italy as a whole reveals a country, admittedly in the process of change, but only slowly. From 1870, when the per capita income of a population of 26,800,000 people was $1,499 per year (a quarter below the average Western European rate), it increased to $1,785 by 1900 and $2,564 by 1913. In comparison with the start of the century there was some progress therefore, but the figures remained far below those of Northern Europeans (an Englishman, for example, could expect more than double the income of an Italian).[2] It is hard of course to give an exact value to these figures, but we do know that below a certain threshold—about $1,000 in 1913—consumer choices are much reduced, since almost the entire amount goes on basic needs, which does not remove the fact that such choices can contain wide disparities due, for example, to territorial factors—very important in the Italian case—or to traditional divides, such as differences between town and country.

I would also like to draw attention to another important factor, not always duly considered where consumption is concerned, and that is demography. The 19th century saw the end of the *ancien régime*, characterized by high birth and high mortality rates, and the introduction of a new one, typical of today's advanced countries, characterized by low birth rates and longer life expectancy. In Italy the death rate fell rapidly between 1870 and 1913 (from 30 to 19 per thousand inhabitants), while the birth rate came down slowly (from 37 to 32). The average lifespan rose from 35 years in 1880 (having long been around the 30 to 32 mark) to 43 years by 1900 and 47 by 1910.[3] As a consequence there was a sharp increase in population density and readjustment in relative age groups. The reasons for this are many and interdependent, linked not only to the industrial revolution and agricultural progress, but also to sociocultural factors as well as the advance of technical and scientific knowledge. The burgeoning demographic pressure thus broke traditional bonds for good, spurring on waves of migration to the new industrial centres or emigration to foreign parts. This in its turn upset traditional consumption patterns that in many cases had not changed for centuries, favouring the adoption of new ones. What is more, as Massimo Livi Bacci has pointed out, the modern ongoing demographic

Table 1 Consumption per inhabitant for some types of food, 1861–1985 (annual average, kilograms)

Years	Cereals				Fruit and vegetables							
	Wheat	Maize	Rice	Barley and Rye	Potatoes	Dried Legumes	Fresh Legumes	Tomatoes	Greens	Fresh Fruit	Citrus Fruit	Dried Fruit
1861–70	127.7	37.1	10.0	5.6	24.4	11.4	1.6	9.6	31.3	14.5	7.0	35.6
1871–80	127.9	50.4	14.5	5.5	25.8	13.5	2.3	10.7	34.0	18.0	8.8	33.1
1881–90	110.0	33.0	11.4	4.1	22.3	10.8	2.5	12.8	34.6	21.3	10.1	26.6
1891–900	109.9	30.6	8.4	3.8	20.5	10.5	3.0	16.9	40.2	21.3	8.3	25.2
1901–10	146.9	32.8	13.3	4.9	34.0	13.7	2.7	18.1	43.8	25.2	11.2	30.8
1911–20	154.9	27.9	15.1	4.6	25.7	13.9	2.5	20.6	58.7	30.6	14.2	24.9
1921–30	180.3	31.4	10.4	4.3	30.1	12.0	3.0	20.8	70.9	30.8	9.8	19.6
1931–40	165.4	31.2	12.2	4.3	38.1	12.2	4.3	15.9	57.7	26.4	10.2	13.0
1941–50	139.1	19.1	10.9	4.2	34.3	5.3	5.1	17.6	60.8	30.5	9.5	9.8
1951–60	159.3	9.4	8.9	3.9	38.4	5.3	8.9	20.2	61.7	52.6	11.4	10.1
1961–70	166.2	5.7	7.2	2.2	44.7	5.4	9.4	37.1	90.4	86.6	22.7	11.9
1971–80	173.7	–	6.3	–	41.6	4.1	11.0	44.3	93.5	76.3	34.8	7.1
1981–85	165.2	–	6.7	–	42.6	3.7	12.3	53.1	93.3	78.2	37.0	7.0

Years	Meat				Fish		Dairy products		
	Beef & Veal	Pork	Goat, Lamb and Mutton	Other	Fresh	Dried & Preserved	Eggs	Milk	Cheese
1861–70	3.7	3.9	1.6	3.5	1.5	0.9	6.8	24.3	1.3
1871–80	4.8	4.8	1.8	3.6	1.7	1.3	6.5	26.6	2.3
1881–90	5.9	5.5	2.1	3.5	2.2	1.4	5.7	31.5	3.1
1891–900	6.0	5.1	1.7	3.0	2.6	1.5	4.9	31.9	2.9

(Continued)

Table 1 Continued

Years	Meat				Fish		Dairy products		
	Beef & Veal	Pork	Goat, Lamb and Mutton	Other	Fresh	Dried & Preserved	Eggs	Milk	Cheese
1901–10	5.7	4.4	1.4	3.1	2.5	1.1	5.1	34.0	3.5
1911–20	7.7	5.4	1.5	3.7	2.3	1.4	6.3	32.5	4.2
1921–30	9.8	5.3	1.4	4.2	3.1	2.3	6.5	35.5	4.4
1931–40	9.0	5.3	1.2	4.9	4.0	2.0	7.2	38.1	5.1
1941–50	5.3	3.4	0.9	4.0	2.9	1.3	5.1	36.2	4.4
1951–60	9.1	5.8	0.9	6.0	4.9	2.4	7.6	54.2	7.8
1961–70	19.6	8.1	0.9	13.9	6.7	2.6	9.6	64.4	9.3
1971–80	24.2	16.0	1.2	23.1	7.6	2.0	11.4	75.9	12.3
1981–85	25.2	22.5	1.4	26.7	9.6	2.2	11.6	84.3	15.3

Years	Fats and Oils				Sugar/ Coffee			Alcoholic drinks (litres)			*Daily Calories (number)*
	Olive oil	Seed oil	Butter	Suet & Lard	Sugar	Coffee	Chicory	Wine	Beer	Absolute alcohol (pure)	
1861–70	6.9	–	0.3	2.7	2.2	0.4	–	83.9	0.2	0.4	2,628
1871–80	8.3	–	0.5	3.5	2.6	0.4	0.1	90.4	0.4	0.4	2,647
1881–90	5.2	0.6	0.6	4.0	2.7	0.5	0.1	95.4	0.7	0.8	2,197
1891–900	5.4	0.6	0.7	3.6	2.4	0.4	0.1	89.2	0.5	0.5	2,119
1901–10	5.4	1.0	0.8	3.2	3.3	0.6	0.2	119.6	1.1	0.5	2,817

1911–20	4.5	1.0	1.1	3.9	4.6	1.0	0.1	112.1	2.0	0.5	2,694
1921–30	6.6	2.1	1.1	3.8	7.9	1.2	0.2	112.7	3.3	0.6	2,834
1931–40	5.9	1.6	1.2	3.7	7.5	0.8	0.2	88.2	1.3	0.2	2,641
1941–50	3.9	0.6	1.0	2.4	7.7	0.4	0.3	74.8	1.7	0.4	2,171
1951–60	6.2	3.2	1.5	1.4	16.7	1.5	0.3	100.6	3.7	0.9	2,418
1961–70	9.6	6.9	1.8	1.6	25.0	2.5	0.3	110.5	9.2	1.5	2,897
1971–80	11.1	10.2	2.1	2.3	29.4	3.4	–	102.1	14.3	–	3,259
1981–85	10.7	10.5	2.2	3.2	28.7	4.2	–	92.0	19.9	–	3,190

Source: elaborations on ISTAT, *Sommario di statistiche storiche dell'Italia 1861–1975*. Rome, (1976); Ibid., (*Sommario di statistiche storiche dell'Italia 1926–1985*). Rome 1986.

N. B. Statistical records greatly change over a long period of time, both because of changes in data collection methods, and also through changes of the very objects being studied; data presented here and in following tables try to give the most complete picture of consumption in Italy from Unification to the present.

regime gives the individual more choice. Thanks to many factors—
longer and richer life expectancy, greater mobility, the possibility of
choice where reproduction is concerned and a smaller proportion
of time and resources taken up by childcare (the main, if not only
occupation of women in the past)[4]—it is now possible to plan one's
future to an extent that used to be unthinkable. In short, there is a more
individualized, more autonomous lifestyle, greater freedom (within the
limits afforded by society) and, accordingly, more scope for consumer
choice than has ever been seen before.

What exactly did people consume in the early 20th century? Generally speaking, it is known that where private consumption was
concerned food represented the biggest item on the budget, accounting
for 60 per cent of domestic expenditure in the Giolitti period, and on
the increase. In 1900, for example, it accounted for 40,003 million lire
out of 60,650. Energy and house expenses (8,457 million), clothing
(5,322), transport (667) and everything else (6,201)[5] trailed far behind.
Yet all this money spent on food did not necessarily indicate a rich
and varied diet. Nevertheless, in 1900, every single inhabitant in the
kingdom consumed 123 kilos of wheat, 11 of rice, 25 of potatoes, 16 of
vegetables, 21 of tomatoes, but only 16 kilos of meat (six of them beef)
and four of fresh or preserved fish. Few condiments or fats were
consumed, likewise little cheese or optional additions like sugar or
coffee, with the great exception of wine (100 litres a year) (see Table 1).[6]

Moving from the macro- to the micro-level, that is to families and
individuals, the picture becomes visibly more complicated, and for two
reasons. In the first place, life varied greatly from region to region
because of geographical and historical differences. Secondly, differences in social class (inequality of income and sociocultural conven-
tions) created enormous disparities.

Peasants

Most country people were employed in agriculture, which is reckoned
to have occupied 62 per cent of the active population in 1911.[7]

Living conditions in the country were harsh. Incomes were small and
almost entirely swallowed up by three basic needs: food, shelter, and
clothing. The family budget records that we have access to paint a
desolate picture. For example, in 1890 a farm worker from Ravenna
earned 586 lira and spent 73 per cent on food (half on cereals and only

2 per cent on meat or fish), 17 per cent on the home (of this, 7 per cent for rent), 8 per cent on clothes and 1 per cent on all the rest.[8] An Abruzzi peasant earned less, and spent 83 per cent on food, 12 per cent on rent, 5 per cent on clothes, with nothing left over for anything else. A farm worker from Reggio Emilia fared better, with double the income, divided up expense-wise as 66 per cent on food, 9 per cent on the home, 13 per cent on clothes and 12 per cent for miscellaneous expenses (even leaving him with some savings, whereas many other budgets can be seen as negative, revealing constant states of debt). Statistically the situation was somewhat better for the self-employed (estimated to have numbered 1,700,000 in 1881), tenant farmers, and share-croppers (1,950,000), but dramatic for the farmhands and casual labourers that made up the vast majority (5,790,000).[9]

There are numerous records informing us about the kind of food peasants consumed in the late 19th century. In the Langhe it was usually polenta, vegetables, potatoes, and chestnuts; seldom wheat-based bread, and no meat, except on special occasions or during illness. In Sardinia, a farmhand's diet consisted of two meals: at midday wheat bread and in the evening vegetable soup. Pasquale Villari describes the Puglia peasant's day. On starting work early in the morning each one would receive a blackish, flattened piece of bread weighing a kilo, that he would begin to consume around ten o'clock. In the evening the cook would boil a large pan of water with a little salt in it; the men would line up, each with his own bread cut in slices inside a wooden bowl, on to which the cook poured the salt water with a few drops of oil. That was it: 'saltwater soup'. Villari adds that the meal was so scant that during reaping time the men were given weak wine (made from already crushed grapes and water), so they would have enough strength to face the hard labour.[10] Conditions varied greatly from one area to another and depended on the availability of local products, work contracts, and local cultural traditions.[11] Only one thing was common: the overall low calorie content, consisting above all of carbohydrates, and scarcity of vitamins and protein (leading to diseases and malformations).

Speaking of food in terms of quantity and quality may not necessarily exhaust the argument, however. Few human activities are as full of symbolic meaning as eating and drinking. Various foods have had their part to play in the manifestation of taboos and prejudices, privilege, ritual, and social distinction. Their history epitomizes many cultural constructs in human society, as noted by scholars like Lévi-Strauss who, in his seminal work *The Raw and the Cooked* provides insight into the deep-rooted structures of a community through its food-based metaphors.[12] The fact that peasants had little food available does not signify that it was any less symbolic for them. On the contrary, all country cultures gave enormous importance to food in the organization of social life: festivities were marked by quantity and quality (such as sweetstuffs), which differed from work-day habits. Likewise, different foods distinguished ordinary phases in life's cycle from exceptions (such as illness or religious ceremonies and special occasions). So various kinds of food took on special meanings, a positive value being given to all things associated with 'fat', since it represented a privilege denied many peasants. This led to fatness becoming an allegory for a happy life, as did anything that grew or lived 'high up', like birds or fruit on the trees, unlike anything 'low down', like underground tubers or pigs wallowing in mud.[13] The same was true for the forms of food, the ways of preparing and cooking it, and even the colour (as white was associated with refinement and luxury so white bread was seen as precious and the opposite of the black bread consumed by peasants).[14] Catholic practice, too, had its influence: the rules of diet linked to the liturgical calendar imposed a separation between eating 'fat', as opposed to eating 'lean' that rigorously prohibited meat and at times other animal products in favour of vegetables and fish[15] (not something that concerned persistently hungry peasants).

In a culture strongly associated with growing its own food, a basic commodity like grain, even before becoming edible was sometimes personified, becoming a spirit capable of assuming various meanings and forms, such as a wolf (believed to have been killed in the reaping). Thus, as Frazer tells us, if peasants saw the ears of corn waving in the wind they would say: 'It's the corn wolf passing'; and if by chance a real wolf came into the field they would look at its tail: if it was erect they cursed and tried to kill it, but if it trailed downwards, thus fertilizing the field, they rejoiced, thanked it, and gave it food.[16] This personification continued through late 19th century and beginning of the 20th.

Although held together by certain features, such as an almost sacred respect for food—always so scant and hard to come by—and an attentive, almost symbiotic relationship with the nature and land it shared, peasant culture concerning food differed greatly from area to area, and was to a certain extent self-contained. There was certainly no common 'consumption space' relating to any political or state-based entity; if anything, one needs to examine larger areas with similar geographical and cultural characteristics (think of the kind of economy in the Alpine valleys, unaffected by political boundaries; or the Mediterranean area, though this also presented marked differences within it).[17] Think of the introduction of such 'American' plants as potatoes, peppers, tomatoes, beans, and above all maize, which were however treated and cooked according to local traditions: tomatoes used for sauces, maize not eaten on the cob as in America but ground to flour and cooked to become cornmeal or polenta, while for a long time bread made out of potato flour was tried instead of wheat flour (the result being so vile that the idea was finally abandoned—but from our point of view it is an excellent example of a cultural hybrid). Of course this great variety also makes it difficult to compare the actual living conditions of peasants in Italy with those of their European counterparts, where the average incomes were in any case higher.

How food was consumed was no less significant. It tended to be a collective act, possibly introduced with a prayer, and reinforced social and gender differences, as proved by serving order, choice portions, and hierarchical seating at table: the head of the family in prime position, most important members on either side of him, then all the rest (some, such as the women, might even be excluded from the privilege of eating at such a table). Eating and drinking was an important cultural part of many social events: market and fair visits, village feasts, eating out at the inn, or evening gatherings around the fire.[18]

The second item on the expense list of country people was the home. But what was this home like? It is hard to give a single answer, considering the many different kinds that existed. I can, however, draw attention to two common elements: its close ties with the surrounding area, which involved the almost exclusive use of local building materials, and its link with organized production. So there are Po valley farmsteads: square complexes of red-roofed, terracotta brick buildings around a central yard where the farmer's family lived (usually renting it from the landowner); a large number of dwellings for the farm hands consisting of a big ground-floor kitchen and one/two rooms upstairs for sleeping; then byres with annexed barns and spaces for farming equipment. This was a custom-built arrangement for seven or eight families, reflecting a production system that was already highly differentiated and specialized.[19] Similar in layout, but smaller and diversified, were farms in the South of Italy and areas around Rome, while the dwellings of tenant farmers in central Italy were decidedly more spacious, containing more rooms for the farmer's family, on as many as three floors and with ample communal spaces (wells, outhouses, kitchen gardens, and orchards). Here the families lived in isolation on the land they were cultivating, like a great farming business involving a variety of crops.

Elsewhere, dwellings for really poor, single families were dominant, made with materials like stone, slate, or wood, much smaller in size (often only a stall and one all-purpose room for the family, or at most a ground-floor kitchen and single room on the first floor), huddled together in small mountain villages or scattered about on the estates of absentee landlords—indicative of a backward, inefficient system of agriculture.[20] The barn was an important space not only for work and looking after the animals but also as a social space for meetings, and many artisan and social activities, especially in winter. Proximity with animals has in fact always been a common feature of country life.

Entering an imaginary kitchen—the main room in the house, partly because that is where the fireplace was, so the only heated room—I would be able to see various objects in daily use: earthenware cooking pots, copper cauldrons, tin pans for cooking, drinking pitchers; rudimentary sets of cutlery, plates, dishes, glasses, and cooking utensils (maybe on the rough kitchen table or inside a dresser). In the absence of other spaces, the kitchen was used for a variety of tasks: the women would spin, sew, and weave there, cook, look after the children, lash up brooms; the men would weave baskets, and mend or make farm tools. In other words, it was a production and consumption space at the same time, a space with many functions, adapted to the multifarious needs of the family. In rural Italy, in fact, extended or multiple families cohabited, but above all nuclear families (the average family in the early 20th century consisted of 4.5 members. It must be remembered that the early presence of the nuclear family, like the late marrying age—on average between 25- and 30-year-olds, against the 20 to 25-year-olds in the US, Russia, or Australia—is a characteristic feature of continental Europe, with all the consequences this has on life histories).[21] Such families were strongly hierarchical, with a marked division of duties: the men did the main agricultural work, the women looked after the house and helped in the fields, while the children performed lighter tasks (but all economic and decision-making responsibilities were firmly in the hands of the head of the family or farmer).

Passing on to the bedroom, alongside one or more big beds (where several people would sleep together), there would be trunks or chests holding bedlinen and clothes (shirts, trousers, tunics, jackets, and hats for the men; blouses, skirts, shawls, aprons, and dresses for the women; footwear was often simple clogs). Clothes and sheets were partly made in the home, partly inherited and recycled over and over again, and partly bought cheaply from hawkers or at the fair. The objects present in a peasant's home were therefore the result of both home-made produce and bought items: as in the case of food, clothing was also an important social indicator (as we are reminded by the sumptuary laws, which for centuries imposed special styles and colours concerning attire based on social class). Even for peasants, cutting a fine figure on the social stage was important,[22] especially on special occasions.

Material consumption in the peasants' world, embedded as it was in ancient customs and traditions, was therefore very limited: what was lacking is often more revealing than what was present. This was dramatically true where food is concerned: a primeval, gnawing hunger seems to have been the norm. The list of references, songs and popular proverbs relating to it is never-ending. The Tuscan saying 'He who has food eats, and he who hasn't, must shift for himself' has its Como counterpart 'While bread and wine last don't worry about the future', while a Calabrian maxim declares 'Bread and knife never fill the belly' and Neapolitan wisdom advises 'If you can't eat meat, make do with broth'. And so it goes on. From the ideal of life summed up in the Tuscan 'Eat well, crap well, and don't be afraid of death', to 'A full saucepan means peace in the house', 'Chattering teeth and empty jaws make hunger bite more than cold', 'Hunger makes the teeth bleed' down to the disturbing 'It's dark inside the belly'.

Echoes are not lacking in literature, either. The peasant's plight grimly reminds us of Pinocchio's inexhaustible hunger:

[Pinocchio] started running around the room, rummaging through all the drawers and nooks and crannies in search of a piece of bread, even stale bread or a dry crust, a bone left by the dog, some mouldy polenta, a fish bone, a cherry stone, in fact anything he could chew: but he found nothing, nothing at all.

Meanwhile his hunger got worse and worse, and all he could do was to yawn. He yawned so hard that at times his mouth reached his ears. And after yawning he spat, and felt his stomach churning over.[23]

So Geppetto sacrificed his breakfast—three pears—to the hungry puppet, urging him to eat not just the pulp but the skin and core as well:

I would never have thought, my boy, that you would be so picky and with such a delicate palate. That's bad! In this world we must learn as a child how to eat everything, because you never know what may happen. All sorts of things do![24]

Only at Carnival, the feast of transgression *par excellence*, was there total inversion: deprivation turned into abundance, thrift into profligacy, and even the peasants' harsh world gave way to an orgy of eating and drinking. But not for long, before the dummy or animal representing Carnival was soon chastized for his sins (symbolized by the excesses of eating and drinking) and put to death, making way for Lent with its expiation rituals and fasting—in a ceremony that brought together the ancient Saturnalia and Christian liturgy.

Industrial workers

Living conditions for industrial workers were not much better as a rule. The main difference lay in the fact that their earnings came almost exclusively from wages, and therefore in cash, while consumption of home-made products was very much lower. At the end of the 1800s, a workman in Turin had a family budget showing an overall income to be modest (1,241 lira), but the amount set aside for food still accounted for 74 per cent (of which 40 per cent just for cereals) and the percentage cost for the home was definitely more (23 per cent), while other expenses and clothing were marginal and left a small sum of 102 lira for savings.[25] Later research about Milanese workers just before the outbreak of the First World War showed that only 13 of the 51 families taken into consideration exceeded a daily intake of 3,000 calories (estimated to be necessary for a ten-hour day of heavy labour). Other sources testified that in Milan they ate little meat (in any case mostly offal and umbles, that is inferior quality beef and cow entrails), not much fish (salt cod), but a great deal of milk and low quality dairy products, while the staple food was maize[26]—a situation summed up by the Bergamasque saying, 'Pulènta frègia, furmai che spùsa l'è la baùsa di milanes' [Cold polenta and stinking cheese are delicacies for the Milanese].

Further south things were not much better. In Naples, meat was scarce except for entrails used for frying, and crackling; likewise for fish, mostly salted (dried cod and stockfish). Milk and eggs were avoided because of the high cost, while there was a modest variety of vegetables and cereals. A survey of miners on the Isle of Elba describes their victuals in detail: at work they had an early breakfast (coffee substitute and bread, or bread with either an onion or olives, or bread again with two roasted sardines) and a midday meal (bread, rice soup with either peas, broad beans or greens, and sometimes a little fish). The evening meal was eaten at home and consisted of rice and vegetable soup, bread and a bit of fish. Meat intake was limited to thirty grams per week and wine was almost absent.[27] Once again the diet was monotonous and insufficient. Another survey comparing daily rations confirmed that workers in the north (with good wages) got 23 grams a day of protein and fresh meat against 14 for workers in the south, a ratio reversed for vegetables: 93 grams compared to 129.[28] All this proves that the environment (availability, prices, traditions) had a significant effect on the local life style (for example, a high meat consumption was often associated with a typical workman's diet in northern Europe, while this was less true in Italy).

Does any particular kind of consumer culture emerge for workers, then? The answer is yes. While their living standards were more or less the same as the peasants's in most cases, factory workers started to behave in very different ways. First of all in the demographic field. In the most industrialized towns the birthrate was as much as 30 per cent below the national average (together with a higher mortality rate for both adults and infants), marriages were fewer and formalized at a later age, the rate of illegitimate births was much higher.[29] These factors would suggest—beyond the precarious conditions of sanitation and hygiene—that the burden of family and offspring was less where consumption was concerned and there was more scope for individual consumption.

A second difference lay in spatial mobility. Being a manual worker meant changing jobs continually, due to the precarious nature of the work (without counting the waves of seasonal workers entering towns), which would involve moving house frequently between one job and another, always on the lookout for somewhere to live that suited the fluctuating economic situation and varying size of the family. In such conditions one's attitude to material culture and domestic space was different, tending to be more flexible, less attached to specific places and things, and with fewer emotional ties (very often even the furniture was rented and only a few goods and chattels were taken to the new house). In practice, there was a more 'functional' concept of goods.

This brings in another element: increased contact with other groups and classes, and social mobility. The town obviously offered more opportunities to meet and get to know new habits and customs, in public places, at work, and during festivities and the working conditions were much more flexible than we could possibly imagine today. First, the workers themselves came from peasant backgrounds or had a tradition of crafts behind them. Second, the working life in a factory was very short, the productive period being considered from ages 19 to 40–45 years, after which they would be dismissed due to diminishing productiveness. At that point there was nothing left but to find another job, in a smaller business, as a porter or in haulage, as a custodian and, often where women were concerned, in domestic service.[30] In other words, within a single lifetime, completely different environments and consumption practices would be encountered. This fact brought with it significant fluidity in the formation of a specific consumer culture, certainly greater than that of working classes formed in bygone times and with a bigger weight of numbers (as in the United Kingdom), making geographic generalizations open to question. In fact in Italy, and many other European countries, there still existed an enormous population of unskilled workers with no fixed employment or steady job, who were rarely encouraged to become skilled or settle down, partly due to the tardy arrival of mass production. European workers were, and still are, far less socially mobile than their American counterparts.[31]

I have spoken about workers' houses. It must be said at once that finding a place to live has always been a serious problem for the working classes, due to the scarcity of places available and the high prices involved. Even if the working-class population only represented a small percentage of the whole (it is estimated that in 1901 there were perhaps around 3,500,000 active workers with the possible addition of a certain number of workers listed as craftsmen),[32] they clustered together in certain areas. In Milan in 1901 out of 492,000 inhabitants a good 280,000 belonged to the working class. Accommodation was commonly found in the poorest areas, in blocks of cheap flats in working-class districts on the outskirts, or in run-down inner city areas (often as sublets). A worker's family, usually nuclear, got used to cramped, overcrowded spaces, with an average of three or four occupants to a room.[33] Among the most characteristic urban typologies there are the Milanese *case di ringhiera*: rented multi-storey blocks of flats on the outskirts, equipped with communal railinged balconies facing an inside courtyard, with a structure based on the dwellings of farm labourers. The balconies gave access to many small flats of one or two rooms and to the communal toilet. There was no lighting or drainage. Running water was often found only in the courtyard. These buildings sprang up just outside the ramparts that bounded the central area of the city, from where the poor were being gradually expelled. The same process took place in Turin. Just outside the city tariff boundary, at the start of the 20th century, 'workers' barriers' were set up for new immigrants and workers leaving the centre.[34]

The massive building projects of working-class housing of the type widespread first in English industrial towns, then in Germany and France, were unknown in Italy, as were buildings designed specifically for urban workers. The major exception is found in workers' housing estates, such as the *Nuova Schio* built by Alessandro Rossi of Vicenza, a philanthropist wool manufacturer inspired by a Roman Catholic paternalism, who hoped to overcome class confrontations. His model village, which included gardens, schools, and community services, was designed on the basis of an overall hierarchical subdivision: detached houses for the directors, one-family or two-family houses for office staff, and terraced housing for the workers. It goes without saying that his paternalism bordered on social control and the housing organization was in the factory's interests (above all far removed from the 'dangers' of city life). Many other factory owners followed this example, like the families of Marzotto at Valdagno, Leumann at Collegno, and Crespi at Crespi d'Adda (a village which today is looked after by Unesco as a human heritage site). But there were also those who aimed at a definite integration between the lives of the worker and the peasant, such as Paolo Camerini, who at Piazzola sul Brenta near Padua created factories and furnaces alongside cattle- sheds and fields, and arranged the housing all around.[35] As already stated, however, these were special cases, outside city areas.

The characteristics most associated with the working class, according to a tradition of study stimulated by Edward Thompson's famous book,[36] are sociability, solidarity, and care for one another. In this way families in open-railing houses did not live in isolation but created a network of friends and relations, which also functioned as an exchange of favours and support in times of need. And if in this network we see women as the main protagonists, the men would find alternative spaces for socializing in the taverns (in the family budget examined above, for a worker in Turin the second food item, after cereals, was 'fermented drinks': 91 lira, 8 per cent of the entire wage packet).[37]

Numerous studies have also investigated the iconography of riots and protests, the meanings attributed to food (for example the symbolic value of bread), the rituals of festivals like May Day (with display of working tools), popular songs: everything that went into the creation of a worker's cultural identity—which then coalesced in an association development of a kind that was first mutualistic and then political, even though there was nothing automatic in this progression.[38] Once again material aspects played a significant part in the creation of a worker's culture, including the role played by clothing, or particularly, by working clothes. Much of the iconography we have shows workers dressed in simple, identical clothing (canvas trousers, shirt, jacket or waistcoat, cap—sometimes even bare-chested workers, to symbolize the strength and natural/virile character of the labourer) which make them immediately recognizable as a group. Photographs taken in factories have shown posed images of serious workmen, never smiling, dressed in (all-in-one or two-piece) working overalls or smocks of coarse material, while the women are portrayed in smocks and blouses, frequently with bonnets to cover their hair, as they stand or sit next to their tools.[39] Studies on the French Revolution have stressed the importance of the National Guard uniform in making a citizen,[40] and we all know about the role uniforms played in making a soldier. Well, perhaps workers' uniforms had an identical role from a symbolic point of view, uniting them in a collective whole, easily identifiable even from the outside. It is no coincidence that a clothes metaphor has come to indicate the working class—the blue-collar workers or the 'blue overalls' (from the well-established custom in American factories from the 1930s onwards).

The sociability of the workers should not be over-idealized, however. Historians, perhaps due to a subconscious nostalgia for the community values transpiring from similar life styles, had at length extolled the virtues of the métayage system as a balanced solution for life and work, until recent studies have shown the hierarchical, even authoritarian aspects present in farming families, the difficult conditions women and young people found themselves in, and the cultural conservatism of such a reality.[41] Something of the same has come to light where life in working-class environments is concerned, aided and abetted by the importance given to workers' solidarity in the circulation of socialist ideas.[42]

A lively testimony of the daily life of Milanese workers in the early 20th century is given by documents concerning working-class quarters built by an important welfare institution like the *Società Umanitaria*.[43] In 1906, to address the problem of building speculation it built various blocks of flats to rent out at controlled prices. Buildings, it is noticed, were erected of three or four storeys spaced well apart from one other, avoiding not only the ugly barrack-like constructions typical of the age but also those with a central courtyard and long communal balconies, conducive to the hygienic problems and lack of privacy that tenants were want to complain about. Entering one of the 240 flats, each with its own entrance, one would came into a multi-purpose room of about twenty square metres, or into two rooms: the first was the kitchen, in which you could see a wooden table with four chairs, a dresser, shelves, a cupboard, and a stove/cooker. The second was the bedroom where a large double bed with imposing headboard and side lockers reigned supreme, together with a wardrobe, chest of drawers, two more chairs, and a 'washstand' of iron and porcelain (that is, a washbasin mounted on a metal frame, together with a ewer). The floors were covered with large terracotta tiles. The walls were well painted and decorated with some small pictures. Illumination was guaranteed by hanging gas lights (not very common in working-class houses). Furthermore, each flat had a small room serving as a latrine, which was an even less common feature. Many other services were communal: bathrooms and showers, laundry room, kitchen and restaurant, rooms for breast-feeding babies, meeting and reading rooms, food pantry (wine was strictly forbidden, however). In this way services traditionally shared inside the community were 'institutionalized'.

This description would suggest a decorous way of life satisfied with basic, partly communal services, yet not available to most workers. Even here, however, there was no shortage of problems: in 1909 the inhabitants of the quarter sent a petition to the City Hall to put in order the adjacent roads, which had become almost impassable, to build drains, instal public lighting to guard against serious safety problems, and to regulate the course of the Olona river whose stagnant water was creating hygiene problems during summer.[44] Added to this were small matters related to communal living: frequent disturbances (in the laundry room hung a severe warning: 'it is forbidden to sing, shout or quarrel, under the threat of immediate expulsion'),[45] brawls in the restaurant, furious arguments during communal assemblies (a musket shot was even fired at one tenant).[46] All this conjures up an image of a noisy, smelly world that is a reminder to us that pollution is not just a modern problem, as testified by a custodian of the quarter, Salvatore Sapienza:

> During the summer season one notices enormous numbers of mosquitoes and other insects infesting the air and it is believed that the cause of this is the stagnant water lying alongside the boundary wall of the Fino factory which is right on the road about 30 metres away from the Quarter. The same factory emits disgusting smells which must be harmful to health. To the troublesome health hazards produced by nearby factories is added one which is even more serious, caused by the dense smoke arising from the chimneys of the Fels Firm doll-making factory. It should be noted that since these chimneys are not at the regulation height, the smoke that billows out of them by day and by night (with a favourable wind!) is forced down inside the Quarter with enormous damage to the health of the inhabitants and the appearance of the buildings.[47]

On the subject of smells it must be said that personal hygiene and the cleaning of both house and clothing was limited in the absence of running water. The French historian Alain Corbin writes that in this way, as a result of increasing intolerance of the upper classes towards the stench, from the 19th century onwards, bad smells and the very concept of dirt came to be more and more associated with the idea of poverty.[48] The dividing line between different social classes also passes through the sense of smell.

The living conditions and consumer patterns described above only fit a limited category of workers—those with a certain amount of ready money and the ability to pay a regular rent, in other words the workers' aristocracy. These were usually skilled workers in key jobs such as metalworking and printing, or with professional jobs still linked to specific crafts (estimated at a third of the total).[49] Here consumption might follow the model described above, pursuing the ideal of a decent home, sufficient food intake and with time, expanding to include such areas as amusements and cultural interests, as the printers' bulletin noted in 1912: 'Workers today are not like they used to be, because they love comfort, no longer live in squalor, dress more neatly, have bicycles, and buy newspapers'.[50]

On talk about workers spending money on amusements and cultural interests, the discussion immediately shifts to the 'invention' of free time. Important studies have shown the growth of the perception of time in economic terms (for example with the appearance of clocks in public places), culminating with the Industrial Revolution imposing a rigorous factory discipline of which a fixed timetable was an important part.[51] As a consequence there came to be a definite split between working time, which absorbed the central part of daily life, and non-working or 'free' time, creating a separation between two previously connected and overlapping aspects. Free time was thus not simply leisure time, as the widespread productive mentality called for time to be used differently, but always usefully, in sport, culture, and in increasingly commercialized entertainment.[52] In fact the 19th century saw the birth of an actual free-time industry that offered theatre shows, musicals, books and newspapers, and organized celebrations, sporting activities to take part in or to enjoy as a spectator (such as football or cycling), and trips and outings (since real tourism was still beyond a worker's budget).[53]

These new consumer patterns for workers present a problem, however. Did they represent a progressive extension of consumer habits typical of the other social classes—a trickle down effect revealing itself by raising the tenor of life? Or were there different mechanisms involved for the workers? There is some truth in both these suggestions. No doubt the physical closeness of the middle class and the partial sharing of the same public spaces favoured the spread of similar kinds of behaviour, but we must not forget the impulse given by popular and socialist associations, favouring the spread of education and socially acceptable behaviour (decorum, family care, sobriety) which could improve not only the individual but the working class as a whole. Furthermore, we must not take it for granted that their use and understanding of consumption was the same. The tradition of 'cultural studies' has shown that the acceptance of cultural content and 'high' entertainment by the working classes would only be partial, relating to those parts that could be adapted to their own cultural frame of reference and either adapting or discarding what was perceived as inconsistent.[54] Thus, in Italy, cycling for the worker was a way of getting from place to place more than a sporting activity (unlike middle-class people, who travelled by train, ship, and increasingly by car), while classical music, the finest expression of 'high' culture, could be taken in and appreciated by a working-class listener and perceived with images belonging to his frame of reference—as a music critic commented after sitting next to 'an old workman with calloused hands'.

> The 'Fifth Symphony' conducted by Toscanini, remember? [. . .] Well, at the passage by the double basses,—where the serious notes unfold at a speed almost exceptional for such gigantic instruments, and then seem to frolic and tie themselves up in knots, and then run together in clusters, then stopping themselves a bit at a time, and taking up the headlong pace again to repeat the theme all over again—during that passage my neighbour opened his eyes wide and then—as if the marvellous impression that the musical passage had stirred up in him could not be expressed without images drawn from his own life and what he was familiar with, exclaimed 'orpo (Well I'll be . . . !) pàren machin! (They're just like machines!). For him the idea of sublime beauty could not be separated from his factory floor mentality, from what was esssentially rhythmic in mechanical devices, pistons, gears, engines. At that moment Beethoven's music was for him an incomparably complex, perfectly precise assembly line. Màchin . . .[55]

In this way the cultured critic, by emphasizing his literary superiority with refined prose, rhetorically contrasted it with the simplicity of his neighbour, perhaps unaware that he was setting a traditionally educated musical culture that chiefly took in and appreciated the melodic side against an enjoyment that was instead smitten by the rhythmic aspect. Therefore, to answer the questions raised, in society there are mechanisms of cultural transmission systems that work from the top downwards, but there is no shortage of those working in the opposite way sense, bottom up (think in the alimentary field of some 'poor' peasant dishes elevated to middle-class tables and of the much-appreciated fisherman-style preparations of fish), as well as a push that determines convergence, due to an external common environment. Cultural differences are not to be taken rigidly, as if they were constructions crystallized in time once and for ever, but in an elastic way, flexible, more like a collection of uses and patterns of action linked to everyday practices, capable of building up behaviours according to social status, in a word, what Bourdieu presented as *habitus.*[56]

As mentioned earlier, this type of broadening of consumption actually affected only a relatively restricted swathe of workers in reality. For many others all this was just a mirage with the main concern still being the fulfilment of basic needs. Being out of work was always a lurking threat, and sickness or a serious problem in the family could precipitate a crisis. Furthermore, even for those who had a job there was a precise hierarchy linked to kind of work, size of establishment, and productive sector it belonged to. The workers' world was not free from internal conflicts.

At the same time, some of the hierarchies were not linked to production aspects, the chief one among them being the gender difference. Along a line of continuity with pre-industrial and peasant society, women were employed on a large scale in manufacturing, especially in the textile and clothing sector. Yet they formed a part of the workforce that was downgraded: their work was considered secondary and of a lower quality, they were paid less,[57] and their working life was more limited (usually up to marriage, or more often maternity, when they were more easily dismissed, and not beyond the age of 30 to 35 years). What is more, male workers were hostile towards them because of the fear of cheap competition.[58] Between 1881 and 1911 the proportion of female workers fell rapidly (in Turin it fell from 40 to 28 per cent, a percentage that was lower than Milan but ahead of Bologna and other industrial centres) due to the combined action of major developments in the metalworking sectors (which created a body of specialized workers in the wake of ancient crafts),[59] the introduction of labour laws protecting maternity (which had the perverse effect of increasing the tendency to hire only unmarried women), but also the spread of the need for decorum and the construction of domestic sociability.[60] Women driven out of the job market rarely dedicated themselves completely to looking after the house, however. They usually continued to work at home, adapted themselves to casual work, or frequently, as already noted, went back into domestic service.[61]

This discussion is important in order to avoid making too sharp a contrast between male and female spheres of consumer and social behaviour, identifying the masculine presence as working outside the home and the feminine sphere defined almost solely with reference to the home and family. In the towns there long remained a strong presence of working women, albeit on the decline (in Milan 54 per cent of women had jobs in 1881, 50 per cent in 1901, 42 per cent in 1911).[62] It is interesting to note how in working-class women's lives there were great periods of discontinuity and change according to the different phases of life. This obviously had an effect in terms of consumer choices, with respect to individual consumption linked to social needs (clothing, care of one's personal appearance), which was greater during working life outside the home. It must also be said that when talking about different kinds of consumption we have no data as regards the specific food intake for women. Some inquiries do show, however, that problems concerning undernourishment were particularly evident in women workers, whose body weight was frequently much below the female average.[63]

Another hierarchy concerns age groups: older workers were penalized and children exploited, as child labour was widely in use. The 1901 statistics record that out of a total of 77,000 workers, 18,000 were boys and girls aged between 6 and 15, employed in various jobs (in factories and shops, on building sites, doing itinerant sales, dressmaking, arts and crafts). The papers were full of reports concerning the abuse and maltreatment suffered by these young workers, not only at the hands of employers but adult workmates as well. Restrictive laws were only introduced in 1886, and most importantly in 1902 (when a minimum age of 12 was set for factory work).[64] Here again, the use of children in the workforce, continuing the tradition of having all family members actively employed, had important consequences on consumer patterns. Introduced at such an early age into a working environment, these youngsters left the sphere of family consumption very soon and quickly adapted to 'adult' consumer habits. Life as an infant was brief and even in the family seen as mere preparation for adult life. The family itself expected even the youngest members to make a contribution according to their ability. It was not by chance that current affairs writers condemned the abuses of child labour (and tried to put a brake on its growing use due to its cheapness), but no one thought of prohibiting it.

Consumer practices thus prove to be an indispensable key to interpreting the codes of behaviour and self-representation of the working class.

Middle classes

It is almost impossible to give a single definition of the middle class. The numerous studies devoted to it have all ended up concluding that it would be better to speak of 'middle classes', that is a variety of social categories with distinctive roles and behaviours. Historians have stressed how the class as a whole has been influenced by powerful archetypes, from Werner Sombart who exalted the entrepreneur as a dynamic innovator and champion of social progress to Max Weber, who saw in the class itself a dynamic, evolving element (because of an 'acquisitive' mentality very different from the landowning class), down to Marx himself, who called it revolutionary, up to a certain stage when it became the main target of his political campaign. The problem is that this class, originally identified with artisans and merchants, eventually came to be mainly associated with entrepreneurs and high financiers (owners of the instruments of production, in Marxist terminology), before expanding out of all proportion in the 20th century to include more and more categories of office workers and professionals with widely varying characteristics. Attempts were then made to distinguish them through the use of adjectives (upper, lower, petit bourgeois), but the terminology remained imprecise and loaded with ideological over-tones. Moreover, the 19th-century *bourgeoisie* represented itself using semantic coordinates of an ethical and political nature, seeing itself in a patriotic guise.[65] Again in this case, therefore, resorting to the notion of '*habitus*' may prove useful in identifying collective mentalities and behaviours, rather than referring exclusively to their role in the pro-duction process, to income (partly because some working-class cate-gories earned more than many so-called 'bourgeois') or even to specific ideologies. And here again the consumer practices that gave a form to such behaviours are key factors.

In any case, if for the sake of precision I wished to make an attempt to define and quantify the 'middle classes' in Italy, using the censuses again I could distinguish an upper middle class consisting of land-owners, entrepreneurs, managers, and professionals (estimated at 310,000 in 1901); a solid body of artisans, shopkeepers, and service sector people (1,900,000) to which can be added specific categories such as the military, church, and the like (another 440,000). Finally, there is the group of public and private office workers and teachers (480,000). In all, a matter of 18 per cent of the working population.[66]

What evidence is there concerning the material life of these classes? Unfortunately the great studies and surveys carried out at the turn of the 20th century were inspired by philanthropic, humanitarian motives and concentrated almost entirely on the wretched conditions suffered by the working class, neglecting the comparative aspect. One interesting exception is a study of 1908–1909 on the budgets of various families resident in Troia, near Foggia, which includes some belonging to the middle class (that is, with incomes from two to four times higher than working-class families, and in one case almost nine times higher).[67] It is immediately notice able that once again the major item concerned food, with a percentage varying from 50 to 62 per cent (except for the most affluent family, where it fell to 33 per cent, though corresponding of course to the highest expense in absolute terms). Within the food sector, consumption choices favoured cereals, closely followed however by expensive foods like meat and fish, albeit with great differences, and new items appear like 'condiments', while 'fermented beverages' fall below 6 per cent on average.[68] The home accounted for 14–22 per cent (on average 18 per cent, with a certain stress on heating and lighting, especially for the richest family). What stands out is the amount spent on clothes, which represent on average the second highest family expense, almost 20 per cent (rising to 28 per cent). It is interesting to note how the middle-class budgets do not show any great savings or spending on accessories (in one case there is even a heavy debt), with the exception once again of the most affluent family, that assigned as much as 32 per cent under the heading including, 'moral needs, recreation, health and industrial services, debts, taxes, insurance, etc'.

What can be deduced from all this? Of course the data given is limited and cannot have statistical value. But reading between the lines it could be said that the percentage of budget spent on food appears somewhat elevated, though less in comparison with that spent by the working class. There are possibly more signs of rich food like meat and a greater variety (even if the constant presence of cereals may indicate the importance of local traditions). The home accounts for a significant amount of expense, (albeit not as much as happens with the working class). The major difference appears to be the great attention given to clothes, which in this sample use up a fifth of available resources, revealing a far greater concern with social appearance than is found in other classes. Another observation concerns the purchasing behaviour of the family with the highest income, which shows different priorities, spending less on food and reserving larger quotas of income for representational expenses (lighting and heating, for example), diversifying consumption in favour of services, pleasure, and social life. Diversification within the middle class is therefore quite significant.

Other interesting elements for an understanding of the data can come from international comparisons, particularly through the classic work of Maurice Halbwachs, who attempted to provide empiric demonstration of the consumer habits of the various social classes (with reference to early 20th-century Germany).[69] Studying the uses made of available resources, the French sociologist observed how the budget quota reserved for food by the working class was always high (on average 50–51 per cent), even in the presence of an increase in wages, while home expenses tended to go down with increased income (from 17 down to 15 per cent); which is the opposite to what happened among office workers, who spent less on food (38–41 per cent) and more on the home (18–19 per cent), with the tendency to devote more resources to the home, the greater the income. Contrary to Engel's law (according to which, in general, spending on food diminishes as income rises, to make way for other, non-essential expenses), the choice of purchases appeared different according to social class, even with the same budget. In other words, consumption seems to have been culturally determined.

Comparing all this with Italian data, there are significant differences. First of all on basic necessities, working-class families spent a decidedly greater percentage as proof of their low income level. Expenses on the home, in particular, were on average higher for workers than for the middle class (the opposite to what happened in Germany). This phenomenon can be explained by recalling the difficult housing situation in towns, lack of building projects for working-class homes and strong speculative pressures. Another difference is the quota reserved for food, which in Italy was significantly high for middle-class families too (while home expenses were similar). How can this fact be explained? Again using a cultural logic explanation, it can be state that the importance given to food and pleasure of eating in company were not just features of working-class culture (as was the case in northern Europe) but were shared by all social classes. It is, therefore, a nationwide value. In comparison with other cultures, Italy gives more priority to food and the rituals of eating than anywhere except perhaps France. And this has always been a fixed star of Italian culture, starting with the

Romans, through to medieval times and reaching its zenith with Renaissance banquets: great abundance of sugars and spices, sweet-and-sour flavours, artificially constructed tastes—even after the revolution wrought in the 17th and 18th centuries by French cuisine in search of more natural and delicate flavours and a limitation of spices, which found fertile ground in a land that had always valued vegetables and aromas, giving rise to rich and varied local traditions.[70]

This element—the value given to food in Italian cultural tradition—is of paramount importance and we shall come back to it. For the moment it is enough to observe that it is amply documented from the iconographic perspective in the many art works portraying feasts and banquets, from the Renaissance onwards. Inspiration often came from mythological subjects (think for example of the banquet in honour of Cupid and Psyche in the Te Palace in Mantua)[71] or even more frequently from Biblical and Gospel scenes (representations of such scenes as the Last Supper in the life of Christ are innumerable)—always with a lively attention given to the representation of food. Then, from the 16th century onwards, the taste for still-life scenes took hold throughout Europe, focusing on fruit, vegetables, and various types of food shown most realistically (in the wake of the famous works of Caravaggio or from the 'portraits' by Giuseppe Arcimboldi who even constructed a human face based on nature elements). For centuries these pictures have played an important part first in the decor of wealthy homes, then in less affluent ones also, and are thus very much alive in the cultural imagination, testifying by their presence the artistic transfiguration of food, and thus its symbolic value.

A second element deserves our attention: the role of clothes. Pierre Bourdieu has observed that significant parts of resources are used for motives of prestige. As every class or social segment wants to distinguish itself from the ones next to it—especially if they are inferior—clothing works very well for this purpose. There is no doubt that the legacy of the sumptuary laws carried their weight, as did the need to wear clothes in keeping with the learned professions, held according to a long-standing western tradition to be superior to those in technical subjects (as they were followed in order to uplift the spirit, not just to make money). Hence the importance of wearing distinguished clothes in keeping with the moral code and etiquette of the time, as well as a clean and neat appearance as this was something that was beyond the means of manual workers. It was not by chance that the middle classes came to be known as 'white-collar' workers. In fact, it should be noted that the Italian middle class seemed to give even more weight to this aspect, and thus to their way of dressing in public. This was true right down to the lowest levels of the middle class, whose incomes were not much higher than the top levels of the working class, yet they took pains to dress decorously, at the cost of economic sacrifice and false appearances (the short-sleeved shirts worn by office workers instead of expensive long-sleeved ones). There is an admirable portrait of this in a drama where the leading character is Monsù Travet, an example of a state employee in 19th-century Turin who dangles precariously between what he is and what he appears to be; while in *Demetrio Pianelli*, by Emilio De Marchi, moral condemnation is shown for an office worker who wants to imitate the profligacy of upper-class habits (up to his neck in debt, he commits suicide), in contrast with his honest and thrifty brother who takes his family responsibilities seriously.[72] It should, however, be noted that decorum and a certain uniformity of dress (for example white shirt, waistcoat, tie, and dark suit for men) were in certain cases explicitly required by office regulations, or at least in practice.

So, to the home itself. Middle-class homes were at the centre of significant changes, and to describe these I will refer to the work of two important authors. The first is Simon Schama with his book *The Embarrassment of Riches*. In tracing the origins of Dutch national identity and culture starting from the 17th century, he reveals a dichotomy between the quest for riches and their benefits on one hand and feelings of shame for possessing and enjoying them on the other. The wealthy Dutch merchants and bankers threw themselves into risky dealings that could give abundant returns and accumulate large fortunes but they were troubled at the same time. Would they not in this way lose their souls? The obsession with domestic decorum and cleanliness, so typical of that society, can be explained by their attempt to look for an escape from the 'dirty' world. If the home has always provided shelter, here it goes further in taking on a symbolic value in contrast with the outside world: security versus liberty. Thus the home had to be clean, sober, and uncontaminated by worldly affairs and the lust for wealth, the woman's realm (where she would incarnate these very virtues).[73] Schama's brilliant work, written like a novel and richly illustrated, has suggested to scholars that a new concept of domesticity developed in

northern Europe, a private space, seen as a pivotal value around which
to construct a distinct identity, different from both the aristocracy and
the lower classes. Crossing Britain this new concept would gradually
pervade Europe, to reach 19th-century Italy where it would meet with
a certain tendency to provide a simpler and more private home environment, already present in some realities.[74] The second author is
Pierre Bourdieu, who is interested in homes in a completely different
context (the Kabyles in Algeria). What is interesting is the type of
analysis that he makes of the houses of these Berbers, interpreting
their dwelling spaces as patterns, which clearly let the underlying social
vision shine through, a reproduction of social divisions among the
Kabyles in the spatial structure as well as those between gender and
age groups. The dichotomies of light/shade, inside/outside, high/low,
male/female correspond to the same divisions present in the social
nucleus of the family.[75]

The studies conducted by Schama and Bourdieu are important for
an understanding of the characteristics of middle-class homes in Liberal Italy, which stood out distinctly from those of the peasants and
workers. First of all they immediately seem to be places much more
central to daily life (both in terms of consumption and of time spent in
them). Then they were different not only because they were bigger and
richer, but also because of the special uses to which the rooms were put,
their divisions and hierarchy, which incarnated the cultural and social
structure of the family. These homes were often functional, 'modern'
in style (though not above classical references) and were the first to
welcome mass-produced furniture and decoration. In other words,
these middle-class homes can tell us a great deal about their inhabitants. The first contrast to notice would be between inside and outside:
closed doors, windows, drapes, and curtains protected and separated
the inside environment from the outside; the areas for communication
between the two worlds (for example balconies, porches, and parts
facing the street) became less important to avoid 'contamination'
from the outside world.

Then inside the house there was the separation between public and
private: areas destined for social use, where guests would be enter-
tained, and areas reserved for this new domestic intimacy between the
married couple and their children. The entrance hall introduced visitors into the house, immediately displaying by its furnishings the tastes
and social level of the hosts. Corridors separated the public (drawing

room) from the private (master bedroom, children's bedrooms). In reality the average middle-class family did not indulge very much in social life at home, but preferred to socialize outside the home. However, one study of the Neapolitan elite, conducted on recorded inventories of notaries, shows how at the end of the 19th century both the middle and lower-middle classes invested a great deal in their social spaces. The best furnished rooms were the reception and drawing rooms (the sofas, armchairs, and chairs in the drawing room of an average property owner in Piazza Dante were worth half of the entire furnishings; the drawing room of a pharmacist was worth a third of all the furniture in his seven-room flat) while the private rooms were miserable and neglected.[76] It is possible to see here the striving to imitate the lifestyle of the nobility and the importance of social appearance. Elsewhere the differences are not always so evident, but the public/private dichotomy is just the same. So what is to be seen in these drawing rooms? Sofas, easy- and upright-chairs, mirrors, ornamental furniture, and also some objects endowed with symbolic value: a clock, frequently with a pendulum, combining decorative taste with the call of the machine; a piano to express the role of music in 19th-century middle-class culture (and much called for in the education of little girls); showcases displaying crystalware and silver, symbolic of the family's social status; pictures of various kinds and value, filling the room with family portraits, landscapes, and still-life paintings.[77] The drawing room—in fact the entire home—is full of objects, leaving no empty spaces.

Going along the corridor to enter the private rooms, there are new divisions and hierarchies. The dining room was fairly simple, with a table in the middle and cupboards against the walls where tableware was kept. On the other hand, in the master bedroom there could be often found sumptuous furnishings: a large double bed with tall wood or metal headboard, bedside lockers, chests of drawers, wardrobes, mirrors, religious pictures (even religious devotion seems to have become a private affair). If the family were upper-middle class, there might be some small rooms reserved for the servants (well apart from the master rooms, according to a precise social hierarchy). For the other places the male/female division was complete. The head of the house had a study that was a male-only area. There would be found desks, chairs, closed items of furniture for papers and notepads, bookcases, easy chairs for reading,[78] and then furnishings like inkstands, clocks, working equipment made of silver, everything to conjure up intellectual activity and an attitude of seriousness and dedication (underlined by a choice of wood and leather of dark colours in contrast with the rest of the house). Finally there are the children's bedrooms, strictly divided between male and female, generally furnished with a few essential items. However, the furnishings, and generally speaking all the objects would be different for the various children, more costly for the males than the females and, among the boys most costly for the firstborn. One middle-class Neapolitan family (the Chambeyront) in 1870 spent 1,409 lira on the eldest son (of which 364 for clothing and 405 for education), 1,132 for the second son (371 for clothes and 132 for education) and 817 for the daughter (174 for clothing and only 25 for education) showing a precise family strategy regarding the children's future social standing.[79]

The subject of children leads us to making an important distinction. This was a delicate transition period as regards the idea of childhood. Earlier it was seen that in traditional peasant and worker culture how the small offspring were employed at a very early age to do light work. I was not talking about maltreatment, but simply describing a culture that gave children no special status. Instead, towards the end of the 19th century, within the middle-classes, the idea started to take hold that children were not 'immature adults' but constituted a separate world, with its special requirements and necessities, its own values, sometimes even in contrast with adult ones: creativity, purity, and vulnerability. Therefore, the task of educators was to allow such inner values to come out freely, without forcing children with iron rod discipline, not to mention obliging them to do unsuitable work. In Italy the main champion of this position was Maria Montessori, who founded many schools (the first one was the 'Casa dei bambini' at San Lorenzo in Rome in 1907) and inspired a method which exalted the positive abilities of little children. It is significant that Montessori contested the dogma of original sin: a small child was a pure being, without faults, was even 'father of the man'.[80] This new evaluation of infancy had several consequences. Children were no longer regarded as beings in transition towards the only important phase of life, adulthood. They had their own values and so needed specific spaces (even at home). What is more, they were regarded in a new light where consumption was concerned: now they needed education, entertainment, toys as well as suitable clothes and grooming (no longer to be fobbed off with home-made rag dolls and wooden carts to pull along, or dressed up like miniature adults).[81] It is not surprising that this period saw the birth in Europe and in the United States of an actual industry for products specially aimed at children. Parents and teachers began to think that it was right to buy special things for young children and that an emotional attachment for dolls, playthings, and puppets developed positive attitudes, compensating fears and affective problems, and providing company for little ones.[82] Thus the foundations for child consumption were laid and in a few decades would grow into a real buying frenzy (considered proportional to the affective investment). In this way upper-class children had their own consumer items and entered the world of adult society and consumption much later than their working-class contemporaries.

It has therefore be seen how in a middle-class house there was created an intimate domestic space, far removed from the outside world (the separation between the intimate and the political–business domain was complete). The life of a restricted, nuclear family can be perceived, where the woman had multiple functions and left the handling of public affairs to her husband,[83] and where there was great concern for decorum and morality. Respectability was a must. A historian like Mosse has maintained that such morals (based on a strict control of sexual behaviour with widely different standards for men and women) gave the basis for the spread of political nationalism at the start of the century. At a time when some were having doubts about it, for example in the avant-garde youth movements, patriotism was able to provide an alternative passion that was pure, uncontaminated, ascetic, and to which everyone was able to relate to.[84]

In this picture there are important differences however, first of all linked to the geographical context, as will be seen further on, and then, as has been already noticed, when analysing the consumer habits of the Troia families, dependent on earnings and socio-professional roles.[85] If the families of the most affluent professionals and new class of entrepreneurs tended in different degrees to join together in a leadership elite (including the nobility or its parts), often indulging in conspicuous consumption, other professional groups were inspired differently. This was the case where the commercial class was concerned, which had a strong group mentality. In Naples, as in Turin, traders showed a tendency towards thrift and avoided lavish and showy spending, displaying frugal consumer habits and behaviour. Perhaps the fact of having the working area and domestic space right next to each other created a closed circle of money-saving values and prudent management in the two environments, as a later trade journal seems to suggest:

> We think of them—the children of small shopkeepers—growing up in a house that extends into the shop front, as happens in village stores, where the housewife-shopkeeper plies between the kitchen stove and shop counter, and where the beans she has wrapped up for the last customer are just like the ones she is boiling for her dinner a few feet away. This is not nostalgia for country roots or, deep down, a preference for a rudimentary village economy. It is the pleasure of recognising as alive and well something that really belongs to us, the simple virtues of people with the same way of feeling, thinking, acting and loving, both at home and outside; people who in the perfect circle of each day put everything in its place: thought, feeling, responsibility, work.[86]

To conclude, there only remains one more thing to say, that is to remember the consumer choices associated with social life outside the home. One of the strategies employed by the middle classes to achieve distinction concerns cultural and recreational consumption. Let us start, at least chronologically, with the cultural aspect, through circles, literary groups, and scientific societies. After all, was not the middle class the social group best equipped with 'cultural capital' and the basis, at least according to Gellner, of the well educated and culturally cohesive community necessary for the functioning of modern industrial nations?[87] It is here, in the clubs and coffee houses, that Habermas places the birth of a 'public sphere', the origin of modern public opinion.[88]

Finally, where recreation is concerned there was entertainment transformed and adapted, such as dancing (having been, in the 18th century, the prerogative of the nobility, and now interpreted with a new and different spirit, open to foreign novelties like the waltz and *galop*).[89] Then there was the increasing habit of eating out in *trattorie* and good restaurants, perhaps in the big hotels, which would have attracted the best chefs, once the boast of noble courts and great houses.[90] To round off, there was the main source of entertainment, the theatre. The other big novelties were sporting clubs, which appeared in Italy at the end of the 19th century and developed very quickly. Studies here show how various elements converged in this evolution: military tradition, the new concern for hygiene, reflected patriotism, the search for social status, and desire for solidarity. But there is no doubt that 'mass' phenomena such as cycling, car racing, and tourism (in 1912 the Touring Club already had a hundred thousand members) mirror the values of the incipient mass society: competitiveness, pursuit of pleasure, taste for new techniques, sport business.[91] Sport as spectacle had been born.

Aristocracy

Power needs to be shown. If it is true that it is based on force and consent, it needs to display itself, bring out the inequality in relations, and flaunt the signs and symbols of this diversity. The exhibition of 'symbolic capital' permits its legitimation by society. Is it any wonder that the elite have always tried to stand out, with rich clothes and fine jewels, sumptuous palaces in the city centres, grandiose ceremonies on the occasion of weddings and funerals? For the aristocracy consumption has always seemed to play a key role in legitimizing their position. It need not necessarily be a case of lavish consumption: in a society where savings and thrift are seen as virtues, an austere, spartan lifestyle on the part of notoriously rich entrepreneurs and business people can by contrast perform the same 'ostentatious' function.

This is not to say that the consumption of precious goods, so loaded with symbolic meaning, can escape moral judgement. On the contrary it was stigmatized throughout ancient times, at least in its excessive and wasteful forms. The ancient Greeks claimed that it made men effeminate and unable to perform their duties as armed defenders, the Romans condemned luxury because wealth led to self-interest and detachment from the common good, while Christian tradition distrusted such consumption because it was seen as a continual temptation and threat to salvation. We have to wait till modern times to witness the revaluation of luxury by some academics, taken in the utilitarian sense as a means of commercial promotion and individual well-being (Mandeville, Hume, Smith). In this way luxury escapes moral judgement (which now mainly concerns private behaviour and personal choices) and can enter the economic sphere as a positive element.[92] But a certain ambivalence remains. Luxury is tenaciously associated with sloth and squandering: it is no coincidence that the typical negative stereotype of late 19th-century nobility is that of the idle wastrel.

How many aristocrats were there in early 20th century Italy? And how important were they? From the numerical point of view we know that there were around 8,400 families and that their number was in continuous decline. Territorial distribution was uneven: more numerous in Tuscany, the Naples area, Venetia, Piedmont, Sicily, and Lombardy, 40 per cent of them belonged to urban nobility and patrician families (though this was not the case in southern Italy).[93] Their wealth, often tied up in land and property, diminished with equal rapidity; in Mantua for example, at the start of the century registered legacies for the nobility totalled only a little more than half those for the middle class (a century earlier they would have been greater).[94]

What about their lifestyle? This, instead, showed surprising qualities of continuity, starting with domestic social life, from the tendency towards geographical endogamy, to the survival of some typical professions and to social exclusiveness, which opened up slowly and reluctantly to the new middle-class elite.[95] But if this was true in general, the geographical differences could be enormous.

Meanwhile, it is worth noting that, despite their relative economic decline and dwindling numbers, the impact of this social group on the collective imagination was still very strong at the turn of the century, thanks to their role in history and 'visibility'. Think of their houses. Aristocratic homes tended to house extended families (not just the nobleman and his family, but also other relatives, beginning with unmarried sisters and brothers because of the rights of succession) and many servants. Stately homes in the country also had storage barns, stables, and even shops.[96] It comes as no surprise to find them large and rambling, as they had to combine many practical and symbolic functions. The architecture of the building transmitted clear symbols: its sheer massiveness proclaimed the wealth of the family, the conspicuous heraldic crests recalled their lineage, turrets and imposing facades indicated power. And if it were ever necessary to build a new family home, they would commission a famous architect. *Noblesse oblige.*

Inside were many rooms divided according to the basic principles of day/night, public/private. Here again the age-old multifunctional nature of the environment and mingling with the servants had progressively given way to separation and division. At the same time domestic social life continued to be a prerogative of these families, who used a large part of their domestic space for entertaining guests and enjoying

themselves in company: so we find reception rooms, halls, antecham-
bers, drawing rooms, galleries, boudoirs, games rooms, and ballrooms.
The furnishings were lavish: showpiece furniture, paintings, carpets,
mirrors, sofas, armchairs, and precious ornaments. The furniture in the
receiving rooms of the Marquess Berlingieri of Naples (antechamber,
reception room, main hall, party room) in 1900 was worth more than
two thirds of the furnishings of the whole house and consisted of nine
sofas, ten armchairs, 14 easy chairs, 45 straight-backed chairs, a large
12-place dining table, card tables, a piano, several consoles, crystal
mirrors, carpets, and bronze chandeliers.[97] The amount of seating says
a great deal about the function of these rooms. The same is true for the
costly materials of the furnishings: precious wood for the furniture
(mahogany, rosewood) and marble, satin for sofas and chairs (though
there was no shortage of wooden 'Viennese' chairs), ornaments in
silver, copper, and crystal.[98] The noble *salon* was the area allocated to
social affairs. Here the master of the house would hold audiences—or
better still the lady of the house, because it was really the ladies who
enlivened the most famous 19th-century drawing rooms, creating an
almost political space where the *grandes dames* would gather and socialize. For example, Countess Maffei, several years earlier, would have
'received' between 3 and 6 o'clock in the afternoon, and then after
dinner until all conversation was over, as one guest recalls:

> There were two rooms the Countess allocated for receiving friends. She
> would sit there, without making herself the centre of the conversation but
> letting it fire the patriotic flame of her spirit. The rooms were welcomely
> decked in dark velvet, with that exquisitely simple harmonious taste that
> only real aristocrats know how to achieve. Venetian mirrors, oil paintings
> by Hayez, etchings by Calamatta, and portraits of illustrious friends
> decorated the walls. Fine lacework enhanced sofas and chairs and, by
> the armchair where the Countess sat listening and talking about this and
> that, there were vases on the piano and table, among the candelabras,
> with a profusion of flowers perfuming the air, especially in springtime.
>
> It is not true that in the Maffei drawing room one was bored to tears
> while poets recited their poems, playwrights their plays and economists
> their dissertations, as in *World of Boredom* by Pailleron. On the contrary,
> friends would animatedly discuss current events and now and then
> a serious, patriotic idea would be thrown in to make them think, or
> a witty remark to make them smile. Topics ranged from literature, art,

industry, economics, to philosophy, but everything revolved around the dominant thought—the uprising in Italy. No pedantry was allowed.[99]

Noble houses were not intended to be practical, or even functional: the reception area on the first floor, where the showpiece rooms were concentrated, was usually organized with all the rooms along the same axis, following 16th-century precepts, so that from the entrance hall you could see all the rooms in perspective, producing a spectacular effect.[100] Each room provided its own show of colour: wall tapestries against which large and small paintings stood out in their gilded frames, furniture made of a variety of woods, mirrors reflecting the light filtered through the great windows, heavy crimson curtains, sofas and arm-chairs in shiny satin, wooden floors, large multi-coloured carpets, and frescoed ceilings. A room could have its own particular theme or predominant colour, to suggest a time of day, a season, or a state of mind, as Mario Praz illustrates:

.... in the good season, when the sun shines through the courtyard window in the morning and then beats on the two windows overlooking Piazza Ricci between one and five o'clock in the afternoon, the great hall awakes like Sleeping Beauty in the Wood, opens its eyes and envelops the observer in a harmony of colour. The light from the south-facing window has a purer and fresher splendour, like the glint of a diamond, and the room is filled with joy. The woodwork in the eagle and swan library— warm, feathery maple wood—imitates the translucence of tortoiseshell; the green Aubusson carpet becomes a flowery meadow; the portrait of Foscolo and military picture on the opposite wall, surrounded by arms trophies, throb with an intense relief; and the room's triad of colours— yellow, red, and green—ring out like clarions...

When the chandeliers are lit the colours stand out like a bed of flowers washed by the rain or like summer sunshine bathing everything in its golden, shimmering light suffused by the veil of light dust that often hangs in the air. [. . .] and the house is like a forest bristling with furniture to conjure up strange creatures waiting in ambush: eagles, lions, one-legged swans, sphynxes, mermaids, turtles [. . .]. The house is a Sleeping Beauty wood, a brightly lit ballroom whose doors will soon spring open for the dances, or a solemn church ready, at the sound of the organ, for the procession to advance from the vestry.[101]

Objects were not placed anywhere but, following the advice of widely read manuals, arranged following a single style. In many cases the style itself was adapted to the function of the room. If an entrance hall, it was full of valuable antiques to impress the visitor with the social status of the household, the drawing room and main reception rooms might be furnished in Imperial style with its contrast of light and dark prized woods, sound geometric arrangement, and rich gilded decoration with mythological motifs (an unmistakable sign of prestige and wealth). A Gothic atmosphere suited the aristocrat's study, more severe and monumental, with a prevalence of dark colours, Renaissance style leather armchairs and straight-backed chairs (symbols of sobriety and composure), while the boudoir, or lady's private room, was furnished in the style of Louis XV (rococo, with its delicate inlays and lacquers) or Louis XVI, for a true evocation of 18th-century society. The private bedrooms might continue this nostalgia, with an array of monumental four-poster beds and antique furnishings, or flirt with the more 'bourgeois' Biedermeyer style, with its moderate proportions and simple curvilinear appearance. Of course the rooms in the servants' quarters were very different, far removed from the main areas and in larger houses often relegated to the top floors.

Aristocrats' mansions also contained numerous bathrooms, some of them well equipped with luxuries (from hot water to the novelty of the *bidet* imported from France). After centuries of cleaning oneself without the use of water, because it was feared that water could enter the pores and spread disease—far better, then, to rub down the skin, change one's clothes and dab on lashes of perfume—from the 19th century onwards, medical progress and a different attitude to the body brought a new regard for hygiene: bathing in water came to be no longer linked purely with pleasure as was the case in ancient times, or at most as a cure as had happened more recently, but with health. Hygiene and cleanliness thus became synonymous with discipline and order, associated with the upper classes as opposed to the physical and moral dirtiness of the lower orders.

Another important area in a noble household was the kitchen: large to the extent that it had to satisfy the needs of many (often demanding) individuals, and lavishly equipped with pots, pans, and all kinds of utensils. It was a kitchen mostly inhabited by women, as cooks and maids (as opposed to what were found previously, when the culinary arts of the great families were almost exclusively the prerogative of

men, while women had only cooked for lower ranking families).[102]
Mention of the kitchen naturally brings me to the question of food.
What did aristocrats eat? Or perhaps a more pertinant question would
be: how did aristocrats eat?

In his famous works, Norbert Elias has left an evocative description
that places the spreading of 'good manners' at table and in daily life in
the forefront of civilizing processes. His thesis is simple: the modern
age, starting from the aristocracy (he studied the Versailles of Louis
XIV), witnesses a development of self-control against any display of
emotion and impulse, particularly where cruelty, aggressiveness, and
sexuality are concerned. This control, which gradually spread to the
other social orders, developed side by side with the formation of the
modern State (the only entity to enjoy monopoly over violence)
providing it in fact with an indispensable cultural and social basis.
The rules that regulate daily life, etiquette, and good breeding are
therefore not just simple habits or curiosities from the past: they have
moulded the process of Western civilization and created appropriate
rules of conduct for life in a modern state.[103] Take the case of an
aristocrat's table. The habit of using cutlery for eating is relatively
recent and signals an important transition. Spoons are actually very
ancient implements, already known in Greek and Roman times, albeit
with more specific uses.[104] Knives were also in use and were much
more common, but with them we see an interesting development: in
successive attempts to limit their dangerousness it was suggested they
be used with care, that the tips of their blades be rounded off, and that
they should be held only by the handle when in use. The story of
the fork—a far more modern instrument—is of even greater interest.
Its first public appearance seems to have been in the hands of the
Byzantine Princess Argillo at her wedding in Venice in 955. This
strange, two-pronged gold instrument to convey food to the mouth
provoked amazement and disgust, to the extent that when the Princess
fell ill it was said to be a just punishment from God. The fork reap-
peared much later in the Italian Renaissance courts, then spread to
France and very slowly to the rest of Europe in the 18th century. At the
same time, among the well-to-do there was a multiplication of plates
and glasses, often very costly. Since it became the general practice to use
individual place sets instead of communal ware, the custom of having
everybody eat together from the same dish or pass a drinking vessel
brim-full of wine from one diner to another fell into disuse.[105]

What can be read into these changes? According to Elias they redefine our personal space and create physically 'emotional wall' between us and others, and between us and our own physical being too. This is also true for other aspects regarding the body, increasingly surrounded as it has been by restrictions and taboos (think of sexual relationships or bodily needs, once performed in public without a second thought, or being naked, which now causes shame and embarrassment). It is not so much a contrast between civilization and an imagined natural primitive state, but the fact that there has gradually been built up a network of rules and regulations to prevent excesses and create a disciplined code of behaviour.[106]

Etiquette, at table as elsewhere, was therefore an aspect of upper-class life which was anything but secondary. So, entering an aristocratic dining room at the end of the 19th century, noticiable would have been impressively tall furniture, the upper racks displaying precious plates and glasses, the long wooden table covered with a snow-white table-cloth, as was the tradition to emphasize cleanliness, and a set for each individual consisting of table napkin (to put over the knees to protect one's clothing), plates (of precious metal, white, or decorated china or pottery), an array of (silver) cutlery, glasses (crystal or glass, goblet or bowl, transparent or decorated), as well as salt cellars and other ornamental centrepieces. Among 19th-century novelties was a sense of uniformity due to the use of identical plates and glasses for everyone, all part of a single dinner service, with everything in place before the arrival of the diners, on account of the smaller number of servants available to serve at table. If it looks like a present-day table, apart perhaps from the costly materials and a certain choreographic showiness, this merely demonstrates how it has spread throughout society (it is certainly not the table of peasants, workers, or petit bourgeois).

The arrival of guests
Guests will have started the day with a light breakfast consisting of a cup of black coffee, coffee with milk, or chocolate, and a thin slice of buttered toast, and having already eaten lunch around eleven o'clock or noon, a light meal (made up of a 'thin soup' or an appetiser, followed by a meat dish with vegetables, and perhaps coffee) will expect to eat around six o'clock.[107] In come the serving staff bringing clear soup with rice or noodles or pasta: spaghetti, gnocchi, risotto. Rather than preceding, the appetisers follow, consisting of cold meats or salami, oysters,

small pieces of toast, anchovies or sardines with butter. To follow, the first of the main dishes is brought in, which might be fried, boiled, or steamed (fish or poultry for example). Then follows an 'interlude', an appetising little plateful of pastries filled with meat, stuffing, soufflés and, in summer, cold pies or aspic dishes. The diners are ready at last for the most important course, almost invariably a rich meat roast and side vegetables or, more rarely, a fish dish. To conclude the diners will savour the sweet course (cake, biscuits, pastries, and ice cream) and possibly fruit and cheese. Everything is accompanied by red or white wine—dry or maybe sweet—Italian, or French on important occasions. A really fine meal! And the aesthetic attention given to the food is no less than that given to the table arrangement. The Master of Ceremonies, Feldmann, describes the menu of Count Sanvitale di Fontanellato on an ordinary autumn day in 1884 thus: lunch at eleven o'clock consisting of gnocchi with meat sauce and grilled cutlets, dinner at six in the evening with semolina croquette soup, appetiser, stuffed capon with lasagne, egg in 'basalik', spit-roasted beef, radish salad, dessert, all served on fine china both Italian (Antonibon of Nove, Fusari, and Bianconi) and foreign (Göggingen or Enoch Wood). Far away from the nobles things were slightly different: the eleven servants had simple pasta, veal, and rice on cheap plates.[108]

Though sometimes italianized, many of the dishes served at table had French names (*mousse, omelette, pâté, potage, consommé, blanquette, croquet*), a sign of the indisputed rule of French cuisine. Like aristocrats all over Europe, the Italian aristocracy spoke French fluently, read French novels, and went to the theatre to see French plays (*boulevardières*), while French etiquette provided a model of correct behaviour, *comme il faut* (incidentally, being multi-lingual was a distinctive sign of this cosmopolitan class, which often had more to do with the great European capitals than with neighbouring cities).[109] It has been already noted how French cuisine decreed new rules for taste, reacting against rich Renaissance meals, based on meat and spices, and returning to relative simplicity and naturalness. In Italy this change was emphasized by the chefs of the great city hotels[110] and combined with regional traditions, all very different from one another, so it is impossible to speak of a national 'cucina Italiana'. Also, unification was a long way off. It would take a gastronomic enthusiast from Forlimpopoli, Pellegrino Artusi, with a vast experience of travelling up and down the peninsula on business, to write the first Italian food guide, *Science in the kitchen and the art of eating well.* He collected the culinary traditions of different regions, creating a privileged backbone between Florence and Romagna, to which he added Lombardy, Naples, and other zones of central Italy. His collection does not provide a uniform sample, giving priority as it does to some rich central-north regions, neglecting the south of Italy, and privileging the city rather than the country (even if he did try to adapt some peasant dishes for rich tables),[111] but it did sell well and became a model for later recipe books, which would be more complete from a regional point of view. The work proposed the basis for a 'national' cuisine, and this ambition was reinforced by the rejection of French recipes and exotic terminology, and by exalting national foods and traditions. In other words, the rediscovery of alimentary traditions was part of the nation-building process, and—if you like—paved the culinary road to patriotism.

Escaping from a regional dimension, in cuisine as in anything else, was more wishful thinking than real, however. The noble classes appeared on the scene, seeing themselves as being very different according to the region to which they belonged. Take the case of the Roman aristocracy. Born of princely stock with popes and cardinals among their ancestry, and boasting relations in half of Europe, they presented themselves as a group endowed with great prestige and influence in city life. As Leopardi complained, if these nobles had little interest in civic and political life, they did enjoy a solid economic foundation thanks to the highly re-valued land and property they owned, and displayed a splendid life style unequalled in Italy. With their magnificent palaces, parties, balls, and fashionable clothes set off by a Rome that was a combination of the Eternal City and capital of the new Italy, Roman aristocrats provided a point of reference for everyone but had few imitators (except perhaps among the rich and numerous Tuscan aristocracy).[112]

The Neapolitan nobility also tended to indulge in prestigious consumption, albeit in the presence of a less stable economic basis and to the extent of eroding family fortunes. Despite serious financial problems, in 1901 the aristocrat de'Medici possessed:

15 dress suits,
3 leisure suits,
43 shirts,
77 ties,

2 beaver overcoats,
1 astrakhan trimmed paletot,
5 hats and 2 top hats

while for the little Gaetano Molini a very high personal expenditure
was registered (4,773 lira) which, apart from food, was due to prestige
expenses, such as houses in the country and the city, servants, clothes,
and thermal and marine baths (while only 300 lira went to the tutor for
his education).[113]

The picture seems to have been different for the Piedmontese aristocracy, who kept the family fortunes solvent thanks to careful investments and improvements in land management. They took on a
prominent role in the Italian kingdom, for example in the ranks of
the army or royalty, but did not mix easily, even with the rich middle
class, and maintained a social detachment, if not in public situations,
certainly in where they met and the circles they frequented, where they
lived in the city, where they spent their holidays, and how they conducted their matrimonial strategies. On the public stage an attitude
of *understatement* was appreciated, which valued ownership without
ostentatious display of it. On the eve of the First World War, the tip
of the Turin social pyramid was therefore formed by a parallel yet
separate elite.[114]

Yet another atmosphere was breathed in Milan. Here the nobles
were involved more than elsewhere in mercantile, banking and business
activities, and the social distancing seemed less (even if frequenting the
circles that counted—the Union, the Garden, and the Patriotic Society—reveals a precise hierarchy).[115] A similar public life style linked the
nobility and Ambrosian upper middle class at the start of the century: a
subdued taste in dress (albeit attentive to quality), traditionalist and
disdainful of 'Parisian' fashion, bold colours, or showy jewels. A family
portrait depicts a serious Lady Gallavresi in a high-collared long black
dress, hands at her sides and hair gathered up (while her daughter
Maria, dressed in white, looks more natural as she clings affectionately
to her side). In another portrait Maria Luisa Pirotta Bonacossa is seated
with composure at the edge of a sofa, dressed in black, her hands
resting on her lap, her chestnut hair tied up with a thin red ribbon, as
she looks straight ahead of her. Images of moderation and seriousness.[116] Male portraits are closer to the stereotype, with figures seated
or more often standing, composed and authoritative, without fail in

elegant dark suits, often beside symbols of their work or against the background of the city or their own home. These portraits, commissioned for artists of even good training, make a form of self-representation that reveal a great deal about the cultural values of that social group.

On the subject of art then, how can the portrayal of the Sicilian nobility as it appears in *The Leopard* by Tomasi di Lampedusa possibly be forgotten? Inspired by the personality of an ancestor of the author, the protagonist towers materially and morally above his world: cultured, refined, expert in the things of life, he lives in a sumptuous frescoed palace surrounded by countless precious objects that underline the rank and history of his lineage, but sees his world become decadent in the social climbing of the newly rich middle class and also in the open-mindedness of his nephew who mixes with the new masters. He, Prince Salina, refuses the appointment of Senator in the new Kingdom of Italy: there is no possibility of compromise between the lifestyle and values of the aristocracy and those of the 'bourgeois' of the new age.[117]

In this variety of styles and 'interpretations' of aristocratic culture there are some common areas in the sphere of leisure, which combines amusement and, yet again, distinction. Going to the theatre, for example, was an important social rite carrying with it the need to wear appropriate dress (tails for men, evening dress and jewels for women). Not only was there a distinct circuit of theatres and opera houses, attended by the upper classes, very different from the popular music halls beginning to spring up in the city outskirts, but the social difference was also reinforced by physical separation inside the auditorium itself: nowadays the oldest theatres still keep two separate entrances, each with its own foyer, the main one for the stalls and boxes, and the side entrance for the cheaper seats in the balcony.[118] Other exclusive forms of entertainment, then, included exploring distant lands—very popular in the wake of colonialism—journeys around Europe (Paris, London, Germany, and Switzerland) and holidays in the country, by the lake and at the seaside.

Then there is sport: hiking, mountaineering (the Italian Alpine Club was founded at Turin in 1863 the first president being Baron Perrone di San Martino), and quality sports like hunting and horse jumping most of all.[119] Equestrian sports are the most characteristic of the nobility and give rise to a curious question. If the 19th century saw a great passion for horses, why was the first 'Horse Racing Society' starting at

Florence, Turin, and Pisa created only halfway through the century? During the 1880s there was a great frenzy: each city and holiday resort wanted to have its very own racecourse and built it very wastefully (through private societies whose members were mostly aristocrats and some great factory owners). The point of reference was England more than Paris: the model followed for the architecture and also for the sporting practices and rules was taken strictly from the British Jockey Club (including the spectacular side and the betting business). Even dress was strictly regulated: men had to wear a dark blazer and a Florentine straw hat, the women a light-coloured dress with a collar, wide feathered hat, and lace parasol. Races were great social occasions, splendidly described by D'Annunzio in *Il Piacere*.[120] So stables and racecourses sprang up all over Italy, from Barbaricina and San Rossore at Varese and Leghorn, and had an extraordinary success until the First World War and then again in the inter-war period. It was not just flat racing and trotting, competitions such as horse jumping also became very popular where there were competitors such as 'horseman of horsemen', Federico Caprilli, who set up a high jump record of more than two metres at Turin in 1902 starting off a revolutionary riding style.[121]

How can the explosion of this great passion at the very time that cars began to appear be explained? Is it a form of conservatism, a rejection of new technology perceived as social levelling? The reason may be that it was a form of spectacularization based on exhibitions of archaic practices. Going horse riding and organizing equestrian competitions just when more and more cars were appearing meant underlining the difference between them and the other social classes, reaffirming continuity with the past, and ceremonial typical of times gone by. Anachronism became a sign of distinction, although the aristocracy were quick to adopt technological innovations.

One thing is certain: more so here than for any other group, the consumer space of the aristocracy was manifestly transnational.

2

The State and Public Consumption

Words have their own history, and it is a history that reflects the evolution of a culture. To describe society I have used terms like 'consumption' and 'consumer practices'. I have tried to depict it as a complex system rich in vertical and horizontal connections, in continuous movement, its various components organized within itself as well as in relationship with the outside, each part interacting with and influencing another. And with the term 'consumption' I have implied that in this scenario the individual actors—the consumers—are not passive elements only capable of acting when prompted, but dynamic agents thoroughly aware of the possible consequences of their actions.

A hundred years ago nobody would have used such terms or images—not because they failed to understand social complexity, but because the society of the time seemed more like a pyramid whose most significant elements were the base and the apex. From this derived a substantially two-track logic for which the best description that could be given was linked to this dichotomy: 'poverty' opposed to 'abundance'. If this was the situation, any reforms aimed at improving society would perforce take the form of a fight against poverty.

With this in mind, an important fact to remember—as yet overlooked—is that not all existing forms of consumption are private, in other words bought or produced by individuals, but that some are enjoyed collectively. Whatever is produced by the various economic sectors of the country (agriculture, industry, services, public administration) is used for consumption, be it private (people's expenditures) or public (government spending), and investments. In 1891, household consumption accounted for more than 80 per cent of total expenditure, in 1951 it was 67 per cent and by the '90s it had fallen below 60 per cent more or less everywhere in the western world (in this regard Italy followed the same trend as other European countries at the time).[1] The history of the 20th century is basically this: changing habits in private consumption and progressive expansion in public consumption (and investments).

This discourse brings us to affirm that consumption has always had a central role in government policies. Some academics are in the habit of looking at economics and politics from the supply side, that is assuming that governments take action in order to develop the various productive sectors (agriculture first, industry and services second), and what counts is production. But what about consumption? In my opinion government policies have focused just as much on the side of demand: if through investments they have increased the capital allocated to support growth, through public consumption they have had a strong effect on 'human' capital, influencing private consumption and basically the entire economy. Security, consensus, redistribution, growth. The political motives may have varied, but one thing is certain: we need to be aware of the role played by consumption to understand the directions taken by the economic policies of Liberal Italy, the Fascist regime, and then the Republic.

There were different aims of course, and different terminology, not always emerging explicitly during public debate. Nothing similar to what happened, for example, in post-unification Italy concerning the possible intervention of the State in favour of industrial production (the clash between liberals and protectionists ending decisively on the side of state intervention). But why should the State have interfered in the field of consumption? Did it not aim to guarantee development so that individuals could consume the resources available as they wished, intervening only in the most dramatic cases of poverty or social exclusion?

Differences in consumption were not a sufficient motive for intervening; social disparities had always existed. Endemic poverty in wide swathes of the population was a centuries-old phenomenon, which according to many it was neither possible, nor even desirable to change. The real motive lay in the inability of the single individual, who might be a victim of misfortune (sickness, accident), and in this case should be helped by charity organizations, or else was a social misfit: a lazy beggar, drunkard or good-for-nothing, hence responsible for his own predicament. Pauperism was hotly debated in Italy as elsewhere at the start of the 19th century, reflecting these positions. In reality, however, as industrialization spread, so the features of the problem changed: the conditions of both country and town workers seemed to be worsening dramatically. It was a wide-ranging dilemma, linked to working methods in the factories, to living conditions in the increasingly crowded towns, and to the economic crisis in rural areas. The idea started to take hold that these forms of poverty had a social explanation and were perhaps connected to structural problems in the economy and society itself, not just to the good luck or good will of the single individual. If this were the case would the assistance given by private or religious charity associations be sufficient? Would not some corrective intervention by the State be necessary? Immediately after the creation of the Italian Kingdom (1861–1945) there was already a multiplicity of studies, inquiries, and appeals that denounced the dreadful conditions experienced by town and country workers, and called for public intervention with regard to what was now presented as the 'social question'.[2] In perhaps the most famous investigation, the agrarian inquiry of 1884, Count Stefano Jacini affirmed:

> Now that there is a social question in Europe and therefore also in Italy, if under this name we understand the growing wish of the poor classes to improve their condition, it would be impossible to deny it. However this question does not apply only to the country; it includes all the working classes, in the city as well as the country.[3]

Another problem was to select the right methods for State intervention. The most widely accepted idea was that they ought to be aimed at 'public' consumption, that is those forms of individual welfare that the market was unable to provide. It was not so much a question of increasing expenditure for society as a whole, as was the case with security or defence, for example, but of providing specific benefits and services for individuals: welfare, social security, a decent health service, and education.[4]

Alongside the humanitarian and philanthropic arguments there were other strong motives. As Stefano Cavazza has stressed, since the 19th century the idea of 'mass' had been used as a dimension to describe and define modern society. No longer shapeless and disorganized plebs, it was now a kind of interconnected community with a recognizable shape that had become an active part in the working world, determined to assert its social rights and organize itself into something that counted on the political scene. Having come into being with reference to quantity, the term ended up by taking on a qualitative value. The 'social question' was nourished by the fear that this new mass of people could represent a destabilizing social element, concentrated in the towns and causing an increase in the crime rate (or so it seemed to the eyes of the elite), as well as revolutionizing the meaning of association and even leisure activities.[5] The transition from social to political plane was rapid. The working masses became the proletarian masses inflamed by socialist propaganda. This process can even be seen iconographically: the crowd becomes assertive, the subject of paintings (*The Fourth Estate* by Pellizza da Volpedo, belongs to 1901).[6] It appears in satirical sketches and political posters, no longer part of the background but out in front, no longer an amorphous, blurred accumulation but a spiritual unit around a symbol.[7]

After arguing long in favour of agrarian reform, Jacini continues:

> If discontent with what they are and what they have and a yearning to escape from their condition and climb to a better one, are rife among all classes without exception—imagine what it is like among the lowest and least well off.—Such trends form one of the psychological characteristics of civil society in our time and, as long as they remain within the limits of gratification, they are a good thing and provide a powerful lever for individual and social progress and enhancement. But going beyond these limits they could become the cause of deep unrest and anarchy, leading to regression. So, will modern society be able to stay within the limits of possible gratification?[8]

A possible response for curbing explosive social conflict came from Bismarck's Germany, which had launched an advanced social legislation to contain the influence of the socialist movement and tie the working masses firmly to the State. An example that was different but no less interesting came from England, where social protection instead of being decided from above was the result of cooperation between the Liberal forces and those inspired by Labour, at least during most recent times, and was thus a policy that aimed at the effective integration of the nation's working classes. If we look at Italian figures, expenditure in this sector turns out to be very modest for the entire Liberal period when compared to Germany and England (around 9 per cent of demand). It was not that the Italian state was uncommitted where spending public money was concerned—on the contrary: historically, both Left and Right had made a big effort, but it was principally directed towards the creation of infrastructures (starting with the railways) and building the complex administrative apparatus of the new State. There was precious little room for spending on education, which was left for the most part to local bodies, and almost nothing for redistribution costs. Only during the Giolitti period was there a relative change of direction.

Take welfare. What was the fate of someone who become ill in 19th-century Liberal Italy? It obviously depended on how much they earned. If they were well off they could call in a private doctor and undergo expensive private treatment at home or, if very sick, in the city hospitals. If they were poor they would have to turn to a charity association for help. Predominantly Catholic, these had developed enormously over the centuries, and ran hospitals, charities, and welfare associations. In 1862, a law was passed concerning these charitable institutions, and followed in substance the Savoy ordinance on good works, leaving them wide freedom of action, thus avoiding any financial duties on the part of the new state. Three years later it was established that local bodies should tend to the needs of some categories of 'unfortunates', that is not only the sick but also the poor and destitute by putting them into special institutions. The provinces were to look after certain sick people (the mentally ill and handicapped), the town councils were to take on the burden of hospital expenses and welfare of paupers and orphans, together with the help of charitable congregations (from whom our poor individual would have sought assistance). In charge of public health was the Ministry for the Interior and those locally responsible were the prefects and mayors. It is interesting to note the inclusion in these provisions of psycho-physical illness, child abandonment, and begging, a sign that the concept of welfare and public order was founded on the control of categories considered social rejects. It was a public health project that controlled and strengthened the social organism in favour of the State, similar to the constitution of a 'Health Police' tried out in Germany.[9]

For further progress we have to await the arrival of Crispi. With the new sanitary reform of 1888 a Health Department was created. At local level there was a general practitioner and midwife for the poor, paid for by the town councils, and a network of provincial doctors responsible for hygiene and preventive care. This shows more concern for country areas (our poor invalid had in fact been penalized if he had lived in the country) as well as a different role for doctors, who were no longer treated as technicians or consultants but as state officials. It signalled the formal recognition of decades of efforts by professional associations to have the public role of doctors recognized, which included their entry as leaders of the health institutions instead of the

administrative personnel. Charitable associations became public institutions, laying the foundations for modernizing the by now inadequate
hospital structures—the Policlinico hospital in Rome was established,
together with many minor hospitals, and those receiving assistance
rose from 345,000 in 1885 to 503,000 in 1902.[10] During the Giolitti
period attention was centred on the fight against diseases like tuberculosis, cholera, and especially malaria against which the distribution of
free quinine from tobacconists was ordered.[11] The focus then moved
on to hygiene and prevention, thanks to the birth of 'social medicine' (it
must also be remembered that public opinion was passionately following scientific progress, in microbiology for example with the researches
of Louis Pasteur and Robert Koch, or those linked to the new clinical
trends). The impact of these reforms was of great importance, witnessing the growing role that medicine was assuming in mid-19th-century
Italian society. These were the first steps in the process of 'medicaliza-
tion' and created a growing demand in health consumption. And to
these direct interventions would be added those made in the city for
'hygienic purposes': clearing out old, run-down areas, creating squares
and broadways (like the Umberto I project carried out in Naples
between 1888 and 1894 to clean up the slums after the latest cholera
epidemic). Foucault has written interestingly about ways to control the
'social body' by means of a public hygiene policy, which first appeared
in 18-19th-century Paris.[12] At the start of the 20th century, the Italian
poor could therefore rely on a slightly better sanitary and hospital
system. They probably did not become ill so often, thanks to prevention
measures and structural changes in the urban context. Above all they
saw medicine in a different light and began to consider the new
expenses for health and hygiene as important.

It is no coincidence that during the last decades of the 19th century
the new pharmaceutical industry developed, with its epicentre in
German chemical firms, which ran parallel to and partly replaced the
home-made preparations of the pharmacists with sugar-coated pills,
syrups, and pre-packed tablets: names like Aspirin, patented by Bayer
in 1899 became familiar to everybody, and local industries also multiplied, such as those of Emilio Schiapparelli in Turin (the first to produce
acetylsalicylic acid in Italy), Cesare Serono in Rome, and Carlo Erba
in Milan. A new consumer sector was born: that of pharmaceutical
products on a broad commercial scale.

The situation was perhaps worse on the social security side. Until the end of the 19th century the only help available for a worker would be the support of a privately run mutual assistance company. These were very numerous (more than 6,700 at the turn of the century) and often inspired by Socialist or Catholic ideologies (and therefore basically anti-state). It was only in 1898, in line with strong industrial development, together with the political birth of the Turati socialists, that regulations were passed such as obligatory insurance against accidents for industrial workers, and invalid and old-age pensions (optional and with scant success) and then, with Giolitti, the National Insurance Institute and a legislation that safeguarded the work of minors and limited that of women: on the whole, restricted and tardy rulings compared with those of the European countries from which inspiration was drawn.[13]

I turn now to consider education. What could a child of that time look forward to? The well-to-do classes, as I have shown, could afford private teachers and could send their children to educational institutes beyond the elementary level (college preparatory or technical schools) right up to university level (with a preference for law or medicine). It is known that education, 'human capital', was always the strong point of the upper classes. The Casati law of 1859 had established the obligation for two years of elementary education, extended to four years by the Coppino law of 1877, but with scant success in the country regions and the south of Italy, mostly because the financial responsibility rested with town councils (who could not or would not spend much on education). A definite improvement was recorded when the state was called in to shoulder this burden, with the Daneo-Credaro law of 1911. In that year, the level of illiteracy in Italy was still 38 per cent (from a minimum of 11 per cent in Piedmont to a maximum of 70 in Calabria); of the child population of school age 76 per cent attended primary school, 12 per cent continued to secondary school, and only 1 per cent went on to university.[14] In this case, too, the numbers were low for Italian young people, when compared to their European contemporaries (and with it also a lower tendency for cultural consumption: for example there is a direct correspondence between the numbers going to school and book sales, especially during the early stages of becoming literate). It goes without saying that things were worse for girls, especially at the higher levels of education. However a certain effort was being made in this direction, with the growing allocation of resources.[15]

In reality, when the inhabitants of the Italian Kingdom thought about consumption and the state, their first idea was certainly not about the limited amount of public spending: like two-faced Janus, the state gave on one side and took away on the other, but not from everybody in equal measure. Taxes have always been a pillar of governmental politics, linked as they are to the very basis of democracy (going back to the American 'no taxation without representation'), and of course naturally interwoven with consumption. Up to the First World War, half of the bulk of state and local revenues came from direct taxes (land and to increasingly extent property taxes) and half from indirect taxes, essentially made up of taxes on consumption. This affected various products in the form of manufacturing taxes: tobacco, salt, milled products (from 1868 to 1884), spirits, and sugar; there were also consumer tariffs collected at the local level and, from 1878 protection policies, new tariff custom houses. Also, for some products there was a state monopoly tax: tobacco, salt, gunpowder, quinine and—the great hope of the poor—the lottery.[16] It can be seen, therefore, that taxes weighed heavily on types of consumer products that played a big part in the budgets of the lower classes. It is no coincidence that some serious episodes of violence were in some way linked to tax policy (post-unification banditry, revolts against the tax on milled products, the 1898 unrest). It has been calculated that the 'regressive' taxes, weighing so heavily on the lowest incomes, cut into almost half of the total revenue.[17] And it must be added that the overall fiscal pressure of Liberal Italy was proportionally greater than it was in following periods.[18]

What is the resulting overall picture when the policy from the consumers' point of view is observed? Despite all the uncertainties and waverings of Liberal Italy there emerges in the long run a clear-cut orientation. It is that of a state that understands the importance of a public consumption policy, at the start penetrating more from the qualitative rather than the quantitative point of view, so to say: beyond the actual expenditure a 'cultural' basis was set for consumption such as health and education. In other words, that social consumer practices begin to enter into the political area. It is evident that the provisions adopted would have the aim of controlling the country and the 'social body' no less than making the nation stronger. Growth and patriotism are woven together and reinforce each other. Again what Jacini writes at the very end of his study is enlightening:

As regards pauperism, it cannot be said to be general in the Italian countryside, in the true sense of the word, but it does exist; it is the miserable condition of the agrarian classes which can be extensively found more or less all over Italy. We must therefore offer a remedy, as far as possible, with all our might. It is like an enemy fortress which has reared its ugly head in the middle of our homeland. This fortress must be eradicated and expelled from new Italy whenever possible. But to succeed in this we must first surround it with seige works, and then attack it not from one side only but all sides at once, throwing into the campaign all the forces we have, without exception. Proceed in any other way and the assault would be repulsed.[19]

It is therefore no surprise that the main attention was at first directed towards the education sector, the only one capable of making sure that there would be the widespread and standard instruction necessary to achieve agricultural progress and especially to make the industrial sector work (it was not by chance that the only significant social security interventions were intended for industrial workers, partly thanks to pressure from the socialist movement).[20] All this perfectly supplements and integrates the bulk of public spending, that is to say the formidable task of creating infrastructure and investments. The burden of this spectacular thrust towards development would be shouldered largely by the working classes, since the most widespread consumer goods would be taxed; imposed by the privileged few who were running the country. This also had the effect of partially redirecting private consumers wherever possible. One could say that this period saw the beginning of the creation of a 'national space' to direct consumer choices.

From the point of view of Italian consumers this policy had heavy costs, which differed according to social class and even gender. Costs that were not just economic: in the eyes of the town or country worker the presence of the state loomed every day whenever a purchase was made of some primary need (salt, sugar, tobacco, wine—while luxury goods were exempt). This would fuelled a distrust and resentment for the state, felt even in large numbers of the population that were not politically orientated. Very little was offered in exchange, in terms of education, welfare, and social security.

3

The World of Production

Which are more important, the consumers or the producers? The question is inevitable the moment it is realized that consumer practices are of course the result of cultural processes, but that they inevitably must take into account the material factors that condition them. I could take as an example the historical background and geography of a given society and, for the modern age in particular, that set of elements covered by the term 'production'. The relationship linking production and consumption is obviously one of reciprocal influence (and so our question risks being of the type 'Which came first, the chicken or the egg?'). Economists, who are among the intellectuals most concerned with the question, have traditionally come down in favour of giving more weight to the producers.

Classical economists like Adam Smith and Ricardo concentrated on production. Marx moved in the same direction, but recognized the distinction between use value for a commodity (linked to its effective use with time) and its exchange value (linked to its market price), and lingered on the penchant of capitalist economy for producing large quantities of merchandise. These standpoints are hardly surprising considering the background of the early phases of the Industrial Revolution, while the complex economic developments that followed saw the flowering of neoclassical tendencies (Marshall, Walras and Pareto), which gave more attention to market dynamics. They in fact highlighted the link between consumer demand and producer supply: each wanting the maximum benefit (to satisfy a need or to make a profit, respectively) and their ideal meeting point signified market equilibrium. The consumers are very much present, even if represented in an ideal and rational form. In the following analysis we notice how the producer's power to control the market increases in the presence of situations like monopoly and oligopoly. It is not surprising that such positions have been heavily criticized because they underestimated the historical and social factors. There are famous protests: Max Weber read capitalism in the light of religious and ascetic inspiration in favour of accumulation; or, a mirror of a society with a well-consolidated economic elite, Veblen observed the new role of wealth that linked social status to conspicuous consumption. Starting with the theories of Keynes who attributed to consumption, beyond that of the State, a fundamental role in guaranteeing economic growth, the consumers gained their revenge, especially during the post-war period with intellectuals such as Duesenberry and Katona. The first, noted for his theory of 'demonstration effect', explained that consumption becomes fundamental in a modern society characterized by a high level of social mobility to indicate one's own social condition. The second saw consumption as a real force behind the new mass society, where the consumer is a subject guided not only by prices and incomes, but also by habits and future prospects. The time factor is central even in more recent analyses. Friedman thought of consumption as a constant share of a permanent income. Modigliani used the whole lifelong earnings as a benchmark for consumption. Naturally starting with 1960–1970s, however, there developed a strong critical current against consumption, which even affected the economists. Nevertheless it is interesting to note here that the role of the consumer has grown and become more evident with the passage of time. From a passive and manipulated subject the consumer has gradually acquired an active and dynamic role on the economic stage, almost equal to that of the producers so that, the sector that deals with marketing, market research, and consumer analyses has spread enormously. Furthermore, another figure is progressively coming to light, the 'mediator' in this relationship, that is the dealer. Therefore in the long run the 'cultural role' of the consumer is decidedly changed and perhaps the best image of the producer-consumer interaction, rather than a more or less balanced bilateral link, is that of a circle where the various participants, including the 'mediators', influence each other in turn and negotiate their positions—all against the background of a culture that will determine the final meaning of these practices.[1]

I now return to the question asked as the beginning of the chapter—how important in Italy were producers with respect to consumer processes during the historic interval between the end of the 19th century and the start of the 20th? I would say supremely important, because they produced or at least made the production effectively available for the market (also thanks to the commercial intermediates, which we shall discuss further on); consumer choice, with all the differentiations that we have already seen, took place *de facto* within this productive scenario. There are two important modifying factors. The first is imports from abroad. Italy passed through its first industrial surge in this period, a typical transformation economy with few raw materials. In the European picture it appeared to be a country caught in mid-stream between a traditional and an industrialized economy. Exports were mostly agricultural produce, fabrics (with silk—the 'golden thread'—always to the fore) and foodstuffs. It imported wheat, raw and semi-processed materials, and finished industrial products.[2] Many luxury consumer goods came from abroad. However, the opening in the Italian economy was fairly limited and one could not say that in this period foreign produce played a decisive role in overall consumption (with the obvious exception of consumption by the elite, given their cosmopolitan character and economic resources).

The second is self-consumption. This is a delicate topic because, mainly in pre-industrial society or the early phases of industrialization, many activities linked to production did not pass through the market, that is goods were not bought or sold, so did not show up officially. Statistics made to register market transactions, did not record work performed at home, domestic work, or services exchanged through networks of friends and relatives, which put together would have accounted for a quota of roughly 20–25 per cent of consumption.[3] The economist Federico Caffè joked about this fact, saying that if he were to marry his housemaid he would diminish the national income. We must be aware that of economic statistics, apart from their technical reliability, reflect only one facet of society; and also that a part of consumption, especially in the form of services is constantly being underestimated (this is chiefly true for the working classes and it also explains one of the deep meanings of class or neighbourly solidarity).

Nevertheless, there are some long-term tendencies concerning consumer products. In the first place there was a transition from primary material consumption to industrialized goods, the most outstanding example being food. At the end of the 19th century, just over 33 per cent of all consumed products came from agriculture and another 30 per cent from the food industry. Sixty years later the situation had almost reversed, with the food industry in the first place and primary agricultural produce down to 16 per cent.[4] This means that many operations performed in the family environment (cleaning, cutting, preserving, cooking) had been taken over by the food industry, for reasons which were social (changes revealed inside the family and an increase in work for women outside the home), economic (better opportunities to earn) and technological (new techniques to preserve and process food). In the second place it is clear that consumers were giving more attention to new products, for example those offered by the chemical industry (soaps, detergents), to machines and transport (bicycles, motorcycles, cars), and partly to printed material, with various products linked to increasing school attendance. However, consumption of these goods was in the long run very small and did not significantly impact on the general equilibrium. Finally there was a tendency to move from perishables to preservable goods, though even in this case it is only at the early stages and must wait until after the Second World War to see any significant changes.[5] Considering the clout shown by some national industries in consumer processes it is worthwhile looking into their characteristics and what they had to offer the multifaceted consumer world.

I shall start with the food industry and try to imagine sneaking into a well stocked pantry at the start of the 20th century. What do I find? It is all very strange: even if some typical foods are recognizable, the majority of the products have unfamiliar shapes, colours and packaging (Hartley's words spring to mind: 'the past is a foreign country'). Many foods are stored in glass jars; others are packed in wooden boxes and tightly wrapped in cloth or paper. Foods which are dried or salted (like fish) dominate; from the ceiling hang sausages of various shapes and sizes, while on the shelves sit well-covered blocks of more or less mature cheese. We are at once struck by the preponderance of dried products, including fruit and vegetables, rather than fresh food, just as we notice the absence of any standardizing among the products. Looking in the apple basket we do not see two alike (and many are small or damaged). In the coolest corner we notice the most perishable goods: poultry and other meat, eggs, milk, and butter; below there are oil containers and several crates of bottled wine, all unlabelled and corked manually, while standing nearby is a half-full demijohn acquired from a reliable cellar. Another thing that strikes the eye in this rich pantry is the lack of product labels: here it is evidently local, unnamed produce or industrial goods sold loose at a nearby shop. I also notice the amount of primary material (like flour), used as a base for domestic preparation and a variety of products, and also herbs and several products from nearby gardens. Finally, on the highest shelves there is a splendid display of

Table 2 Private consumption supply, selected years (%)

Production sectors	Year 1891	1911	1938	1951
Agriculture	32.6	31.8	15.3	16.1
Extraction	0.3	0.3	0.7	0.9
Food	30.9	27.5	31.4	33.4
Tobacco	1.9	1.9	3.8	3.8
Textiles	2.6	3.6	3.3	3.8
Clothing	5.2	5.1	5.4	6.7
Furs and leather	4.1	4.2	2.7	2.8
Wood, furniture	0.2	0.6	0.7	1.0
Metalwork	0.4	0.8	2.3	4.3
Mechanics	0.4	0.4	0.8	0.1
Non-metallic minerals	0.3	0.7	2.0	2.8
Chemicals	0.0	0.2	0.2	0.7
Coal and oil derivatives	0.0	0.1	0.1	0.7
Rubber	0.0	0.1	0.1	0.7
Paper	0.2	0.6	1.3	2.5
Other manufacturing	0.1	0.1	1.1	0.1
Construction				
Electricity, gas, water	0.2	0.5	1.4	1.3
Commerce	3.0	4.6	2.8	2.0
Transport	2.1	2.7	7.0	3.3
Communications	0.1	0.2	0.5	1.2
Credit and insurance	0.3	0.4	1.4	0.9
Various services	7.3	5.7	5.3	6.4
Public administration				
Building rentals	7.8	8.0	10.4	5.2
Total	100.0	100.0	100.0	100.0

Source: *I conti economici dell'Italia*, edited by G.M. Rey, vol. III, *Il conto risorse e impieghi (1891, 1911, 1938, 1951)*, Rome-Bari, Laterza (2003), p. XLV (tab. 18).

home-made preserves: jams, jellies, fruit in liqueur, sauces, tomato preserves (and several others we are unable to identify).

The contents of this pantry reveal much about the food industry. Besides a reminder of the importance of self-consumption, it confirms that production has a local character: almost all the food products were made within a radius of fifty miles or so, within the same region at most. In fact the food sector, albeit the most important for total production (in 1911 it reached a total value of 854 millions, which was more than the mechanical industry) and involving even more man-hours when compared with more advanced sectors, was still very small on average (5 employees per operating unit) and on the whole proved to be behind the times from a technical point of view, often placed half way between industry and crafts (or industry and farming).[6] Small producers served their own area and were neither interested nor had the productive capacity to expand, with a few exceptions concerning luxury items or products destined for the export market.

Nevertheless, these years represent a crucial transformation period. The shock wave of the Industrial Revolution, starting with the mechanical and textile industries, was beginning to make itself felt in food transformation too, with new processing techniques, new machines and new industrial products (such as chemicals) to use during the different stages of production. The result is that some firms managed to make the quantum leap and begin to mechanically produce enormous quantities of food, much more standardized and decidedly cheaper products thanks to economies of scale. Was it easy, then? Absolutely not. Selling small quantities of home-made products to local customers, who know us through habit and word-of-mouth, involves very different mechanisms from those used for selling large quantities of industrial products to unknown customers far away in national and international markets. Big producers must take into account problems linked to distribution and, above all, to *marketing* (even if they had never even heard the word before). In this way an aspect took shape that would transform the history of consumption in the 20th century: branding.

What is a brand? The question may sound ironic to the ears of 21st-century consumers, exposed every day to hundreds of logos. Its meaning has known with the passage of time a complex evolution and widening range of meanings; initially it was simply a trademark: the name or symbol of a commercial item produced by a firm, often protected under a legal register. Naturally, giving distinctive names was nothing new, but in the ever-expanding market created thanks to modern transport and the Industrial Revolution, this has taken on a completely different meaning having become a means of characterizing goods and, if possible, enhancing their sales. A brand has two basic functions. The first is informative: it lets you know the characteristics of the product, its functions and contents even before you buy it; the second is evaluative: it provides a kind of 'added value' with respect to the product itself, telling us how this specific article rates in the market, and what status value it can give—make us feel fashionable, rich, modern, or part of a definite social group.[7]

Creating a brand is essentially based on advertising, a phenomenon that not by chance was taking its first steps also in Italy at this time. It was, however, publicity concerning above all the first aspect of advertising, that is information. On pages of magazines giving space to an increasing number of 'ads' (pull-out supplements at first), there appeared illustrations, each with a small picture of the product and a lengthy description. This is hardly surprising, since in this first phase the most important thing was to introduce buyers to the product and make its use clear, as well as explaining how and why to use it. This also accounts for the amount of writing on the ad (the age also witnessed the first posters, though they were not greatly used by the food industry). Another important aspect was the *packaging*,—again an unknown term although many had already realized that the external package of the product (shape, colour, printed logo) played an important part in giving it character and should stay the same over time. If the whole mechanism worked, and it was possible to distribute the goods quite extensively, it was hoped that the consumers themselves would ask for that specific product and, in the long run, form an attachment to the brand.

Going back to my pantry to check on the presence of branded products, and looking more carefully, I now see several industrial packages (having failed to switch on the light before!)

A whole shelf is taken up by pasta and pastries. Beside home produce I can see pasta from Buitoni (a family firm founded in 1827 at Sansepolcro, near Arezzo, very early to mechanize and makers of new products such as glutinate and diet pasta), from the Abruzzese Filippo De Cecco, from Barilla of Parma (created in 1877) and from Agnesi of Oneglia, as well as several brands from the area between Naples and Salerno (with producers such as Vicinanza, Scaramella, Rocco, and Pepe).[8] Among the sweet products biscuits immediately strike the eye, a typical English speciality; but we also notice some boxes of Lazzaroni almond biscuits (one of the first Italian industries in the sector, thanks to the English machines the ex-Garibaldi supporter Luigi Lazzaroni had brought into his father's factory—he was one of the first to attach great importance to the requirements of the external packaging, which in fact we notice immediately), as well as 'English' biscuits made by the Tuscans Marinai and Guelfi (the latter went so far as to disguise himself as a charcoal dealer to spy on the top-secret English machines, and on his return to Italy made his own manufacturing machinery). Then there are large quantities of chocolate, nearly all coming from Turin: we see Caffarel hazelnut chocolate, Venchi chocolate-coated sugared almonds, chocolates made by Moriondo & Gariglio, and even Talmone (the biggest Italian firm, founded in 1850 and already bought by Tobler of Bern in 1905: Swiss competition is very fierce).[9] Perhaps there will also be a glimpse of Perugina products, a small Perugia firm, jointly bought by a branch of Buitoni and the Spagnoli family.

A prominent sector at the time was that of preserves, connected as they are with the need to conserve perishable food such as fruit and vegetables (we have already noticed the large number of jars in the pantry). Looking around, we see that the label most present is Cirio: we discover it on tins of peeled tomatoes, vegetable preserves, tins of fish products (side by side, however, with those of the Genoese firm Angelo Parodi) and even on boxes of fresh fruit. Yet this only represents a tiny part of Francesco Cirio's activities. This entrepreneur from Nizza Monferrato was a real pioneer of the Italian food industry. He started with exports: fruit, vegetables, and even eggs, poultry, cheeses, and wines to be transported to northern Europe in special refrigerator wagons invented by himself. A preservatives firm in Turin was added to this in 1856, the first round of an industrial expansion to southern Italy, Venetia, Tuscany and even abroad, which gradually embraced many collateral activities: railway wagons, flour mills, fertilizers, cheesemaking, and model farms. The Cirio empire (founded not by chance on imports–exports, given that the home market was unable to absorb all he had to offer) overshot itself and had to get through many difficulties at the start of the century when, scaled down, it passed to the Signorini brothers. As well as Cirio I see other preserves with the labels of Del Gaizo, Polli, and Arrigoni.

What about cheese? On close examination many are found to be of local origin and difficult to classify; but there are already some well-known types, such as Parmesan grana and Roman pecorino, produce of medium-sized firms that have reached the national market and created a set of distinctive recognizable names. Then there are the Lombard cheeses labelled Locatelli, Cademartori, Invernizzi, and Galbani's 'Bel Paese'; yet again butter and milk from the Latterie Soresinesi (an example of a large cooperative firm) and Polenghi Lombardo. On the other hand I do not see any brands of olive oil; during this period oil was in effect still a home produce (and frequently of a quality so poor that it was used not for food but as fuel, lubricant, or for soap making). The first great producers were beginning to appear, however, making more highly appreciated oil of low acidity (besides the various Apulian firms, we remember Bertolli of Lucca and Escoffier from Liguria). The same is true for rice: cultivated on the Po valley plain for centuries, and only recently an industrial product, polished to make it keep better (the first brands were Bolgè and Lombardi). After a good look the only produce in our pantry that can be called 'industrial' in today's sense appears to be flour, turned out by a widespread milling industry, which by this time was well advanced, and sugar, particularly expensive in Italy through being produced by an oligopolistic sector supported by high revenue tariffs (we can wager that the original packages will bear the name Eridania or Società Ligure Lombarda).[10]

There is no shortage of foreign brands: some of 'colonial' concern and coffee, which I would expect to see; others however indicate a series of 'new' food products: meat extract, broth concentrate, condensed or dried milk (Liebig, Knorr, Nestlé).[11] Finally, there is wine in a crate next to the demijohn. The house owners have many bottles of wine from various parts of Italy, perhaps the most prevalent being Piedmont, with brands that I no longer recognize, some of which bear the names of aristocratic families. What strikes me most, however, are the sparkling wines: Contratto, Bosca, and Gancia (who is said to have created the first Italian *spumante* in 1865) and fortified wines like vermouth (Cinzano, Cora, Martini & Rossi—one of the first brands to systematically use advertising—and Campari, started as a successful bitter served in a Milanese bar) and finally marsala (Florio, coming from one of the biggest and most modern wineries in Italy, although the brand name was created in Sicily by Englishmen like Ingham and Whitaker). It is a pity that my hosts are not beer drinkers, otherwise

I would have seen the first bottles of Peroni, Wührer, Pedavena, Poretti, and Menabrea.

I leave this Pantagruelic pantry with the satisfaction that I have learned many things concerning the tastes, social, and financial position of my hosts, the residential area (based on the local produce) and even the technological level of the food industry at that time as well as the place occupied by Italian production in the international market. To tell the truth, I move away partly because that rich cellar is also full of powerful odours, coming from salt cod, mature salami, slightly mouldy cheese, half-opened wine, fermented preserves, dried pasta and more besides—certainly unlike any pantry of today.

Going through the other rooms of the house and looking at the furniture there is a prevalence of well-made handicraft work. This is hardly surprising in a country with a powerful and widespread tradition of craftsmanship (45,000 firms working just with wood were recorded in 1911). Few people could afford furniture made by fashionable artists like Vittorio Ducrot of Palermo who specialized in luxury furnishings for big hotels, yachts, mansions, and reception houses (like Montecitorio) or Mariano Coppedé of Florence, specialist in inlaid furniture desired even by royal families. But everybody was able to call in the local carpenter to make furniture for the home. In reality, the first mass-produced furniture was already available but was only used by less well-off social classes: not very attractive, generally made of simple pieces joined together, and with a poor finish. The first case of attention being given to the aesthetics of industrial furniture (that is industrial design) was probably that of the 'Viennese' chair designed by the Austrian Michael Thonet in 1859. He used the technique of steam-bending wood, inspired by boatbuilders, to create beechwood chairs of simple and refined lines. Light in weight and easy to dismantle and ship, they are still sold today and are the most widespread item of furniture in the world (they are to be seen in the drawing room of the Marquess Berlingieri).[12] This is, however, an exceptional case. It is important to underline how at that time everybody considered industrial products to be inferior goods, and absolutely out of place in a dignified home, partly because what had always been valued was gifted craftsmanship—and partly because they really were of poor quality. Many years would have to pass before standards emerged for furniture, even if in the production centre created north of Milan, in the Brianza, they were experimenting with remarkably better techniques.

Things were a little different for British-made items, synonymous as they were with elegance and modernity. The English Industrial Revolution is often thought of as a huge tide of cotton canvas, industrial machinery, coal mines, steam engines, modern transport, enclosures, without paying attention to the fact that English wealth was for the best part based on producing consumer goods, needed by the lively home market and exported all over the world. Biscuits, spirits, colonial products, sauces, chinaware, household fabrics, cutlery, shirts and ready-made suits (especially for men), sheets, and clothes of fine wool: on this and much more besides rested the power of the British Empire. These signs of distinction are easily seen in Italian homes too: for example Wedgwood pottery, among the first to experiment with forms of advertising such as honouring high profile aristocratics or exhibiting in the centre of London.[13]

Ability in this sector was not lacking in Italy either: just think of china (the 'white gold') manufactured by the Richard Ginori firm, founded by the noble Florentine family, Ginori, in 1735 and producer of objects of the highest quality; or while in the realm of household goods, of the numerous glass and crystal makers whose most ancient traditions went back to the Middle Ages. Nevertheless this very example pinpoints the essence of the problem: the Venetian master glassworkers, like those others in Tuscany and Liguria, remained behind the times, clinging to ancient working processes (very secret and protected) that enabled them to create outstanding multicoloured glassware, artistic lamps, and unique ornaments, but did not allow them to make standard perfume bottles or 'plain' glass for syringes and pharmaceutical phials, nor even, because of prices that could not compete with Germany or France, small objects for daily use. The expertise shown by the most advanced foreign industries (in other words, cross-border influences) and consumer orientation together created a formidable impulse towards an industrial transformation which, at its best, combined new skills with ancient 'know-how' and craftsmanship that were to lay the foundations of the future 'Made in Italy'.

Consumers and producers are therefore part of the same process, and where consumption is concerned it is important to bear in mind its economic function as well as its cultural and political aspects.

4

Commercial Spaces

Behold the beautiful evening, friend of the criminal: it slinks in like an accomplice, with wolf's step; the sky slowly closes, like a great alcove, and turns the impatient man into a beast. O evening, dear evening, desired by one whose arms, without lying, can say: 'We have worked hard again today'.—It is the evening which gives some uplift to the spirit devoured by a wild pain, to the obstinate thinker wrinkling his brow, to the bowed-down workman returning to his bed.

Meanwhile sickly demons are heavily awakening, as if they were men of business, and while flying, crash into shutters and canopies. Through the light tormented by the wind prostitution is rekindled in the streets and like an anthill unlocks all its exits. Everywhere an occult pathway opens, just like an enemy attempting a sudden attack: the mud city shakes in its bosom like a worm stealing a man's food. Here and there we hear kitchens hissing, theatres bellowing, orchestra buzzing; whores and ruffians (their accomplices) swearing in the fixed-price restaurants, where gambling is the main attraction; the thieves, who never rest, will soon begin their work: which is to gently force open doors and safes, to get through a few days, to clothe their lovers.

Pull yourself together, my soul, in this grave moment and try to close your ears to that great roaring.[1]

From an attic above the roofs of 19th-century Paris, Baudelaire contemplated with fascination and disquiet the birth of the modern metropolis. He observed manual labourers, industrial workers, artists, the crowd continually moving in the wide streets perfected by the geometry of the 'Prefect of the Seine', Haussmann. He observed the army of derelicts, the old, beggars, thieves, prostitutes, all inexorably caught up in the tentacled city. And he saw the crowded places of the city: restaurants, theatres, ballrooms, gambling halls. Old Paris was disappearing, lamented the poet, and it was not clear whether the new one replacing it was better or worse. It was certainly marked by two phenomena: frenzied speed, which was becoming the key symbol of urban life, and commercialization which was everywhere, urging people to work till they dropped, rob and steal, or prostitute themselves.

The artist wanted to ignore the city's 'roaring', but was unable to detach himself from the spectacle.

Nineteenth-century Paris must really have been a splendid spectacle; only London, the capital of the widest empire, could rival it for wealth and power, or perhaps multinational Vienna to a certain extent.[2] Many years later, in 1935, an exile such as Walter Benjamin was also struck by the fascination of the French city and wrote about it as the epitome of the 19th-century capital, making precise reference to Baudelaire. According to the Berlin philosopher, the 'shocks' felt by continually living in the city (lights, noises, encounters, novel situations) had forged out a new sensitivity, more nervous and unstable, typified by the *'flaneur'*, a new figure who would stroll about with an 'outsider's stare'. Through the crowd, he would see the city like a phantasmagoric spectacle that found its most complete creation in consumer spaces such as arcades, the *flaneur's* 'last resort', where selling is the spectacle.[3]

Several years before George Simmel, also from Berlin, had perspicaciously seen similar traits in metropolitan life. In particular, he had drawn attention to the (blasé) attitude and detachment of the town dweller, who uses it to defend himself against the sensory overstimulation which constantly assails him. Simmel saw his solitude, which is the other side of increased freedom from social control, and above all he saw the central position of money. In the city everything is based on money, which measures everything and transforms quality into quantity, time into money, coarsening relationships into bargaining.[4]

All this seems to have physically materialized in the great bazaars and 'novelty shops' specializing in female underwear, and especially in the arcades, the first shopping galleries that appeared in Paris at the end of the 18th century. In places like the Palais Royal gallery (1789), the Delorme arcade (1808), or the Colbert gallery (1826) all seemed directed towards consumption. Notice that they were covered passageways from one street to the other, sumptuously paved and furnished; entering them did not necessarily mean that someone wanted to make a purchase; all they did was to encourage them to walk through pausing here and there in front of the dazzling shop windows, which arrayed themselves one after another, interspersed with cafés, restaurants, and theatres. Their explicit aim might have been to provide people with places to meet and converse, but their commercial function was implicitly provided by the architecture. Here was a faceless and ever-changing throng; attractions created by all kinds of noise, sound and light; a place to be immersed in a scenographic atmosphere. Everything could be bought or sold here (including sex, since with time some of them ended up being frequented by prostitutes in search of customers).

The attraction of these places was also supplied by technology. Constructed in the 19th century with a modern covering of iron and glass, they allowed a soft light to filter in by day while in the evening they were illuminated by the dazzling brightness of gas lighting, which strongly contrasted the half shadow of the rest of the city. Schivelbusch records the magical effect on the first customers of the brightly lit windows of cafés and shops (up to that time it had been technically difficult to manufacture such large sheets of plate glass). The great windows seemed to have become stages where an unending script was acted out for passers by, while the entire street was transformed into a wide open theatre.[5] Or it might have been the scenes themselves that were adapting to the new technology, using it to light up the stage while keeping the stalls in darkness to mark the contrast and accentuate the stage illusion.[6]

Shopping arcades spread rapidly throughout the main European cities, becoming centres of attraction and showpieces. In the 19th century in Paris alone one could count a hundred and fifty, and they multiplied in London (Piccadilly Arcade, Burlington Arcade),[7] and also in Italy, where several big arcades were built during the last decade of the 19th century, such as those created in Turin, Genoa (Mazzini Gallery), and Naples (Umberto I Gallery). In contrast with the original galleries these constructions were much bigger and more monumental, to the extent that the original commercial intention of creating the character of a refined drawing room now combined with that of self display. Let us take the biggest, the neoclassical Vittorio Emanuele II gallery of Milan, designed by Giuseppe Mengoni and built between 1865 and 1877. It is the largest of its kind in the world with an enormous central dome and four lateral branches, while at the main entrances there are two triumphal arches dedicated to the king. It is obvious that the wish here was to create a monument to represent the ambitions of a growing city, so much so that when the private company that started the work failed, it was the council that bought the property and shouldered the enormous expenses needed for its completion. There remains the significant fact, however, that the most majestic architecture created to give dignity and prestige to bourgeois Milan was neither a civil monument (these had already been dedicated to the heroes of the Risorgimento) nor a government palace, a museum, nor a traditional work of art, but a shopping arcade, where places were immediately taken by the most prestigious shops of the city and fashionable bars (like the 'Camparino'). In this way social prestige and economic progress revealed themselves in a commercial form.

Ideally, the next step along the road to development would be the department stores. Unlike the shopping arcade, formed by a motley collection of firms, the department store is a single unit (in fact partly derived from 'novelty shops' and partly from large bazaars displaying the widest range of wares). The Bon Marché of Aristide Boucicault in Paris (1852) is the recognized prototype of this kind, the best known and most copied, and which was to become in a few decades the chief company for direct sales to the customer. Set up in a grandiose building with hallmarks of modernity, it spread out before the eyes of the customer a profuseness of exotic, luxury, and everyday goods; interspersed by grand staircases, passages, and stairs; a choreographic draping of multicoloured fabrics, curtains and carpets; a sparkling of showcases, lights and mirrors; and then sounds, music, elegant salespeople, presents for the customers, special offers, flowers for the ladies, discounted goods, balloons for the children, bars, restaurants, rest rooms and much more besides; a magical and self-sufficient universe to dazzle the most jaded of eyes. The formula quickly caught on in Paris (Magasin de Louvre, Le Printemps, La Samaritaine) and throughout Europe, with famous places like Harrods in London, and later on Kaufhaus des Westens in Berlin. It even came to roost in Italy. At the same time the first department stores opened in the United States: Macy's, Bloomingdale, Wanamaker, and Marshall Field.[8]

Contemporaries were in no doubt: the department store marked a turning point in the history of consumer culture and commerce. Even intellectuals and writers took notice and Émile Zola, as we remember took inspiration from it for his famous novel. The same reaction was felt in Italy where the Bocconi brothers looked to the French example to open the first department store, Aux Villes d'Italie, in Milan in 1877 (with a French name, as desired by the Francophile culture of the time and perhaps as an indirect tribute to the original model).

At this point, several questions arise. If this way of selling came both from the arcades and from commercial formulas already in existence why did it have such an impact on the collective imagination of the time? And why do academics of today substantially agree in considering it a breakaway from what was there before? And again, what happens in the Italian case?

To answer all this I must take a step backwards and return to what had hitherto been the standards of commercial activity, that is shops and markets.

Markets and shops

I have already stated that commerce is a basic element in the consumption cycle, for its connections on one hand with the world of production and on the other with that of the consumer. It has the function of mediator *par excellence*, but it is actually more. With its original formulas (shopping arcades and department stores are one example) it exerts a specific influence on the consumer world, on the quality and quantity of goods available on the market, on the methods and time spent in buying, on the cultural and symbolic meaning of the goods, as well as the economic value of the articles. Being close to the consumers it is very sensitive to their needs and reactions, and can set up a 'negotiating' relationship with them. It can also act as a stimulus or brake with regard to manufacturing industries and sometimes even competes with them. A long tradition of studies has led us to consider advertising as the main link between producers and consumers and as the basic drive for buying but this actually underestimates the role of commercial spaces, which are not just 'neutral containers' but instead influence consumer behaviour just as much as they determine the practical method of purchasing and create a framework of meaning and value round the goods. The scant attention given to these spaces by historiography is unjustified. The history of consumption is also the history of commerce.

Fairs and small shops are very ancient forms of commerce. Fairs have been an identifying element in economic and social life for centuries, even if, as has been observed, their frequency was possibly more an indication of inadequate structuring in the trade market than a sign of how well it was flourishing; in fact some highly developed areas from the marketing point of view, like Venice, did not have important fairs.[9] Be that as it may, almost up to the 19th century fairs were important occasions for buying and selling, for meeting people and frequently for celebration (the most important were those of Senigallia and Bergamo).

The development of rail and sea transport then decreased the importance of such manifestations in favour of more stable structures, such as local markets. These, too, have plied their trade in the main streets and squares of the towns and villages since time immemorial, but are now becoming specialized and divided by rank, type, zone, and kind of customer.

Urban development had a big effect on these structures: provision needs for the city grew rapidly and led to the construction of covered markets, maybe following the example of the great Halles Centrales of Paris. The most significant example is the Mercato Centrale of Florence: constructed in the ancient area of the Camaldoli of San Lorenzo, it is one of the buildings designed to 'modernize' the face of Florence, which had become the capital of the Kingdom for a while. The little medieval houses were knocked down to make way for a large canopy of cast iron, glass, and steel, for which the architect Giuseppe Mengoni was commissioned in 1870. The result as a whole was positive, because the new building harmonized fairly well with its surroundings, thanks to a basic framework of classical-shaped arches, a covering, which guaranteed plenty of light inside, and an ample space unimpeded by heavy supporting structures. Many similar buildings sprang up in Italian cities, usually near railway goods yards, visibly indicating the rational and industrial processes that commerce was experiencing (especially on the wholesale side).[10] As already said, this did not lead to the disappearance of traditional street markets, but their evolution.

Shops also have a very long history and for many centuries hardly changed at all, with limited internal space, open to the street, simple furnishings inside and a shop rear where handicraft or sales back-up work was often done. Little by little during the 18th century but more completely in the 19th, the old shop became a modern store as we know it today: a more spacious, more specialized place. There was however much heterogeneity in the aspect of these places, often half way between the places where goods were sold, and where they were produced or stored, taking into account the flourishing presence of craftsman's work that greatly limited the sales of ready-made goods (especially at the start, as already noted, the latter were on principle considered to be of inferior quality: it was tradition that created 'value' and tradition was on the side of craftsmanship). Furthermore, a great deal of commerce passed through the hands of itinerant salesmen, whether in the regular markets with improvised stalls or simply 'wandering streetside trading', performed in many ways to help eke out meagre earnings, right down to forms that verged on begging.[11]

In the urban centres involved in this new building development there was a proliferation of shops selling luxuries (fabrics, clothing, china and pottery, jewellery), cafés imitating luxuriously aristocratic furnishings, chemists with preciously inlaid wooden shelving. It is difficult to give an exact count of this commercial élite, but it can be imagined that there are a restricted number of shops, even in the biggest cities (a fact that reflected the limitations of luxury commerce). But what did these shops look like? Observing photographs of those times there is immediately an image of luxury and elegance, whether they show the sober outside with a prominent sign (the shop windows were not the main feature for this type of visible communication, and were often opaque or lacking in interest) or the inside. For example, in shops selling fabric or haberdashery there would be wide counters separating the space reserved for the salespeople from the space reserved for the customers (or more precisely, 'lady customers'). Against the walls are cupboards, towering wooden shelving, drawers, and storerooms indicating the presence of a great quantity of goods; all around are refined furnishings (curtains, carpets, lamps, ornaments, chairs, mirrors) reminiscent of a drawing room.[12] However, in the foreground there is always a salesman showing a product to an elegant lady: and he is the real protagonist, the inescapable means through whom the sales must take place, the animator of this public space. He is the expert and advisor, partly because most of the goods are not on display and it is he who will make them 'appear'. It is not the done thing to show the prices, either.

But this scene was the exception and not the rule in the portrayal of Italian commerce, as Eduardo De Filippo recalls with piercing irony (referring moreover to a later period): 'Has not the province always been the support of the shops of the Main Street? When did the aristocracy or the elegant gentry ever keep the tradespeople alive? In every city there are two, or at least three shops that succeed in fooling the gentleman; for him the others do not even exist.'[13]

For the 965,000 employed in commerce recorded in 1911, the situation must have been very different. The spaces were narrower and less refined, the salespeople were often the shopkeepers themselves, probably helped by members of the family. The furnishings were reduced to bare necessities: there was the counter and some cupboards or containers for the merchandize.[14] Massimo Bontempelli remembers a typical shop thus:

> at the corner where the street enters a little square, and in a house whose front is all darkened by bare branches of ivy and by symmetrically intricate reddish incrustations, there opens (and closes every evening) a salt and tobacco shop. [...]
>
> In this place—and this is important following the narrative—they also sell, besides salt and tobacco, glasses of brandy to the men, picture postcards to the women, liquorice to the children, and tins of old food to those lacking in life skills.[15]

And Luigi Pirandello is even more detailed when describing the inside of a wine shop:

> I went into that *Bottiglieria*, I, a non-drinker of wine, just to keep a foreign friend company, who seems unable to go to bed without the spiritual comfort, every evening, of a glassful of the good stuff.
>
> There were two rooms with an archway between. One lower and the other three steps higher, both equally gloomy, with walls covered halfway up with wooden skirting. The first room had faded, stained, and dusty racks to hold the liqueurs and spirits, and an old wine bar counter in front, the other where we sat down, had just a circuit of squat yellow-painted tables and four light bulbs hanging from the ceiling, on string and small paddles [...]
>
> Meanwhile other customers had come in. Some, in the other room, were playing cards. Every now and then, there were shouts, swearing, and then nothing.[16]

Literary testimonies are prolific. They confirm what was apparent in the photographic evidence concerning shops of the time, found in many illustrated history books about the cities (a very popular subject, to judge from the quantity of publications available in bookshops)[17] and from the rich photograhic archives we have at our disposal.[18] The impression we get is unmistakable: poor non-specialized places. But what if it is mistaken? After all, literary sources are a free transposition of reality, as everyone knows; an interpretation, maybe with a realistic tone, but still an interpretation. And the photographs? In effect even these are less 'objective' and impartial than they seem to be.[19] The shot might have frozen a certain moment in one's life, maybe an unusual one, or be specifically looking for moments dramatic for their visual impact, and thus catch only a partial aspect of reality. Besides (as can be seen from studying professional photographs that are of course the bulk of what has come down to us from that period), they follow precise 'stylistic' rules, in the choice of subject, composition, close-ups, or backgrounds. In a word, they are 'contrived', which is aggravated by the fact, that the observers find themselves in a situation far removed in time, space, and culture from the objects depicted. A black and white photograph showing a Neapolitan macaroni maker, his shop consisting of a low dresser placed just outside the main door of his house together with a rickety table and chair, and the smiling salesman behind the dresser and two customers eating from plates held in their hands[20]—or a slightly faded picture of the Vairo wine cellar café in Turin, where the customers seated inside are waving at the photographer with glasses upraised[21]—or again the set-piece banquet of a water-melon seller in Naples shown holding sliced melons, surrounded by luscious green foliage and a rich display of ripe fruit on his barrow, as if he was an actor in the middle of a scene.[22] These photographs can either bring a nostalgic smile, while gazing at a world that no longer exists, or maybe uplift the spirit us because of the changes for the better that have occurred. Besides, even present-day values have changed: what may look like poverty today was perhaps normality for them; what may seems quaint was probably commonplace for them. Belonging to the here and now, not there and then no one can be an objective and detached spectator. There is no answer to this dilemma, of course. It just has to rembered that it exists.

Department stores: a European model?

One day in early 20th-century Milan, the elegant lady enjoying a stroll by the Cathedral would have come upon an extraordinary sight. Unlike the usual small shops, here was a palatial building all set up for shoppers and shopping. In front stood a spacious portico supported by dark red granite columns and surmounted by a dome at each end. Its huge gallery windows, like luxurious tableaux promising extraordinary delights, were richly illuminated, as if to communicate with the fabulous interior she can catch a glimpse of as she stands outside. The temptation to go in is irresistible . . . and here we are, in the main hall where a lavish spectacle strikes the eye, an enormous open space full of showcases, stands, and merchandize, and above, another three floors with balconies running all around, and a grand central staircase dominating the scene. High overhead, the stained glass ceiling allows a dream-like light to filter through. White and gold are the prevalent colours, contrasting with the polished wood floors and counters, and the vivid colours of carpets and curtains, the whole show enhanced by dazzling crystal, mirrors, and chandeliers. There are objects for sale everywhere, not hidden away in cupboards or storerooms, but alluringly displayed on tables or peeking behind showcase glass, ready to be touched or felt freely—since the elegant sales girls stand by discreetly ready to give assistance, while the price is easily seen on the display label. How exciting to wander through these open spaces. In the 'lingerie' department—one of the largest—countless items are neatly set out on low wooden counters and many protrude from inside open-fronted cupboards. In the woollen department can be found rack after rack of ready-to-wear clothes, obviously the latest Paris fashion, while drapes of multicoloured fabrics festoon the walls. In the perfume and trinkets departments you walk among large illuminated showcases full of jewellery and beauty products, and in the women's clothing department among smartly dressed display dummies and lofty crystal glass showcases, with characteristically curved surfaces framing expensive clothes, furs, hats, and feathers. But that is not all. This fine lady would not have believed her eyes when she reached the tableware department, with its plethora of glasses, china, glass, and cutlery on display, all famous brands. Then there is the toy department, abounding in tricycles, wooden carts, rocking horses, dolls, masks, and coloured blocks. Has she had enough? No problem. On the top floor she can relax in an elegant lounge overlooking the Cathedral, listen to music over a cup of tea or visit the hairdressing salon. Are her purchases weighing her down? The store provides a home delivery service and, if she likes, she can make her selection from the comfort of her own home using the illustrated catalogue. As she leaves, casts she one last glance at the Dudovich posters hanging on the walls. Without doubt those elegant, stylish figures facing the world so confidently are none other than herself![23]

It was not just the department store of the Bocconi brothers, ex-dealers in fabrics from Lodi, that provided such a spectacle. No less prestigious were the centres opened in other Italian cities (Turin, Genoa, Bologna, Florence, Naples, Palermo) and above all the ultra-modern store in Rome's piazza Colonna (inaugurated in 1877). The high-arched commercial building did not look at all out of place in the commercial heart of the city, close to the Chigi Palace, as if claiming the honour due to a department store. Naples, then, was the choice of the Bocconi's chief competitors, the Grandi Magazzini Mele which Emidio Mele had opened in 1889 on the ground floor of the brand new Borghesia Palace in via S. Brigida, a stone's throw from the San Carlo theatre. Here again the owners' aim was to acquire a middle-class clientele sensitive to the demands of taste and fashion, their motto being 'the best bargains', and they were ahead of the times with many new ideas, for example employing the services of a professional commercial artist.[24] Neither was there any shortage of well-run minor emporia in most big cities, with interesting cases in the cooperative world too (the first coop store appeared in Turin in 1853). Outlets of the Turin Cooperative Alliance, Cooperative Union of Milan, and Military Union of Rome were some of the most thriving stores of the time.[25]

Of course, the dazzling facade actually concealed a complex reality. Based on a high volume of sales, quick merchandize turnover, fixed prices, and no obligation for customers to buy anything, the selling strategy required a huge administrative machine.[26] In 1900, the Bocconi stores employed no less than three thousand men and women to perform all tasks from selling to delivering, warehousing to accountancy. What presented itself as trade's counterpart to the mass manufacturing industries shared with them the same kind of labour problems. Working in the department stores concealed a reality of strict discipline, piecework wages, precariousness, and limited career prospects for the great majority of the (mostly male) employees. Relations could be difficult not only with their superiors but with the customers too.[27] As in Baudelaire's vision, even this symbol of urban modernity, attractive as it was, had a dark ambiguous side.

The question was asked earlier on as to why the department stores have made such an impact on the collective imagination. By now there is plenty of evidence and can summarized as follows.

First, department stores seem to have embodied the myth of progress and widespread passion for novelty in the late 19th, early 20th century (at least until the horrors of the First World War shattered faith in the 'wonders' of progress). Just like the Excelsior Ballroom, they had shown the triumph of light over dark, being the first buildings not only to use electric lighting, but also to install the marvels of hydraulic lifts, central heating, gigantic mirrors, and plate glass (often ordered from abroad) soon to be followed by escalators—ostentatiously placed right in the middle of the building. After all, an outstanding part of the department store's appeal had to be provided by technology. But the sense of novelty does not stop here: the merchandize itself played its part, being replaced, renewed and recreated all the time, according to the dictates of the latest fashion—in a perennial process of innovation. The department store had, par excellence, come to represent urban modernity.

Second, it is here that the process of making a spectacular display of the merchandize is fully realized. Its presence all in one place, in large amounts and immediately accessible, induces a sense of wonder at its uniqueness. The 'container', that is the store itself, is fashioned to fascinate the visitor with its grandeur, wealth, convenience, and attractiveness—characteristics reflected by the goods on display, which seem even better because of their pleasant surroundings (as Miller observes, it is not only the merchandize that is on sale but the very concept of consumption).[28] I enjoy myself where I go shopping means I enjoy going shopping. As a result, the concept of consumption merges imperceptibly with the concept of pleasure.

Third, the importance that the new consumer places take on in the city leads us to redefine urban spaces. A circle is thus created combining consumption with leisure essential in the definition of the modern metropolis, including as it does commercial emporia, arcades, and shopping streets alongside places of commercialized entertainment such as theatres, cafés, and sports centres. This helps to define a new hierarchy in urban spaces, added value being accorded to spaces associated with buying and selling, as they increasingly become places to meet socially, 'promenade' and attract tourists (no doubt to the detriment of traditional places associated with civic and religious power). It is interesting to note that this phenomenon has its epicentres in the major European capitals such as Paris, and London, emphasizing the transnational nature of consumer culture.

Fourth, these new spaces have social connotations. They are not aristocratic and certainly not working class, but belong to the bourgeoisie, reflecting its values and consumer practices. The burgeoning growth of this social sector due to the effects of industrial development has produced with time a stratification of clientele with a widening towards the bottom (white-collar petit bourgeois). It has led to a phenomenon defined as the democratization of luxury, which is not simply the reinstating of aristocratic consumption at a lower level, but a combination of the search for distinction with values such as saving and efficiency.

Be that as it may, one element could still be missing. I will try to discover it with some considerations on the department store:

> It is superfluous to describe in detail the grandeur of the 'Department store'. We can all see it for ourselves. [...] A Bernini or a Vanvitelli did not have to obey orders concerning height, numbers of floors, display windows, covered yards, the (near) abolition of pillars and marble to replace them with cast iron columns and beams made of iron or reinforced concrete. [...] But, age for age, purpose for purpose—if instead of comparing it to the austere environment of a Greek or Roman theatre we compare it with the lavish decoration of a large auditorium for modern entertainment, we must acknowledge that the department stores of today provide such a plethora of wonders as to create a vision of beauty.[29]

And on a poster advertising the reopening of La Rinascente:

> ... a great happening in the city, as important as the opening night at La Scala, when, in all her pride and elegance, a beautiful lady, wearing an incredible head-dress of huge white feathers, will move regally towards a person who will offer her, on a velvet cushion, the keys that will open the doors to so many wonders, so long awaited.[30]

What terminology has been used when talking about the department stores? What mental images does it conjure up? That is the point. To a certain extent the eager customers already knew what to expect of this new consumer space; they knew they would be enjoying a great show, anticipating the enthralling sights and sounds to come. They knew them already—from the theatre. The theatre was the matrix from which to model new experiences, an 'Urtext', a dictionary to update with new expressions. See how the show provided by a department store is just like a play full of light, technicality, costumes, colour, music, and decoration. The customers are the audience; the space protected and limited, as in the theatre; the artistically prepared showcases, like scenery, hide from sight the hard work going on behind; the anticipation of a pleasant, enjoyable, (albeit not too taxing) experience is identical. The department store does indeed mimic the theatre, which is why it was immediately understood and accepted.[31]

And, as in the theatre, it is women who took on a major role. Assiduous theatre-goers (and main readers of theatre reviews), women made up most of the audience, in the same way as they became the main consumers. And if on the stage the artistes were symbols of great fascination but also doubtful morality, in the same way the saleswomen, actresses on the department store stage, became needed and admired but also subject to severe moral criticism because of being removed from a traditional wifely role. The massive presence of women from the very start of the consumer age, at a time when the idea continued to prevail that a woman's role should be confined within the private domestic area, cannot simply be explained by stressing the safe and respectable aspects of the department stores,[32] but because, thanks to their association with the theatre, they appeared to be culturally appropriate for women—places to project themselves.

The advent of women on the public scene (which, as Habermas reminds, had been the exclusive prerogative of men for centuries) did, however suffer counter-attacks. Alluring and alarming at the same time, it gave rise to negative stereotypes: actresses were often portrayed as the equivalent of prostitutes (public women, in fact),[33] female consumers as kleptomaniacs—both categories seen as breaking the moral code even before breaking the law. Notwithstanding this, women succeeded in winning a public space for themselves, which became important in defining their identity—in the world of the theatre as in that of the consumer, creating thus a 'genderized' space. The show becomes part of life, and life part of the show.

PART II

Fascism

5

The Regime

The beautiful dancer flops down on the bed in the metropolitan Grand Hotel, wrinkling the smooth surface of the coverlet into a thousand creases. She wears a silk dressing gown with rich decoration at the cuffs and all round the neckline. Her make-up is striking: arched eyebrows, long black eyelashes, powder, rouge and (no doubt) exquisite perfume. The room is splendidly furnished in art décor style, with fine velvet curtains right down to the floor, gilt-inlaid furniture, deeply-padded comfortable armchairs, artistic lamps, scenic pictures, flowers everywhere. But this is certainly unable to console the lady as she lifts the telephone receiver with pensive air. At which point the dashing baron, dark suited and brushed-back hair, bursts in and throws himself down at her feet passionately declaring his love. He (John Barrymore) gazes intensely at her while she (Greta Garbo) looks into the distance. She repulses him: 'You must go now. I wish to be left alone'.[1] The mysterious ending to the story does not dull the effect on the male and female audience in the stalls, carried away as they are by that enchanted world. The old caretaker of the Metropol has to shoo everyone out and so the youths crowd towards the exit in their home-made clothes of coarse cloth, imitation leather shoes, and fashion accessories from cheap chain stores. They go away on foot; some take the tram. The caretaker wheezes himself astride his old Bianchi and starts to pedal squeakily homeward. Every evening it is the same story.

The economist Simon Kuznets spent years asking himself the meaning of the expression 'modern economic growth'.[2] When is a nation able to call itself developed in the sense that we mean today? When does the industrial sector take the lead? Or when does domestic and per capita production increase steadily and significantly? The complex picture of social, economic, and cultural factors the academic paints to explain his theory seems to fit inter-war Italy rather well, due partly to the fact that more or less everyone agrees that it was at this precise moment that the country became industrialized (at the end of the 1930s industry actually overtook agriculture where gross domestic product was concerned). This evaluation is confirmed by illustrations of the times (films, photographs, and advertisements). It leaves the impression of a distancing from the previous period. They seem closer and more 'modern'.

As well as confirming that Italy had entered a new cultural and economic phase (the dramatic impact of the First World War must not be forgotten), Kuznets's analysis holds particular interest for us where consumption is concerned. What general factors have influenced its growth in modern economies? The prerequisite has obviously been the increase in per capita earnings, which is to say a steady rise in the economic resources available for every family. Be that as it may, an increase in wealth does not necessarily mean an increase in consumption. In the past 'excessive' consumption was often linked to negative connotations such as waste and dissipation, as seen earlier. Historically many societies conceived wealth more in terms of accumulation than consumption, whereas in these modern economies most of the wealth available is spent, not saved. All are therefore faced with a high propensity to consume. Where does this come from?

It is possible to subdivide into three large categories the factors that affect consumption over a long period of time.[3] The first category concerns changes in living conditions. To start with, due to a growing specialization and division of labour, urbanization has brought about increases in the consumption of commercial products, especially noteworthy in the case of goods once produced within the family, such as food, and clothing. Besides, many of these goods and services cost more in towns due to transport and distribution costs, increasing the impact on the family. Finally, the closeness of different social groups, cultural separation from traditions, and the typical openness of urban culture all lead to increases in new kinds of consumption as, for example in the culture and entertainment sector.

A second important factor, frequently underrated, is linked to different social patterns and changes in the distribution of earnings. The formation of quite a large class of dependent workers out of what was once a self-sufficient class of craftsmen, traders, and farmers, has inflated consumer trends. Business people used to have a strong inclination towards saving, since in this way they increased their capital together with their chances of market success (which perhaps accounts for the austere lifestyle apparent in some professional categories such as bankers and shopkeepers). Employed people are more likely to invest in themselves and their children (i.e. human capital), spending on education and culture, while professionals and managers have a tendency towards even greater consumer habits, not only to meet greater needs linked to education and training, but also to display their higher living standards. Then whenever, through redistribution policies, there are increased earnings for some less affluent levels of society, this has led to further increases in basic consumption.

The third factor is technological progress, which is of great importance since it is able to bring extensive changes into traditional consumer habits and introduce new categories of products. The attraction of new kinds of goods has given enormous drive towards greater consumption on one hand and towards an increasing variety of purchased goods on the other (the great diversity between the consumption structure in Italy at the beginning and at the end of the 20th century lies precisely in the increase in items outside the basic food-home-clothing trio).

It is certainly possible to recognize these characteristics in 1920s and 1930s Italy—urban consolidation, middle-class expansion, impact of new technology. But the most distinctive trait of that period is found in politics, with Fascism, which brought an end to Liberal government, established a regime of propaganda and mobilization such as Italians had never seen before, proclaimed the advent of corporate economics, and explicitly entered the arena of consumption.

Autarchy, gender, race

First of all the figures: by 1938 the per capita GDP for an Italian stood at 3,819 lire (having increased at a rate of 0.9 per cent, per year in comparison with 1911) while private consumption per capita was equal to 2,586 lire (increase of 0.7 per cent, per year).[4] Consumption had therefore increased less than earnings (contrary to what had happened during the Liberal period and would happen again later). However the amount devoted to consumption was distributed in a different way, most noticeably in the net decrease in the percentage spent on food consumption (down ten points and shown to be around 50 per cent). Footwear and clothing show some loss (down to 9 per cent), while there was increased expenditure on the home, beauty, and hygiene, and, most of all, durable goods and transport (from 4 to 11 per cent).[5] We are therefore confronted by greater diversity, though worthy of note is the strong squeeze on food, despite there being no drastic variations in the content of the food basket. Wheat is still in the lead, even if slightly down, next to maize, potatoes, and dried vegetables; garden vegetables and fruit are going down, while the presence of expensive food like meat, sugar, and coffee remains scarce, and wine consumption varies greatly. That the diet was becoming less rich is confirmed by counting the calories of an average daily meal, which are seen to have been lower than they were in the preceding decade.[6] Similar conclusions are confirmed by an analysis of the family budget for the period, emphasizing the continuation of differences due to divides of a social and geographical (regional, town/country) nature as well as class and even gender.[7]

An international comparison confirms the huge gap: in 1930, for example, the per capita earnings in Italy, measured in dollars were 2,900, compared with almost 4,000 in Germany, 4,500 in France and 5,400 in Great Britain; by 1938 this had climbed to 3,300 (but in Germany had reached 5,000 and in Britain 6,300, while France remained unchanged). The average earnings throughout Europe were 4,817 dollars, so Italy still appears to have been a relatively poor country.[8]

To judge from the campaigns carried out by the regime, it could be said that a full-scale revolution had been started in the economic field, its foundations in corporate organization and its apex in innumerable 'battles' being fought on behalf of the nation (the battle for grain, for the defence of the Lira, for integral drainages: every economic measure was brandished to become a propaganda slogan). In actual fact the regime's policy was very much more cautious and sustained. During a period of history characterized by instability and one crisis after another, of which the 1929 one tested the Western economy most severely, Fascism made a definite choice in favour of industry, which it helped with safeguards for new institutes (such as IRI). It was a policy of industrial concentration and—what is most interesting—with a strongly protectionist slant which encouraged the replacement of imports with national products. Therefore when a new battle was fanfared in 1936, this time for self-sufficiency in response to sanctions proclaimed by the League of Nations following Italy's invasion of Ethiopia, the regime simply gave political authority to a protectionist line that had long been in existence through customs controls and tariffs.[9]

This has been unanimously condemned by historians. It is seen to have damaged a transforming economy such as Italy's was. It favoured some sectors to the detriment of others. It imposed on the consumers more expensive Italian products or poor-quality substitutes.[10] This is all true. But the discussion does not end here: if seen from the consumers' point of view it takes on a different meaning and reveals an even more significant and lasting impact.

It is perfectly clear why Fascism's attitude towards the development of consumption was unfavourable: its priorities were elsewhere. However, to support Italian industry and combat the sanctions, a campaign to support Italian products was built up and sustained in order to give enhanced value to the merchandize—its Italian quality. Buying Italian goods was not wasteful. It fulfilled a patriotic duty. Leafing through magazines and pamphlets of the time (and don't forget that during the 1920s radio transmissions began, unleashing incredible collective obsessions such as the hunt for Perugina stickers), this phenomenon of 'Italianization' is easily observed.[11] There was an enormous burst of patriotic language. In one advertisement Italy offers to the world—represented by an array of flags—its 'best product: Fernet-Branca'. In others are extolled the virtues of Sniafiocco's 'national cotton', 'the material of Independence' of Lenasel, artificial fibres manufactured by Chatillon, or Lanital, the synthetic wool created by Antonio Ferretti. Later on, Italviscosa did not use half-hearted phrases: a skein of its fabric is draped over the Winged Victory of Samothrace and it is stated in no uncertain terms that 'The certainty of victory lies in the power of Italian labour'. 'Italians prefer Italian products', say a Motta panettone, Siare valve radio, and Stenogenol tonic. Words like 'national produce' and 'made in Italy' appear in more or less all big company advertisements, starting with FIAT, steamship lines (like Lloyds of Trieste, where four enormous Italian liners plough the seas all over the globe) and airlines (where a modern Ala Littoria plane whizzes over an old steam train); right up to 'the epitome of Italian cigarettes: Principe Piemonte', in competition with Macedonia. Another expedient is to hark back to 'Roman style', so there are elegant men's suits ('Caesar style, elegance, distinction'), Etrusca eau de Cologne ('ancient essence of sacred herbs in a limpid amphora') or 'Impero' ('the most Italian, the best!'), while Radiomarelli presents models like the Vertumno, with alternating statues and mythological touches in the background.[12]

The use of the patriotic lever to promote output is neither new, nor limited to Italy. In the Fascist context, however, this policy had the effect of raising consumption to the status of being a full contributor to the nation's development—thus partly giving the lie to the distinction made by certain militant advertisers between 'warrior' and 'merchant'—as well as creating an explicitly 'national' consumer ideal.[13] It has been seen how consumption had previously included characteristics that were both local and transnational. Fascism provided the thrust to create an identity and profile which was typical of an 'Italian' consumer.

This brings with it two further considerations. The first concerns the role that gender took on in this policy. Self-sufficiency affected the consumer ideal, as we have said, and became an integral part of family life. As such it spoke directly to women, since it was usually their task to deal with the shopping and manage the family as if it were a small business. They were expected to be as thrifty as possible, avoid wastage, and buy national products—doing their very best to find Italian substitutes for everything. Magazine columns and household management manuals taught them how to be almost completely self-sufficient, with advice on recipes containing easily found ingredients, food preservation, hygiene, gardening, preparing syrups and liqueurs, restoring furniture, first aid, care of domestic pets, stain removal, eliminating bad smells, simple repairs, how to make perfumes and cosmetics, medicines and infusions, how to combat mosquitoes, how to get rid of ants, forecast the weather (by observing insects, birds and spiders), how to prevent sea-sickness, bad nerves, and much more.[14] The autarchic battle was fought in the trenches of the home with women in the front line. Victoria de Grazia maintains that it was the Fascist regime that nationalized Italian women for the first time, since the policies of the preceding Liberal regimes had been exclusively aimed at the menfolk (integration in civilian and military life, extending suffrage, etc.). The Fascist State instead was concerned with giving women a precise role within the family for the elevation and advancement of the Italian race. To this end it created both positive incentives (social assistance, maternity support) and repressive measures (removal from certain kinds of jobs, discouragement from higher education, exclusion from politics).[15] In this scenario consumer policy takes on an important aspect of Fascist politics with respect to women. It goes without saying that it was chiefly conceived for middle-class women, seeing that working class and peasant families were largely excluded from the consumption of non-basics.[16]

The second consideration concerns the boundaries of this ideal consumer space. I have defined it as national, but I could also call it Mediterranean or Imperial. There was obviously an effort to create an integral space that would include Italy and the Mediterranean and this applied to all kinds of consumption. For example, the first gastronomic guide for the whole of Italy was published in 1931 by the Touring Club, and it presented the country as a compilation of tourist attractions and gastronomic marvels, where each and every region and village could present its specific offering (we are a far cry from Artusi's centre-north dominion).[17] Capatti and Montanari have indeed observed how the centre of political gravity, moving towards the Mediterranean (later accentuated by the alliance with nordic Germany) led to a re-evaluation of Italy's southern image. With its beaches, sunshine, first fruits, fresh fish, pasta, and oil, the South was to become central to the image of consumer Italy, as proposed both inside and outside the country.[18] But there is even more to be said. There was an attempt to create a national consumer space expanded to include the colonies too. For all those unable to visit them, the colonies were represented through images shown in the Luce cinema newsreels, photographs in newspapers and magazines, through public speeches, and in a more tangible way through the exotic merchandize (especially coffee and bananas) that was arriving on the markets from Africa. There are various examples of advertisements for these products. One of the best known is of a Somali banana, 'bread for the gods', which shows an Italian child eating a banana as her mother looks on contentedly, with an enormous bunch of fruit in the foreground and words written about the vigour the bananas would give to some 'primitive tribes', together with the fact that they had been produced in Somalia by 'Italian colonists' thanks to help from the Fascist government.[19] Among other things another variable enters here. Italians were used to differentiating consumption in terms of class and gender, and now race appears as well. Many products were advertised by appealing to positive stereotypes of 'natives'. In another banana advertisement a smiling African boy is doing the offering ('The Colonies' gift to the Motherland').[20] In another, Moretti sports equipment is being transported by three African boys, this time just sketched out. A different case is one for Fatma perfumes, showing a beautiful Italian standing out in the middle of a desert surrounded by palm trees (colonized and colonizers obviously never appear together and their roles are kept well apart).[21] These advertisements—and the numerous products with names and images redolent of Africa—are by no means irrelevant in the construction of a national 'sovereign' identity with respect to the colonial population, because they visually underline the racial differences. Finally, do not underestimate the presence in Italian cities of shops selling colonial produce, coffee makers and roasters with exotic names, frequently furnished with colonial images and objects to create for all consumers a kind of familiarity with Africa, integrating overseas products and backgrounds into everyday life (some of these places have survived to the present day). In short the construction of a colonial image was also passed on through consumer products.[22]

Emigration

At this point it is worth recalling briefly that the consumption of 'national' products is not limited to Italy and the colonies. In fact, starting in the late 19th century it followed in the wake of waves of Italian immigrants across Europe and America, where a significant demand for typical products was created. The Italian government had favoured this interchange for motives that were both economic and political. It was a way of keeping ties with Italian communities abroad, reinforcing their sense of identity, and mobilizing them in favour of the homeland in case of need. This explains why consular offices and chambers of commerce went well beyond the mere economic side and proved themselves an integral part of diplomatic activity (while the importance of exportation should not be underestimated, since it boosted the food industry: companies such as Buitoni, Bertolli and Martini & Rossi actually made their fortunes in foreign markets).

Now for a look at the Italo-Americans, one of the most studied cases where historiography is concerned. During Fascism, when pride in their ethnic roots was created (after the discrimination they had long suffered from the Anglo-Saxon groups), one of the ways to display this renewed nationalism was by increasing consumption of Italian products. During the Ethiopia campaign there was a great mobilization of the large enclaves of Italians in New York and Chicago, encouraging them to buy goods imported from Italy so as to counteract the effects of the sanctions. Calls to 'buy Italian' multiplied in the newspapers and on the radio, partly sponsored by local importers and retailers.[23] Apart from the fairly positive results of these campaigns, the long-term effect was to reinforce the idea—in case there was any need—that one's ethnic identity is partly made up of what one consumes.

When I speak about consumer models, I do not mean just the products themselves since, as it has been seen, their significance rests equally on the customs that go with their use. This is very evident in the case of the Italo-American. It was not just a case of consuming pasta, tomatoes, olive oil, wine, and bread, but more about how they were consumed: with the family, all sitting around one table, or on certain occasions with all the relatives (and this in a country like the United States where, generally speaking, such practices are not so common). Equally important was the domestic preparation of 'genuine' products, the handing down of typical recipes, the giving of food to friends and relations. In practice 'Italian-style eating' meant giving substance to values such as family, the group, being together, and homeliness, and this explains the persistent emphasis on food and its rituals within the definition of Italian ethnicity, as recorded by Donna Gabaccia.[24] Any difference lay in the fact that America was a land of plenty, where even 'poor Italians' could eat whatever they liked. Hasia Diner has even maintained that the emigrants were able to fulfil their dream of eating the same food as the élites, overcoming class barriers. White bread, meat, and precious products were within their reach (enabling many of them, in fact, to embark on profitable commercial activities).[25]

Of course this does not mean to say that consuming Italian products carried with it any real replication of identity. Apart from the first generation of emigrants, all their descendants construed images of Italian tradition based on local memory, which was progressively contaminated by other regional or even other ethnic influences, and above all by American products and habits, leading to a marked fusion of alimentary and cultural elements. There was also the tension between wishing to preserve their own ethnic identity and wanting to integrate within the host community, which often led to split behaviour (traditional within the private and domestic environment, Americanized in the public sphere).[26] Any discussion of the characteristics of emigration would obviously be long and complex; all we wish to do here is to emphasize, yet again, the cultural role of consumption.

Fascist consumption policy

An episode often quoted to demonstrate the analogy between the laws of nature and human society is Townsend's dogs and goats theorem, which Polanyi recalls in his most famous work. During the 16th century on a forgotten island in the Juan Fernandez archipelago off the coast of Chile some goats were let loose by Spaniards to provide food for possible future trips. Free from obstacles and predators the goats multiplied all too rapidly, to the extent that they became convenient supplies for the local corsairs. The annoyed Spaniards then landed some dogs. These also quickly multiplied and began to hunt the goats. The end result was that the number of goats stabilized. Many remained, but not too many because a lot of them ended up in the jaws of the dogs, which in their turn were unable to hunt indiscriminately because the younger and faster goats took refuge on unassailable peaks. Nature was therefore able to provide a new equilibrium. Notwithstanding its popularity it seems that this story is not completely true. The goats were landed on the island but seem to have established themselves on inaccessible cliffs far from the beach. The dogs were actually cats (and did not multiply); it was fat seals that prospered on the beach. To sum up, many celebrated theories (from Malthus to Darwin) were probably inspired by a somewhat tame story.[27]

Polanyi cites this story as proof of the fact that there is no such thing as a 'self-regulating' market and that it is at best a social invention, as well as confirmation of the principle that the existence of a 'natural' balance between supply and demand is nothing but an abstraction.

However, even the most absent-minded of consumers living during the twenty years of Fascism would have had no need to listen to any ideological or naturalist diatribe to understand that the market for consumer goods was governed by complicated mechanisms that were anything but 'natural', and to realize that the state was making its voice heard more and more. Not only was it attempting to steer private consumption in the direction it wanted, through the self-sufficiency ploy and promotion of national goods, but it appeared to be getting more and more involved in the supply of public goods and not only for propaganda purposes: percentage-wise, public consumption doubled between 1911 and 1938, leaping up to 18 per cent of domestic demand).[28]

Years	Private consumption	Public consumption / Government expenditure (collective consumption from 1971)	Total	Private consumption %	Public consumption %	Total %
Millions of 1938 lire (constant prices)						
1861–70	47,216	2,116	49,332	95.7	4.3	100
1871–80	50,898	1,795	52,693	96.6	3.4	100
1881–90	53,289	2,031	55,320	96.3	3.7	100
1891–900	56,881	2,586	59,467	95.7	4.3	100
1901–10	68,677	2,797	71,474	96.1	3.9	100
1911–20	81,733	14,409	96,142	85.0	15.0	100
1921–30	97,196	7,303	104,499	93.0	7.0	100
1931–40	106,009	13,177	119,188	88.9	11.1	100
1941–50	97,520	18,574	116,094	84.0	16.0	100
Millions of 1938 lire (constant prices)						
1951–60	13,267	3,019	16,286	81.5	18.5	100
1961–70	22,648	4,475	27,123	83.5	16.5	100
Millions of euro-lire; millions of euro from 1999 (current prices)						
1971–80	73,169	16,571	89,740	81.5	18.5	100
1981–90	265,538	89,301	354,839	74.8	25.2	100
1991–2000	565,815	185,344	751,159	75.3	24.7	100
		[2001–2005 item details]				
		Medical 83,294				
		Education 56,176				
		Public admin, general services 38,440				
		Public order 24,977				
		Defence 17,700				
		Economical affairs 16,780				
		Social protection 12,374				
		Recreation and culture 6,490				
		Territory structure and housing 5,598				
		Environmental protection 3,247				
		Association activity 1,977				
2001–05	782,367	267,053	1,049,420	74.6	25.4	100

Source: elaborations on ISTAT, *Sommario di statistiche storiche dell'Italia 1861–1975*, Rome (1976); Ibid., *Contabilità nazionale. Conti economici nazionali. Anni 1970–2005*, Rome (2007).

The question concerning public consumption is important. As we have already seen, it is true that the Liberal governments had already taken an interest in it, but with Fascism this spending acquired a new focus. One doubt that might have assailed our consumer—and us too—is the following: was this trend typical of the Fascist regime or was it something more or less common to all Western countries? Was it Mussolini's statist creed that created this 'Fascist consumption policy', or was it propaganda that inflated and gave political flavour to things that were going on in liberal and democratic regimes as well? Once more, when talking about consumption it is not really possible to judge by merely singling out the national level: Fascist action must be placed within a general transnational context.

Looking at it in retrospect it seems obvious that there would be an upward trend in public spending, a significant proportion of which would be public consumption. This fact is widely attributed to the greater complexity of modern society, which carries with it increasing control and intervention by the state, a need for greater effort in providing infrastructures, and so on. A classic study in this regard, by Adolf Wagner, links increases in spending with increased earnings. The State keeps spending more and more because it is called upon to 'correct' imbalances in industrial development, for example as regards urbanization and the environment, and as a response to the growing demand for social services (the limit being the level of fiscal imposition that the citizens will support). However, this growth is not constant over a period of time, but comes in fits and starts: Peacock and Wiseman have observed that during a serious crisis—war for example—spending soars and then, when the storm is over, comes down but never returns to the previous levels, perhaps because people prefer to keep some of the social services and safeguards that have been introduced. This is the so-called 'displacement effect'. After every crisis the spending level stabilizes at a slightly higher level (some maintain that the high level of social protection in Europe is perhaps an offshoot of the traumatic experiences European citizens endured within the span of a few decades).[29]

Fascist policy therefore fits in with a much more general conduct, linked to the industrial development of the nation. Within this framework, however, it made some specific choices. It can be seen how in Italy, as opposed to other European countries, the displacement effect was almost non-existent (or at least came later). This was due to a certain backwardness but also to the fact that Fascism rapidly redirected public spending, pursuing political ends and reducing spending on welfare assistance and social security, which had greatly increased after the war (especially during the three-year period of 1920–22), while giving priority to other expenditure, especially military spending—at least until the end of the 1920s.

A clear example of this policy is given by education. The percentage spent was almost lower during Fascism than it had been under the preceding liberal governments. The maximum quota was reached during 1933–1934, when it represented 2.4 per cent of the GDP (it was 1.8 per cent in 1912). But there were important differences. The first was its management, now mostly in the hands of the State, which had ousted local authorities; the second was the increasingly political nature of education. This was not so much the case with the Gentile reform of 1923, which aimed at building up a hierarchical and élitist education system (with humanistic subjects and classical high school at the top), but rather with the creation during the 1930s of a complex 'Fascist' education system, where schools were teamed up with youth organizations, which dealt with sports and paramilitary preparation, recreation, and cultural competition (thanks to the National Balilla, later Italian Lictorian Youth). The Gentile reform was increasingly disregarded, and Bottai, the Education Minister from 1936 to 1943, worked hard at a complex project of reorganization, which enhanced technical education so as to create an intermediate level of skilled workers. If Bottai's ambitious plans were not completely fulfilled, it was more due to insufficient funding than to the war.

For a young boy elementary education was by and large assured (according to available data). Nevertheless his academic career would still be strongly influenced by the social standing of his family. To have any hopes of going to a classical high school, and university after that, he would have to belong to the élite. Otherwise the choice would be for a lower educational level, such as a scientific high school or a training college (however, secondary education enrolment doubled in the span of a few years and by 1936 represented 8 per cent of the corresponding age group). For the majority of cases it was limited to a few years at school, then it was out to work, participating however in the numerous para-scholastic organizations according to age: *Figli della Lupa* (Sons of the She-Wolf), Balilla, Vanguard, and male Fascist university groups. Instead, in a girl's case the prospect of spending many years at school was decidedly less, partly because of family and social pressures. Her educational experience would also be different. She might set her sights on going to a girls' high school, but not so much the university. She would join different organizations (Little Italians, Young Italy, Young Fascists). Yet in the long run female education was to increase enormously, as required by industry and the growing service sector, though the regime imposed restrictions on various managerial professions and the use of female labour.[30]

This was to be expected. The use of education as a course of action to transform society, and youth in particular, to create a 'new man' completely moulded by the regime is common in totalitarianism. It offers a broad preparation but provides a political type of education, 'Fascist' in this case, which above all else reinforced divisions of class and gender.

Welfare assistance and social security policy was more innovative. During Fascism, private company and category insurances operated within the health system structure, resulting in disjointed, piecemeal assistance schemes covering two thirds of the population. Concern for the integrity of the race forced the authorities to make insurance obligatory for some categories of workers and, during the last few years (1943), to widen health insurance through a central institute called INFAM. Further provision was made to reorganize the health service in the hospitals (1938) and for the entire regime a campaign was conducted to wipe out diseases like tuberculosis and malaria, with good results.[31]

Social security grew in parallel. Some important reforms were actually planned during the pre-Fascist period as well as during and after the war, to alleviate the serious social crisis. Compulsory accident insurance was extended to farm workers and, in 1919, the old age pension and invalid insurance schemes for employees were launched, together with the first safeguards against unemployment.[32] The Fascists then added numerous laws, officially because they saw social security as the positive result of collaboration between employer and employee, ratified by the corporative system, and in actual fact because it created a useful tool for social control and political orienting. One of the novelties introduced was the creation of centralized, state-controlled agencies to manage social security. Institutes were created for employees of local authorities (INADEL), public bodies (ENFDEP), and the State (ENFPAS), while in 1933 two big institutes came into being—INFPS for pensions and INFAIL for accidents to private work-ers.[33] The creation of these agencies is interesting because it made it possible to centralize social security while allowing a certain economy and flexibility in its management. For this reason the agencies survived the regime and were to form the basis of welfare assistance and the social services in Italy after the war. Furthermore these great institu-tions provided important territorial control centres, guaranteeing many jobs and some prestigious positions, as well as lending themselves easily to a system of patronage, something else that would survive into the post-war years.

There is another aspect of Fascist public consumption to bear in mind, and that is the specific regulations relating to women. When speaking of its autarchic approach it has already been seen how the regime saw a new role for women in the state. Recall here how the pro-maternity policy was not only maintained by insistent propaganda (contrasting the healthy, full-blooded Italian mother with the slightly-built, neurotic modern woman). Numerous laws were passed to support working women: extending regulations against night work for women and children; almost revolutionary laws on maternity, allowing two months of compulsory paid leave, as well as a prolonged period of optional absence, breast-feeding permits and also a cash bonus when the baby was born.[34] To this was added the creation of nursery schools, pediatric advisors, and specialized clinics—all of which also had the effect of improving medical assistance during pregnancy and the early stages of life—and the blanket coverage of welfare assistance provided since 1925 by ONMI (*Opera nazionale per la maternità e l'infanzia*) (National Assistance for Mothers and Infants).[35] And there could added many other provisions, from family allowances (since 1934) giving assistance for large families (including higher wages for fathers).

So how can my questions be answered? Without doubt the Fascist regime gradually stimulated public spending, starting with the military, but also civil later on (during the 1930s total spending exceeded 30 per cent of the GDP, something that happened in Germany but not in countries like France and Great Britain).[36] Where civil spending is concerned an important phenomenon is witnessed: redistributive spending (welfare assistance and social security) during the 1930s ex-ceeded the amount spent on education. This fact could be interpreted as a delayed 'displacement' effect, but the characteristics of this expen-diture show that a political choice was being proposed. The aim was to benefit specific groups, women in the first place but including industrial workers (who were partly compensated for the heavy wage-cuts they had suffered after the Lira was stabilized, and not offset by equally efficient discipline where prices were concerned) and civil servants (as part of a policy of broadening out the wage scale in favour of directors) so as to integrate them in the regime. In this way public spending became a tool for attaining political consent.

Collective consumption

In the daily life of a family living during Fascism it was not just private consumption and basic services that were guaranteed by the State. Increasingly involved were other forms of 'collective' consumption by state-controlled agencies, private bodies and party-controlled associations (so not technically public consumption, that is, paid for by the State, even if there was relatively little difference, seeing the increasing overlap between state and Fascist party). Consumption is increasingly linked to leisure time: education, sports, culture, and entertainment. The working man who practised sport or went to the theatre or cinema in his free time, the student who went to art exhibitions or gymnastic displays, the woman who attended courses in first aid or home economics, the farm hand who took part in folk festivals, the clerk who sent his son to seaside camp; all these were trying out new ways of consumption, enjoyed collectively, and either free of charge or at greatly reduced prices. It was very different from public intervention seen as a corrective for certain forms of industrial development which had been the focus of debate in the past. I am not talking here about the most essential goods and services, but about leisure time and the secondary consumption. Why should the state involve itself with this?

The first answer is pragmatic. The importance of clubs and associations for recreation and sport within working-class culture has already been discussed. Socialist parties had pushed strongly in this direction. Following the German Social Democrats' example of keeping their members united in a hostile environment, they had organized a tight network of 'non-political' associations, sports leagues, cultural organizations, newspapers, shows, and welfare assistance agencies: a real 'State within the State'.[37] In Italy, workers' recreation clubs, whether spontaneous or of socialist inspiration, were already widespread and popular. Thus one of the Fascists' first concerns was to make a clean sweep of their opponents' territory, targeting bands, choirs, drama societies, and sports clubs if they gave the slightest hint of socialist sympathies (or even popular Catholic ones at times). In some cases these were disbanded or else absorbed into collateral organizations of the Fascist party, starting with *Opera nazionale dopolavoro* (OND) (National After Work Recreation). Why waste a valuable source of enrolment when it could be persuaded towards your own political ends?

A second stimulus and incentive for these initiatives came instead from the United States, where after-work activities flourished, representing a development of the philanthropic tradition of helping and 'uplifting' workers that had begun in Europe back in the 19th century. It was no coincidence that the original OND nucleus was made up of the workers' leisure clubs run by provincial bodies and companies, created by Fascist trade unions through the incentive of Mario Giani, a technician working for Westinghouse's Italian branch.[38] However a new factor now appeared. All these activities were swallowed up by the state and taken collectively into a government-controlled agency directly entrusted to the Fascist party so as to turn it into an instrument-of-consent organization. So was born what Stefano Cavazza calls 'State leisure time'.[39]

It would be simplistic to think that this operation was merely instrumental, that is to keep a check on the masses and regiment them better. In actual fact it brought about a momentous change. Consumption linked to free time had become important enough to justify official attention. It was not something unnecessary, luxurious, or possibly reserved for a certain élite. In Liberal Italy it would still have sounded like heresy. What had happened?

Researchers like Kern and Corbin have shown that every age and every culture have a specific concept of time.[40] Ever since the 19th century time has been more structured (hours dedicated to different activities strictly separated; take work and rest for example: each with its own allotted period that cannot overlap into the other). It is more measurable (with the use of increasingly refined measuring devices, such as mechanical clocks—since the end of the 19th century even the minutes have been counted). It has accelerated (with modern means of transport the mental images of space/time relations have been changed). It is interiorized (lives are organized around many 'time' signals: alarm clocks, factory hooters, diaries). Even each social class has its own particular vision. Over the aristocrat's unvarying concept of time or the countryman's time regulated by cosmic and natural rhythms, it is middle-class 'calculated' time that has prevailed, where every minute counts and wasting time is condemned (a short step to 'time is money').

If contemporary time is therefore both precious and measurable, it comes as no surprise that one of the longest battles for unions and workers was the one fought to reduce the legal working hours, reduced from 12–15 hours a day to the present 8, and to get holidays and the 'English' Saturday (as regards the latter, it was the Fascists themselves who brought it in, naturally calling it a 'Fascist Saturday'). In this way the workers gained more time for themselves. But what could be done with this increased leisure? Corbin still recalls how the West has inherited two different traditions in this regard: idleness, the individual free time typical of the élites, and recreation, the time for collective activity typical of the working classes. In the eyes of the 20th-century managerial classes, 'idleness' was definitely not right for the common people. At the same time they were convinced of the need to 'usefully employ' leisure time, also prompted by examples coming from the US.[41] And so it is that recreation—the time dedicated to culture and relaxation activities (which could also have significant economic repercussions), becomes a welcome social activity. The die is cast: cultural and recreational consumption takes its place alongside traditional consumption. Fascism did nothing more than consolidate it all, adding its own political connotations.

The impact on education and social control is obvious, but we are only interested in seeing the legitimizing effect it had on all activities linked to leisure, opening the way for them to be included among Fascist ideals.[42] Little wonder that free time activities came to be among the regime's most popular projects.

An example can be given by looking at the regime's action in the theatre sector. Theatre is a good choice because it represents a typical case of cultural consumption reserved for the upper classes, with its possibilities of both passive enjoyment (by the audience) and active enjoyment (by the amateur actors). Well, the regime began in the 1920s by disbanding all musical and dramatic associations considered to have political leanings, and gathering all the rest into the OND, where they all flourished remarkably. From 113 in 1926 they increased to 1,095 by 1929 and over 2,006 a few years later, thanks to a complex structure of support and facilitation.[43] Simultaneously, the *Carri di Tespi*

(Thespian Wagons) were created in 1929, inspired by Giovacchino Forzano. These were travelling theatres continually moving from place to place, giving shows in rural areas where there were no halls. Held up by metal framework, a canopy that could be erected within an hour was transported by lorry overnight to the next venue, erected anew in the morning, filled with long rows of chairs and equipped with external floodlights. In the evening all would be ready for a new show (always free) by professional actors or singers. The performances were absolutely not of the propaganda type, but based on great successes from contemporary Italian theatre or famous operas. In its very first year the Thespian Wagons covered 2,500 kilometres, stopped at 42 different venues and had an audience total of more than 300,000. It is widely seen as one of the regime's most successful initiatives in the cultural field, and the fact that it contained no obvious propaganda did not limit its political value, as this commentary hints:

> It was like a huge carriage, with raised hood, supported by a large triangular pediment on which the Fasces of the Lictors were emblazoned. In the background, splendidly framed, the Fortuny dome stood out against the night sky. [. . .] It all seemed like a gift from the Regime . . .[44]

The most effective propaganda is what is not seen, as Lazarsfeld says.[45] In 1936, the Press and Propaganda Minister in his turn set up theatre shows especially for the Fascist Saturday. This was reserved for workers, junior clerks, itinerant salesmen, and employees with a monthly pay-packet of less than 800 lire. It was a success. From 1937 to 1940 almost a thousand shows were presented to a total audience of a million. From 1937 all activity was reorganized under the umbrella of the Italian Summer Music festival, jointly run by the Minister for Popular Culture, the party, provinces, city councils, and OND. Attendance was really high and audiences totalled two and a half million a year. This time it was a more mixed public, but certain 'protected' social segments (youth, workers, and rural populations) benefited from big price reductions and special ticket distribution. During the same year, factory concerts were also launched, directly organized in the large working plants in the north, in the ports, and mines.[46]

The regime thus brought the theatre, typical consumption of the élite, into a broader swathe of the population within the sphere of a national integration programme (so we come back to the idea of a national consumption space. It is no coincidence that the only requirement for the work being performed was 'Italianness'). And the same could be said for other areas, such as sport, which was meaningful not just for class but for gender too. Think of the impact on Italian society of the (albeit tentative) physical education policy for girls, the public gymnastic displays and participation of female athletes representing Italy in the Berlin Olympics of 1936 (where Ondina Valle won the first ever gold medal in the women's 80 metre hurdles to become a celebrity and new female role model).[47]

At this point many researchers have asked the question: to what extent did all these efforts to widen the horizons of consumption help to reinforce the regime? Opinions differ here. From our point of view it makes more sense to turn the question around. To what extent did the regime make this consumption socially legitimate? Considering the huge numbers involved, the reply is highly positive, seeing that participation always remained voluntary (even if at times it was 'advised'). In this way the regime spread the benefits of 'high' quality consumption, such as the theatre, and popularized more things such as sport, cinema, and the novelty of those years, the radio. But, this does not mean that adhesion was total and homogeneous on the part of the different social classes, who may have interpreted the new experiences in the light of their own specific cultures. In other words, to each their own: everyone could take what they wanted. But what did they want? Observers of organized systems say that joining a voluntary organization depends on two main factors: selective incentives (material ones, for example in our case the possibility of having the benefits of goods and services otherwise beyond the economic resources of the middle-lower classes, and for some the ability to attain positions of power and status) and collective incentives (which could take the form of group solidarity, a sense of belonging, having a specific identity—such as being Italian—and frequently, but not necessarily, accepting the presupposed ideologies of the organization).[48] We can therefore maintain that there were benefits at more than one level, even at the same time, and it is impossible to separate them. One thing is sure, however. By distributing these various kinds of consumption from above, the regime helped to give them a strong veneer of social legitimacy making them seem part of the 'package' of goods and services to which all citizens were entitled.

If any doubt could assail consumers of the time, it was another: did the broadening of consumption have to pass through these collective forms organized from above, or did other ways exist? The doubt was legitimate because in reality, within the very 'media system' created under the Fascist regime, competing models could be seen.

Leafing through illustrated magazines or watching *Luce* cinema news, the continual presence of nobility as role models for consumption is striking. At evening receptions and any kind of inauguration, horse race, film premier or gymnastic exhibition, representatives of the aristocracy (together with those of the Party, of course) would never fail to be present, always sitting right in the front row. His Royal Highness Umberto, Prince of Piedmont would be there on many occasions, tall, refined, smiling, and elegantly dressed in his faultless uniform. Beside him would be Maria José, sophisticated and haughty in her Nordic beauty.[49] And it was not just aristocrats of ancient lineage. The ennobling of Ciano, who also attended innumerable receptions, wearing his black shirt (but always very formal, with commentators referring to him as 'His Excellency Count Ciano') is most telling. Edda Ciano too (or rather 'Countess Edda Ciano Mussolini') was always there: elegant and refined, fashionable, almost ethereal when, for example, as a guest in Berlin in 1938, she strolled around in just a sleeveless white silk dress pulled in at the waist with a black belt, while around her five or six high officials sweltered in their stiff jackets and ties.[50] She was the epitome of an aristocrat, put up as an example to follow at receptions, in her exclusive dresses with trains, fine jewels and furs, and riding in luxury cars. She really made her mark in Fascist Italy.

There was, then, another model, imported from America through popular Hollywood films—the so-called '*telefoni bianchi*' being the Italian version. Here again, a woman is the centre of attention: fair-haired, tall and slim, a striking beauty who lives in a luxury flat, frequents the theatre and cinema, and surrounds herself with symbols of modern city living. Beside her the man is no lesser a figure: elegant, dynamic and self-assured in his cool blazer, he smiles as he raises a cigarette to his lips, or sits at the wheel of his bright shining car. Here, the reference is to an affluent middle class that enjoys individual kinds of consumer products belonging to a commercialized culture.[51] But, here again, it was an impossible model for an inter-war Italy that had to come to terms with the difficult realities of everyday life. America was far away.

On the contrary, Nazi Germany was both geographically and politically close at hand. In this respect it is widely held that the Nazis enforced a rigid policy of private consumption restraints, creating hardships for the people, in order to concentrate economic resources in preparation for war. Researchers like Berghoff now maintain that the picture is more complex, however.[52] Admittedly, some kinds of consumption were limited (butter, margarine, cooking fat, and other foodstuffs, thus depleting the diet). In other cases, however, the regime favoured the growth of symbolic forms of consumption, such as radio, cinema, and mass holidays (through the *Kraft durch Freude*, identical to OND in Italy). It also encouraged the sale of cars (though the *Volkswagen* was not bought by everybody because of its high price) and use of household electrical appliances. In reality the Nazis seemed to fear that a sudden drop in the tenor of material existence, albeit for patriotic motives, might undermine consensus and cause a return to the dramatic scenario of 1918. Because of this, even the savings campaign on the eve of the war was presented as a way of consuming more in the immediate future (with slogans such as 'savings help you buy', 'money saved – dreams come true').[53]

In Italy, conditions were different: there was greater poverty. Because of this, the role of the regime in promoting public and collective consumption was more significant. Besides, greater stress was laid on the nationalistic side of consumption, with all its political repercussions. For both regimes their consumption policies were of enormous significance and the consumers reacted selectively (in many cases both Nazis and Fascists proved reluctant to openly challenge consumer models they considered 'xenophilic' and 'unhealthy'). On the contrary, it was sometimes they who initiated advertising campaigns and created eagerness for new products for private use: technological gadgets for the home, cars, cultural consumption, tourism—without being able to provide them. But this was the moment that paved the way culturally to mass consumption based on technology and the enjoyment of domestic facilities, a condition that would come into effect after the war.

6

Everyday Life during Fascism

History tells us that the meeting at Cajamarca (Peru) in 1532 between the Spanish conqueror Pizarro and the last sovereign of the Incas, Atahualpa, was very dramatic. First to come forward was the chaplain, Valverde, holding a Bible and declaring that the Incas owed obedience because the word of God contained in that book commanded it. The emperor took the book, an object he had never seen before (the Quechuan language was not a written one and documents were recorded using strings with knots called the *quipu*). He inspected it, then held it to his ear and, as he did not see or hear any words, threw it scornfully to the ground, calling Valverde an imposter. This was the signal for the Spanish to attack. With their guns they spread panic and routed the large Inca army. Atahualpa himself was captured, forcibly baptized, and garrotted.[1]

One thing is sure: even without this sacrilegious act, the Spanish conquest would have gone ahead anyway. This fact, however, points to a significant culture clash and reminds us that even the simplest everyday objects can be understood and used only within a context that gives them meaning. It is necessary to learn their use and realize the cultural value of this use. They mean nothing on their own, and the more complex and more technological they become, the longer it takes to include them in the surrounding 'system of objects', to use an expression by Baudrillard (that is, within the well-coded system of signs and meanings that makes up the 'language' of our modern mediatic society).[2]

Talking about technology, Kuznets reminds us what a powerful incentive it is for getting people consume more since it urges them to want new and different things, as well as broadening the scope of their choices. But it is important to note that even a technological thing is not a 'black box', a mechanism that only works when a button is pushed. It is an apparatus or process that becomes active in certain cultural contexts that presume a certain level of knowledge, the spread of other means of technology, the presence of support services, and so forth.[3] Recent studies have emphasized the interaction of this process:

the equipment does not impose its own rigid way of use, because it is the users that will negotiate methods and meanings of use, changing and interpreting it differently according to their culture or even their sex. This is not about technical determinism but about a real sociocultural process.[4]

Whichever way it is looked at the phenomena, there is no doubt that technical progress is fundamental to consumption processes, especially in today's world (for some, it is perhaps the element that most characterizes of our age). So why not go and look for the objects that best embody this aspect in the period under examination, that is to say during Fascism?

Home

To conduct my research I have selected an upper middle-class home in a big city, owing to the high cost of new technology (which means that I would not have discovered anything in a working-class or lower middle-class home) and also because it is more likely to be found in a metropolitan environment. The wide social separations of the classes is yet another reason, again marked by similar material indicators, which are very strong and visible (a characteristic more or less found throughout Europe rather than the United States, even though the actual social inequalities are less defined in Europe).[5]

I must wait until the owners of the house go out. It is morning and out through the main door of the elegant block of flats comes the husband. I cannot avoid taking a look at his clothes. His complete suit of jacket and trousers is certainly tailor-made (partly because during Fascism ready-made suits accounted for only 20 per cent of the total of suits made and were often of poor quality and highly priced).[6] I can wager that all other items are factory made, however, starting with the shirt that lies under his tie. In fact shirt-making was the first department to become industrial, thanks to collar sizes (proportional to chest and shoulders), while conventional sizes came later, through the need for military uniforms. Important shirtmaking firms appeared in Milan and Turin (with manufacturers like Carlo De Micheli, Vincenzo Boero, and Isaia Levi), even though the most famous were still English. Notice the soft collar, perhaps attached by buttons. (Shirts were sold together with spare collars and cuffs.) Clothing had to last. The waterproof or trenchcoat is also manufactured, reminding one of its origins in the trenches of World War One, and it might have come from a specialized zone of Empoli or maybe San Giorgio of Genoa.[7] Then there is the hat, the typical sign of belonging to the middle class (workmen wore a cap). The hat he is wearing is made of felt or animal hair. It may have come from Monza, where they have specialized in this craft since the 17th century, and where there are big firms (Cambiaghi, Ricci, and Paleari); or from the Biella factory of the Barbisio brothers in Piedmont—or, if of the best quality, from Borsalino of Alessandria. If it happens to be summer he will probably be wearing a fine straw hat made in Florence, from where, for more than two centuries, this product has been exported all over the world. I cannot see his shoes. They are hidden under gaiters or galoshes (because of the cold, but also because the 'genuine Italian' leather is not of good quality at this time). Off he goes at last, round the corner.

Immediately afterwards I see the maid come out (easily recognizable by her humble, 'country' look. She wears a sort of blue shirt and low-heeled shoes). She is taking two children to school, both wearing black smocks. The girl has a pink rosette, the boy a big white collar, blue rosette, and short trousers (worn until he is adolescent) peeping out underneath his smock. They are late and almost running, as they are likely to go all the way to school on foot.

I have to wait a while for the wife to come out. She is elegant, in a fairly clinging rustling dress decorated with tiny flowers, over which she wears a long dark jacket with a small fur collar. Her outfit would be sober if it were not for two details: the little plain-coloured hat worn at an angle (even this is a sign of class: common people went bare-headed or would wear a knotted kerchief), and the sheer stockings with the centre back seam (probably from the Milanese Santagostino firm, the biggest manufacturer at the time). Stockings and dress remind us of the important evolution in fabrics that occurred during the 1930s with the introduction of artificial fibres. The exceptional development of companies like Snia-Viscosa led by Riccardo Gualino, or Soie de Chatillon, the brainchild of Leopoldo Parodi Delfino, raised the sector to second place at world level, producing rayon (from cellulose), flock, lanital, and other products that gave a strong boost to textiles and ready-made clothes.[8] Among other things this made it possible to produce good-quality clothing at reasonable prices, even during the protectionist regime.[9] Going back to our lady, I see she is a follower of fashion, something by no means scorned by the regime (as long as it was 'Italian' in taste and material). She probably reads certain magazines to keep herself up to date (naturally *La Donna* by Mondadori or *Lei* by Rizzoli or, if she is very sophisticated, *Lidel* by Lydia De Liguoro).[10] Her clothing is certainly the work of one of the many local dressmakers or a tailor-made product from a fashion house (the first serious centre of sartorial quality was formed around Rome and Florence—where the 'shoemaker' Ferragamo distinguished himself with his wedge heels using cork when leather was in short supply[11]—while a second, more industrial centre, was between Milan and Turin). But this is only at the dawn of what would become the Italian fashion system.

The field is finally clear and I can go in. I am immediately struck by how neat and clean everything is inside, conveying an air of decorum. Goodness knows what a job it is to keep everything in such perfect order! By good fortune between the two wars the chemical industry made colossal advances and offered new consumer products for domestic cleaning and laundry (the sector leader in Italy being Mira Lanza, from the merger of two pre-existing firms specializing in soap and candles, while giants from abroad were still unknown, such as Procter & Gamble in America, Henkel in Germany, and Lever in England). And there is no shortage of other products: all the rage at the moment are refreshing drinks (such as fizzy orangeade: San Pellegrino was the first to launch this), effervescent mineral water like 'Vichy' obtained by adding in succession two coloured packets of salts, and Idrolitina made by the Bologna restaurant owner Arturo Gazzoni.[12]

In the kitchen, I immediately notice a majestic, shining white 'new' object in the middle of the room. It is the cooking stove. On the ample range are the hotplates (concentric cast iron rings), with a perennial pan of hot water on one of them. Below is a large oven and a hatch where wood or coal can be put in. It is square-cut and modern in shape, easy to use and heats the kitchen much better than the old cooker made of bricks with a hood above it. The drawback is the high price of a thousand lire (much more than an office worker's monthly salary). In 1935 a civil servant at a subsidiary level would not reach a gross annual income of 10,000 lire, an executive would earn between 7,000 and 14,000 lire. Only a director could hope to reach 15–20,000 lire).[13] On one side is a heavy old heating stove, but nearby there is a new electric heater (which is probably rarely switched on, given the high cost of electricity—and you can tell because the room is a little chilly). There is no shortage of electrical gadgets. A kettle is visible and perhaps there is something else in the white cupboard. However, when I look up I am aware of the (dim) light that the lamp sheds over the large table and linoleum floor.[14] But what I nearly missed is the fact that in this house there are other important 'modern' services. There is running water, electricity and, seeing that it is a fairly new and a good quality house, probably gas as well.

This is an important point in our history of consumption. Some of the goods and services which we consider an integral part of current living standards belong to the category of 'natural monopolies'. This means sectors where a single operator works more efficiently and is thus considered the basic supplier to the community and accorded a special regime of rules and prices. In the United States they have preferred to trust private companies and impose very strict regulations. Instead, in Europe they entrust the management to public, state-controlled companies. In Italy the great performers are local agencies. During the Giolitti era, after an important law of 1903, there was a spread of municipal agencies dealing with electricity (the most lucrative sector), gas, water supplies, and urban transport (the sector making the greatest loss). So ends a debate on monopolies that started in the late nineteenth century. In some big cities, public services thus assured are fundamental for the work of urbanization, becoming like a banner for many administrations. Fascism maintained these institutions without increasing them, partly due to the political mistrust it often nurtured towards agencies that had come about due to socialist inspiration, and partly through the state's centralizing policy.[15] There was naturally no lack of exceptions to state control. Without doubt the most sensational is Edison, a real bulwark of Italian capitalism. Besides supplying electricity, during the 1930s it also landed the job of supplying gas to Milan and had enormous gasholders built in Bovisa, a working-class area to the north of the city. As already noted,[16] this altered the urban landscape completely. In a magnificent picture painted in 1943, Mario Sironi depicts the enormous dark red mass of a gasholder in the centre with two tall chimneys and other industrial buildings beside it. Down below a solitary workman is passing on a bicycle. It is a telling portrayal of the new urban outskirts.[17]

To return to the kitchen, it is a feminine space, dedicated to the work associated with the woman's social role rather than as a housewife. After the tremendous mobilization of the female workforce in the First World War the return home involved the middle classes as much as the

Table 4 Average annual consumer prices for some products and services, 1861–1985 (current lire)

Years	Bread (kg)	Pasta (kg)	Rice (kg)	Potatoes (kg)	Butter (kg)	Olive oil (litre)	Wine (litre)	Roasted coffee (kg)	Sugar (kg)	Beef (kg)	Milk (litre)
1861–70	0.47	0.72	0.59	0.13	2.47	1.37	0.62	2.17	1.33	1.06	0.24
1871–80	0.58	0.90	0.77	0.17	3.10	1.46	0.65	3.50	1.43	1.39	0.29
1881–90	0.45	0.68	0.70	0.14	2.85	1.36	0.59	3.42	1.51	1.50	0.31
1891–900	0.44	0.63	0.72	0.12	2.79	1.35	0.51	4.19	1.55	1.58	0.28
1901–10	0.43	0.62	0.68	0.15	2.92	1.46	0.46	3.35	1.47	1.66	0.28
1911–20	0.64	0.98	1.03	0.33	6.69	3.64	1.15	7.96	2.75	4.88	0.60
1921–30	2.19	3.29	3.08	0.87	19.33	9.12	2.41	29.09	6.82	13.56	1.51
1931–40	2.06	2.96	2.30	0.65	14.16	6.82	1.86	32.27	6.50	10.99	1.16
1941–50	96.00	150.20	207.60	40.40	1,144.60	506.40	95.20	1,307.00	327.20	805.00	64.40
1951–60	130.30	197.10	183.60	47.90	1,190.90	579.80	122.40	2,029.40	255.90	1,145.20	78.90
1961–70	159.40	236.30	232.40	75.20	1,470.10	735.50	147.00	2,169.00	228.30	1,723.70	112.40
1971–80	378.00	471.40	567.70	237.90	3,070.10	1,570.20	327.00	4,969.60	464.90	4,432.90	283.20
1981–85	1,172.40	1,416.20	1,574.00	587.00	7,389.00	3,091.00	822.40	10,135.80	1,109.80	11,491.80	773.00

Years	Worsted for men's suits (m)	Worsted for women's suits (m)	Men's shoes (pair)	Women's shoes (pair)	Domestic brand cigarettes (pack of 10)	Average railway travel	Stamp for a letter	City bus ticket	Electrical energy (kWh)	Gas (m3)	Radio (or TV) license
1861–70	–	–	–	–	–	–	0.20	–	–	–	–
1871–80	–	–	–	–	–	–	0.20	–	–	–	–
1881–90	–	–	–	–	–	–	0.20	0.10	–	–	–
1891–900	–	–	–	–	–	–	0.20	0.10	–	–	–
1901–10	–	–	–	–	0.19	4.16	0.16	0.10	–	–	–
1911–20	28.34	19.52	38.49	38.71	0.41	5.14	0.16	0.14	0.53	0.33	–
1921–30	64.05	36.16	55.69	50.74	1.29	14.04	0.50	0.45	1.28	0.78	52.20
1931–40	63.70	33.36	49.95	47.74	1.71	15.80	0.50	0.50	1.83	0.63	79.60
1941–50	4,792.00	2,626.20	4,527.00	3,802.40	57.85	210.84	12.33	14.00	21.14	17.97	1,754.00
1951–60	5,628.30	2,888.60	5,153.90	4,478.00	80.58	404.12	24.96	27.60	40.13	30.00	2,450.00
1961–70	6,852.30	3,699.30	6,146.20	5,423.60	88.09	583.50	38.77	56.80	40.45	38.06	3,400.00
1971–80	14,397.10	8,954.70	18,292.60	16,460.00	96.00	1,037.50	112.18	120.00	34.51	72.28	3,531.00
1981–85	35,740.00	23,764.40	54,774.60	49,762.20	107.50	2,800.00	365.83	385.00	96.34	251.73	3,603.00

Coefficients to convert lire (2006 = 1): 1870 = 1; 1880 = 7,896.04; 1890 = 6,715.62; 1900 = 7,133.54; 1910 = 7,537.94; 1920 = 6,889.60; 1930 = 1,887.16; 1940 = 1,543.64; 1940 = 1,255.13; 1950 = 31.54; 1960 = 22.35; 1970 = 15.27; 1980 = 4.11; 1985 = 2.15 (cf. ISTAT, *Il valore della moneta in Italia dal 1861 al 2006*, Rome (2007)).

Source: cf. Table 1.

workers. Fascism reinforced the trend to quit work after marriage or one's first child. In 1931 Turin the percentage of women employed in industry was 42 per cent up to the age of 20 (as against 47 per cent for men), but this fell drastically to 26 per cent for ages from 21 to 34, and yet again to 14 per cent beyond 35 years of age, while men stayed constantly close to 50 per cent.[18] In the kitchen, therefore, I find signs of the traditional activities related to domestic self-sufficiency, attention to food and clothing, but in different forms. In one corner there is a Singer sewing machine (but it could easily be a Necchi). It is black, fitted to a little table, and operated by a cast-iron pedal. Despite costing around a thousand lire it was a most important appliance for the household economy as it enabled the wife to make simple clothes, sew, mend and patch nearly everything. This was hugely important in an age that insisted on the virtue of saving (one of the regime's slogans warned: 'Indigestion kills more than hunger'). The sewing machine represents the mechanized version of an age-old feminine culture.

Nearby is an electric iron. It is one of the first and surely cost a lot. Before leaving I cannot resist having a look inside the dresser and—thank goodness for that—there's the pasta! For one moment I feared that Marinetti's bold call for the creation of a *Cucina futurista* (futurist cooking) banning pasta might have been put into practice, but it is not the case. The provocations of intellectuals work better in the drawing room than in the kitchen.[19]

The childrens' rooms hold no surprises—I can tell that there are only two children, which is in keeping with the country's descending demographic trend whereby, despite all the regime campaigns, families decreased from 4.5 members in 1891 to 4.2 in 1936.[20] The drawing room, across the hall, has the same solemn format I have already met in the past: armchairs and sofas, heavy furniture, decorated carpets on a wooden parquet floor, a great many ornaments, side tables. The furniture is still more hand-made than mass-produced (even though in Europe there are now completely mechanized factories like the Deutsche Werkstätte at Dresden) and it reflects traditional tastes. And just think, that this is the period of Bauhaus, Wright, Mies van der Rohe, Le Corbusier, to quote a few names, but also of functionalist architecture and Milan's Triennale experiments.[21] But these are things reserved for the élite. There are, however, no less than three objects to remind us that we have entered into a new age of mass communication: the gramophone, radio, and telephone, with the place of honour reserved for the radio. It is a Radiomarelli Vertumno model receiving long, medium, and short waves. Fairly big and heavy, it is made of dark wood below and light wood above. There is a central panel of pale cloth protected by a grating. At the sides are two knobs to move the frequency indicator. Despite being a modern invention it blends in with the traditional wooden furniture. However, its impact on family life was massive as it introduced new forms of music (half the transmissions were dedicated to music), the latest news with radio newsreels, and entertainment, culture, and even propaganda programmes. The radio transmitted a taste for songs and live sports events, created new personalities, made the voices of the powerful familiar and punctuated the rhythm of the day. This family is lucky to have one, seeing how costly they were (this model sold at 1,100 lire while the 'Radioballilla', costing a third of this, was not invented until 1937); then there was the license to be paid for as well. As a result, listening often became collective in OND centres, country schools, and public buildings.[22]

The radio increased people's taste for music in the home, heralding the way for the gramophone. There is one here, in an elegant little case with a wind-up handle made by Edison-Bell (the trumpet bell has disappeared by now). Nearby are replacement needles and several 78 rpm records: EMI, Decca, Pathé, Deutsche Grammophon, and His Master's Voice (with its famous trademark, the little dog listening to a trumpet gramophone). Most of them are operas and dance music. There are also records by Enrico Caruso, the first recording star, who sold a million copies between 1901 and 1904 (they are real collector's items! But I had better leave them where they are). Before my eyes I can see the way 'canned music' revolutionized musical entertainment, replacing live performances and greatly increasing demand. A new market was created, powered by big international industries and sustained by continuous advertising.[23] The low level of family incomes greatly restricted the spread of new equipment. I am reminded of this when I see a black telephone with a dial (white telephones were only found in films), and a party line. Even this was an object few could afford.[24] The average Italian spent only 19 lire a year on entertainment (70 per cent went to the cinema, the real passion of the age). It may well be true that the only categories to increase during this period were transport and the durable new commodities, but the prices were high enough to restrict their use to upper social levels. This is why the numbers were significantly lower than in other major European countries. Italians with a radio license were one fifth of the total for France and only one tenth of the German total. Where the telephone was concerned, the difference was enormous (during 1938, 40 million calls in Italy, 960 million in France and almost 3 billion in Germany).[25] Being an owner of new technology was thus an almost distinctive sign of class.

Finally, a look at the bathroom. There is an enormous bath-water heater, a real luxury. Beside the big cast-iron bath there are several products lined up on a shelf: Marseilles soap (for clothes or personal use), Palmolive and Lanza toilet soap, Gibbs hair cream ('keep your hair in order'), Colgate toothpaste (as well as Email Diamant: 'without me| loved mouth| no shine'), a Parma Violets perfume, a box of ten Gillette razor blades 'within everyone's reach'. High up on one wall a tightly closed cabinet can be seen, full of medicinal products, which by now have become an increasingly important family need (there is absorbent cotton wool, tincture of iodine, cod liver oil, and much publicized products like aspirin, Formitrol for the throat, Rim laxative, S. Pellegrino magnesia).[26] I am called out by the sound of a car horn. It is time to go.

Transport

> We believe that the magnificence of the world has been enriched by a new beauty: the beauty of high speed. A racing car, its bonnet decorated with snake-like tubes hissing explosively... roaring and whizzing along like a hail of bullets, more beautiful than the Winged Victory of Samothrace.[27]

Marinetti and the Futurists were the first Italians to exalt the fascination of speed and the automobile, which they elevated to the masculine status symbol of technical progress and modern beauty.[28] Their enthusiasm was shared by very many others right from the start, however. Cars miraculously condensed the conquest of time and space, enabling people to travel great distances and in much less time, and they satisfied the passion for new technology and the desire to show off one's status.

The Italian car industry got going in good time. During the 1920s there were as many as 36 car-manufacturing firms, some decidedly industrial, others boasting a high standard of craftsmanship. There was the Isotta Fraschini, most elegant and avant-garde, the epitome of a luxury car. There were sports cars created by Alfieri Maserati, the mechanical genius from Bologna, winners of prestigious races like the Targa Florio in 1926. There were Alfa Romeos, also winners of many international victories (linked with the names of champions like Antonio Ascari, Enzo Ferrari, and Giuseppe Campari). There were the prestigious cars (including the outstanding Dilambda), created by Vincenzo Lancia, a factory owner's son with a passion for driving. Last but not least, there was the greatest firm of all, Giovanni Agnelli and Vittorio Valletta's FIAT, the first Italian company to make a production-line car (the Tipo Zero of 1912). The company expanded greatly, thanks to wartime contracts, and from the 1920s dominated the market with its 501, 508, and 509 models. It was in fact a Fiat 508, the famous 'Ballilla' saloon, which caught the Italian people's attention in the street. I can imagine it stopping by the roadside to wait for someone and being able to admire it in all its beauty: gleaming black, with big chrome headlights and high mudguards. It is the two-door model with a 995 c.c. engine and three gears, and is capable of 85 km/hr. It is not very roomy, but four people can fit in it. I notice the folding front seats inside, the cloth furnishings, the roll-up blind for the back window, the side windows that can be wound down. The two external spare wheels, the rear-view mirror, the stop light and exterior luggage rack, as well as the chromework, were all extras to be paid for even then. The basic model was launched in 1932 and cost 10,800 lire, which was less than the competition but beyond middle-class means (even the master and mistress of the house I have just visited, in spite of their comfortable income, cannot afford one—perhaps later on they might be able, on the hire-purchase, to get a Fiat 500 'Topolino', which cost a little less).

It is no surprise that cars continued to be luxury items in Italy. By 1938 the number in circulation totalled 289,000 (seven for every hundred inhabitants and the figure had not even doubled in a decade), against 1,818,000 for France and 1,272,000 in Germany[29]—not to mention the United States. In all it is calculated that there were 450,000 drivers (fewer than 15,000 of them women), and all residing in big cities like Milan, Rome and Turin.[30]

Nevertheless, the Fascist regime pushed for mass motorization and encouraged improvements in road links. The first stretch of the Milan-lakes highway was inaugurated in 1942, the first motorway in Europe. Built by Piero Puricelli it was, according to Fascist propaganda, a reawakening of Italy's engineering genius. To this was added a tremendous publicity drive, not only where cars were directly involved, but also the motorways themselves (in an original advertisement of 'L'illustrazione Italiana' a black strip of road surface rises up to create an almost human shape with motorway trunks and branches springing out of its hand. The caption reads 'Drivers and motorcyclists! Using the motorways means saving your time, money and machines'). Fuels and lubricants also received attention (an advertisement for the Italo-American Esso company shows a cowboy with a whip and colt 45 in his hands, taming a roaring lion: 'Esso the super fuel. Controlling power. With Esso there is no more risk of pinking in your engine'). Added to all this was the attention given to sports events and car rallies on the radio and in the newspapers.[31]

But all this was a dream for the average Italian, just as it was a dream to use the other highly advertised forms of transport like the steamship. The daily newspapers of the time were full of pictures of great liners, not carrying emigrants and poor transatlantic passengers, but looking like luxury hotels. During the 'cruises', that is organized tours lasting several weeks, there would be a frenetic social life: grand balls in sumptuous surroundings, dinners, musical performances, games, discussions, sport, lazy relaxation. Best evening clothes and most refined jewels could be seen in gorgeous modern surroundings. A voyage on a luxury liner became one of the highest and most exclusive forms of worldly pleasure.[32] All the rest could do was to become mere 'onlookers' from the outside, which was no less exciting, as is illustrated in the scene in Fellini's *Amarcord*, when the enormous Rex, holder of the transatlantic speed record, with decks and portholes all illuminated, appears for a brief moment before slipping back into the dark night.[33]

Even more selective was the clientele for air transport, even though flying was the other great passion at the time. Transatlantic flights, the Italo Balbo, and Francesco De Pinedo exploits and the many models available from national industries (Fiat, Caproni, Macchi, Savoia-Marchetti) fed a myth but did not create a market. In 1938, Italian airline passengers numbered little more than 100,000.[34] The regime concentrated its efforts more on military than civil aviation.

This leaves the trains. With more than 157 million passengers in 1938 they were certainly the most used means of transport for work and personal reasons, including the main holidays of the middle classes.[35] In the wake of the nobility and upper middle classes, the middle classes as a whole discovered the fascination of untouched nature, well represented by the craze for mountain trips (seen as physically and morally regenerating), as well as thermal and maritime spas that were becoming better and better equipped, modelled on the English city of Bath, famous for its Roman baths, and the Belgian example of Spa, which provides the synonym for thermal bath resorts.[36] But once again the working classes were left out, only able to take advantage of regime initiatives like third-class excursion trains with 80 per cent discount[37] to discover, at least to some extent, the benefits of seaside holidays, sun, and sport as proclaimed by the Fascist health campaigns.

Distracting me from these thoughts is the arrival of a bicycle as it squeaks past. This was everyone's means of transport: factory workers, country folk, city clerks. It was around in all types and colours, from expensive 'English' bicycles to factory-made ones by Edoardo Bianchi and Giovanni Tommaselli or Prinetti and Stucchi (who also made more costly motorcycles), up to the many hand-crafted ones which were adjusted time and again to make them last as long as possible. The roads were full of bicycles zig-zagging in all directions (in 1933 there were already 3.5 million in circulation).[38] All factories had large cycle racks at the entrance and bicycle spare parts shops could be found at every corner. For many people this was the best bit of technology they could afford.

Popular department stores

There is one last sector to consider: commercial enterprises. The first thing to say is that there were no drastic breaks with the previous period. The number of retailers had increased. By 1938 there were 1,220,000, of whom 220,000 were travelling salesmen, two thirds involved in the food sector and one third elsewhere, in 530,000 outlets.[39] This indicates two things: first, the presence of a vast network of small shops (on average employing two people) and second, the fact that the food sector led by a long way.

Frankly, it is not a homogeneous category. Some interesting fiscal data delineates a real hierarchy in luxury. They show that food shops were the most widespread but also the poorest. The average gross returns per annum averaged 12,000 lire in 1930 (similar to a good wage for a clerk). Grocers (19,000 lire) did better than delicatessens, bakers, or fishmongers. Worst of all were the greengrocers and fruiterers (only 6,500 lire). Half way up can be seen the varying catering sector, while close to the top were hoteliers (a good 39,500 lire a year); in between were pastrycooks, cafés, and bars (between 16,000 and 21,000 lire); lowest of all came the *trattorie* (10,000 lire). Shops selling non-food items were richer on average (21,000 lire). At the peak we find fabric shops (40,000 lire) ahead of shops selling luggage, furs, hardware, haberdashery, underwear, pots and pans, and trinkets (all above 18,000 lire). Lowest of all were stationers, booksellers, and electrical suppliers (around 14,000 lire).[40]

This series of numbers draws a very clear picture of a triangle where consumption by the affluent classes (guaranteeing good incomes for those concerned) is at the apex—hotels, precious items like fabric, underwear and haberdashery, luggage and furs, and among foodstuffs the most costly colonial products—reminiscent of travel, domestic luxuries and clothes. Halfway down the triangle come cafés and bars for social life, pots and hardware for decent household equipment and not much spent on education. At the bottom is consumption for strictly prime necessities, especially foodstuffs, and at most one restaurant visit. The consumer places provide a faithful mirror of society. Not to be forgotten is the fact that this tight commercial structure is also explained by demographic dynamics and by territory population density in particular (a fact that from the historical point of view categorizes most European countries, unlike America).

Popular department stores

But what about the big department stores that had so caught the imagination at the start of the century? The numbers clearly show that there was no expansion. In 1938 they represented only 0.8 per cent of all sales (a fifth of Germany's and a seventh of Great Britain's), and things were no better for the few chains of specialized shops in Italy; generally sales outlets of successful industrial firms (like Richard Ginori, Olivetti, Perugina, Motta, and Varese shoemakers) or bookstores (Treves, Bocca, Ricordi, and Bemporad). Among the commercial firms to make their mark were Morassutti (hardware), Bertelli (perfumes), Franzi (luggage), and Unica (sweets). The last mentioned was an ambitious attempt to merge several trademarks like Moriondo & Gariglio with Talmone, through the efforts of the financier Riccardo Gualino (the company was to pass first to IRI and then to Venchi). These were naturally joined by many existing local and town businesses, as well as cooperatives and company sales outlets, including the railway workers' Provvida, which was the outstanding one.[41]

The main cause of this passivity lay in the low purchasing power of the consumers, accentuated by recurrent economic crises, and wage freezes imposed by the regime. But it was more than this. Fascism soon applied a policy of economic control. In 1926 a law stipulated that a license was obligatory in order to start up a shop. The license was issued by the city council after a careful evaluation of the actual need for such a shop, considering demographic and urban aspects, as well as the existence of other similar shops and street markets in the area.[42] A few years later a similar law came out for factories, but without the same impact, partly because of the fight put up by Confindustria, with the result that it was suspended at the outbreak of war. Due to the difficulties of the 1930s the new law served very little to rationalize a growth that did not exist. On the contrary, the regulations became an instrument to bind together the host of recalcitrant dealers. They in their turn accepted the new rules partly because they were worried about something new: one-price (or popular) stores.

The oldest photo of the new emporia is the one showing the entrance of the first Upim store, launched 22nd October 1928 in Verona. The upper half-circle of an ancient entrance arch is filled with a white sign bearing 'upim' in black cursive script. Display windows full of goods appear below. It was all very different from the magnificence displayed by Rinascente, but in the same vein as the message that the new retailers wanted to broadcast, as seen written elsewhere: 'stores for everybody'. There are relatively few images to testify to their origins, perhaps because of their modest appearance, and their merging into the common place urban landscape (we are not very impressed by everyday things—neither were the photographers).[43] However, it is known that the first Upim offered 4,000 fixed-price items to its customers (selling at 2, 3 or 4 lire), falling back on a formula invented by the American Frank W. Woolworth in 1879 and, as a result of the economic crisis, widely imitated in Europe between the two wars. It was the initiative of Senatore Borletti, the owner of Rinascente, who in fact created a parallel chain (UPIM, The Milan one-price store) to distinguish the two brands. Upim served a working-class, petit bourgeois clientele. Its furnishings were functional and it aimed at widely consumed items. It developed according to a different geography (in the centre of average-sized towns, with their great vitality as in all Europe, and in semi-central zones of the big ones). At the same time it projected a veneer of social status (its posters were designed by Dudovich and it gave an idea of practical fashion, care of the female body, and journeys—by train, probably). In substance it enabled consumers stricken by the wage squeeze and the depression to build up a varied shopping basket, of lower price and quality, but answering equally well to a by now well introduced consumption pattern of a 'Western' standard of living. It was a very important success. At the eve of the Second World War the Borletti company managed 5 branches of Rinascente and 57 Upim stores.[44]

The public response stimulated the Monzino brothers, former managers of Rinascente and above all related to Ferdinando Borletti, to set up a competing firm called Standa. (It was originally Standard Sams, but was later altered because it seemed too 'English'). Despite the financial and personal connections between the two companies, or perhaps because of them, conflict soon broke out. On one side was Rinascente, confident in its strong development and the political influence of Senatore Borletti. On the other side was Standa, which, capable and uninhibited, already managed to create branch numbers equivalent to half of Upim's in just a decade. But these goings on, combined with pressure from shopkeepers and a desire to impose itself on the part of the Fascist regime, spurred the regime into stepping in. It first passed a law extending the need to get a licence to department stores, obtainable in this case from the Prefecture (in 1938). It then imposed a 'pact' between firms in the market (in 1941), establishing a maximum number of 177 branches on national territory, divided between Upim (76), Standa (44) and PTB (33), thus creating a real oligopoly.[45] All this stunted the growth of large-scale distribution and created an increasing shortfall compared with the major European countries.

Regarding the third protagonist, the PTB (*'Per Tutte le Borse'*) (For All Purses), this too had its headquarters in Milan and was formed in 1937 involving Anglo-American capital. Its aim was to create a variety of offered items still at a reasonable price but of better quality than the others, in order to attract a middle-class clientele, who scorned the more popular emporia. The business strategy was based on limiting the number of articles and a very efficient organization (for example, it was sufficient to have one salesperson for every seven metres of counter space instead of three as in Upim and Standa). The growth was lightning fast, but was quickly blocked by seizure of the foreign capital (organized by a confiscator nominated by the Fascist trade unions).[46]

It took the First World War to freeze a complicated situation, the same war that would soon worsen people's living conditions dramatically—shortage of prime necessities, bomb destruction, price controls, black market—so much so that a poverty-stricken destiny seemed inevitable. An inescapable fate eternally ordained from above, as the actor in *Napoli milionaria!* bitterly comments on:

GENNARO Then there's price control.... It's my idea that price control was created for the use and consumption of him and her, and so-and- so.... They're only professors because they can hold a pen and take advantage of us, materially and morally; morally first and materially second.... It's like this. Price control in essence means: 'as you don't know how to live, get out of my way and I'll teach you!' But the sure thing is, people do know how to live.... It's all to their good to say people are lazy, illiterate, childish.... They know how to grab and keep things, and that makes them bosses. [...]

People and professors are on opposite sides. The professors grab what they think is theirs and the people grab what they can. But then you get the feeling you own nothing, no roads, no buildings, no homes, no gardens, nothing is yours... these professors take everything they can, they grab what they want, and you're left with nothing, not even a stone. So at this point it's war. [...]

PEPE (*confesses candidly*) Don Gennà, I don't know what you're talking about...

GENNARO And if you did, we wouldn't be in this mess.[47]

PART III

The Economic Miracle

7

Society during the Golden Age of Capitalism

The consumer revolution

They had waited outside for hours. In the neighbourhood it had been on everyone's lips for months. The crowd was so thick that the police had to intervene to organize entrance shifts. Some even felt sick in the crush but recovered in time and they all went in. It was well worth the wait! According to the newspapers there were 'God's gifts from all over the world': sharks' fins, swallows' nests, Neapolitan mozzarella, all kinds of boxes and tins, meat in clear film wrapping, an entire department dedicated to quick-frozen food (thank goodness for the fridge!), not to mention 'normal' food at bargain prices. The customers were ecstatic. An elderly lady stopped a manager to enthuse: 'My relatives in America have for years told me of these wonderful stores. . . . I have prayed over the years that I might see one and shop in it before I must pass on. . . . believe me, this is the answer to all my prayers', while some wag lectured another: 'Just remember this next time you vote, they don't have any of these in Russia'. It was just like having America in Italy. One's first visit to the Supermarket was unforgettable.[1]

If the decade between the end of the 19th century and the First World War were the years of the 'great transformation', the years 1945–73 were the 'golden age' of capitalism.[2] Per capita earnings throughout the whole world grew by 2.9 per cent while national earnings and exports increased even more. The best performances were in Western Europe (as well as in Asian countries like Japan, South Korea, and Taiwan). In terms of wealth, the separation between world leaders (the United States) and western Europe decreased significantly from 1950 to 1973: the pursuit, or 'catch-up', had begun.

There were many reasons for this fortuitous situation, some structural and some due to circumstances. First of all came market liberalization and the integration of the productive system into a single economic space overseen by international institutions firmly anchored to the dollar, which unleashed an unprecedented flow of goods and capital. The role of the United States cannot be underestimated in this process, due to its far-sighted leadership, the aid it gave to Europe during the post-war crisis, the dynamic spread of new production (and consumer) models and the thrust for integration it gave western politics and economics. From this point of view researchers like Maddison have held that the split into opposing political blocs had an important function in economic development too. It defused dangerous tensions between neighbouring nations, thrusting them into a wider plan, and in its anti-Soviet stance forced through greater cooperation and integration among countries inside the Atlantic bloc (where the Common Market momentously came into being in 1957).[3]

Equally important were the economic policies conscientiously worked out to promote development both within individual countries and at international level (for example, towards countries freshly liberated from colonial domination). The promises of such policies were clear: development lies essentially in a quantitative type of economic growth, which will lead to a higher standard of consumption, improve the quality of life, and reduce unemployment and social conflict, so that the prime objectives are investment in both fixed capital and human (education, professional training) capital.[4]

A third element is provided by the unexpected room for change and economic growth, which was opened up by the reconstruction. The typical resistance to change held out by social institutions and cultural habits was overthrown at a stroke as a result of the war, which swept away antiquated institutions, privileged classes, rich corporations, and ancient families, together with many of the poor. Wide chasms opened within managerial classes in countries where regimes had been compromised (though it would not be the total renewal many were hoping for). In certain cases, even the structural damage turned out to be a positive incentive. It is not by chance that the countries that registered the best economic performance were those that had ended up defeated and the worst damaged by the conflict: Japan, Germany, and Italy. This is recorded in Hannah Arendt's lucid words about destruction being the stimulus for reconstruction and the accumulation of new wealth. It can indeed lead to:

> a booming prosperity which, as postwar Germany illustrates, feeds nor on the abundance of material goods or on anything stable and given but on the process of production and consumption itself. Under modern

conditions, not destruction but conservation spells ruin because the very durability of conserved objects is the greatest impediment to the turnover process, whose constant gain in speed is the only constancy left wherever it has taken hold.[5]

So it was that from 1950 to 1973 Italy and Germany shared an exceptional average growth of 5 per cent, well above the European average. In 1973, in fact, Italy tripled its per capita earnings to 10,600 dollars, while in 1950 it had been least among European nations with its 3,500 dollars a head (compared to 6,900 in Great Britain, 5,200 in France, and 3,900 in the still-suffering Germany, not to mention the traditionally prosperous small northern European nations). By now it was very close to the European average, and to the leading nations (12,000 dollars Great Britain and Germany, 13,000 France).[6] Now it finally made sense to compare it with its rich neighbours and there were economic conditions for wide-ranging changes in consumption.

But that is not all. As had happened at the end of the 19th century, halfway through the 20th, the demographic aspect was again fundamental element for understanding the dynamics triggering profound changes in consumption. The post-war generation gave origin to the 'baby boom', a small demographic eruption that led to a rapid increase in the population (there were 47.5 million inhabitants in Italy in 1951 and more than 54 million by 1971) above all in the youngest generation. In effect, as Massimo Livi Bacci informs us, we are faced with a new phase in 20th-century demography. The Second World War brought to a close the first period, characterized as it was by a high mortality rate resulting from the First, the great transatlantic migrations, and demographic isolation. This second phase, instead, saw demographic increase hand-in-hand with economic growth for western countries and the renewal of migration, both internal and international, especially within Europe. This came to an end at the beginning of the 1970s with more demographic stagnation.[7] Meanwhile, for the quarter century following the Second World War the mortality rate continued to decrease, and for a couple of decades the fertility rate reversed its steady decline.[8] This not only allowed a population increase but also indicated a significant rise in life expectancy (an important indicator of better living standards). In Italy life expectancy was 72.1 years in 1970, slightly less than in France, but more than in Germany or Great Britain—whereas up to then it had been decidedly less, faithfully reflecting the divergence in the socioeconomic conditions.[9] And it is important to observe how the improvement was more marked for women than for men.[10]

As already mentioned, the other important demographic phenomenon was the revival of migration movements. Certainly it was nothing like the tremendous migrations at the start of the century. The movements now were from south to north, from southern to northern Europe (Germany in pole position) and also, in countries like Italy and Spain, with their internal divide economically, from the poorest regions to the most industrialized ones. In fact the migrations were caused by the industrial boom, which in Italy alone induced 1.7 million people to abandon the countryside to look for work in factories or small businesses (agricultural activity plunged within a single generation. Within twenty years the number of farm workers fell from 8 to 3 million).[11] All this brought about a change in the demographic profile of the average Italian with immediate consequences on consumption. The presence of new young couples who got married, had children, created a family nucleus, lived in places geographically far away from their original families and found it easy to move from place to place, gave origin to a strong demand for consumer goods. There were, therefore, social foundations for the changes in consumption patterns.

That is not all. Inextricably linked to social and economic factors is cultural change, and the older generation of the time was bewildered. Thousands of people had abandoned their familiar rural horizons to come suddenly into contact with unfamiliar surroundings and a very different urban culture. Roles began to be redefined within the family, based on gender and age. Sudden wealth mixed up the old boundaries of class and status. Traditional institutions were increasingly less sources of reference and legitimization in comparison with the mass media. Unfamiliar consumer objects appeared every day and the meaning of their use could vary. But what was most troublesome was that after the hard years of reconstruction and the lessons learned from saving, there spread, like a fever or sickness, a widespread expectancy that everybody's condition could become better and a prosperous existence was possible with a life full of 'things'. It was a dream coming from far-off America, as in the tale by Moravia in which a retired clerk's family one day finds a new piece of merchandize in a shop:

Now the product could be clearly seen: happiness. The three Milones, like everybody in the world, had always heard about this product, but had never seen it.

It had been talked about all around as if it were something very rare. Of a rarity so completely legendary that it gave one doubts about its actual existence. It is true that illustrated magazines every now and then published long articles, with accompanying photographs, where it was stated that happiness in the United States was, if not common, at least accessible. But it is known that America is far away and journalists invent so many things. [...]

In the window [...] happiness, like so many Easter eggs, arranged in order of size, for every pocket. They were small, they were medium, and they were gigantic, perhaps only pretend ones, put there for publicity. Every happiness had its own clever card with its price written in elegant script. [...] 'And why,' said the old man with irritation, 'after years and years of being told that there is no happiness in Italy, that we are short of it, and it costs too much to import it ... here all of a sudden a shop opens which sells absolutely nothing else. [...] ... and you know what importing means? It means spending precious money... money that should have been used to buy corn ... the country is perishing with hunger... we need corn... no, Sir... those few dollars that we managed to scrape together have been spent on this stuff, this happiness!' [...]

'But we need happiness as well,' the daughter observed.

'It is superfluous,' the old man replied. 'Before all else we must think of eating... bread first, happiness after... but this is already a perverse country: happiness first, then bread ... '.[12]

In the Italy of the economic miracle the time had come to 'buy' happiness. No doubt through the spread of a model of individual well-being, where private consumption was the real sign of success and social integration (exactly as it was in America). Or perhaps because the cultural conditions of mass consumption had already been put in place during Fascism, without the actual means to pay for it.

But, more prosaically, what were Italians buying? Can a miracle be taught about with respect to consumption? Definitely so. A numerical value is enough to sum up the situation. Per capita private consumption took sixty-six years to double (from 1890 to 1956), but only another fourteen years to double itself again.[13] In overall terms, consumer spending was more than 10,000 billion in 1950, but verging on 30 billion in 1970. This was an enormous jump which allowed consumption to rise at a record pace, though staying below the rate for gross domestic product and investments (a fact that lessened the propensity to consume and favoured accumulation and development instead).[14] And everything was based on stable prices and greater productivity, which together allowed an increase in consumer purchasing power and industrial profits.

Within this increase, confrontation by a revolution in the mainstream trend can be discerned. For the first time, food shopping ceased to absorb most of the available resources but fell to well below 50 per cent (in 1970 it was 44 per cent of the total). Above all, diet changed dramatically. On the whole, most food items increased, but with significant exceptions. What decreased was the 'people's' food, such as brown rice, dried vegetables (giving way to fresh), lard and suet (butter and oil instead), meat from sheep and goats. What increased, even exploded, was the consumption of food for the 'rich', once too expensive and limited to the élite. In comparison with the 1930s, all dairy products (milk, cheese, and eggs) doubled. Wine consumption increased, and beer even more, but what increased most of all were three symbolic products: beef, sugar, and coffee. The average housewife of 1970 finally enjoyed a choice of food that was rich and varied. The miserable ingredients of the past were put aside, although this did not mean she rejected some of the characteristic foods of traditional Italian cooking; in fact she consumed 173 kilograms of wheat and 47 kilograms of tomatoes a year. If fresh vegetables and potatoes were fairly well represented on her table (10 and 45 kilograms respectively), there was a decided push for meat: 36 kilograms a year, of which 25 were beef (during Fascism it was 8–9) and 11 pork, accompanied by 11 kilograms of cheese, 11 of eggs and 67 litres of milk (not much fish: only 7 kilograms a year). All these numbers would have been unimaginable up to two decades earlier. The consumer then discovered such a passion for condiments that she used lots of oil (11 litres of olive oil and almost the same for the new seed oil) and butter (2 kilograms). Everything was accompanied by 114 litres of wine, still the national drink, since beer was only a tenth of this. But above all there was a passion for sweets and coffee, a little cup accounting for the consumption of 3 kilos of coffee a year (during Fascism it was just under one kilogram and at the start of the century it had only reached half a kilo) and sugar came to 28 kilograms a year (four times what it was during the Fascist period, ten times more than the early 1900s) (See Table 1). And she was a consumer who appreciated a rich and varied diet, with many sweet, high-calorie foods, and with a high consumption rate of fresh products. To conclude, the years of the economic miracle marked a real bonanza in the abundance of food together with unfettered optimism.

So what did our consumer do with the money left over? The percentage of shopping for shoes and clothing stayed around 9 per cent and a similar trend for household shopping, around 12 per cent of the total. We find increases, instead, for other forms of consumption: transport and communication (10 per cent), durable goods (6 per cent), spending on health and hygiene (8 per cent) and other goods and services (11 per cent). This provides another glimpse of growth. The triad of basic consumption appears to have been sharply reduced in percentage, with a sharp decline on food, while spending on the house and clothing remained substantially stable. The other varieties of consumption covered 35 per cent of available income. So a shift can be seen in choice and a progressive exchange of the traditional shopping quota on food for private motoring, durable goods (furnishings and electrical household basics), bodily health and beauty, and the purchase of services (See Table 5).[15] The primary novelty in this family picture is the presence of durable goods. A survey by the Bank of Italy in 1966 describes a precise order of priorities. First place (almost joint), goes to refrigerators and televisions (owned by 60 per cent of families); well behind come washing machines (32 per cent) and cars (31 per cent), then vacuum cleaners (16 per cent), motorcycles (14 per cent) and finally a small number of dish-washers (1 per cent).[16] Choices were not uniform, however, if different levels of earnings are compared. The poorest families tended to favour a TV slightly more than a fridge (while the order was reversed for the well-to-do) and they spent an inordinate amount of their earnings on these two products. Vacuum cleaners were less common, while the percentage of men with a motorcycle was greater. Significantly, commodities like dishwashers were only found among a few very rich families, as status symbols. It would take ten more years before the spread of televisions and refrigerators became general, being present, that is, in more than 90 per cent of families, with a sufficiently uniform distribution for each level of earnings.[17] If the situation in Italy is compared with six other major European countries as regards spending on food, house, durable goods, and services, Italy always came last. Even for the most popular goods the difference was large (in 1965 Italy for every 100 inhabitants there were 12 televisions, compared with 25 in Great Britain, 19 in Germany,

Table 5 Domestic private consumption by groups of commodities, 1861–1985 (annual average, constant prices)

Years	Food and drinks	Tobacco	Shoes and clothing	House	Fuel and electrical energy	Furniture furnishings etc,	Hygiene health, medical	Transport and communications	Other goods and services	Total	Final consumption abroad by residents (+)	Final consumption in Italy by non-residents (−)	Total final consumption
Millions of 1938 lire													
1861–70	30,270	2,323	3,931	6,043	304	1,744	734	200	1,667	47,216	–	–	47,216
1871–80	33,163	2,595	4,037	6,460	323	1,724	669	227	1,700	50,898	–	–	50,898
1881–90	33,910	2,370	4,860	7,061	341	1,887	710	331	1,819	53,289	–	–	53,289
1891–900	35,428	2,208	5,194	7,660	392	2,023	958	527	2,493	56,881	–	–	56,881
1901–10	42,845	2,391	5,994	8,485	519	2,796	1,153	970	3,524	68,677	–	–	68,677
1911–20	50,755	3,029	6,284	9,278	792	3,607	1,534	1,718	4,736	81,733	–	–	81,733
1921–30	57,062	3,908	10,171	9,965	1,299	4,103	1,966	2,645	6,075	97,196	–	–	97,196
1931–40	55,194	3,572	13,423	11,591	2,110	4,875	3,194	3,980	8,070	106,009	–	–	106,009
1941–50	48,432	3,835	10,714	12,501	2,896	4,698	3,509	3,853	7,022	97,520	–	–	97,520
Billions of 1963 lire													
1951–60	6,022	499	1,275	1,554	339	747	788	773	1,479	13,476	–	−209	13,267
1961–70	9,745	799	2,134	2,133	747	1,416	1,541	2,091	2,602	23,208	–	−560	22,648
Billions of 1970 lire													
1971–80	15,403	1,603	4,273	4,394	1,667	3,202	2,238	5,003	9,289	47,072	345	−1,551	45,866
1981–85	17,116	2,015	4,473	4,990	2,214	3,506	2,984	6,506	11,571	55,377	408	−2,110	53,675

Source: cf. Table 1.

and 13 in France while the total number of vehicles in circulation were 5.5 million, compared with 10 in France and 9 in Great Britain and Germany and the engines were much smaller on average).[18]

This last data could be confusing and casts a shadow on an otherwise brightly lit picture, an impression reinforced by the curious imbalance we observe among the sources. Reconstructions by researchers and journalists present this period as a sort of golden age, using terms like 'miracle' and 'economic boom'. Oral memories of today even hearken back to a happy age of human solidarity, now lost, and new consumer goods loaded with meaning and personal fulfilment. But the contemporary sources had a very different tone, exposing the unpleasant living conditions of immigrants, the disasters due to building speculation, the arrogance and ignorance of the *nouveau riches*, the hard toil and daily sacrifices that attended the workers' lives, which were made up of hope rather than fulfilment.[19] So who is right? It may be too difficult to analyse long-term developments from everyday life and at the time perhaps people noted their problems more than their gains. Or perhaps the age has since been idealized ('the mythical 1950s', 'the fabulous 1960s') in positive contrast with the following period of crisis and stagnation, or in conflict with today's reality.[20] Every country needs myths.

The focus on consumption perhaps allows me to address this issue. Looking at Italian family consumption rates we can draw the following conclusions. There was a long post-war period characterized by a modest lifestyle and little hope for change (curiously even this has been removed from the collective memory).[21] Things improved later than in other European countries (in fact the miracle started in Italy at the end of the 1950s, unlike in countries like Germany and Belgium, which were the first to attract migratory flows). Besides, when it did arrive, it was selective. That is the point: it did not apply to everybody. An extensive European inquiry into family budgets in 1963–1964 (involving 10,000 Italian families) reveals not only Italy's relative tardiness, but above all a precise social stratification in the spread of durable goods. Middle-class families spent three times more on cars than working class ones did, 44 per cent, (compared with 13 per cent of workers, 14 per cent of farmers and 3 per cent of farm labourers); 79 per cent had a television (compared with 48 per cent of manual workers and barely 11 per cent of farm labourers); 58 per cent had a telephone (against 20 per cent of manual workers) and so on.[22] As Giuseppe

Maione observes, if we make a detailed comparison of office workers' families similar in income and number of children, there were many similarities, for example where cars were concerned. While there were marked differences in the case of manual workers' families (only half or even only a third of Italian homes had a car compared with Germany and France). Moreover things were even worse for land workers. In essence, at the height of the 'miracle', it was the middle class that made great leaps in consumption, while many urban and rural workers were largely excluded,[23] unlike that which was happening in northern Europe, where the increases in consumption involved a wide strata of the working classes. The data therefore suggest a deep distortion in consumer habits in Italy, plus, we mustn't forget the historical and geographical divides, whereby all southern regions were greatly—often dramatically —below the average consumer levels, central regions were close to the average, and the northwest regions at least a quarter above.[24] The same phenomenon, therefore, was experienced differently by those who took part in it, and all this also throws a contrasting light on the contemporary debate concerning 'distorted' consumption and the dynamics that led to the 'autumn of discontent' (1968).

During the miracle years, Italy was still the country of a thousand faces. However, the great changes that swept through the period rearranged many balances, redefined differences and recharged social classes with new identities. At Fiat, would a worker coming from the south share the same culture as the son of a worker from Turin earning the same wage? Would a middle-class lady exhibit the same values if she lived in an industrial city in the north rather than the countryside in the south? Where, from a social and cultural perspective do you place a man of property who has fallen on hard times or a small-time craftsman who has amassed an inordinate fortune within a very short period?

The answers to these questions are important because material culture plays an important part in constructing new identities and materializing values and behaviours, becoming the means of determining how one relates to society and tries to be part of it. For this reason, in order to grasp the novelties and characteristics of the time, I will not describe consumption using class differences as pointers, though they still existed, has been shown. I shall instead choose profiles and personalities to illustrate the process of superimposing values and creating multiple identities.

Immigrants

Hundreds of people arrived every day at the station platforms of Milan, Turin, and Genoa on the 'trains of hope'. Photos and films of the 1950s and '60s show us streams of decently dressed, intense-looking new-comers getting off trains, carrying all sorts of parcels and cumbersome suitcases tied up with string.[25] As confirmed by oral witnesses, they never let themselves be parted from their case-loads of memories: clothing, footware, photographs, addresses of friends and relations already there in the north, lucky charms, and homecooked specialities. Before them the promise of a better future.

In this transition from one geographical location to another, one (rural) culture to another (urban) one, it is easier to see what material culture means. Immigrants change much that is material, but at the same time symbolic. Thanks to material objects they give sense to reality, interweave social relations, communicate and stand out as individuals. A single item has no meaning on its own but only within the culture that produced it and, as Daniel Roche reminds us, 'it contains specific knowledge together with a certain amount of extra meaning'.[26] In other words, objects structure our lives and reify per-sonal tastes, social behaviour, and culture. Besides, Lévi-Strauss had already identified three fundamental systems of social communication: through women (that is relationships), words (mythologies and beliefs), and commodities themselves.[27] The immigrants left behind a great deal more than material objects: not just a big rural house but a structure built on well-defined social hierarchies; not just sturdy rustic furniture, they had inherited or made themselves, but an economy based on self-sufficiency; not just home-made food served in spacious kitchens but, as Mary Douglas would say, meals that followed precise cultural patterns of succession and combinations (savoury/sweet, hot/cold);[28] not just simple clothes carefully divided into working and best but distinctive personal and social elements (though some of these had to be in their cases, perhaps the best ones or those more suitable for 'city life'). They would go on to buy new objects embodying different values and behaviours.

These immigrants would have come from an extremely wide range of locations. Arriving from various geographic regions, many had been wage-earning farm hands, but there were also a good many small-time rural property owners. They came from large and small villages, and there was no shortage of townsfolk, both working and middle class (intellectuals looking for work with newspapers or northern publishers, for example). The first waves were chiefly young men, but women and children soon followed. They were labelled 'southerners' a term that actually concealed enormous cultural and material differences and says more about the attitude of the northerners, who lumped them all together in a generic 'otherness' (as happened years later when the first immigrants started arriving from outside the Common Market, indistinctly seen as 'North Africans' or 'Moroccans').

No matter where they came from, or what their cultural background was, the immigrants experienced many new things. The first was mobility. Obviously geographic first of all, which plunged them into a different reality. This was not generally a total leap into the dark, thanks to the supportive network of friends and relations who had migrated before them, and helped them find their first place to live and temporary work (finding a good job in a big factory was not as easy as they said it would be back home—a little job in a shop or on a building site was more obtainable, especially if it was undeclared). The shock of the northern cities was therefore powerful but not too traumatic, as it was softened by this family network that offered a certain support and recreated ways and means of making social contacts linked to memories of home (as well as consumption. Think of the shops, *trattorie*, and restaurants offering northeners typical food from central and southern Italy, thus supplying some sort of economic integration).

But there was one thing that immediately caught the attention, encapsulating all the meanings of mobility until it became symbolic of the 'Italian dream': a car. Or better a cheap car, starting with the Fiat 600 that appeared in 1955. What did they see—immigrant or not—in this little car? I can imagine I am making my way among the crowd thronging into a Fiat salesroom of the time to have a close look at it. The 600 appears as a gleaming white object with soft rounded lines, narrow metal trimming, and ample windows. For its limited size (1.4m high, 1.3m wide, and 3.2m long) it appears roomy inside, with four comfortable seats. As the would-be customers admiringly observe, the engine is at the back, while the bonnet has (a little) luggage space next to the spare wheel. The 633 cc. engine gives a maximum speed of 60 mph.—not much perhaps, but a good speed for those days, and consumption of course is very low, at 50 miles per gallon. This car is the answer to a dream, because it was the first car designed with everyone in mind. Not that the price is really that affordable: 590,000 lire (70–80,000 lire maximum was a good month's wage for a workman), even if the salesman going around keeps on promising that payment can be made in twenty-four convenient instalments. The impression is good, however, and nobody pays any attention to the know-all who tells everyone that the car runs well but has an overheating problem when climbing steep gradients. Nobody listens to him, as they lovingly pat and gaze at this gem of technology which might soon be theirs. Even if it is smaller, it is still the icon seen so many times in American films. Photos are on show all around. In one there is a man at the wheel, with three happy girls in the passenger seats. In others the 600 appears in various colours, by the beach, on a quayside, in the mountains. I am struck by one poster in particular, designed by Felice Casorati to launch the sale of the car: a geometric nocturnal Turin, all dark blue, dotted with little lights, out of which rises the Mole Antonelliana monument with dark mountains in the background. High above is the moon, the River Po a golden ribbon in the distance, and in the foreground a 600, bright and resplendent with its lights turned on, surrounded by men, women and children—an image which presents the car as the epitome of harmony between technology (electric lights, headlights, street lights), nature (moon, mountains, river), and humanity (the city, people, passengers inside the car).[29] Perhaps the 600 was all this: the dream of a new world, unlimited freedom of movement (perhaps part of the first wave of mass tourism or to enjoy a holiday break) and unaccustomed personal liberty. The language spoken by this object seems to have been understood, judging from the ecstatic faces of office clerks and manual workers who never tired of admiring it. It talks of status symbols, material improvements in one's living standards, a sense of fulfilment seen for the first time more from consuming than from working, of the satisfaction of immigrants who could display proof of their success with a life richer in material objects when they returned home in summer.

The success of the 600 (after three years there were already about 400,000 on the road) caused new models to be proposed: the 600 *multipla*, a curiously shaped sort of people carrier with six seats and, in 1957, an even smaller economy car: the 500, originally a two-seater. What was to become the most symbolic car of all had very Spartan characteristics, both in its external bodywork (none of the chromework so highly valued during the 1950s), and interior (no small levers or extras, just a bench behind the two seats). It was a 'no frills' car but had a metal exterior of a pleasing rounded shape. It held the road well, could get up a fairly good speed (56 mph) and, last but not least, it cost less than any other car, 415,000 lire for the most basic of all the versions that began to appear (economical, normal, sport, America, convertible, soft top, station wagon, Abarth—in production up to 1973, it would sell 3.8 million cars).[30]

But how many of our enthusiastic neighbours could actually buy a car? How many immigrants could make their dreams a reality? We know that for many of them it would remain just that—a dream. Statistical data have it that the diffusion of the car began slowly. In 1950 there were barely 340,000, by 1956 just over a million. Starting with the 1960s, however, a more marked growth began, which accelerated incredibly after the middle of the decade, when every year traffic increased by a million vehicles: 5.5 million in 1965, 10 million by 1970. This last figure starts to close in on the major European countries[31] and is matched by increased family spending on travel. I had better stop here and take this topic up again later. The little salesroom scene has given me food for thought.

First of all we observe how it was that cars provoked divergent attitudes. It is noticeable with all 'new' commodities, because it is not just a question of passing from one product to another, but of modifying the values and attitudes that particular product gives expression to. The car was the contemporary icon of the new urban and industrial landscape. It expressed spatial and social mobility. It attested to the value of individuality. It inaugurated new ways of working and consuming. All these made the product more desirable for Italians. But just as it was starting to become a widespread consumer commodity, here was something to arouse criticism and objection. The car was assailed by moral doubt. Non-commissioned officers in the army (up to the rank of warrant officer) in 1958 were still not allowed to buy one. Priests and monks could do so only with the explicit authorization of their superiors (in Milan, on Archbishop Schuster's orders all ecclesiastics were forbidden to drive, until permission was granted by Cardinal Montini in 1954), and there were even more rigorous restrictions for friars and feminine orders. I will not even begin to discuss women, since in newspapers and conversations they were long the subject of jokes, not to mention academic arguments about their natural inability to drive on account of being emotional, inattentive, and averse to anything technical. The same was true for young people, they were considered too immature to drive.[32]

All the categories quoted were obviously those most targeted by social controls. The car was viewed as a means of escape from them, a way of transporting these presumably weak individuals to unknown places, out of the 'benevolent' control of authority. Thus, in reality and even more through imagination the car became a place for sin and illicit sex. Moreover, the car was dangerous. It embodied speed. Those against the car imagined thousands of people carriers hurtling at unheard-of speeds along the brand new motorways (the Autostrada del Sole, begun in 1956, was opened in 1964)[33] making hazardous manoeuvres, unable to put the brake on their natural instincts. Urban speed was contrasted with rural slowness. Public debate had it that, because of this, fatal accidents were increasing out of proportion, involving reckless drivers and innocent pedestrians. The role of chance or obsolete road conditions was never even mentioned. It was always the drivers' fault (so they tried to exorcise danger with Saint Rita's blessing of the car). Not to speak of the stress that came from negotiating city traffic (in a famous advertisement the actor Ernesto Calindri sits at a little table in the street calmly drinking an *aperitif*, while cars whizz all around him. 'Cynar, against the wear and tear of modern life'). Giorgio Bocca has left us a telling tale of a motorist, actually a taxi driver, caught up in Milan's infernal traffic:

> Now my man, lively, warmed to the heat of battle, goes at the red traffic light like a bull at a stockade, slips through, swerves, breaks away. Swearing and yelling abuse, he threatens death and destruction: 'Idiot, go drive your grandmother.' 'Get out of the way, dimwit, or I'll give you a haircut!' And when we get to via Turati he suddenly stops, leans out of the window, raises his hand against a 600 blocking his way and, in an apoplectic fit, yells: 'Women go home'. An outburst of horn blowing makes him move on, but he turns round to explain: 'I only just missed them ... Two women, did you see? Clackety clack, clackety clack, they never look where they are going!'[34]

The car did not only overturn mechanisms relating to social control, it also affected gender. Historians have only recently started to pay attention to the creation of the male image, since it used to be taken for granted (or was simply part of general 'norms').[35] In actual fact, masculine identity has also been through specific processes in its formation. For example, during the twentieth century, one of the role models for masculine identity was still the soldier. Think of Fascism with its proliferation of uniforms and military jargon even in peacetime. But what kind of models followed it? According to some academics the period of the 1950s and '60s was central to the construction of a new masculine identity, because mass culture—with its stress on consumption and a supposed 'feminization' of society—put traditional roles in doubt. It was no coincidence that frequent sex scandals, challenges to the traditional separation of the sexes, and the first timid admittance to homosexuality emerged during this period. All this created widespread angst concerning the male's individual role, leading to a reaction with the discovery of new roles such as anti-conformist artists, cowboys in western films, action men, sports heroes, playboys, and young rebels.[36] It was the beginning of a process that would lead to an interpretation of masculinity based on the physical 'look' and therefore to more awareness of specific aspects of posture, clothing, and parlance. As a result there is no doubt that in this process of creating masculinity anew some objects would be given pride of place, notably the car. We have only to think of the film *Il sorpasso* (The overtaking) by Dino Risi to understand how a car can communicate many traits of identity: self confidence and assertiveness, exuberance, mechanical ability, and so on.[37] Advertising agencies were not slow to catch on and frequently associated the car with female figures.

The other observation these would-be car owners inspires concerns the role that object like the car played in their consumer habits. Considering its cost and social significance it is clearly a luxury item, and after all, historically speaking, luxury has had a precise meaning as a status symbol in defining affluent classes. But what meaning did it have as it entered the world of middle- and lower-class consumption? What kind of logic was there in the purchase of a highly expensive durable commodity by an immigrant working in a small business or a worker in the heavy metal industry? In other words, what modern categories define luxury? This is a very important point because it concerns not only cars but the whole process of 'democratizing' luxury spear-headed by mass production and increased earnings. So let us take a big step back, long ago and far away in fact.

An alluringly mysterious painting by Gottfried Lindauer[38] is displayed in the Auckland art gallery. The scene takes place at Aotearoa (New Zealand). An ancient warrior with his hands behind his back is kneeling on some cloths spread on the ground. He is clad only in a kind of skirt and his face is completely covered with tattoos. A naked child stands in front of him feeding him food on a little stick. Behind them can be seen a hut with a mask displayed in the doorway, and there are mountains in the background against a grey sky. The man is definitely not a prisoner, but rather a person of a certain rank judging from his attire, and the whole scene suggests a sacred ritual. What can we interpret from all this?

Tattooing was a potentially dangerous activity in Polynesia because it was seen as imitating the work of the gods and involved the shedding of blood. Tattooed individuals (who covered their bodies with pictures in order to keep a check on divine power) were subjected to taboos and severe restrictions. In particular they were not allowed to touch ordinary things, like cooked food, because they neutralized divine power. This explains why the tattooed dignitary is being fed by the child. It is to avoid violating the taboo. It has always been suspected that everyday objects had a *certain* if only *symbolic* value, no less important than that of sacred or precious objects. Be that as it may, anthropologists have often observed a dualism in the economic sphere between the luxurious or prestigious on one side and what is associated with everyday life on the other. The two categories do not intersect, so the respective commodities are incompatible, associated with different practices and cannot be interchanged. In many cultures, in fact, there exists an explicit division concerning the goods available, generally corresponding to a social divide.[39]

Albeit not of the same order as the ones we have just seen, of course, economists have noticed that differences still exist where modern societies are concerned too (without going so far as to imitate Polynesian practices). It has already be seen, when analysing consumer choices in Italy during the post-war period, how higher earnings caused less spending on food and increased spending on other things, more or less confirming Engel's Law, though things were not so simple in reality, not all goods being equal. For some, demand was quite stable (that is, non-elastic, as in the case of basic needs),[40] while for others it could be highly variable (that is, elastic, as in the case of luxury goods). This variability is due to many factors, such as the amount we consume, the presence of substitutes, the social and individual value we assign to their use, the fact that they are linked to commodities we already have (like fuel for cars), the amount of income we use up in order to acquire them (for durable, expensive items like cars there is a high degree of elasticity). Then there is the time factor, which suggests it is hard to change our habits over the short term but easier to do so over the long term. It can be said, therefore, that there is a dual process in consumption. Basic spending, as on food (non-elastic consumption), rises rapidly up to a certain income level then slows down and finally, if earnings start to rise again, it stabilizes and even begins to show a slight decrease (people are not in the habit of buying larger quantities of bread with every wage increase). Things are different where luxury goods are concerned. There is a continual increase related to the larger income, not directly proportional but constant (therefore, if income increases, people will buy more and more luxury goods). This means that the inclusion of luxury goods in an ordinary family budget sets off complex buying strategies, which answers our questions about modern categories. Families will redistribute available resources to include expensive luxury goods, perhaps limiting the consumption of other supposedly basic items. The final result may appear incongruous, since it is actually driven by two different kinds of logic at the same time. In a certain sense, democratizing luxuries makes quality more important than quantity, and this upsets the balance. It also means that for certain goods there exists a real limit, while for others consumption could go on indefinitely.

To return to the immigrants discussed earlier, it is recognized that it would have been too difficult for many of them to buy a car, due to the expense. However, this does not mean that they were excluded from being motorized, just that they would have followed a different course. The first step would have been a motorcycle. At the beginning of the 1960s, if only 13 per cent of manual workers owned a car (against 44 per cent of clerks), 25 per cent had a motorcycle, double that of clerks, and the percentage among farmers and farm labourers rose to 34 per cent.[41] It was certainly no niche phenomenon. In 1960 there were still twice as many motorcycles as cars (they were overtaken in 1964). All kinds of vehicles used the Italian roads, which in many cases were just beaten tracks. There were old pre-war motorcycles, inventive adaptations, bicycles fitted with Cucciolo or Mosquito engines and two great novelties, the Piaggio Vespa and Innocenti Lambretta. When it first appeared in 1946 the Vespa provoked a great deal of controversy. It was completely different from the traditional motorcycle: its ample, rounded bodywork enclosed all the mechanical parts, covered the engine, hid the small wheels and guaranteed comfortable seating for two people. It did not make the driver dirty and the driving position was more dignified (though to traditionalists it looked like a 'loo on wheels'). Catching on immediately, even among middle-class youth, and helped by an affordable starting price (80,000 lire), its success was shared by another Italian scooter, the Lambretta. Made in Lombardy but advertised with American style slogans, the Lambretta was slimmer and cheaper. Vespa and Lambretta drivers became two diehard factions. The originality of these motorcycles turned them into real icons well beyond national boundaries, and they were adopted as symbols of transgression even by the 'mods', a youth subculture popular in London during the 1960s. To sum up, in the early 1960s, as the prerogative of workers, farmers, and young people (who used it in different ways: means of transport, meant means of escape), a motorcycle became the alternative to a car, which was the prerogative of the urban middle classes.

Immigration studies leave no doubt about what the other priority was, together with a car: it was a house.[42] Owning a house became symbolic of putting down new roots, guranteeing stability and a future, and corresponded to having a fixed job in a factory. This is confirmed by the immigrants themselves:

> With a house I feel safe. If I own land but have to pay rent, what good does it do me? (44-year-old).
>
> My ideal was an office job, but first of all a house! Then little by little I set up first a small shoe shop and then a butcher's (38-year-old).
>
> When you set up house, it is for ever, to settle down once and for all. If you have a house you feel stronger. Human beings are made to look ahead. If you own a house and land, you're something else (38-year-old).
>
> I keep saving because I want to get married and have children without my wife having to go to work. She will stay at home and be a lady. If I had some hard cash I would become a travelling shoe salesman with a small van. I know what it is like to live in a fairly unpleasant place, only my mother working, with many sisters to support. I want a better life. I want to have a house, even if it will take a lot of money (23-year-old).
>
> I saved up because I wanted to get a house for my daughter. I demolished the old house and rebuilt it. I bought a TV, refrigerator and stove: Now I spend all my money on food [...] (65-year-old).[43]

But it was not easy to buy a real house. It was easy to make do in somewhat rundown, temporary lodgings in the inner city but more often a solution was sought outside town. Consequently, thousands of illegal habitations sprang up on the outskirts, consisting partly of brickwork and partly of metal sheeting and planks, surrounding urban centres like a belt. Even the prefabs erected immediately after the war for refugees were reoccupied. Around some cities they were called 'townships' or '*borgate*' as in Rome; in others '*coree*' (Koreas) as in Milan (recalling the hardships caused by the Korean War). As time went on they would be absorbed into city areas and change their appearance (some, however, remained run-down, were gradually taken over by socially disreputable types, and later passed on to new immigrants). But this would take decades and meanwhile the occupiers faced a very difficult reality, obviously unable to fly away on brooms, as surrealistically shown by De Sica in the film *Miracolo a Milano*.[44] Partly due to the formidable pressures applied by building speculators, no city administration was capable of handling the emergency, take Turin, as an example. It ended up by concentrating more than half of the immigrants into a small area and came to be known as the 'third city' of the south, chaotically mushrooming out towards the two strips of adjacent communes (in twenty years land rent increased by fifteen times in the centre, and thirty times on the outskirts). Milan had similar problems. The planned dramatic destruction of historic parts of the city to build new roads (the so-called *Racchetta*), which luckily never went ahead, combined with huge peripheral redevelopment: 900,000 new rooms, many of them built with repeated dispensation from planning rules (the 'Ambrosian Rite' as the newspapers called it). Rome was also assailed by a massive influx from the centre and south, and illegal practices made the building of condominiums and blocks of flats outnumber legal ones, and were responsible for a third of the accommodation available in the sprawling outskirts.[45]

Efforts to acquire a dwelling place were very strong among the urban working classes. The above-quoted European survey of 1963–1964 shows that blue-collar workers were slightly ahead of white-collar workers in owning somewhere to live, 31 against 29 per cent, even if they contented themselves with decidedly smaller flats, despite having a more extensive family nucleus, and much more precarious housing conditions (only 44 per cent of workers' houses had a bath). The password doing the rounds was crystal clear: get a house, never mind the condition.

What was the catalyst behind all this? In the 1960s, Francesco Alberoni was already going against the grain in his reading of why immigrants wanted new consumer goods (house, car, high-tech objects). He said it had nothing to do with imitating the buying habits of higher classes, nor was it a form of ostentation, or even a sign of alienation brought about by consumerism. Immigrants are conscious performers (an *agency*, as Stuart Hall would say) and their choice is to seek integration in 'modern' society through consumer goods. New acquisitions communicate new values. A television is symbolic of escape from a restricted, closed community. A car or motorcycle means independence, and spatial, social mobility. The house itself, not that dusty old thing inherited back in the south and shared with other family units, but a small, new, albeit modest flat, where a new domestic life for the family nucleus, a hitherto unknown intimacy and a new spatial hierarchy can be created.[46] It represents a form of individual integration outside social organization. Within the chaotic realities of urban life during the economic miracle, material possessions represented the rejection of a miserable past and the realization of the 'Italian dream'.

Women (and men)

What was the consequence of all these housing changes? And what effects did they have on the female identity? To search for an answer, I am catapulted into a flat near the outskirts of a large city. It is newly built, in a small cube-shaped condominium not very beautiful from an aesthetic viewpoint (and I suspect that it is also made of second-rate materials), but for now it has the attraction of being modern.

I am in the hallway, a small square area with a big mirror and a coat stand to one side. There is a grey SIP dial telephone on a tiny table and oriental prints hanging on the walls. The long corridor that led to the rooms, dividing them functionally, has gone. Everything is small. Everything is different. A door on our right opens on to a small room with a large table in the middle covered with a fancy tablecloth and with chairs around it. On either side are two low pieces of furniture made of light coloured wood, probably the remnants of an old dresser, but closed and not displaying glasses and tableware as they used to. I look for the kitchen. Where is it? To my great surprise it has vanished, or rather turned into a long narrow alley with a window at the end (certainly to get the maximum use out of the space available). This place is really interesting, however, because it is full of all the newest technical products: all new electrical appliances! They are all white and perfectly aligned, opposite a row of hanging cupboards. A Rex model 720 cooker is at the far end. It has a thermostatic oven, roasting jack, spit-roast grill, and a generous top with four burners. A bit like previous economical cooking ranges, it does however conceal some new functions. But my attention is drawn to two great novelties, the washing machine and the fridge. The washing machine (originally called the washer) is a Candy Automatic. It has square-cut lines, twelve washing programmes and a spin drier of 550 revs a minute (and cost 160,000 lire). It does everything on its own, is very simple to use, and soon makes one forget the hard grind of washing by hand (one newspaper calculated that the time dedicated to laundry went down from 7 to 4 hours a week, and that electrical appliances all together gave a saving of 17.5 hours of physical work, equal to 7 years of one's life span).[47] 'Thank you, Candy', sang the advertisement, showing the mark of a lipsticked kiss near the porthole. Near a little formica table (a new material that 'fears neither time nor use') towers the Ignis refrigerator. Its rounded lines, typical of the 1950s, reveal that it was the first electrical appliance to enter into the home. The capacity is 200 litres, the door is mechanically opened with a handle and the interior is divided into neat little compartments. It is not cheap, costing 200,000 lire, but the price will come down significantly within ten years or so.

Let me have a look at these gleaming white objects. What does their presence signify? Technology within the home is certainly nothing new, but I have the impression of having come to a turning point. One of the first things to consider is the use of time. In the wake of studies by Gary Becker, some economists have maintained that time itself is an important variable when trying to understand the workings of a family unit, and have divided domestic appliances into two categories: those cutting down on time (*time-saving*) and those making us spend time, or rather use it for entertainment (*time-spending*).[48] Domestic appliances like the washing machine, vacuum cleaner, and refrigerator come under the first category; radios, record players, and televisions are in the second. In a certain sense, it is like applying the categories of production and consumption to the domestic sphere. The family adapts itself to the technology found throughout society. But there are some complications.

The first applies to gender. Since domestic work is culturally linked to the female role, *time-saving* electrical appliances fall into the sphere of women's activities (and are placed in the space dedicated to them). They are 'feminine objects' just as cars are 'masculine objects' (not all goods carry similar characterizations of gender. Some are neutral. The boundaries may also shift according to class or social group. Yet every culture provides a fairly accurate map of the consumer goods it considers appropriate for each gender).[49] Consequently, the little value traditionally attributed to women's work is said to have delayed the introduction of quite a few domestic appliances. All countries, in effect, have registered a well-defined pattern for their diffusion: apart from radios and stoves/ovens, already fairly common before the war, the first to appear during the 1950s in Italian and other European homes was the refrigerator, which saved shopping time but was above all an obvious saving in food consumption. Second place instead is split between television and washing machine (end of 1950s—early 1960s).

There will be a delay of at least another decade for the dishwasher, and even longer for the spin-drier—probably incorporated in the washing machine to save space. Therefore the need to lighten the burden on women does not seem to have been a powerful spur for encouraging the spread of new equipment. *Home automation* progressed much more slowly than *office automation*. Girls and women could always dream of the future they saw on the TV and in the American cartoon *The Jetsons*, where the family of the future travels by spaceship and lives in a house where everything is automatic. To make anything move all they have to do is push a button and the work is all done by a (female) robot.[50]

All this is not enough to explain when and how the use of electrical domestic appliances proliferated. As already observed, they represent a category of goods created for social reasons.[51] Not simply the successors of durable goods of the past, they have been invented, produced, and sold in the name of new values (to substitute work or provide domestic entertainment). Their presence is linked to a large number of social and material factors. Among the material ones are pricing and marketing policies on the part of businesses, and level of family income and credit rating, as well as public policies where gas, water, and electricity supplies or fiscal buying incentives/restrictions are concerned. Among the cultural ones are the symbolic aspects linked to the use of these appliances, starting with advertisements and newspaper reports. Above all this, however, is the new dimension of domesticity that took hold of the nuclear family. In general the functions performed by these new appliances had already been widely available at the industrial level for some time (washing and drying of clothes, freezing of food, etc. and the same goes for entertainment with movies and concerts) so they could already be enjoyed outside the family. Some had even been tried out at the collective level (think, for example, of the creation of cooperative dry-cleaners or condominial washing machines and similar experiments). But the political and cultural exaltation of the intimate family, wrapped up in itself, where everything revolved around privacy and anything of significance is related to the family experience (glossy magazines of the time made fortunes out of the private lives of the good and great), brought these functions into the family, which became a small inward-looking universe, especially where women were concerned. The electrical appliances defined the family more and more as a self-sufficient unit of production and consumption, creating an intimacy and rituality that regulated the rhythm of domestic life and ended by defining new status levels.[52]

There is no doubt that continual exposure to the American way of life, with its middle-class style of consumption, was an important point of reference for this construct (it is no coincidence that the most advanced appliances came from the United States, and in many cases those made in Italy were their adaptation to a less affluent reality).[53] This, however, must also have been the result of past developments. We have already recorded the importance of demographic dynamics: the smaller family (the Italian average for 1961 was 3.6 members, but it was already below 3 in many urban situations) could undo the traditional social ties that had been necessary in the previous network of family, friends, and relations. The new family had fewer children, enjoyed the benefits of the social services and could provide itself with goods and services to a previously unthinkable extent. It was therefore more autonomous and independent and could construct its own domestic space. The number of family nuclei remained high, but at the same time there was a strong increase in smaller families and a decrease in large and extended ones. Another basic element was the question of income. It is not a coincidence that the major transformations occurred within the middle classes, which were the real beneficiaries of the economic miracle and expanded enormously. They now made up a third of the population, so that the whole of society was no longer represented by a triangle as it had been half a century before, but more like a pentagon with a broad base, wide central body, and a vertex that was still narrow.[54] The model presented by the urban middle classes thus became a benchmark, which in the middle to long term also influenced working-class family culture.

How did all this affect women's roles? Inside the family as described and considering the part they played in transforming domestic life, what did the new electric appliances represent for a woman? Advertising used no half measures in presenting them as instruments of freedom from toil, means of self-realization and the conquest of new space for herself and her family. Newspaper articles and many oral testimonies say the same. You can hear in their words a sense of liberation from previously unacknowledged drudgery ('I'm only a humble country woman. When I used to do the washing, I tell you, the effort was killing me . . . ').[55] Although some maintain that the higher standards of cleanliness and tidiness that resulted ended by nullifying the conquest,[56] the time saved could be used for personal care, pleasure, other kinds of work or, in fact, improving domestic performance (one Candy television advertisement shows the lady of the house playing with her children, with the porthole outline always in the foreground: while the woman enjoys herself, the appliance continues to 'wash, wash, wash . . . rinse, rinse, rinse . . . dry, dry, dry', and all better than Tic, the awful robot of the future).[57] Modern studies agree in maintaining that the introduction of electric appliances did little to change either role divisions within the family or society's opinion of the housewife. On the contrary it often created a multiplication of roles and responsibilities around the female figure, loading her with both domestic and outside duties.[58] It is interesting to note the same ambivalence that we have already seen in connection with cars. It was not always easy at first to accept electric appliances for the home. Many women feared that they were in some way dangerous, or at least useless, perhaps even 'dangerous competition', capable of casting doubt on their housewifely virtues. The washing machine is practical but it ruins and tears things, you know . . . If you want a really clean wash, it has to be done by hand . . . The new detergents wash well but are harmful. In any case laundry from the washing machine certainly doesn't smell as fresh as it used to . . . The refrigerator is handy but it needs a lot of looking after and has to be cleaned with vinegar-based solutions. The floor is done quickly with the polisher but doesn't have a good finish (better go over it again by hand with a soft cloth). The vacuum cleaner doesn't get all the dust from the corners and it is noisy as well. The changes brought about by these objects caused anxiety because they chipped away at a traditional social role.[59] In time, however, it would be partly through these very electric appliances that the identity of the 'modern house-wife' would be defined: thriftier, more efficient, more competent, and more attentive to the various needs of all the family members com-pared to the housewife of old.

I cannot tear my eyes away from these fascinating white objects. How many changes were wrought by their arrival on the scene! Look-ing at them again, I am reminded of the words of Arjun Appadurai: it is true that our understanding of the meaning of things is necessarily conditioned by a cultural and social network (we would never under-stand the meaning of an electric appliance without referring to the spatial values of the home, the concept of domesticity or the social divisions of roles between the sexes, for a start). Yet things have their own language too, derived from their shapes and uses, their 'trajec-tories', that is displacements in space and, we may add, in time (the same kitchen appliance in an underdeveloped African country could imply something entirely different in terms of status. If it were to be found in a kitchen of the future it would have yet another!).[60] Modern western societies have developed communications separating 'things' from 'words'. The first are mute, passive, and only brought to life by people, the second are active and communicative by themselves. This comparison has not always been true in the West and it is certainly not true in other cultures, as noted by Marcel Mauss.[61] In actual fact, the question is not so cut and dried: even *things* communicate. So, how do these objects communicate with their physical form? To begin with, their insistence on and rigorous use of the colour white is a reminder to us to be clean and tidy, conjuring up the idea of a washbasin and bath just to show how hygienic they are. White is the colour associated with these two objects. Then their shape: they seem to be enveloping boxes, the shape of cubes, or rectangular solids, with only a few simple controls. Comparing this with what is seen in the car (rev counters and speed-ometers, warnings for oil, water, and lights), there are no indicators to tell us how it is working (temperature, electric consumption, motor condition). It is as if the mechanical heart of this equipment is hidden behind the pure white bodywork. The controls are minimal and simple in the extreme: for the refrigerator, on/off and defrost on/off; for the washing machine, a knob to turn and select the right programme and a button to start it. It is all automatic ('Candy knows what to do', 'Candy Automatic does it all on its own: what a wash you do for me | thank you Candy | you do it all by yourself' as the advertisement on the Carosello Tv programme went). Here is an interesting point. The mechanics of a car are visibly exposed and call for user involvement. In domestic appliances on the contrary, they are hidden and do not need any form of interaction. In this way can be seen how technological products use a different language and create a different relationship for the male psyche (culturally characterized by explicit technical references) and for the female (who is instead attentive to 'humane', personal, and family values).[62] By playing down their technical aspects, it was possible to make the new appliances more acceptable to women, presenting them as some sort of friendly furniture (in some advertisements they were actually referred to as 'friends').[63]

Leaving the kitchenette I will explore some more in the bedroom. Here, instead, very little has changed. The big double bed takes up most of the space. On one side there is a large square wardrobe with several doors. Facing us is a low piece of furniture with a framed mirror. Through the window a working crane and the outlines of other blocks of flats can be seen. It is like being on a building site. The room itself has a cosy, intimate aspect, reminding us of days gone by, even with the modern furniture. It is certainly still an important room in the context of the home, and reflects the weight of family tradition. Opening the wardrobe we see the husband's side. There is an elegant evening suit, and then jackets and work outfits of grey and blue following the day/evening division. The finest clothes are tailor-made by hand, like many of the jackets, but many of the trousers are ready-made (and one notes a more casual cut for some garments, perhaps inspired by American style). There are also two coats and a raincoat (something on the decline). On the top shelf are a couple of hats and a neat row of perfectly ironed shirts, all ready-made (in fact the most widely sold of off-the-shelf clothing). Hanging behind the door is an array of sober-coloured ties with stripes or geometric patterns.[64] In the other side one more unusual: clothes and underwear of different cuts and fashions, but also many skirts and blouses (an item strongly on the increase) and the novelty of slacks. Of course, there is a coat, an overcoat and a raincoat. To conclude, a smart, practical wardrobe, certainly richer than it would have been in the past, which includes a lot of good clothes, either hand-made or bought in a *boutique*, reminiscent of French fashion.[65] But something in a drawer attracts my attention. Here, in fact, beside the most intimate items, where I would not presume to rummage,[66] I find costume jewellery (real jewellery, if it exists, will be hidden elsewhere) and above all cosmetics.

It is not that the widespread use of cosmetics as a distinctive sign of femininity had been lacking in the past. But from the 19th century at least, make-up had been associated with women seen in public places, and so of dubious morals (actresses, prostitutes).[67] During the 1950s the push towards private domesticity, supported by strong morally-inspired campaigns, was certainly unfavourable to the social spread of cosmetics, even if it has to be said that they were used by entertainment stars and upper-class women, who flaunted fiery-red lipstick, well-defined eyebrows and coloured eye shadow. It is as if cosmetic care had something to do with class. Yet it was in these years, and with full force in the following decade, that the process of democratizing luxuries gained a foothold even here, in this case favouring the spread of cosmetics in the middle class, aided and abetted by new forms of distribution and marketing strategies that offered products at much lower prices. This process was associated with the new emphasis given to the female body, which also found expression in the advertising field, together with the new social roles women were being called on to perform. We must not forget that the speeded up urbanization was multiplying occasions for social contact (while, as Alberoni notes, women had traditionally felt less adequate in public life), and that though it had a very low employment level in a European perspective, even Italy had a brief boom in female employment between 1958 and 1963, mainly where young girls and women (that is until marriage or the birth of children) were concerned.[68] Among the various cosmetics, the one that took on symbolic value, perhaps because of its sexual allusions was lipstick. It is here before my eyes in an elegant gold-plated case with a bright red lipstick inside. It is the flamboyant symbol of women's new ambitions. During a television inquiry in 1963 a young man says to presenter Ugo Zatterin: 'girls don't want country boys, they go off to factories, put on lipstick and that's the end of it'.[69]

Women's magazines like "Gioia" waited until 1959 before running the first lipstick advertisements, and the agony columns advised that cosmetics be used with moderation, and always accompanied by a morally irreproachable manner.[70] Cosmetics, together with costume jewellery and clothes, were therefore a means of constructing a more sensual, more outgoing female figure, who makes the most of herself instead of being self-effacing in favour of the family. It is not by chance that ever since 1968 they have been used as symbolic provocation against conventionalism.

All this, of course, has nothing to do with the lady of the house although she has several bottles of perfume on her dressing table. One is immediately recognizable. It is Chanel No. 5, the perfume of Marilyn Monroe, film star icon of the time. It is not surprising. During this period there was a small boom for spending on hygiene and beauty care, a symptom of the importance given to the social graces (final stage in the spread of good manners, as Elias would say). So there was a surge in the production of perfumed soap ('Camay, for a complexion that turns heads'),[71] deodorants, tubs of talcum powder (Roberts: 'the magical finishing touch to your toilette'), Vidal bath foam (to make us feel as fresh and free as white horses galloping along the seashore, as a Carosello slot suggested), shampoo, hair cream (Linetti: the one mistake made by the infallible Inspector Rock was not to use it), toothpaste (like Pasta del Capitano or Chlorodont, which gave an enviable advantage: 'with a mouth like yours, you can say anything you like!').

There was also a vast array of special products for domestic hygiene, starting with floor wax (the Grey one is famous for its entertaining television tributes: from the Brutos, Ciccio and Franco, and Ave Ninchi). Then there was the fierce competition between the detergents: from Angelino's amusing animated cartoons advertising Supertrim, and Ava's Calimero—the little chick who was not black but only dirty—on to a band of armed knights fighting to defend cleanliness: Mister X (Dixan) defends the magic formula of his detergent against the baddies with the same ardour as the White Lancer (Ajax). Later on situations became post-modern: a fully-dressed man walks smilingly into a tub to soak and demonstrate that there is no such thing as impossible dirt (Bio Presto), while actor Paolo Ferrari will spend years vainly trying to exchange two ordinary packets of detergent for one of Dash.

Advertising agencies were quick to take advantage of the greater role of hygiene and body care, which also tied in with the ancient 'social' role of smells in fixing class divisions. But perfume takes us back to much deeper meanings and ancestral traditions. Since ancient times it has symbolized purity and the soul contrasted with the corruption of the physical body, and many myths relate to how young people were transformed into fragrant plants, as in the case of Myrrh the Cyprus king's daughter. Spurred on by Aphrodite, she lay with her own father and was turned into a plant (which also reminds us of the erotic connotations associated with perfume). Equally widespread was the practice of anointing statues of gods with oils and fragrant essences. To a certain extent all this was transmitted to ensuing religious tradition, which on special occasions does not disdain the penetrating perfume of incense, while on the secular side 'bad smells' are always associated with bestiality, the opposite of civility. From the twentieth century, frequent baths, and showers later, have ensured bodily cleanliness and purity, with the added assurance that perfuming oneself afterwards aspires to a kind of transfiguration, answering the desire to achieve perfect beauty in all aspects of the flesh.[72] Whether she indulges in these reflections, or whether she just considers perfume a luxury she can afford, the lady of this house has plenty of toilet water and fruit essences on display. The same cannot be said for her companion, who only has one bottle of perfume, with a dry, lemony, nay Hesperidian fragrance, as they still say today in perfume shops to remind you of the fabulous gardens of the Hesperides, who tended the fruits of paradise aided by the dragon Ladon.[73] Only one bottle, then, and used sparingly to avoid the risk of being thought effeminate.

The game of matching consumer goods to gender prompts me to look at a handsome wrist watch lying on the bedside locker, next to a Sisal coupon and a pack of Nazionale 'esportazione' cigarettes. It is a Zenith watch made of steel with a round case. There is an extraordinary history behind this object. Even a couple of generations ago, no gentleman would have dreamt of wearing such a peculiarity as a wrist watch. They had been in existence for some time but were small and made of precious materials, a jewellery item for women. Men carried pocket watches which were much more robust, kept exact time and had many functions. It was the Great War with its need to be precise and practical that caused the spread of wrist watches among the officers and men (probably carried in a metal case or leather pouch to protect the delicate glass and china parts). As a result this device began to take on 'masculine' characteristics. The case became bigger, chrome plate and steel took the place of gold and functions multiplied (starting with a second hand). It became waterproof and finally automatic. The message passed from aesthetics and preciousness to technical functioning. During the 1930s, the chief watch manufacturers, among them Hans Wilsdorf, the founder of Rolex, competed with one another to show the precision and reliability of their products, advertising how adaptable they were to any profession. In Italy the smallness of the market was an obstacle to the spread of these new models. It wasn't until the 1950s that the first significant sales materialized (with the Omega, Longines, and Zenith brands), while high-class Swiss watches remained the privilege of an elite (the post-war classic Rolex Oyster cost 180,000 lire).[74] Later, during the 1960s the real boom came, extending wrist watche sales among the middle classes, and first of all among men. For them it became a basic commodity both from the symbolic point of view, because it represented working time, and from the practical point of view given the greater cultural restrictions on male clothing (few accessories were permitted, cosmetics were absolutely forbidden, jewellery was severely limited—no more than a thin gold chain or unobtrusive bracelet, tiepin, or ring).[75] By the end of the decade this watch was to be superceded in a certain sense, thanks to the introduction of electronic technology first (with American Timex and Japanese Seiko) and quartz crystal later, drastically bringing prices down and enabling everybody to buy a watch. Another ten years and the Swiss SMH with its colourful and low-priced Swatch, would transform this object into a simple fashion accessory (not to mention the fact that the luxury watch sector was boosted at the same time). Its long journey through class and gender comes to a close here. So let me put the watch down and leave this room.

The door next to it is shut, which is a shame; I will have to come back later. To compensate there is the bathroom right beside it, so I will go in at once. It is just as I expected: white, with some accessories in pastel shades; functional, with a careful arrangement of bathtub, wash-basin, toilet and bidet in a limited space. I notice the small modern cupboard with a mirror above the wash-basin, the new gas-operated water heater, the laundry basket half-hidden between the bidet and the wall, a bowl in the bathtub, a hair-drier lying on a shelf together with bars of soap, shampoo, and bath foam. Is that all? I am just about to leave when I realize that I am in the presence of a second revolution after mechanization: the plastic one. The bowl we see in the tub is made of isotactic polypropylene, a name somewhat difficult to remember and thus changed into the commercial Montecatini name of 'moplen'. It is the amazing invention of Giulio Natta (Nobel Prize 1963). Starting with low cost hydrocarbons, he produced a polymer with a regular spatial structure suitable for industrial manufacture. Articles made of this are of all shapes, as well as being unbreakable, resistant, and lightweight. They first entered the home as simple, colourful objects for everyday use, such as bowls, plates, cups, tubs, combs, dustpans, boxes, pails, broom handles, carpet beaters, colanders, and the casing of small electrical appliances (hair-driers, extractors, blenders, fans, pocket radios). They had a different identity and function from objects made with traditional materials and created a new domestic landscape (a chemist would explain that polymerization has a long history going back to the nineteenth century, and he would also say which objects 'conceal' PVC, celluloid, Bakelite, and formica—like the kitchen bowl—as well as nylon and plexiglass).[76] Because they were easy to manage and worked well, there was a practical and economical reason for the spread of these objects, linked to their cheapness (a plastic object was as little as a third the price of the same thing made of wood, pottery, or metal).

There was also a symbolic reason for the popularity of these plastic objects. They embodied a fascination with everything modern in an age attracted by the future and technological progress (culminating in the lunar landing of 1969: no coincidence that it also marked the height of success for science fiction). It also represented man's Promethean desire to control nature and matter, bending it into unexpected shapes and sizes. To conclude, it was an example of the aesthetics of modernity which, ignoring the past, was only interested in itself. It was, in short, the icon of the future, but with a fascination that was ambiguous, especially in Europe (perhaps a little less in the United States).[77] There was no concern as yet about its polluting the environment, its safety or its toxic potential, which would all explode later, but only about its own characteristics, as Roland Barthes wrote:

> It is essentially an alchemic material [...] more than a substance, plastic is the idea itself of its infinite transformations; and as is shown by its common name, it is ubiquity made visible [...]. In the poetic order of great substances it is an ugly material, halfway between the softness of rubber and the flat hardness of metal. It does not reach any true product of the mineral order like foam or fibre. It is a substance *gone bad*. Into whatever state plastic is reduced it has a fluffy appearance, somewhat

cloudy, pasty-coloured and frozen. It is unable to reach the triumphant smoothness of nature. And, above all, it is betrayed by the sound that comes out of it, empty and flat at the same time [...].[78]

Therefore, to the traditional symbolic structuring of the home into public/private, masculine/feminine, etc. (which we still find here) some new, diametrically opposed values are added. The first revolves around the category of functionality and determines the entire set up of the home, finding its greatest expression in mechanization as shown by electrical appliances (thus corresponding to the efficient/inefficient dichotomy). The second corresponds to the contrast between natural and artificial. Everything that harks back to nature and tradition has more value than what is modern and artificial. Prized furniture comes from noble materials like wood, marble, or even glass and metal, definitely not from plastic (and the same contrast is found between natural fibres like silk, linen, cotton or wool, and artificial or mixed fibres).[79] As Baudrillard observes, this is, of course, a purely ideological and cultural conception of 'nature'. The wood found in furniture is very different from its natural state, because it has been treated, bent, painted, and polished to make it behave differently (that is, it does not age, go mouldy, stain, break or get worm-eaten). And what about 'unnatural' metal, glass, or paper, man-made for centuries, but accepted by virtue of having been around since who knows when? If human surroundings have always been constructed why, he adds, does stone have to be more authentic ('noble' indeed) than cement?[80] To sum up, the presence of plastic brings out a profound value in contemporary culture which, naturally, gives direction and design to the domestic landscape of objects. We also observe that while the mechanization and motorization have inspired a profusion of literary and artistic works, plastic, which has changed our everyday lives to no less a measure, is rarely present in the artistic panorama, and when it is, it almost always has negative overtones.

So how could such a controversial material have been brought into Italian families? The choice was inspirational, using a popular comedian and larger-than-life figure like Gino Bramieri, and creating comic spots in the much-loved Carosello programme to conjure up a reassuring, homely atmosphere. The 'armchair adventurer', instead of working, confronts—in his sleep—all kinds of evil-doers. He duels with the musketeers against the cardinal's guards. He lets himself into secret laboratories like James Bond. He gets up to all sorts of tricks. Luckily, when he wakes up, it is to a safe little home, full of useful, unbreakable objects ('Mo . . . mo . . . mo . . . Moplen!'). The fame that followed this opened the door to new products, which came into the home with their bright colours: red, green, blue (in strong contrast to the light or dark brown of wood, the white/cream or pastel-coloured walls and the dark colours or fancy designs of the sofas) bringing their functional shapes and muffled sounds with them.

On the subject of noise, even this has changed, though not just due to plastics. Gone are the creaking parquets and old furniture, all thrown away; the ticking pendulum clock, left out for the street cleaners; the piercing doorbell and the deafening alarm clock. Even the telephone has a gentler ring, not to mention the fact that the continual racket of street noises is no longer heard. Everything has become softer and more 'urbane', not necessarily more silent, but the sounds have changed. Instead of the loud sharp noises of the past there is a bland and continuous background drone made by the buzz of recharging electric motors, the indistinct mechanical hum from outside, and music, or words and music in continuation! Where does it all come from? I will now return to the house.

The sound has guided us through the hall and into the living room, or perhaps I should call it the parlour because it is very different from the large majestic space it used to be, and smaller than the master bedroom. In the room I see a small sofa and two armchairs of pale pink velvet, with spindly legs like metal-pointed reversed cones. They are arranged around a shiny low table of nondescript material with some magazines on top. In the background white floor-length curtains, gathered and frilled into ample drapes, permit daylight to filter through. On one side a low cocktail cabinet in the same style hides a little surprise. When you open its door a hidden light illuminates the mirror-lined interior. Inside there is a wide range of drinks, chiefly aperitifs according to the taste of the time (Punt e Mes, Biancosarti, Martini, Cinzano Soda), bitters like Ramazzotti and China Martini, and 'the brandy that creates the right atmosphere' (black label Vecchia Romagna, naturally).[81] What is really different, however, is the absence of the showy character old living rooms had, made as they were for social life and showing off one's status with the help of countless precious ornaments (all vanished, together with the piano, fireplace, grandfather clock, and big oil paintings), even if the new furniture happens to be fairly expensive, even more than the electric appliances, and paid for by instalments. This parlour is arranged like stalls in a theatre. The divan and armchairs in fact face a wall occupied by a modern piece of fitted furniture, with some shelves for books and others containing bits and pieces or closed behind with wooden flaps or glass fronts. On one of them there is a radiogram (where the music is coming from), and beside it is a pile of 33 rpm vinyl records (LPs of classical music). Enthroned in the centre is a large, heavy piece of apparatus: the television set.

This is why the arrangement of furniture and furnishings has changed so much. It is no longer a place dedicated to social life, for conversation and reception of friends, but a space specializing in cultural consumption. Of course, it is as yet a very limited consumption. For the entire culture/show 'package' the typical Italian family of 1970 spent 6 per cent of its budget, basically making it the last of the consumer goods, coming after hygiene/sanitary expenses. Nevertheless, it was taking on a special role because of its continual transformations and the formidable cultural impact it brought in its wake. It goes without saying that the media concealed deep differences, which underline social divisions (79 per cent of clerks had televisions in the 1960s, for example, against 48 per cent of manual workers) and the typical town/country divide (only 16 per cent of farmers and 11 per cent for farm labourers had one, meaning it was urban consumption).[82]

We know that spending on culture and entertainment had always been there. In Liberal Italy the predominant form was the theatre which, though remaining essentially élitist, was a clear reflection of the culture of the time. It then passed to the cinema, which during the 1930s had already become the first real form of mass entertainment, carrying with it aspirations and new models of lifestyle. At this point two important phenomena can be seen. The first is the development of 'domestic' cultural consumption, that is the tendency for consumers to spend less and less outside (live shows, cinema, sports events) and more and more in their own homes. It can be seen here how the cultural values of privacy and domesticity have played a powerful role in directing cultural choices. The radio was the first of the important mass media to push in this direction. Before the war the number of radio license holders had never reached two million (it was still mostly collective listening), after the war it soared and from 1957 to 1959 it reached a peak of six million license holders, before descending equally

Table 6 Cultural and tourism consumption, 1861–1985

Years	Average annual culture and entertainment spending (millions of current lire; millions of euro from 2000)			Tourism (average annual data in thousands)			
	Theatre and music	Cinema	Sport	Rail passengers	Ship passengers	Air passengers	Cars in circulation[1]
1861–70	–	–	–	–	1,195	–	–
1871–80	–	–	–	–	1,035	–	–
1881–90	–	–	–	–	–	–	–
1891–900	–	–	–	–	1,009	–	–
1901–10[2]	–	–	–	88,630	1,635	–	–
1911–20	–	–	–	97,801	2,351	–	–
1921–30	–	–	–	123,376	8,026	31	99
1931–40[3]	109	597	36	133,949	8,043	113	242
1941–50	2,483	21,170	2,167	297,970	6,399	440	190
1951–60	8,467	104,660	9,224	381,469	8,929	1,330	1,039
1961–70	12,354	157,011	23,577	344,674	16,198	8,677	6,081
1971–80	46,187	322,490	88,236	376,096	26,083	22,630	5,100
1981–90	264,330	525,764	419,034	398,438	41,056	34,596	22,878
1991–2000	659,673	873,556	715,691	448,176	63,617	64,091	30,460
2001–05[4]	456	753	315	494,261	65,469	100,090	33,807

Source: elaborations on ISTAT, *Sommario di statistiche storiche dell'Italia 1861–1975*, Rome (1976); Ibid. *Sommario di statistiche storiche 1926–1985*, Rome (1986); Ibid. *Annuario statistico italiano*, years 1985–2006.

[1] Vehicles that had paid road tax.
[2] Train passenger records for 1906–1910.
[3] Culture records for 1936–1940.
[4] Data records for 2001–2004.

rapidly during the next decade. Television came next and spread like lightning. From its beginnings in 1954 up to 1970 it registered almost 10 million license holders. The transfer of the public from one means to the other and the 'privatization' of consumption is evident, as testified by the large number of TV sets sold.[83]

The second phenomenon is the creation of mixed consumption due to the increased media available. This means that to understand the dynamics in progress we can no longer refer to the consumption of just one means, as had happened previously, when the social characteristics of the users were very clear-cut. Instead we have to refer to a cross-section of several media, characterized differently according to reference groups. Therefore people do not go to the theatre or the cinema any more, but to the cinema every now and then, and to the theatre (almost never); they frequently listen to the radio and (always) watch TV. Can we create a map of these kinds of cultural consumption? Indeed we can, including printed paper as well. With reference to habitual consumers, according to various surveys, the highest circulation at the start of the 1970s was for newspapers (at least once a week). Immediately after that comes television, which in 1965 already reached 40 per cent of the population every day and within ten years had leapt to 65 per cent (the overtaking would actually occur during the 1970s). Then there are weekly magazines, which were widely read during the period in question (60 per cent), after which comes the radio with a seesaw progress. In the lowest parts of the table, but on the increase, there are monthly magazines and books, growing slowly (though also the sector with the biggest number of non-consumers, with less than one book a year: 75–80 per cent). Last of all comes the cinema, which after a good run during the 1950s (a quarter of the audiences went there at least once a week), plunged to 14 per cent habitual filmgoers by 1973.[84] The picture that emerges is of overlapping consumption where the various media were concerned, varying according to levels of education, gender, age, and income, almost as if there were a completely different public on show. Academics have racked their brains trying to classify groups and subgroups of users (as have advertisers, even more, in their search for the most suitable means for targeting a certain public). In this picture, notice how the whole sector of printed paper is privileged, even if the quantity levels varied greatly—for one reason through improvements in education of course (increased compulsory school attendance, one middle school, and campaigns against pockets of illiteracy). There is also an overlapping and mutual reinforcement among the various means (*cross-fertilization*), whereby the glossy magazines showed more and more interest in television (stimulating consumption); picture stories all the rage, half-way between cinema and comics; television repeating radio pro-grammes, and so on. However one thing is shared by all these media. They all converged towards the creation of a virtuous (or vicious?) circle to reinforce consumer culture, if only to sell themselves—even books appeared in cheap pocket editions and started to be sold at newsagents.[85]

It is time to scrutinize the newcomer, television, more closely. In appearance, this valve-operated Telefunken has a great big case in wood-coloured exterior finish with a bulging screen and four control knobs at the bottom. It takes a while to warm up and has to be worked at to get a good signal (there was little choice anyway, at the start just one channel transmitting 32 hours a week, and two channels from 1961).When it is switched off there remains a persistent luminous spot in the middle. For the record, when it came out in 1954 it cost more than 200,000 lire (not to mention the RAI license on top of that). But for the lucky owners of this apparatus it is worth the trouble and expense. It brings the whole world into the home in a flash, a bevvy of pretty young announcers, newscasters, Italo-American presenters, yelling singers, old and new comedians. It is a far cry from the fabulous, glossy cinema world of Hollywood and nearer to everyday reality. Television personalities have something familiar and ordinary about them, partly because they are seen every day and partly because they infiltrate the home and are part of the atmosphere. Then, of course, some of the most popular programmes (not cultural or educational, as the directors may have hoped) like the quiz show *Lascia o raddoppia?* (Double or quits?), actually present completely ordinary people, the man in the street. Who knows, one day any ordinary person might make it and suddenly become rich and famous.[86]

Television seems to have miraculously combined the assets of the cinema (images displayed, contents accessible to a vast public, pro-grammes from all over the world) with those of the radio (useful, free and readily available information once the set was bought). If cinema and radio had revealed a universe of information and entertainment, now television had brought all this conveniently into the home. In a word, everybody would understand the meaning of an expression like 'global village' (even without reading McLuhan). The viewing levels soared high up and stayed there. Within Europe, Italy has always been a country with high levels of television consumption, even after education and income got close to the Community average (it has been suggested that the reason for this may be because literacy was achieved late, during the post-war period when television already existed. Many people were unable to develop a reading habit in time and 'jumped' directly to television).

As has been said these new media reinforced consumer culture. Thanks to its incredible hold and coverage, television did this in two ways: indirectly, by showing in its programmes a world of desirable—and available—goods; and directly, despite the moralistic and didactic style of its beginnings, by introducing advertising with *Carosello*. This interlude became a very popular programme. Children would not go to bed without seeing it first, and parents and grandparents also lapped it up. It brought with it sparkling, snappy language, launched or relaunched actors, directors, imaginary characters, and triggered the association of each product with a slogan and catchy tune (a real fad of the times). Its effectiveness lay not only in the quality of the programmes (Totò, Peppino De Filippo, Dario Fo, Fabrizi, Gassman, Manfredi and many other famous actors appeared in them), but also in its message.[87] It was the triumphant phase of advertising: new, within limits, entertaining, and instructive (in the sense that it launched new products and explained how to use them, as with plastic for example). To conclude, the first consumption it launched was advertising itself.

As I am sitting here so comfortably, it is a perfect time to have a quick look at the coffee table magazines before I go. There is *Epoca*, with its splendid photographic features inspired by *Life* magazine, and offering the Italian family quality information. Underneath there are some women's periodicals: the popular picture story '*Grand Hotel*' and '*Annabella*' and '*Gioia*' magazines. Leafing through one of them I come across:

> The perfect hostess must be able to handle any problem, even an 'emergency meal' for guests round the television [. . .] To simplify things, this time we propose exquisite, appetizing dishes that can be served in bowls, on skewers, or even (don't be shocked) without forks.[88]

A reader's letter:
Question: Can I ever be the wife my husband expects me to be? (Fiancée on eve of wedding). Reply: a few basic rules. For example: always make your husband feel he is your protector; never contradict him in public; know how to say 'I'm wrong' with good grace; listen to him without showing impatience; never propose any expense he cannot afford [...] self-esteem is the first quality in a man even when he becomes a loving husband".[89]

Reader:
Question: "Do you think a girl can become a radio-technician if she studies hard? [...] I would hate to be held up to ridicule" (Damiana). Reply: nowadays there are women magistrates, nuclear physicists, and airline pilots. Be brave then and never forget to do things seriously.[90]

Many husbands forced to remain alone in town while the family is on holiday want to eat in their own homes at least once a day. So the wife, before leaving, should restock the pantry well...Here are provisions for two weeks: First course: 2 cans of soup; 2 of meat-filled ravioli; 2 of pasta and beans [...]. Main course: 2 tins of boiled beef; 2 of braised meat; 2 of veal in aspic; 2 of frankfurters; 2 of tunny in oil [...]. Monday. Soup [...]. Boiled meat with spinach: open the tin of meat and invert it over the plate [...].[91]

These magazines were as widely and avidly read as they were lambasted for their content and the female image they were held to convey. But apart from the notable differences between them, closer study reveals a certain liveliness on topics such as morality and consumption. It is also interesting to observe how in the course of ten years or so there was a gradual shift from didactics and entertainment to decidedly commercial intent (as well as entertainment). Some inquiries and oral testimonies have also shed light on a most important aspect: how they were received by their readers. There was not necessarily a watering down of the messages but an active re-elaboration. For example they were used to produce replies in front of difficult family situations, or to establish contacts and social exchanges among women sharing the same interests, or else to create space for relaxation based on specific time needs.[92] These magazines were also used to construct new identities, therefore. They pointed out differentiating strategies, becoming part of the sort of bricolage that makes use of material culture to create new models of everyday life, designing different cultural landscapes from those handed down by class-bound tradition.

We should remember that the sociocultural situation exemplified by the family described earlier is only one possible direction to take a look at, for all its cultural prominence at the time and the stress put on it by the media. It was defined by economic and social barriers, as shown, and was certainly not for people living in do-it-yourself homes on the poor out-skirts of town, in overcrowded conditions and unable to afford even the smallest of comforts. Nor was it the direction taken by people living in deserted rural areas where many families had to find a new equilibrium around the 'abandoned' wives of emigrants, relying on the money sent home from other countries. Emigrant women, too, had different reac-tions when faced by the new domesticity and its symbols. Some accepted it, at least as an ideal, seeing it as a form of liberation and conquest of independence (probably together with their first wage packets). Others rejected it and carried on in the traditional way, maybe even reinforcing it. Then there were others who accepted it selectively, so that some goods and practices came to be incorporated in behaviour still dominated by the ethics of self-denial rather than the temptation of consumerism.[93]

Young people

I am standing in front of the door that was closed before. Now I can push it open and enter. How different this room is from the others! I am immediately struck by the blue walls and bright light hanging from the ceiling. Gone is that essence of perfect order and cleanliness that reigns in the rest of the house, replaced by 'creative' disorder (the lady of the house would surely not approve). It is the (probably teenage) son's room. There is a big poster hanging above the bed, stuck to the wall with adhesive tape. It is the photo of a boy sitting on the bonnet of a car, with jeans, white t-shirt, half open windcheater, cigarette in mouth, and an insolent smile: James Dean. There is a table with a small lamp next to the bed with a bit of everything on it: a tiny portable radio, text-books, exercise books, newspaper cuttings, Coccoina paste pot, a packet of chewing gum, biros and other types of pen (one has a ship moving up and down in transparent liquid), comics (*Intrepido*, *Tex*), magazines like *Ciao Amici*, *Giovani* and *Big* (then *Ciao 2001*), which discuss music, young people's problems, and how boring adult radio and TV programmes are. On a shelf in front of a multi-volumed boys' encyclopedia is a Geloso tape recorder (somewhat in disuse by the look of it, even if it did cost 28,000 lire) and a portable Lesa record player with many 45 rpm discs beside it (all the latest hits). Thrown into a basket, old playthings stick out: *Topo Gigio*, a Disney Donald Duck, battered toy soldiers, little metal cars, marbles and a box of Lego bricks (which have taken the place of the old meccano, against Dad's wishes—just as the Barbie doll, icon of a new femininity, has ousted Mum's beloved rag doll). In the little wardrobe facing the bed is a strange medley of clothing: some almost 'classical', that is jackets, trousers, and white shirts; others somewhat different: blue jeans, (Levi's 501 to be precise), white and striped tee shirts, one windcheater with zips and another of black leather.

The objects in this room send out a clear message. Here is a space and material culture in contrast with the rest of the home and constructed around an age difference. The 'otherness' of childhood with respect to maturity was already recognized in the past, but the actual construction of a youth identity only appeared during these years.[94] Of course, looking back at history, it is highly evident that there had already been a specific interest in youth since the late 19th century at least (if not the Romantic period), and that it had really thrived in avant-garde 20th-century movements. Perhaps the most significant moment came with the exaltation given to it by the Fascist and Nazi movements, keen to be seen young, in contrast—both politically and age-wise—with their 'old' opponents ('Youth, youth| Spring of beauty' as the Fascist anthem went). And it must not be thought that this emphasis was only instrumental, to bind the young to them. As academics like Mosse and De Felice have suggested, it fully reflected the characteristics of the movements and their ideological connotations.[95] It is true, however, that it was only from the 1950s and 1960s onwards that the young saw themselves as a generation, in the sense that they found themselves with a common identity, created shared cultural forms, and developed their own understanding of reality, which was to lead to social and political commitment in the future.[96] The reasons for this change are partly linked to the overall transformations that were going on (geographic mobility loosening traditional bonds, urban migration, increased demographic weight, more disposable income, more students).[97] It was also partly due to a cultural transformation that affected the West (starting in the United States and northern

Europe actually, and reaching Italy later) and looked at the world of the young with different, more attentive eyes. The developing cultural industries were an influential part of this, as they saw in the young age group potential new clients and began to produce goods aimed at their needs. A 1964 survey estimated that 6.6 million young Italians had a good 250 billion lire available, which they spent respectively on non-essentials like drinks, cigarettes (50 billion); Vespas and Lambrettas (another 50 billion); clothes, cosmetics, and hairdressers (25 billion); music (23.5 billion, of which 12 on records, 5 on record players, 6.5 on juke-box tokens); transport by motorcycle, bicycle, and car (22 billion); cinema and sports events (21 billion); books, newspapers, magazines, and comics (20.5 billion); and other things (38 billion).[98]

What has been observed for other 'new' entities is naturally also true for the young, of course with their multifaceted, volatile and complex identities, stratified according to income, geographical urban and gender divides (the spending listed above could only concern middle-class youth and exclude those from the working class and rural backgrounds), so generalizations must therefore be treated with caution.[99] Nevertheless, the impression remains that in this construction the reference to material culture has played a highly relevant role, both as codified within the group and as a form of social self-representation, that is giving visibility to the juvenile subculture. All well, then? Absolutely not.

On 10th October 1956 two brothers not much over twenty years of age, Arturo and Egidio Santato, apparently with mental problems, entered the elementary school of Terrazzano di Rho, a village near Milan, armed with pistols and tubes of explosives. They took three teachers and 97 children hostage, threatening to kill them. Using a loud-hailer through a window, one of the kidnappers bargained for the payment of a ransom in front of dozens of photographers and reporters. He asked for two hundred million to be deposited on the roof by helicopter ('to start a new life', as he said at his trial). He then asked, in order, for food, TV cameras, photo-electric cells, and ten live hens. The negotiations dragged on. The police lined up. The authorities, a priest and detective Tom Ponzi arrived. Finally a female teacher attempted to disarm one of the bandits and the children started screaming. It was the signal to take action. One brave citizen (who was killed) and police officers scrambled up the stairs and broke in, putting an end to the kidnapping.[100] This unusual act of violence upset the whole country, not only for the potential consequences but also for the brutal and 'cinema-like' nature of the kidnap. Arguments immediately broke out attributing the event to the damaging influence of films and magazines with violent content. Public opinion polls revealed that a large majority of the population agreed and were in favour of some sort of censorship on messages that 'portrayed a life of pleasure and luxury, where riches easily come by were squandered, and made audiences of all ages and situations dream of things beyond the reach of the vast majority of people'. And it was maintained that the people most strongly influenced were 'abnormal or born criminals' and 'all youngsters and adults with an infantile mentality' even more so.[101] The young were particularly vulnerable because of their 'desire to enjoy themselves at all costs', and 'earn a lot with little effort', together with their selfishness and 'inability to make sacrifices'.[102] It all went to confirm public opinion's growing belief in the emergence of juvenile delinquency: deviant and disrespectful behaviour, episodes of hooliganism and criminal acts large and small seemed indicative of the position of the young in society. The media gave a lot of space to the exploits of 'lost youth' and the polls revealed a stern judgement on the part of adults. These young delinquents were not victims of society but had been spoilt by permissive parents. They had little desire to work and were unduly influenced by films and comics. To sum up, they only wanted the pleasurable side of modern society, as consumers, and not the necessary prerequisites of self-denial and hard work.[103]

What was the real truth? Judiciary statistics provide us with a controversial picture. The increase in juvenile crime may have been part of the general increase recorded during the post-war period, but many distinctions need to be made. They show a sharp decrease in wilful murder, reaching a historic minimum during the 1961–70 decade, albeit accompanied by a high number of manslaughter cases. Also decreasing were personal injury and abuse. A sharp increase in theft was revealed, and robbery continued at a high rate (crimes against the family and morality were also characteristic of the period).

In essence, it is the picture recorded by all western countries, in that increased well-being became the cause of a subsequent rise in crime against property (theft, fraud, etc.) and a lessening of crimes against the person (murder, violence, etc.). More material riches and ostentation of consumer goods were certainly strong incentives for crime, just as more laws determined by an increasingly regulated social life put

law-breaking on the increase. Violence, which had been a daily presence in the not so distant past, largely disappeared from contemporary
experience, as for example collective violence (revolts, lynchings, etc.)
and all that remained were private cases, as further evidence of the
tendency for social life to become a private affair.[104] Equally, violence
against offenders, or rather, against the bodies of offenders, was gradually being made illegal, and the death penalty limited or abolished
almost everywhere. It was the last step in the process masterfully
delineated by Foucault concerning the modern age, going from the
discontinuation of horrific kinds of torture (through which the sovereign would spectacularly re-establish his challenged power) to the
creation of total institutions like modern prisons where refined new
forms of punishment can be practised.[105]

But to return to the young people of the time, in Italy at least, they
did not seem to have a leading role in criminal activities.[106] What was
the cause of all this panic then? The 'natural' link between young
delinquents and the cinema/literature formed by public opinion may
be more of a cause than an effect. The post-war period saw the success
of films about young rebels, from *Gioventù perduta* (Lost Youth), *I vinti*
(The Vanquished), *Gioventù alla sbarra* (Youth Behind Bars) to American
productions that made a sensation, such as *Blackboard Jungle*, James
Dean films *East of Eden* and *Rebel Without a Cause*, or *On the Waterfront*
with Marlon Brando, as well as a host of detective and *noir* films full of
rough young gangsters. Literature drew on French existentialism and
its condemned youth. Comics were filled with dubious masked characters like Batman and Spider Man.[107] Perhaps the hidden side was
emerging of a society keen to show itself as positive and bent on
progress, claiming to have turned over a new leaf after the war and
cast the darkness behind it. Be that as it may, here there is an interesting
cultural mechanism at work, producing a recurrent stereotype of youth
out of control, with a social debate constructed around it—not a
particular interpretation of reality by public opinion (it is a long way
off Habermas), but a construction of practices and discourses that form
the meaning of their objects, as Foucault says. Anything relevant (cases
of hooliganism, juvenile transgression, wild dancing, alcohol abuse) was
isolated and made the subject of public debate. Everything else faded
into insignificance.

All this had already happened in other countries, and in more
exaggerated forms.[108] In Great Britain, for example, they had

witnessed with concern the birth of many youth subcultures (Teddy boys, mods, rockers, followed by punks, skinheads, and Rastafarians) together with the violence associated with them. Analysing the phenomenon, sociologists like Stanley Cohen and Stuart Hall concluded that social reactions were out of proportion and only had one explanation: moral panic. The fears aroused by the young (and in the British context also by black immigrants) were in reality projections of the deep-rooted disquiet that held society in its clutches and originated in the transformations in progress. These were admittedly creating better welfare and faith in the future but greatly undermining traditional values and behaviours. The disquiet latched on to people that most embodied the challenges of the new times, that is the young, and demonized their behaviour, automatically labelling them as guilty.[109] In Italy the situation was not so extreme, at least up to 1968, but the reactions were very similar.

For their part, young people saw things quite differently. Their behaviour was a way of expressing themselves as individuals, enjoying themselves, and being together. They started by constructing their identity around certain objects and places. The first is precisely where I am now, the little room conceived as 'somewhere else' with respect to the rest of the home. It was where they could escape from their parents, study, listen to music, and meet and chat with their friends. This was particularly important for girls, who were subject to much tighter limitations than boys of their age when it came to going out, especially in the evenings.[110] However, the young saw their space as being chiefly outside the home. Indeed, one could say that they built it as the complete reverse of family life, partly for practical reasons and partly as a cultural choice. Where could the boy who lives here be at this moment? As it is the afternoon, he is probably not at school. The first obvious guess, after what has been said, is that he is at the cinema. In fact during the 1950s the cinema already tended to be a means of entertainment frequented mainly by the young (over 65 per cent went at least once a week) and the trend intensified later.[111] And of course, at least where the upper classes were concerned, they would go around on a Vespa or Lambretta, just as much icons of freedom as of mobility.[112]

A second possibility is that he is in a bar playing pinball or putting coins in a juke-box (another precious pair of American imports), or dancing either in some commercial place (dance hall, discotheque) or even somewhere private where there is another symbolic element, a record player (maybe at a friend's house, where he has brought along some records and paid his share towards buying orangeade or Coca Cola).[113] Music had become the real language of youth. After the first wild boogie-woogies and institutionalizing of jazz as a form of intellectual music, it was the arrival of rock'n'roll that gave voice to the young. From America and Great Britain came the new stars, like the Beatles, Rolling Stones, Doors, and Rokes, as well as many others. Even melodious Italian songs tried to adapt.[114] June 24th 1965 saw the arrival of the Beatles in Milan. There had already been 3,000 fans waiting at the station for them the evening before, but the group had given them the slip in four red Alfa Romeo sports cars. The afternoon concert was attended by 7,000 young people while more than 20,000 came to the evening one. The singers wore jackets, ties, and white shirts, but had long hair. Paul McCartney stepped up to the microphone, shouted 'ciao', and broke into *Twist and Shout*. There was pure delirium. Parents were shocked at the sight of their offspring dancing wildly, mini-skirted girls screaming, floods of tears and all the fainting. In Rome's Piazza di Spagna long-haired beatniks assembled, affronting tourists and passers by, but telling newspaper reporters that they were doing nothing wrong by chatting and listening to music. After all, in their time, even the grown-ups had enjoyed themselves and, anyway, there was no need to confuse 'beat' with 'yea-yea'.[115]

I have discussed objects and spaces, but among objects the distinctive signals were clothing, accessories, and hairstyle. Boys had long hair and wore blue jeans (introduced by Teddy boys into Italy), tight jackets, sweaters, and striped tops or white or coloured shirts. Girls had long or page boy, short-cut hair and wore mini-skirts, jeans like the boys, showy belts and boots or high-heeled shoes. They loved geometric fancy patterns, 'cosmonaut' appeal (silvery hues, futuristic shapes), and powerful colour combinations. Furthermore, they used lots of make-up and vivid eye shadow, a little like disco girls. With its taste for the exotic and oriental, and shirts, jackets, trousers, skirts, and bandannas, all covered with flowers, the hippy movement soon came to Italy and spread like wildfire.[116] Their clothing clearly showed the search for new aesthetic as well as new political models, trying to be different and anti-traditional in order to show their independence and rejecting everything formal both in dress code and social behaviour.

It was also practical and sexy, rediscovering and drawing attention to the human body, both male and female. Note, by the way, how in all these items a growing role was played by plastics: plastic necklaces, bracelets, purses, and various accessories. Synthetic fibres were present in many items of clothing and above all in a brand new product: tights. After nylon stockings, here they were on the market, invented by Du Pont in a light elastic polyurethane fibre, elastam. The firm put the article on the market as medical stockings but the success of the mini-skirt, launched by Mary Quant during so-called 'Swinging London', quickly converted it into an important item of clothing, because it was so practical and also because of its modesty. In Italy it was Omsa, publicized by the Kessler twins, who promoted the item.

How is this to be interpreted all this? As a form of sociopolitical protest? Yet young Italians, during inquiries and interviews, did not use a language that was particularly 'revolutionary'. They spoke about their desire for freedom and how they liked being together. Just another display of consumerism among the young? The great differences and continual variations make me reject a merely passive acceptance of prefabricated models. In reality the young were using hybridizing and assembling processes. To explain mythical thinking, in his book *The Savage Mind* Lévi-Strauss turns to a *bricolage* analogy. For his own purposes the 'savage' uses a little of all the objects and materials that come to hand, even when they are not really suitable. He puts them together, rearranges them over and over again, modifies them, and eventually throws them away and looks for something else.[117] According to some sociologists young people do just this. They assemble different materials (perhaps from the media, fashion, consumer advertising, examples set by people of their own age, or from their own personal inspiration) and create something completely new, a new set of rituals. In this way objects change meaning because they have been taken out of context, transformed, or exaggerated. Unusual hair-styles are exhibited, variations in traditional clothing (like short skirts or the same blue jeans that started out as working clothes) and consumer symbols, outside their original context, take on the role of recognition signals. And in this way, with the aim of creating a specific identity different from its origins, a 'style' is born communicating to the outside world this 'otherness' (if only within a particular social order and with all the usual differences due to class, age, or gender).[118] In this way, with their active reworking of consumer messages, the young give a foretaste of future fashions.

By the way, an observation often repeated in the news is that the Italy of the time seems to have been overrun by a wave of 'youthism'. This certainly has cultural as well as demographic roots, but it could also be linked to something else. Italy is historically a country of low social mobility. Some comparative studies conducted in those years show lower social mobility than in other European countries, despite the great changes. It is calculated that rising forms of mobility involved only 21 per cent of the population, compared with 32 per cent in Germany, 28 per cent in France, 27 per cent in Great Britain, not to mention 38 per cent for the United States and 45 per cent for Japan.[119] One may surmise that, in the absence of efficient exchange mechanisms, the upset caused by the war and an albeit limited cleansing of sectors compromised by Fascism provided a unique opportunity for a degree of renewal in the ruling class. The result was that many people, even those quite or very young, were able to occupy important positions in more or less all sectors of public and private life, contributing to the impression of a young, forward-looking society.[120]

All this talk about 'juvenile deviation' brings one thing to mind: not all consumption is equally approved of by society and not all consumption is legal. The line marking the boundary is not always unambiguous, however, and changes with time. The rules of the game frequently undergo cycles of tolerance or restriction. As Roberta Sassatelli has observed, what clearly results is that certain types of consumption are socially regulated and cannot be used by individuals just as they please, so that we may speak about a 'tamed' hedonism.[121] Take alcohol for example. As seen earlier, at the start of the twentieth century, wine was an important part of the diet of farming and factory workers. Abuse of it was severely stigmatized, however, and contrasted with middle-class drinks such as coffee, which kept the head clear and was a work stimulant. Tirades against alcoholism were a constant part of campaigns to 'moralise' the working class, but there was never any actual prohibition.[122]

The tobacco story is equally ambiguous. Used by sorcerers in pre-Columbian societies for healing and religious ceremonies, it completely changed meaning when imported into Europe, where it became a luxury item for the affluent classes but also spread among the poor, for whom it acquired a role similar to alcohol, quelling pangs of hunger and creating a mild euphoria. Its later expansion was linked to the firms that produced and marketed it (there is no coincidence in the fact that it spread slowly in Asia and even more slowly in Africa). Distributed to soldiers in the form of cigarettes, it became a symbol of vitality, dynamism, and sociability, and it may be for this reason that it also began to be appreciated by women from the 1950s onwards. The last phase in time sees a burgeoning health campaign and mild prohibitionism in the second half of the twentieth century (significantly preceded by the strict anti-smoking campaigns in Nazi Germany).[123]

What is there to say about paid sex? Always disapproved of, prostitution continued to exist on the legal fringes of society. It could be practised but not 'solicited'. If anything, we can observe here the typical strategy of concentrating such activities in controllable areas. In Italy it was the 'closed houses' (abolished in 1958 by the Merlin law),[124] the other important strategy being medical control. Then there are the illegal, but nevertheless widespread forms of consumption, starting with drugs. Even here, however, western history is fairly complicated. For example in Great Britain opium had been imported from Turkey for centuries and freely sold as a base for medicinal preparations. During the nineteenth century production boomed thanks to its cultivation in India (and lucrative exportation to countries like China). The British began to look at the substance differently, as an exotic, temptingly pleasurable drug, dandies and sophisticated writers spreading an ambiguous image of it. Consumption rocketed, as did moralizing campaigns, until in 1920 opium was declared illegal except for medicinal use.[125] The boundaries were mobile, therefore, without taking into account that the various social groups adopted different practices and attributed different meanings to it.

I leave the house satisfied, but somewhat bewildered. The landscapes of consumption are like quicksilver. The goods I have seen have told me a lot about redefining social and spatial traditions; about disorientation, continuous negotiation, resistance, and identity building; about different meanings that these selfsame objects can assume at the same time (academics talk about multi-accentuation, and I am reminded of certain Andy Warhol paintings: a tin of Campbell's soup repeated ad infinitum, but looking closely it is apparent that each tin is slightly different, and the whole thing suggests both a sense of approval and fulfilment, as well as mockery and criticism). The goods discussed reveal that it is in everyday things that practises, relationships, and meanings are forged, and that the 'great transformation' of the 1950s–70s affected not only factory, town, and country, but the home as well. It was here that it gave voice to the young, activated female emancipation in many little ways and changed the aspirations of immigrants. In conclusion it produced new identities and at the same time, important new economic subjects whose choices were to become determining for the way the country was structured where production and distribution are concerned. All the conditions are present for change to enter the political arena.

8

Politics, Culture, and Welfare State

It was during the 1950s that something new happened in public and political debate: the term consumption started to appear. Not that consumer culture had been politically absent in previous historical phases, as noted above, but it now took on a more pivotal role and higher profile. The role of consumption in the ongoing processes of growth and transformation was so evident that it could not be ignored. The problem, if any, was how to judge and (from the political angle perhaps) govern it.

Judging by what intellectuals, politicians, and economists were saying, there was a chorus of critical voices. Protagonists in the public sphere were left bewildered and perplexed by the changes that had occurred in the course of a very few years. What was consumer culture all about? Why were Italians on a perpetual buying spree? Why were they so enthusiastic about television? The explanations put forward take their cue from contemporary debate. (To paraphrase Ruth Benedict: no adult looks at the world with virgin eyes.)[1]

Many ignored the issue, since nothing very important in politics and economics was involved. It had no direct connection with any ideology, movement or party, and was at most inspired by American ways of doing things. What consequences could there be from watching *Il Musichiere* (The Music Man) on television or buying an all-purpose mixer? Others, however, feared that the changes in everyday life would have a long-term influence and would eventually become the norm, as Giorgio Bocca warns in his popular newspaper inquiries:

> Italy is made and Italians more or less. What the Medici's Pope-King, Dante's Emperor-Messiah, Machiavelli's Prince, Cavour's Piemontese bureaucracy and Mussolini's Fascists all failed to accomplish is coming together through the auspices of the consumer civilisation and its television oracle. Before long the Italians will be a compact people with identical customs, habits and ideals, from Sicily to the Alps. They will dress, think, eat and enjoy themselves all in the same way, as the small screen dictates and imposes.[2]

Not everyone agreed, however. Particularly influential at the time were the economists, who were taking part in projects to direct economic growth, like the Vanoni plan and programming policies. Their analysis speaks of 'distorting consumption'. Italians were giving priority to luxury goods, typical of the most highly developed countries, instead of buying essential things first. They were rushing to buy cars, electrical appliances, televisions, while still living in shacks or houses without toilets or bathrooms, and eating inadequate meals. There was also too much emphasis on private, individually enjoyed consumption, instead of the collective consumption of prime necessities, on behalf of which the state had a duty to intervene. For this reason it was suggested that luxury products should be limited or postponed and primary consumption developed during this phase.[3] This was like saying that whenever Italians had the chance to become consumers, they chose badly. It should also be borne in mind that the concept of 'development as growth', as defined by Arndt, was widely accepted internationally. According to the writer, a country's well-being automatically depends on its economic growth rate (measured by the GDP) with the result that investment has absolute priority. From this point of view excessive consumption, by limiting saving, 'burns up precious resources'.[4] Moreover, saving, as opposed to consumption, has an historically ethical and virtuous aura about it (especially when practised by others).

No greater understanding came from the political parties. The great white whale of the Christian Democrat party had many factions in it yet harboured a sense of distrust towards worldly forms of consumption that might overshadow the role of the Church, insidiously undermining the institutions and very bedrock of Catholic values, though it was only from the 1960s that the first debate on the effects of 'Americanization' began.[5] The Communist Party was equally dubious about any actual improvement for the working class or, generally speaking, about the ability of capitalism to promote any real development. Consumer culture was seen as a trap, a fatal illusion spread about by the new media; fighting it was part of the struggle against monopolistic capitalism. But studies on the daily habits of party members, especially young ones, reveal a progressive insinuation of new styles and a fascination with cinema and television because, as Gundle has shown, despite the hard line taken by the party leaders and the sense of being different that was cultivated within the organization, its members were still part of society and influenced by it.[6]

The frame of reference for much of this discussion is given by the heated intellectual debate that raged during the 1950s and '60s concerning these very issues. The essential benchmarks are the works of Adorno, Horkheimer, and the Frankfurt School, and especially the famous *Dialectic of Enlightenment*, where consumer culture is discussed as a compulsory and unrestrained form of consumption induced by the culture industry. It becomes the new opium of the people, dazzling the workers and tempting them to spend their earnings on ever-changing consumer goods in an ongoing circle. It is the way modern capitalism even manages to suck the working class into its whirling mechanisms. Before long Marcuse will draw attention to the process leading to the manipulation of needs and creation of an amorphous mass of conformists, with the aim of ensuring authoritarian control from above; while Debord maintains that everything has turned into a gigantic spectacle, in the East as well as in the West, and that consumption as spectacle is the main mechanism for exercising power in contemporary society. Baudrillard will complete these reflections: the experiences deriving from consumer culture are now more satisfying than real ones, with the result that these 'simulacra' supplant reality. The pretence conjured up by the merchandise makes us lose the ability to distinguish between what is real and what is false. And albeit with a non-Marxist slant, and careful attention to the new sociopsychological studies on advertising, the work of American academics like Galbraith and Packard also recommended a critical analysis of the workings of the affluent society, which seemed destined to overflow rapidly from the United States to Europe.[7]

In Italy, a dissident voice making itself heard a few years later is that of Pier Paolo Pasolini. In a famous article in the '*Corriere della Sera*' he uses the metaphor of the vanishing fireflies to show that while ideological battles raged and the Government tried to use its repressive powers, something dramatic was happening within Italian society. Just like the fireflies, swept away by pollution, so the old agricultural and paleocapitalistic universe was all giving way to something totally 'other' and new: the consumer civilization.[8] An 'anthropological' transformation of the Italians had taken place, starting with the middle classes:

> speaking in anthropological terms, the 'middle classes' have changed radically: their positive values are no longer the clerical and reactionary ones of the past but (as yet unnamed and purely existential) values of the

hedonistic ideology of consumer culture and the consequential Ameri-can-style modernistic tolerance. It is Power itself—through so-called 'development' producing superfluous goods, imposing consumption mania, fashion and non-stop information (especially, and overpower-ingly, by means of television) —that has created such values, cynically throwing traditional values overboard, together with the Church, which was the symbol of them.[9]

Pasolini knew the 'language of things'. As a movie director as well as writer, he saw the world in a different light. A light that enabled him to view Yemen not as medievally picturesque, full of tall red houses with precious white friezes, or elegant architecture standing out against the desert, but the horrible expression of incipient modernity: huddled slum dwellings, pretentious modern skyscrapers, plastic objects, radios, tin cans, t-shirts. 'The language of new things, which in Yemen—as in my youth—is childish babble, for you Gennariello, has become articu-lated, logical and normal dialogue'.[10] Italian cities tell the same story: the old working-class outskirts have gone, supplanted by soulless limbos; instead of reminding us of the continuity of humanist tradition, city centres only remind us of the problem of how to preserve them physically; the countryside no longer reminds us of where civilization came from, but only of weekends and holiday homes.[11] Unfortunately, the language of things is powerful and unstoppable, he confesses to his young friend:

> The point is this: my culture (with its aestheticism) makes me critical of modern 'things' understood as linguistic signs. Your culture, instead, makes you accept those modern things as if they were natural and listen to their teachings as if they were absolute.
>
> I might try to tarnish, or at least cast doubt upon, all you are taught by parents, teachers, television, newspapers, and especially boys of your own age. But I am absolutely powerless against the teaching you have been and are getting from things.[12]

Here the writer shifts his attention from an analysis of political and ideological aspects to those concerning everyday changes, and he has insightfully caught their transformations. It is, of course, always a question of changes brought about by a power that is even stronger than political power, changes he is led to reject from a human, political, cultural, and even aesthetic point of view. In his view there is no hope for the future, which he presents as apocalyptic, and all he can do is take refuge in the dream of a timeless, mythical peasant past, very different from what it was in reality. But his observations, even in a semiological key, raise great interest.[13]

After this, rapidly increasing studies 'on the field' provided other perspectives. There are surveys like Alberoni's concerning the way consumer goods are received (by no coincidence combining theoretical analysis with empirical inquiries promoted by companies), opinion polls, surveys concerning immigrants in Turin and Milan or people still living in the country. These studies have a kind of emic approach, as some ethnographers would say, that is listening to subjects' voices and maintaining that their self-representations are valid, instead of forcing a thesis from outside based on researchers' own values and rules (according to an etic approach). Let us take the interesting research carried out in 1959 by Lidia De Rita among the poor villagers in Basilicata, to elicit their reactions to the first television programmes they had seen. When asked about the usefulness of television (the only programmes appreciated were entertainment ones), the replies were enlightening:

'Do you think TV teaches you anything?'
'You bet! But you can see the world as well. Then there's kids' television that teaches a lot. If we had electricity I'd buy a TV set for a bit of company.'

(Interview no. 9): 'So, have they broadcast anything useful?'
'Just like the movies: you see the harvesting, how it's done . . .'
'Have you learnt anything, then?'
'A bit . . . But we already know it all.'
'So television isn't any good, is it . . . ?'
'Well, it's better than nothing! It makes you think.'

(Interview no. 63): 'Do you think TV is useful?'
'It teaches you.'
'Does it? But not always, I think. Which programmes teach you the most?'
'All of them: *The Music Man, Double or Quits*, films, sport.'
'What do you learn from watching *The Music Man* ?'
'It's fun. I like it'.[14]

About *Carosello*, which for the most part advertised products beyond their means:

(Interview no. 18): 'What about *Carosello*. Do you like it?'
'Of course I like *Carosello*!' (adamantly).
'Why?'
'Well, we see lots and lots of things... because if I go into a shop and I want something, I can't explain, because I don't know how to. But with TV...'[15]

The composition written by 12-year-old Rosaria, on the subject of *which TV programme you liked best* says it all:

> I liked me Carosello best because there is lots of singerers, but there was Aurello Fero who sang the song as if he was like me. Claiudio Villo, Villo, Domenico, Madugno, Villo Pizzo are the four singerers I seed. I only seen this television and it is very nice. I only seed it once and can't say no more because I come, watch a little and goed away.[16]

Television was not regarded by these rural people as superfluous or a luxury, but as something good that would enable them to get a better knowledge of the world (the fact one of them failed to appreciate the distinction proposed by the interviewer between useful and nonuseful programmes is significant: for him all of them were equally important). And it was a knowledge that allowed them to 'articulate' what they knew, clarify their needs, and call things by their right names. A second aspect that comes out of the research is that there is a continuous dialogue about the most popular programmes. There is talk, discussion, memories, repeated phrases, and snatches of music. In practice, the new forms of cultural consumption stimulated communication and new ways of socializing among the audiences. Finally, what emerges is the core aspect of entertainment, something that perhaps reflects new importance for individuals and their needs in contrast with traditional ethics, which were based only on duty and the importance of sacrifice.[17] What can be seen here, which is missing in many authoritative studies, is a new consumer culture, one that is born out of new objects, develops on an everyday level, involves families and individuals, forms transverse identities, creates different value priorities, gives voice to new subjects, and invents new kinds of language and symbolism. It is this culture (apart from the glaring inequalities in income already mentioned) which explains why Italians bought consumer goods following behaviour models similar to those of richer countries. And all this would be repeated later in less developed countries, defying any economic forecast.

Yet despite different voices being raised, as we said at the beginning, the overriding tone was critical and opposed to consumer culture. On paper, that is, because politics in particular is based not only on rhetoric and debate but also on pragmatism. In fact one section of the DC was not slow to understand the political significance that strong economic growth could have in stabilizing the country, whatever form it might take, including consumption. For many it was the true, and possibly the only concrete answer in those historical circumstances to solve more or less all the problems. Better living standards could in fact relax social tensions, create cross-section consensus, and bind society together across the class divides. The American recipe of social integration through consumption became a guideline and consumer goods turned into an important indicator of attained affluence, and a measure of social mobility. DC politician Giulio Andreotti gives a clear explanation of this fact in a posthumous argument with Pasolini, who had criticized a policy too imbued with materialistic values, 'bread' inspired only by 'development' that was incapable of bringing real 'progress':

> Perhaps unlike the young generation which, as such, had never known the underdevelopment there was before, we took great pride in collective economic growth. We were shocked by the headlong rush of many who, in the name of criticising consumption, railed against the eleven million electrical appliances that had come into family use. I instead remember my mother's hands all cracked through doing the laundry, so I saw the washing machine as a saving grace for the family.
> [...] I was perhaps stubbornly rooted in the conviction that without bread life was never safe.[18]

Riding the tiger of development was the best recipe for the country—and for the government as well, all the more since beside the unbridled and somewhat anarchic growth (economic programming schemes quickly fell out of date) there was available an enormous apparatus of state industries and, above all, the powerful lever of public consumption. Fascism had brought the sphere of consumption firmly into the political debate and it was impossible to turn back. The need to redistribute income and ensure social justice, expressed by both Christian Democrats and left-wingers, would be able to find full expression through this channel. This is how the construction of a welfare state became the linchpin for maintaining balance in the Republic.

Speaking of welfare, three important aspects need to be remembered. The first, as already said, is continuity with the preceding periods. It has been shown how public consumption had been a widely debated issue since at least the turn of the century and how policies related to it were an important part of governments in the Liberal epoch and even more during Fascism. Republican Italy inherited an impressive set of regulations and institutions which seem to have remained unaltered (the big state-controlled agencies created by the regime simply dropped the 'f' standing for 'Fascist': INFPS became INPS, INFAIL became INAIL and so forth). But the guiding inspiration for the Republican governments had a fundamental difference: benefits were no longer to be aimed at specific categories (industrial workers, civil servants, pregnant women, etc.) but were basically for everybody. An exclusive policy was replaced by an inclusive one, and redistribution and social equality became central aspects of it.

The motivations behind this change bring me to the second point. Welfare was considered an important element in post-war democracy. It was no coincidence that it came officially into being with the famous report that William Beveridge published in 1942, at the height of the Second World War, contrasting the contemporary '*warfare state*' with a future order of peace and well-being (*welfare state*) which would guarantee freedom from the five 'giant evils': want, disease, ignorance, squalor, and idleness.[19] A few years later a Cambridge sociologist, Thomas Marshall, includes this observation in a seminal reading of history. The making of citizenship goes through three phases. The first is the recognition of civil rights (the rights of the individual linked to freedom of speech, thought, expression of faith, and personal freedom, together with the major collective rights of political and trade union association), which started to be put into effect around the eighteenth century; the second is the acquisition of political rights (the right to elect and be elected), which came piecemeal during the nineteenth century with the gradual extension of universal suffrage; the third was the social rights of citizenship (education and basic services for all), which belongs to the twentieth century. It is only through the enjoyment of all three kinds of rights that one can be a full member of a community.[20] Marshall's theories have been subjected to a barrage of well-grounded criticism (starting with the fact that they are too evolutionistic and only centred around the British experience), but they have had enormous echoes and been in many ways an ideal model for the construction of the welfare state.[21]

The third point brings me back to mainland Europe. The structural model for welfare spending that took shape in Italy was very similar to that of the major European countries, both in the allocation of resources and in its timing. There is no doubt here that harmonizing policies and 'demonstration effects' were at work in the European Community. If, apart from their cultural heritage, there is one element that strongly characterizes European countries abroad, it is probably the common reference to the welfare state—some talk about a real European model revolving around the State (where the citizen comes before the consumer).[22] It is important to stress, therefore, that the welfare state was constructed not only on requirements based on domestic policy but within a clearly international frame of reference. And the economic miracle gave governments ample financial resources to invest in sectors where tardiness was noticed with respect to the rest of Europe (education and national insurance). It was here, too, that the foundations of European integration were laid.[23]

With these premises there was a great surge in public spending. One could say that the modern Italian welfare state was literally built during the 1950–73 period. Some percentage of spending decreased (institutional, such as administration and defence); in other cases it increased (education and especially transfers to health, social assistance, and insurance). This means that the presence of the state in these sectors lightened corresponding private spending, thus favouring the expansion of certain kinds of consumption and freeing up resources for other uses. But I must proceed in order.

What school prospects faced a youngster in the 1960s, perhaps one from the home discussed earlier? In some ways he is lucky. Post-war governments invested a great deal in education, so that the level of spending rose immediately after the war in comparison with the Fascist period, and there was another leap during the 1960s when spending on education, in constant currency, for the first time exceeded spending on public works.[24] There were several reasons for this policy. One was an aspect of social equity and another was practical. The level of illiteracy and early school leaving was still relatively high in Italy, at the very time when the economic boom was calling for a better-qualified workforce. Basic and technical education was therefore seen as a prerequisite for increased employment and the formation of the 'human capital' that various theorists considered no less necessary than the investments guaranteeing economic development.[25] Our youngster will have begun his academic career in elementary school (it was only in 1968 that state kindergartens were introduced, followed by nursery schools in 1971, too late for him). Elementary schools were organized according to the old model: five years of attendance and a demanding final exam. But here is the big novelty: in the past, having reached this point, he would have been obliged to choose between continuing his studies or doing occupational training (the path for most lower-middle class children). Now one could, nay had to, enrol in the single middle-years school. Introduced in 1962, it was one of the major reforms of the central-left government and perhaps the greatest intervention in the field of education in the entire Republican period. In this way the length of compulsory education was increased to eight years, favouring access to higher studies (from 1950 to 1970 secondary level pupils quadrupled from fewer than 400,000 to more than 1.6 million). The timing of this reform was also decisive because it was introduced at a time of economic expansion, reinforcing the idea that education played an important part in social mobility. This is why our the fictional boy's parents (discussed earlier) have insisted on his attending a course of upper-secondary school studies, a school sector which in spite of all the good intentions, had not yet experienced change and continued to be divided into technical-occupational institutions and high schools.[26]

The young boy has therefore chosen a technical institute ('so as to have a trade under your belt,' as his father suggested). But while he is at school something happens. Great unrest invades the school and university world, and students take to the streets on demo after demo, either by themselves or together with demonstrating workers. They talk about the right to study, demand that obsolete courses be changed, notionistic, rote learning cease, authoritarian teachers be replaced and studies be disconnected from the existing 'power system'. The authorities do what they can to cope with the wave of demands, but instead of producing comprehensive reforms (which would need new ideas, political agreement, practical application, and resources—there is no such thing as a free meal), they issue, one after another, temporary, stop-gap provisions and petty piecemeal laws. So it transpires that the technical-occupational course becomes 'experimentally' longer, while even the dreaded *maturità* (matriculation) exam changes 'temporarily', and a later provision permits university entrance.[27] This is a fine state of affairs! Who would have said this young boy would get as far as university? The boy is enthusiastic and enrols in a science faculty, even though he would have liked to study humanities, which is all the rage. His first impression is a strange one, however. The university he has started to attend was created for a restricted elite. Though overwhelmed by a tide in flood, it still has not become a school for the masses. The lecture halls are inadequate and always full to capacity. The academic staff hold their lectures assisted by a small army of discontented, underpaid assistants. There are few laboratories, and even fewer grants and scholarships. Many students who, like ours, have come a long way, are finding themselves in difficulty. Luckily the atmosphere is stimulating. There is plenty of discussion about study and politics, and he has made a lot of friends (including girls: by now 40 per cent of students are female).[28] During his second year enthusiasm wanes. Maintenance costs in the city are high. More flexibility in the choice of courses (another petty regulation) may have opened up new prospects but it has also lengthened the time span. A lot of the courses seem neither useful nor interesting, not forgetting that it would be a good thing to bring some money home. Then there is another doubt which the student does not dare to confide to his parents, namely that in the modern world of media a traditional education is not as important as it used to be. And, even worse, that piece of paper at the end will not guarantee social mobility. The boy has come to the conclusion that social selection thrown out of the door by law has come back in through the window. Culture is still a privilege. Other friends in his situation forge ahead, but he does not and decides to drop out. Nor is his story an isolated case, seeing that the number of graduates is much smaller than the number of drop-outs and foot-dragging *fuori corso* students.[29]

If the typical student of the time was in any case fortunate, for those on welfare it was like hitting the jackpot. Never in the country's history had the State offered so much. I will begin with health. What happens to a national health patient when he is sick? First to consider is continuity with what had gone on before. The patient had probably been enrolled in one of the many public or professional medical insurance schemes (with widely different levels of performance and assistance). The assigned doctor would have provided the first diagnosis and more severe cases would go to hospital (even this being paid partly by the medical insurance and partly by public funds). It was therefore a very fragmented and dishomogeneous system based on insurance, where private and public were continually interwoven (the Health Ministry was only created in 1958). The drive towards a more rational system was also linked to the change in pathology. The age of the big parasitic and infectious diseases such as tuberculosis and malaria was over, partly thanks to new medicines. On the contrary degenerative diseases like cancer and arteriosclerosis, or diseases of the cardiovascular system, were increasing so that medical treatment had to change and the emphasis shifted in favour of prevention. But there were huge interests at stake (public health spending from 1962 to 1972 rose from 3 to over 5 per cent of the GDP) and reforms were continually postponed. Finally, in 1968 the hospital system (IPAB) changed, to be converted into public law agencies. Ten more years of debate would be needed before complete health reform would be achieved, following the creation of the 'regions'. Inspired by the British example, the National Health Service was created in 1978, the key points being the organization of all welfare and health services in local units (USL), compulsory enrolment for all, equality of treatment, family protection, and responsibility for preventive care. Special attention was reserved for problem cases such as the physically handicapped, drug addiction, and pschiatric illness.[30] Of course the last-mentioned provisions have to be seen not only in their political and organizational aspects but also as part of an actual new 'culture' of the body, as well as the expansion of medical culture that went back a long time.[31]

However, the main expense was for neither health nor education. The real characteristic of the period was the high increase in redistribution costs. As happened in other European countries too, within public spending the 'exhaustive' expenses, that is what the state pays directly to meet benefits and services (education and health, but also housing and collective services) decreased in percentage, while there was an increase in money transfers (pensions, family allowance), that is the redistribution of money among different subjects. This happened partly because it was relatively easier to do and also because it did not increase the visible presence of the state in the market, so was more acceptable even to free traders.[32] It could also be argued that it was part of the return to privatization: better give the money to families for them to spend (also in favour of private concerns) than provide collective goods and services.

In actual fact, even in the real field of assistance (invalids, the physically handicapped) the situation was the one inherited from

Fascism, with a multitude of institutions, benevolent funds and different agencies looking after it with widely differing results (which explains why it was called the 'welfare jungle'). Its strong point, however was national insurance, entrusted to the big government-controlled agencies. Pensions for the employed improved rapidly, progressing during 1968–69 from being a contributive system to a retributive one (after 40 years of contributions, one could retire with a pension worth 80 per cent of one's last salary, which was then index-linked). Retirement pensions were introduced (obtainable after 35 years of contributions, and much less for some categories of civil servants—the so-called 'baby pensioners'). Old-age pensions were created, given to anybody over 65 years of age who was without any other income. National insurance was then broadened to various categories of self-employed workers (farmers, craftsmen, traders), frequently in the presence of very small contributions. There also remained special arrangements for some categories that guaranteed substantial privileges. If the subsidies for those laid off or unemployed are added, given in increasing measure through the reformed redundancy fund scheme (CIG) when firms got into difficulties, it is easy to understand how the budgets of agencies like INPS (National Insurance) began to go seriously adrift.[33]

Why did all this happen? There was undoubtedly an idealistic, egalitarian drive to lessen disproportion and relax social tension. There was the fact that these decisions had been made during a healthy period of labour expansion, which had made it seem that the basic source of contributions would go on expanding, so that bigger and bigger concessions were possible (the 1970s' crisis was to undermine this belief). But there were also politically motivated reasons. It became a way of acquiring consent so as to get specific social groups on board or, especially during the 1970s, it represented concessions to public demands by a weakened central-left coalition. The reverse side of the coin was a happy-go-lucky attitude to the running of the social security agencies, which had become real centres of power and source of votes, symbolic of party-led interests in managing the public resources (with shocking examples of degeneration as exemplified by the inflation of disability pensions).[34] Welfare assistance therefore got broader and broader, becoming all-inclusive, but without giving the same protection to everyone.

My fictional welfare recipient has been moderately gratified; however, a sword of Damocles hangs over his head. Who is paying for all this? To a large extent, he is, through taxes and national insurance contributions. The entire proceeds of revenues grew rapidly during the post-war period, sixfold from 1950 to 1970 and tenfold by 1980, thanks to greater affluence for the individual, the quotas of the employed (more easily taxable) work, and the increases in prices. The major tax reforms came between 1971 and 1973, when IVA (VAT) was introduced together with new progressive income taxes (especially IRPEF and IRPEG—Personal Income Tax and Corporation Tax). From now on direct taxes exceeded indirect taxes in Italy, as they did elsewhere. In parallel a formidable increase in social contributions was registered (in 1970 equal to 26,000,000 million against 40,000,000 million state revenues).[35] The charging process was not very satisfactory however, on account of problems caused by inefficient organization and political convenience, whereby some categories ended up highly taxed and others found evasion easy. To put it simply some welfare recipients pay their taxes, while his others has dodge them. The proceeds collected were not enough to warrant expanding this welfare system, not to mention the growing overall expenses of a highly interventionist State. So this is where phenomena of 'budgetry illusions'[36] came in, together with increasing doubts concerning the real beneficiaries of the redistribution (which worked horizontally, between categories as well as vertically), and here, too, was the basis for increasing public debt to act as a source of 'painless' financing, the interest on which would explode from the 1970s onwards.

As revealed by Brosio and Marchese, this was the painful point, because in actual fact the overall spending structure was very similar to that of other European countries. In Italy during 1970 it equalled 34 per cent of the GDP (compared with 39 per cent for Great Britain and Germany and 43 per cent for France). Of this quota 11 per cent was transferred (nearly all to pensions), one point less to institutional expenses and defence, and the same again to services (including education 4 per cent, health 4 per cent and housing 1 per cent),[37] 5 per cent to economic interventions (subsidies, etc), and 2 per cent to interest quotas. The distribution was very similar in the other countries, including the pensions part. However, within a decade Italy rose to the top of the spending classification (51 per cent of the GDP) on account of the growth of more or less all the factors, but pensions in particular (the most important item, equal to 13 per cent) and the interest quotas.[38] Despite these figures, many welfare recipients are not at all convinced they are any better off than their European counterparts. They feel that the services there are receiving are often low in quality, and the organization of them is inefficient, so that they have to use 'parallel' channels to get certain things,[39] while their pensions are barely sufficient (after all 80 per cent of a low salary does not amount to much). They argue that there is a problem of service quality as well as quantity, that the increases in public spending are partly due to purely budget-based factors, that all these numbers are percentages and therefore reflect very different real transfers to the people (and decidedly lower in Italy than elsewhere). They are never satisfied! Or maybe they just expects too much.

9

Advertising and Production

Whoever had one can remember her well. She was soft and colourful, made of rubber, with a black and white body, partly covered with flowers, an ever-smiling mouth, big eyes, and pink ears and udders. Even her horns were not frightening and all the children loved her (and sang along 'tolon tolon, tolon tolon . . . eh oh!'). She was Carolina the Cow, a gadget which one got by collecting a big number of coupons found in Invernizzi processed cheese. The tale is told about a theft in Padua where two boys stole a grocery van (including all the gift coupons), but were arrested because they traded them in at a delicatessen to get Carolina the Cow.[1] This popular animal, with familiar comforting appearance, big soft round body (to symbolize the end of poverty) and rubbery material (hygienic and technological), miraculously represented the transition from a 'rural' past to an 'industrial' present. And this was equally true for its material essence and the product it was symbolically linked with: packaged processed cheese, an industrial invention, perfectly white, homogeneous and digestible, in sealed individual portions. Conjuring up an idyllic image of nature served to dispel fears about the future: tradition giving reassurance over modernity. The success of this character was also a sign of things to come in the food world.

The tale of Carolina is interesting for another reason too. It reminds us of the role of advertising during this period. The growth of private consumption and launching of new products were spurring more and more companies to use forms of advertising, but there was something more as well, the shift from an industrial strategy focused mainly on the product (*product-oriented*) to one giving more attention to the selling side and the market (*market-oriented*). In other words it was the triumph of a set of policies related to sales that included, but did not stop at, advertising, and also involved pricing, selling strategies, branding, consumer research, and so forth, all under the name of *marketing*, which spread across Europe from America.[2] According to Richard Tedlow's timeline, the importance of these policies depended on the historical moment. The first stage of the market, geographical fragmentation (approximately up to 1880), was characterized by the absence of a unified market and the prevalence of local products sold loose, except for rare exceptions. The second stage, unification (from the end of the 19th to halfway through the 20th century), depended on modern means of transport and communication, and saw the growth of a truly national market, with big companies and famous brands capable of selling to the entire population. Finally, the third stage, a segmented market, corresponded to the mature process, first appearing during the last decades of the 20th century. In this model the consumer is ever more demanding and differentiated (by income, age, and culture), competition between companies is merciless and the media and advertising play a highly important role. It is not enough to produce; it is increasingly important to know how to sell.[3]

It was within this change of perspective, which had only concerned a limited number of food and textile firms before, that investment in advertising began to grow in Italy too, though remaining on the whole far more contained than in other countries. At the same time, the great increase in available media helped to give advertising a social visibility it had not had before. As a result more and more studies and analyses define it as a reflection or stimulus of the changes, a suggestive, alluring and manipulating mechanism. But what is it really? It may have been nothing more than a 'literary field', to use a Foucaultian term, that is a historical and concrete 'discourse' through which knowledge is communicated as a text. It is therefore constructed in time, has its own traditions and narrative forms, its own fashions, as well as its own theoretical, practical, and national, but above all international (American) points of reference. Indeed, it is often self-referencing. It also has its own specific economic dimension determined by the investments it receives from industry, giving it size and shape, so doing research on consumption based only on advertising itself is risky and can create a somewhat distorted picture. The contents may be an original creation by the agency with little reference to contemporary customs or they may reflect a specific request by the investors. Worse still, investments in advertising concern products and sectors in a selective way (the automobile industry, which does the most commissioning, is over-advertised, while widely used products that cost very little are completely absent, for example). With all this—indeed, because of all this—advertising represents an important means of creating an identity in contemporary society. Advertising is a narrative.

As said before many things changed a lot during this period[4] and advertising methods changed radically. From a technological aspect, spectacular posters such as those by Leonetto Cappiello and Fortunato Depero, or the ones Dudovich created for la Rinascente, now seemed obsolete. The emphasis was no longer on the creative drive of the designer-artist alone but on a precise division of labour in the agency, between the art director who looked after the images, and the copywriter who wrote slogans, texts, and even the musical jingles. To the first Italian agencies of the 1930s (and the very special one founded in Turin by Armando Testi in 1946) would be added, in early 1950s Milan, branches of the great American and British firms (J. Walter Thompson to start with, and then Lintas, McCann-Erickson, Young & Rubicam), which brought with them rich contracts with American companies and a set of working techniques that were a master class for Italy and the rest of the world as well.

The early posters were also obsolete from a scientific aspect. Advertising theory at the start of the century had been mainly based on psychology.[5] It was believed that a poster should impress the consumer using a strong and continually repeated message, in order to exert great persuasive power (the same theories were used in First World War propaganda). Its success depended almost entirely on how stimulating it was, the receiver being easily conditioned. In the United States research in applied psychology soon brought about a greater interest in experimentation (partly because advertising agencies had discovered the strange fact that consumers put up 'resistance' and would not rush out to buy, or to vote, as they were supposed to). It was suspected that consumers were 'filtering' the messages, not only on account of their individual tastes and preferences (as the psychological approach suggested), but also their social position, income, gender, age, and education. There was no such thing as a typical consumer, but many different groups with different lifestyles. It was in fact the sociological approach, which ushered in a heyday of research in this field, thanks to the techniques of quantitative analysis developed by Gallup and Nielsen between the two wars. The first research institute in Italy was Doxa, founded in 1946 by Pierpaolo Luzzatto Fegiz with the support of IBM,[6] but there was also a real boom of initiatives financed by the industrial world, including Misura, directed by Francesco Alberoni and sponsored by Bassetti, which specialized in motivational research (in the 1970s psychology would cleverly combine both quantitative and qualitative aspects).[7] In other words, as advertising is a science as well as a technique, before creating any message, careful inquiries into the market have to be made.

Lastly, the old posters were obsolete because of the language. Slogans and images had changed and were being simplified to adapt to the current communication styles, a mass public and different means of communication, so that the campaign itself had to know how to 'talk' through the printed word (which still collected the lion's share of investments), television (where advertising was strictly limited to *Carosello*), the radio and, to a lesser extent, roadside posters and cinema screen time. Furthermore, talking about advertising, we note how it was the channel connecting not only industry and media, but also industry and politics. The public advertising agency, SIPRA's habit of conceding prime television spots and space in party-linked (or at least party-sympathizing) newspapers, in an all-in 'packet', so as to guarantee a form of financing, is well known.

If consumers showed themselves unwilling to bend to preconceived theories, so did businessmen. The historic model of British style industrialization envisaged progressive growth from small- and medium-sized firms to large managerial companies and from 'traditional', labour-intensive sectors to 'modern', capital-intensive sectors. In Italy things were somewhat different. Large-scale industry hardly ever took over completely, except in some specific sectors (culminating at the end of the 1960s, and the following crisis landed them in serious difficulties). Instead, there was widespread success for small-time, 'Manchester-style' businesses. It was during the 1950s, in northern regions that wine cellars and workshops filled up with low-cost, secondhand lathes, cutting tools and machinery, and factory workers and craftsmen started to supplement their wages with extra jobs or became cheap sub-contractors to bigger firms. The traditional sectors (those producing consumer goods, in fact) held on to their important role and evolved in their turn. Furthermore, the highly productive industrial triangle was progressively extended to new areas, in north east and central Italy, where the labour division tended to be horizontal rather than vertical, family connections continued to exist, and there were strong links with the territory (Alfred Marshall's industrial districts). By adding to this the international expansion that characterized the period and strong interaction with European Community countries like Germany and France (so that some academics talk of export-led growth), the whole picture is in front of us and it helps begin to understand how it was Italian entrepreneurs themselves who created the boom in consumer goods.[8]

Of course in such dynamic sectors as the chemical and mechanical industries the big companies, including state-run ones, were certainly making their presence felt. But it was a complex scenario. Take the chemical industry' role played by Montecatini in producing plastics and synthetic fibres, which were then used in many end-products, has been shown The most spectacular growth was in detergents, however, partly helped by the spread of washing machines. There are both technological and commercial reasons for this. Synthetic detergents were spreading far and wide (researched in Germany before the war, then mostly patented in the United States) and an international war broke out among the leading world groups to secure market shares, in which enormous sums had been invested and major advertising agencies were mobilized.[9] American Procter & Gamble, launching Tide, was the first, followed during the 1960s by Dash (which would become the Italian leader). Unilever produced Omo first and Bio Presto later. Colgate-Palmolive put out Olà, Ajax, and Ariel (the first 'second generation' detergent based on enzymes). The German Henkel also secured a good place with Dixan as did the Italian Mira Lanza firm, an old Genoese maker of soap and candles, which prospered thanks to Ava detergent and the little chick Calimero, while Bologna-based Panigal made its mark with the 'Sole' brand. The phenomenon puzzled a lot of people. What was the meaning of this great boom in humble little products destined for housewives? Was it connected with the new idea of a clean home? Was it the triumph of technology in every single aspect of daily life? Did it have any influence on the role of women? As always, technology and economics played their part in the cultural picture. The final result would be supremacy for consumer products like cleansing agents and household detergents together with the early establishment of international oligopolies (by the end of the 1960s big groups already controlled two thirds of the Italian market).

Things were different for the mechanical industries. Fiat, which was admired earlier as a prime example, easily met the needs of the domestic market. Of the cars on the road in Italy, 80 per cent were still Italian in 1975 (63 per cent of them were Fiat, followed by Lancia-Autobianchi, Alfa Romeo, and Innocenti). And things were even better for motorcycles. Piaggio's Vespa, manufactured at Pontedera by a firm with a great aeronautical tradition, was selling in Italy and abroad; Lambretta was turned out by Innocenti from an impressive factory in Milan up to 1971; while more custom-built high performance motorcyles (Malaguti, Guzzi, Gilera, and Ducati) launched Italian brands into the sporting world.[10]

The most original innovations, however, came from the field of electrical appliances. It is here that we come across a number of people, all of them outside big business, who can be seen as embodying the economic miracle. At Comerio, near Varese, Giovanni Borghi set up a small factory making cookers and water heaters and in 1950 started to make modern, square-cut, small, yet highly useful refrigerators, using automation and avant-garde technology, such as cooling with compressors (produced by Necchi and Fiat) and new insulation materials like polyurethane. It was a dazzling success, which placed Ignis at the top of the domestic market and in 1970 helped Italy to become the world's leading manufacturer of refrigerators, alongside the United States. The same thing happened with washing machines: on one side the dynamic, extrovert Borghi, great sports sponsor, on the other the discreet Eden Fumagalli of Brugherio, in the Brianza, who was co-founder with the Candy company family, a company producing washing machines smaller and simpler to use than the American or German, and best of all, less expensive. He, too, started out from small beginnings, adapting his mechanical workshop to the new needs of production— exactly as happened in the north east with Riccardo Zoppas at Conegliano Veneto (who made the first all-Italian dishwasher), and Lino Zanussi at Pordenone who enlarged his workshop to produce various electrical appliances, while Indesit of Turin became another of Italy's great success stories. Aristide Merloni began his activities at Fabriano in the Marches. From a country background, but with experience at Pinerolo behind him, he went from making kitchen scales and small cookers to electrical appliances with the Ariston brand name.[11]

The above-mentioned firms exported half their output and satisfied three quarters of the home market (even more if we consider the widespread practice of manufacturing products for non-Italian brands) in the face of such competition as Bosch and Philips. Two things brought them all together. The first was extensive recourse to advertising, necessary for launching new products, explaining how they worked and even more why they were needed in a modern home, where the part they played in creating a new vision of domesticity was by no means negligible.[12] The second was their inability to consolidate their position on the market after a lightning expansion, and the collapse of many of them when the market became saturated and the competition fiercer.[13]

Talking about consumer goods immediately brings the food sector to mind, which during these years underwent really important changes. So what if I return to the fictional kitchen introduced earlier? Here I am, catapulted back to compare a 1960s pantry with the turn-of-the-century one. I am immediately aware that everything in this kitchenette is in perfect order, with no smells, dust, or dirt. In fact, I cannot even see the food. It will be in the cupboards hanging on the walls, so I shall open one. Here I am, faced with a triumph of Italian tradition. Well stacked, one above the other, I can see several packets of pasta by Barilla, Agnese, and Amato—spaghetti and spaghettini, macaroni, penne, farfalle, rigatoni, fettuccine, tortellini—then Buitoni with its small bran and gluten pasta. Beside all this stands everything necessary to make good pasta sauces: tins of Cirio peeled tomatoes, De Rica ready-made pulped and creamed tomatoes, tubes of tomato concentrate (next to Calvé mayonnaise), jars of herbs, and other aromatics. In front of everything there are the unmistakable packets of Star cubes: ten magical little cubes which ensure a high quality broth when dissolved in hot water or improve the taste of any dish when a little is added. Pasta and conserves are the two pillars of a food sector worth about a tenth of the GDP, which has increased at the expense of agriculture, that is natural, non-processed produce. During these years the pasta industry underwent a considerable restructuring, with the success of a few big firms at the expense of countless little ones. To make sure of the leadership Pietro Barilla put a great deal of effort into the advertising: an easily identified logo, packaging in equally recognizable blue boxes, a constant presence in newspapers and on television (entrusted to the CPV company), targeting the modern woman ('there is a Great Cook inside you . . . and Barilla will reveal her'), and counting on outstanding testimonials, from the singer Mina for example.[14]

The canning sector was particularly innovative, with the Fossati family starting Star from a small wholesale trading company in meat, to become one of the leading European groups challenging the German and Swiss cube monopolies. The surge in demand for preserved tomato (worth four fifths of the sector) further developed Cirio as well as De Rica from Emilia (whose products—to judge by the advertisement—even Silvester the cat would not dare to harm when in hot pursuit of Tweety Pie). But there are more tins in the pantry: Arrigoni peas and beans (cleaned and already boiled, legumes were back in favour thanks to their ease of preparation), and a pile of red tins with a nice Swiss cow on top. This is the Simmenthal meat in gelatine, created by the Sada family from Crescenzago outside Milan. It started out as canned food for the army and succeeded in converting its image from soldiers' 'rations' into a convenient family lunch, taking advantage of both sport (as sponsor for the Milan basketball team, eternally at war with its arch rival Ignis from Varese) and advertising (the comedian Walter Chiari persuading us with a wink and a smile: 'Be cool: eat more meat, eat more Simmenthal'). The promotion focused on how practical and healthy it was, backed up by dieticians and repeated in all the women's magazines: eating more meat puts you in better physical shape. For this reason other brands were also successful, like Manzotin ('home-cooked meat'), which went on to launch Rio Mare tinned tuna, and Montana by Cremonini from Modena (which instead trusted its advertising fortune to Gringo, a tough western guy—'Down here with the herd and the cowboys| there is always one too many'—invariably ending with a tremendous gunfight à la High Noon).[15]

As well as the ready-ground Paulista coffee (made famous by the spot with the mysterious horseman and Carmencita in the boundless Pampas), together with flour, rice, and a good reserve of sugar, in the cabinet there is a neat row of condiments: vinegar, olive oil made by Bertolli, Dante, or Sasso (each insisting on its quality and lightness; Sasso oil became famous for its 'no more belly' slogan); and the novelty of seed oil: witness a fine tin of Topazio oil (to be succeeded by Olio Cuore, thanks to which actor Nino Castelnuovo will go on vaulting over fences for ever) and various other seed oils following on. Consumption of these oils boomed in a very short space of time. In 1950 it was less than a litre per person but by 1970 had reached 10 litres, equalling olive oil (which meanwhile had 'only' doubled). Seed oils cost less and were suitable to all kinds of cooking (frying replaced the poor person's habit of boiling) and were pushed by powerful publicity often, even here, the work of foreign multinationals. They were accompanied by another new product: Gradina margarine, launched in 1954 by Unilever (which had just acquired Gaslini-Arrigoni in Italy). The product was presented as completely vegetable, healthy, light, and a cheaper replacement for butter (which, in fact, was one of the few foodstuffs that did not increase). An advert from 1958 shows a housewife serving spaghetti to a child and her husband who compliments her: 'Good girl—how right you were—Gradina's really good' (and all for 60 lire a 100-gram package). Here we have the first hint of a health philosophy that would fully assert itself in the next few years.

Opening the next cupboard, instead of food there are thick glass beakers and white crockery (practical and pleasing to look at, but less showy than in the past—the 'best' sets, wedding presents, are stored elsewhere). There is cutlery and every kind of utensil, a Bialetti coffee maker (the man with the moustache), accurate scales, a San Giorgio Proteus (the Italian version of an American food processor, perhaps a Kitchen Aid with countless accessories for blending, cutting, and mincing)—equipment that was to change both the consistency and appearance of food.[16] It is almost like being in a laboratory; the art of cooking seems to have turned into a study in precision, with recipes and times to be followed to the last letter, almost as were being in one of those mythical American kitchens (probably the hostess's dream). Gone are the copper pans and earthenware cooking pots. Here instead is a well-equipped set of pots and pans, frying pans, casseroles, baking tins and pie dishes of steel, aluminium, and the new tempered glass (the famous Pyrex, the first time kitchen ware could actually be brought to the table!)—it will be a bit longer before the ones with non-stick bottom linings of Teflon are seen (at least until Du Pont places the new material on the market in a big way). A Lagostina stainless steel pressure cooker is enthroned in front of everything. Manufactured by a firm from Omegna, which started out by making tableware, it is the embodiment of the new kitchen, allowing the preparation of elaborate dishes while saving time and money and making everything tender and appetizing. It is safe and technological, long-lasting and easy to clean. To sum up, it 'interprets' traditional recipes with a minimum of effort. What it also does, however, is bring out the contradiction between a culinary style that cherishes the past and home-made things while being in love with technology at the same time. But the 'Linea' advertisement on TV, created with a single stroke of the pen, is so attractive![17]

Here is the third cabinet. How heavenly for a sweet tooth! It is evident why sugar consumption tripled from the post-war years reaching 28 kilograms per person by 1970! It is also the reason why the average daily calorie intake exceeded the 3000 level.[18] In fact, here is an impressive number of biscuits, sweets, and snacks, seeing that the sector grew by almost 8 per cent between the 1950s and '60s, targeting children in particular. In front there is a huge Motta Panettone (but it could easily have been an Alemagna). The panettone is the hallmark of the economic miracle that transformed an ordinary Milanese cake into the symbol of Christmas. Motta and Alemagna both expanded during the post-war period, when sugar and prime materials were again available, creating a vast distribution network and helping to change Italians' eating habits. Another big protagonist of the time was Pavesi of Novara, already famous for its little biscuits called Pavesini. Pavesi launched two great innovations, the first being the *autogrills* (motorway restaurants), refreshment facilities along the motorways with their futuristic architecture punctuating the scenery and catching the imagination of the 1960s (the first to open was on the Turin–Milan stretch in 1950). The second innovation was its crackers, another new product of American origin: crisp, light, and with low calorie content (contrary to what would happen abroad, the crackers started to be used instead of bread in the Italian diet—just like many centuries before, when maize was prepared according to local tradition and turned into polenta). Topo Gigio, the mouse puppet advertising Pavesini, became one of the most popular characters (alongside Calimero and Pippo the hippopotamus), soon to be emulated by the valiant Lancillotto who created chaos but left everything tidy, and later by the ravenous Joe Condor.

If all these great names were soon to enter into the sphere of state-owned SME corporation, it would not happen to another one, again from Piedmont—Ferrero—which built its fortune on a creamy spread consisting of cocoa and local hazel nuts. It calls itself Nutella, and here it is in a fine glass container that clearly displays what is inside and can be used afterwards as a drinking glass. There are other boxes of biscuits, too: Doria snowdrops ('Tacabanda'), Saiwa (a Genoese firm that would grow rapidly) and Plasmon for babies (associated with the curious figure of a gladiator or half-naked Roman about to hammer and chisel a marble column). Then there are chocolate snacks by Talmone of '*Miguel so' mi*'(owned by Venchi, after a project to create a chocolate pole with Gualino failed during the 1920s—but later on it will be managed by Sindona), and finally the sweets: Dufour, Alemagna Charms, ('Sweets for our time'), the Ambrosoli ones with honey (perhaps because of the persuasive little chorus '*Bella dolce mammina. Dacci la caramellina...*' ('Sweet pretty little mummy. Give us the pretty little sweet....'). In one corner there is a packet of Orzoro, soluble barley for infants, conjuring up scarecrow figures, and lastly a canister of Fabbri black cherries, associated with a famous pirate advertisement.[19]

It is interesting to note how commercial strategies paid a lot of attention to age and gender. Cooking products, whether completely cooked or more often half prepared (conserves, condiments, dry pasta, baking powders, cake and pudding mixes), went straight for the house-wife. They could be identified through their packaging, which was 'technical', disposable, communicative and functional. Sweet products instead targeted children and the advertising shows this, often with puppets and animated cartoons, lively coloured packages of cardboard or plastic derivatives (relegating Grandma's beautiful boxes to the attic). It was not until the 1970–80s, however, that the sweets sector, the second most important among foodstuffs, would try for bigger increases among adult consumers. In the period we are examining children were expected to grow quickly, eat and be happy, and not suffer the privations associated with the past generations. There were, then, food products aimed at the young in general. First came ice cream, with Algida—a firm with factories in Campania and Sardinia—in the lead. Ice creams and water ices belong to a very ancient Italian tradition, of course (in 1775 Filippo Baldini wrote a specific treatise about water ices complete with recipes and doses).[20] The problem here is how to include them in industrialised production which favours 'ice cream that can be eaten in the street', laden with social connotations, full of energy and social daring ('Can I say something? There's an Algida down there that's making my mouth water'). The second product was gum, that is chew-ing gum. In the United States it had had a long tradition partly to do with the military, since it was included in the official rations given out during the Second World War, on the grounds that it cleaned the teeth, partly mitigated hunger and thirst, kept attention awake and relaxed the nerves. Associations with popular culture followed, especially in sport and music. Out of all this, in 1946, the two Perfetti brothers of Lainate had the idea of using their Dolcificio Lombardo plant to make an American type gum with an American name, Brooklyn, 'the gum from the bridge'. It was the start of a great commercial success in Italy, as it had been in America (with Wrigley's). But it would have deep repercussions on the Mexican forests where latex gum was produced, though on a smaller scale to what had happened during previous centuries where coffee and tobacco were concerned.[21]

I will now open the refrigerator. How different from the old larder where the household had had to be contented with dried stuff! This is the realm of fresh produce, with a profusion of citrus and other fruit, vegetables and tomatoes, consumed in quantities never seen before, with increases of 30 or even 50 per cent in two decades.[22] I can now see a balance between the two mainstays of the kitchen: heat for cooking and cold for conservation. Whereas the stove/cooker had entered the domestic scene many decades before, determining culinary practices, now it is the refrigerator that makes its presence felt, switching the diet towards highly perishable food.[23] The next find is fish (not much, the yearly consumption per person was 7 kilograms compared with 20 for beef), already cut meat: slices, steak (or rather beefsteak, another British word to add to the list, together with cocktail, snack, picnic, shaker, party, bar, toast, etc.), which will become an essential part of a 'typical' lunch (in the middle of the day—first course pasta, second course probably sliced meat and vegetables, cheese: optional, dessert: fruit and coffee or, on occasion, cake). The evening meal is a lighter, simpler menu. There is also a Negronetto salame (it is bound to be there after the success of the Silver Valley sheriff), eggs, butter, and Gradina margarine (I could have bet on that!). Then an enormous quantity of cheese, inside a plastic cheese box; some big pieces wrapped in white paper, others already packaged: Locatelli, Galbani, Invernizzi, and Auricchio, processed cheese in cubes, fresh and mature, in single portions or family packs. It is no surprise that this is one of the leading items in the food sector. In the bottle rack there is wine that has already been opened (I can't read the label: perhaps Folonari or an Asti, or Riccadonna sparkling wine), a Dreher and a Peroni beer (with its allusion to the blonde mirage in the desert), a bottle of Recoaro mineral water (Lora water acclaimed by Captain *Trinchetto* (Foremast) who always exaggerated a little: 'Pipe down Trinchetto!')—San Pellegrino and Sangemini for babies were doing well (although the mineral water boom is yet to come). Of course there are two small bottles of Coca Cola. What about milk? Here it is, in a most modern tetrapak (composite of cardboard lined with polythene) packet, that has just replaced the traditional glass bottle, and next to it is a packet of the very latest UHT milk (ultra high temperature), that is, brought for a few seconds to 140 degrees to make it keep for a long time. Such is progress.

Compared to the old larder here there are various industrial, trademarked foods (as well as many loose products, like meat and fish, fruit and vegetables, cakes and specialities). This transition led to more standardized products where shape, colour, and taste are concerned. Biscuits are invariably all the same (cooked in the same way, with the same shape and colour, and all with an identical taste). The same is true for fresh produce (cheese no longer has the old crust, malodorous creamy centre and the mould that appeared as soon as it was opened). In fact, it could be said that all strong smells have disappeared. The new concern for hygiene and cleanliness discussed already is fully confirmed here. Wrappings take on a conspicuous role, for both communication purposes and protection and hygiene for the products, and they use new materials too. The inevitable consequence is a certain delocalization of the foodstuffs, following the centralization of production plants. But there is no need to exaggerate. If there is one aspect that characterizes Italian food it is its high fragmentation: there are few medium-sized to large industrial plants in the middle of a host of small to microscopic-sized local producers, often of extremely high quality with the result that the 1960s' pantry contains a mixture of loose produce, local commodities coming from semi-home-made origins and packaged foodstuffs from big industries (a small per cent of which are multinational). There is no shortage of the usual equivocal attitude towards anything new, especially after the explosion of various scandals linked to food sophistication—particularly where meat cubes were concerned—which gave rise to consumer boycotts and calls for tighter controls.[24] The new products, often selectively targeting certain kinds of customers, have not altogether ousted traditional cooking methods. The increasing consumption of sugar and meat has not undermined the use of pasta in the daily diet. On the contrary, the food industry has exalted typical food products, especially those from the south, and launched them onto the domestic market (continuing a practice already started during Fascism).[25] And this is where the myth of the 'Mediterranean diet' comes in, proposed by the American dietician Anael Keys in 1962. Impressed by the longevity of Cilento peasants, he sent out a health message to his fellow citizens to the effect that, both healthwise and culturally, it was better to use olive oil, eat less animal protein and more pasta, fresh fruit, and vegetables (a diet poor peasants surely followed, but through necessity and not always even then, but which was suggested as a means of restoring balance to the hypercalorific diet so typical of the United States and northern Europe).[26] On the whole, the different eating habits that separated north and south remained. In the 1960s there was still a 15 per cent difference in favour of the north, most significant where meat and sugar were concerned, but tending to diminish (it would flatten out completely in the 1980s, though maintaining some local peculiarities). The same can be said for a comparison between the Italian diet and the more calorific ones of the major European countries (where the weight of cultural differences continued to be felt).[27]

The simultaneous presence of big and small, delocalized and highly local, industrial and home-based processes, often with age-old traditions behind them and the ability to make quality goods at reasonable prices, seems to have been a characteristic of Italy's industrial development—for better or worse. This will also be found in another important sector, clothing.

I have already had a chance to observe this fictional family's clothes during an earlier domestic raid. Clothing has got better and increased in variety. The family is spending more, but from the technical, stylistic, and wearability point of view, and with more variety in sizes, the manufacturing industries have also made a lot of progress, to the extent that ready-made clothes are no longer synonymous with paltry, badly made garments. Tailors and dressmakers still existed, of course, as did high-quality artisan boutiques, but their role slowly diminished (in 1959 the Italian clothing industry produced only a few million garments, compared with 20 million in France and 35 million in Germany).[28] Among the first firms to launch ready-to-wear clothing was Apem (for Rinascente), Rosier, and Vogue Italiana in Milan, Max Mara in Reggio Emilia, Spagnoli in Perugia, and then big textile companies like Marzotto (with the Fuso d'oro trademark), Lanerossi (Lebole), and Rivetti *Gruppo finanziario tessile Gft* (Textile financial group GFT), for menswear (Facis and Sidi), and women (Cori), for which they consulted the famous high fashion dressmaker Biki.[29] It should also be pointed out that behind the ready-made clothing there was a long-standing textile industry, located in Lombardy and Piedmont, capable of providing wool, cotton, and silk fabrics as well as high quality synthetic fibres.

What was missing, however, was a market for high fashion Italian clothes, which could come anywhere near the undisputed capital of fashion, Paris, with its great houses like Dior and Pierre Cardin—though Italy did boast tailors and craftsmen much appreciated and well known abroad. The first efforts to create a typically Italian style went back to Fascist days and during the post-war years initiatives to create alternative catwalks to the French ones multiplied. Standing out among the many efforts to attract foreign (especially American) buyers is the attempt by Giovanni Battista Giorgini, an Italian buyer for such big American stores as Neiman Marcus, who organized the 1951 Fashion Show in Florence. On the Pitti Palace catwalk paraded big names in Italian tailoring, starting with the Florentine Emilio Pucci, but internal rivalry soon created a split between Florence (specializing in knitwear and high quality ready-made clothing) and Rome, where the accent was exclusively on high fashion (with names like Simonetta and Fontana)—while textile fairs remained in Milan (Mitam) and Turin for mass-produced clothes (Samia). The Italian fashion world had a polycentric birth but was immediately quite successful because of the quality of the fabric, poise of the models, elegant yet practical style, and competitive prices compared with Paris.

Nevertheless, there was no shortage of problems. The world of high fashion, elite by definition, remained a world apart with respect to the ready-to-wear industry, which also continued to grow, maintaining good sartorial standards (many firms still practised finishing by hand).[30] Basically there is still a reminder of the traditional social separation between the elitist creations of skilled craftsmen, expensive, original, excellently made and always different, and industrially turned out mass-produced clothes, which were cheap, reasonably well made but with scant regard for fashion. The market was changing, however. Consumers were becoming more affluent and demanding, and when they bought ready-made clothes they wanted them to be fashionable. Quality and price were not enough; one's clothes had to express much more from the individual and social point of view, they had to be a means of conveying 'distinction' as Bourdieu would say. There was more and more talk about democraticizing luxury, and 'fashion' presented itself as added value for all clothing. Women, for example, were giving clothes an increasingly personalized touch. A 1971 Doxa survey revealed how active women were in interpreting the concept of 'fashion', which they built up using several sources (different from what the experts would have predicted). First they studied magazines and found them useful for information and advice (62 per cent); then went window-shopping to see how clothes looked when they were on (59 per cent). Some way behind followed proposals from the world of high fashion, suggestions from tailors and the big stores, and what they saw well-dressed women wearing (around 40 per cent). Advice from favourite shopkeepers and friends also played its part.[31] In other words there was a great variety of information gleaned from press, fashion, and shopping sources but also from the street and personal evaluation. What can be said about the young then, who invented their own fashion or anti-fashion, continually changing points of reference and starting to buy from small shops specializing in 'youth wear', such as boutiques that managed to obtain limited quantities of the latest style garments and accessories in record time, using specialized workshops, where such items as blue jeans, mini skirts, tops, sweaters, battle tunics, and windcheaters could be found? Sales data from 1973 confirm new buying habits. There was an increase in casual wear for men and women (heavy jackets, tank tops, jeans). Knitwear enjoyed a real boom (with pullovers and sweaters), while ground was being lost by traditional clothing (overcoats, raincoats, women's dresses and suits, and men's shirts). By now the ready-made industry was responsible for 90 per cent of the sales of menswear and 80 per cent of women's.[32]

One last step was needed to consolidate development and make sure of the new public: the creation of an intermediate fashion level capable of combining the creativity and quality typical of high fashion with the advantages of mass production, thanks to direct contact between fashion and industry. This breakthrough came at the beginning of the 1970s, with the advent of a new figure, the fashion designer. Neither captain of industry nor traditional tailor, he would devise collections, each bearing the stamp of his own particular style, work together with the textile firms, follow the making of his creations step by step, and present them at highly publicized fashion shows. He would also be familiar with the specialized press and deal with the buyers and distribution aspects. In this way textile and clothing firms were able to meet the needs of a new kind of customer, who refused to be dictated to by high fashion and was looking not just for something nice to wear, but for her own personal style and a possible way of being (all at relatively accessible prices).[33] In a Milan that could offer modern infrastructure, adequate trade fair space for display purposes (Milanovendemoda, Modit), media attention, international connections, closeness to industry and a variegated hinterland of quality tailoring, the 'fashion system' came into being and the first designer labels made their mark: Gianni Versace, Giorgio Armani, Valentino Garavani, and many others.[34]

The same thing happened in the furnishings sectors. The coffee grinder in the kitchen, in the shape of a little dome (Subalpina), this functional looking washing machine, and plastic kitchen utensils (Kartell) but also, having a quick look outside the room, the armchair in the boy's room made entirely of plastic (Artemide), the elegant table lamp and ceiling light fixture (Arteluce), the streamlined sofa (Arteflex), the small electric fan (Vortice), the simple, modern chairs (Cassina)... all shapes of industrial design that give meaning to this house.

Once again, the origins can be traced back to the period between the two wars, with the work of architects like Terragni, who designed houses but also chairs in metal tubing, or Gio Ponti who designed new pottery for Richard Ginori and launched the Domus Nova low-cost line of furniture for Rinascente. During the 1950s and 1960s architects worked increasingly with small-time craftsmen as well as big firms, or created new companies themselves. Combining creativity with mass production became the password. An aesthetic trend rigorously based on simplicity of form and design was established, beating down costs and highlighting an object's material and technological content. It was the line, later known as 'Italian design' and, like fashion, had its strong points in flexible, high quality material, great personalities (Albini, the Castiglioni brothers, Gardella, Magistretti, Sottsass, Zanuso, and many others), 'institutional' initiatives (the Milan Triennial, Trade Fairs, Rinascente's 'Golden Compass' prize) and specialized publishing (*'Domus, Abitare, Casabella'*).[35] They designed objects for everyday use that transformed the aesthetics of the domestic landscape, drawing attention to humble ordinary objects and giving them a new importance (even a corkscrew or a plastic colander can enhance the home). The message they gave out was that all human space is important and anything can have an aesthetic dimension, thus breaking—or at least tarnishing—the taboo whereby aesthetic value was an exclusive prerogative of the social elite who could afford such costly items. It is no coincidence that many of the protagonists in this revolution were engaged in politics. The same process took place outside the home where, thanks to Pininfarina, Bertone, and Giugiaro later, magnificent cars and motorcycles could be seen on the road, while offices were being embellished with elegant furniture, efficient typewriters and calculating machines. Even in the bars espresso coffee machines became symbolic of the Italian look:[36] thus more democratization of luxury and different styles were being offered to the consumer.

The success of Italian design was based on a balance between price and quality, with its strong points in the ability to work with new technological materials like plastic, together with so-called 'noble' materials, and the ability to reinterpret typically artisan or foreign forms in modern terms. An example is Gino Ponti's 1957 Superleggera (Ultralight), a chair inspired by the traditional Chiavari chairs in interlaced wood and cane, but smaller, very lightweight and low in price (around 5,000 lire). Another example is the Ariston Unibloc. The problem was how to adapt the 'American kitchen' (big, modular, and with every possible technical invention) to Italy. Cost was one problem, space the other. Merloni entrusted designer Makio Hasuike with the task of creating a valid alternative, which came into production during the 1960s. It was a built-in kitchen unit with four or five fitted components in which the main electric appliances were encased (refrigerator, oven, and dishwasher), as well as several functional spaces, all covered with a single Franke stainless steel top with cooking burners, sink and generous working surface. Closed, it had the appearance of an aesthetic piece of modern furniture; when opened it revealed high-tech functionality. For the first time all the appliances made up a perfect single unit. The price was competitive, the dimensions modest (from 1 to 2.7 metres) and the aesthetic language alluring.[37]

Made in Italy was ready to take off.

10

Large-scale Distribution and 'American' Supermarkets

Supermarkets

Moscow, July 1959. The Americans prepare an exhibition in the Soviet capital which includes a perfectly functioning house (the 'standard' American home). Nixon and Khrushchev visit it and go into the kitchen. Here the American Vice President proudly points to a dishwasher and several electrical appliances, and explains that everything is designed to make everyday life simpler and more pleasant, using the latest technology (which is not only reserved just for rockets and armaments), and that in America all this is within the reach of the humblest worker. Why not allow people a free choice of the type of house, food, and ideas that they want, Nixon urges an increasingly irritated Khrushchev. . .

Rome, June 1956. The US Department of Agriculture and the National Association of Food Chains prepare an exhibition at EUR of an entire thousand-square-metre supermarket, with all the most modern equipment, shelves, counters, automatic checkouts, and twenty sales-girls circulating with trolleys among the 2,500 articles on display (all offered by American firms) to show how 'self-service' works. In thirteen days 'Supermarkets—USA' is visited by 450,000 people and several commercial operator groups, arousing great interest also among the media.[1]

The Moscow episode (going down in history as the *kitchen debate*) and the Roman supermarket are only two examples of American strategy, which during the 1950–60s aimed at spreading the American way of life as widely as possible, using examples of how the United States were capable of guaranteeing consumer goods in quantity and quality superior to all others, and with an implicit ideological message that the everyday desires of the common man are just as important for the US administration as space exploration or scientific advancement. Furthermore, freedom of choice among different products guaranteed by the market economy is nothing more than a mirror image of the freedom of choice guaranteed by democracy.[2] Economic and political liberties are two sides of the same coin. It implies that a fulfilled life is a life full of 'things' that are bought individually, give satisfaction, and indicate a family's social position in a mobile society.

In this sociological construction the supermarket is an important element. Its spectacular display of every good thing sent from heaven, all to hand, ready to be bought, is but the embodiment of the idea of well-being and limitless abundance. It also constitutes an important new consumer space that transforms daily habits and routines. The King Kullen of Long Island, opened in 1930, is traditionally considered to have been the first modern supermarket. The spread of this commercial structure in the United States experienced a first wave during the great depression, thanks to its competitive prices, while the second wave started during the 1950s, due to an improving quality of life and the baby boom (in 1958 there were already over 20,000 supermarkets). In Europe it spread during post-Second World War years, when important food chain shops (like Tesco's and Sainsbury's in Britain or Tengelmann and Edeka in Germany) adopted the 'American' system, which was more efficient and pleasing to the public.[3]

Things in Italy were a little more complicated. We have seen the difficulties and delays in the development of department stores and popular emporia. The 1971 census ascertained the presence of 1,180,000 commercial enterprises, with 2,700,000 employees, of which 93 per cent were individual firms with 2–5 employees. The bigger companies dealt with the wholesale trade (most located in Lombardy), while large-scale distribution was modest (only 550 department stores and popular stores selling 6.9 per cent of non-food commodities).[4] The commercial world was still characterized by networks of small shops that had actually experienced expansion, owing to the internal migrations (given that many found work here rather than in the big factories) and with the increased purchasing power of the population. It is no surprise that non-food shops grew more quickly than food ones, in order to meet the new consumer needs. Progress was particularly strong in clothing, jewellery, haberdashery, perfumes, luggage items, flowers, sanitary goods, science and sports equipment, stationery, radios, smokers requisites, and anything to do with household goods and furnishings, while difficulties were experienced by general stores, hatters, and shops selling fabrics. The picture reflects improved living standards, more attention to the body and the home, and greater

Table 7 Traditional commerce and large–scale distribution, 1956–2006

Years	Number of traditional food shops	Number of traditional non–food shops	Total
1956–60	413,967	367,275	781,242
1961–70	491,681	506,270	997,951
1971–80	464,682	547,525	1,012,207
1981–90	397,719	636,859	1,034,578
1991–2000	340,861	675,737	1,016,598
2000–05			761,588

Types of business — year 2006	Number selling place	Market share (%)
Hypermarkets	355	13.0
Supermarkets (400/2499 sq. m.)	8,410	41.2
Self service (100–399 sq. m.)	6,495	8.8
Hard Discount	3,220	5.8
Traditional shops	177,000	20.9
Itinerant sellers and others	30,000	10.3
Total food selling	225,480	100.0
Hypermarkets and supermarkets (non–food sales)	–	7.6
Department stores	710	2.1
Large–scale and specialised chain stores	1,946	25.5
Traditional shops	487,000	50.3
Itinerant sellers and others	98,000	14.5
Total non–food selling	587,656	100.0

Source: elaborations on ISTAT, *Sommario di statistiche storiche 1926–1985*, Rome (1986); Ibid. *Annuario statistico italiano*, years 1985–2006; FAID (Federdistribuzione), *Mappa del sistema distributivo italiano*, 2007.

mobility, but it also shows how the clothing industry was expanding (throwing tailors and fabric-selling shops into crisis) and, incidentally, the power of fashion (causing a decline in the wearing of hats). Big changes can be noted in the food sector, too. There were increases for shops selling fresh and highly prized commodities (grocers, fruit and vegetable sellers, dairy shops, bakers, delicatessens, and butchers), while non-specialized sellers of general goods, cooked foods, tripe shops, and bazaars lost ground (and the poor street trader even more so) (See Table 7). So what about the supermarkets? The 1971 census reveals the presence of 607 (two thirds in the north), which affected commercial food consumption by a very modest 3.7 per cent. Yet their very existence had caused pandemonium.

To go back a few years, after the Rome exhibition and isolated attempts to apply the new self-service system (without any great results),[5] the first important supermarket company to make its mark in Italy was again the work of an American, and one of the wealthiest and most prominent men in his country, the millionaire Nelson A. Rockefeller, Standard Oil magnate and potential candidate for the White House. It was one of his New York companies, IBEC (International Basic Economy Corporation), with branches already in South America, which in 1957, opened a firm in Milan with mixed American and Italian capital (together with textile manufacturers Bernardo and Guido Caprotti, Crespi of *Corriere della Sera*, Marco Brunelli, and other minor associates): 'Supermarkets Italiani SPA'.[6] The venture opened in the midst of a thousand difficulties: lengthy bureaucratic procedures to obtain operating licences, strong resistance from small dealers, and concerns of a political nature. But the expertise of the American management and good reception from the public ensured rapid success.

Indeed, the polemics springing out of the pages of the daily newspapers and all the gossip and controversy increased its social impact, which was far greater than its market share actually warranted. So what did supermarkets represent for the Italian society of the time?

To find out, I will follow an elderly lady on her visit to the first shop opened by Supermarkets Italiani in November 1957. Weaving among the Vespas, station wagons and other cars parked outside (no need for a garage yet), we both enter a huge modern building with the word 'Supermarket' inscribed in large letters above it (in English, we note, and combining the sales system with the company name, just to be on the safe side!). By the way, on my journey here I noticed a large number of signs and illuminated advertisements, many of them in white and brightly coloured neon lights, which conferred a futuristic, Americanized aspect to Italian cities of the time: one of the ways commerce changes the urban landscape.

The first impression is of an efficient, well thought-out environment. The large single space is divided into long, regular aisles flanked by rows of shelves holding infinite piles of foodstuffs. The furnishings are simple and functional, signs and colour-coding neatly identifying the various departments. The colours are chiefly metallic and light, the floors polished and everything is spotlessly clean. Fluorescent tubes shed a white light. If the luxurious department stores were modelled on the theatre, here I see a different form of spectacle at work, based on efficiency, technology, and modernity. It has been said that for these characteristics a supermarket is reminiscent of a factory—but a factory dressed up out for a party, I might add. The generally sober profile is in deliberate contrast to the bright colours and variety of packages on display. There is background music and a pleasing atmosphere (as manager Boogaart will record: 'The shop is usually full of husbands and wives. The music plays continually and the entire shop has a holiday atmosphere. Our staff seem to be extraordinarily happy').[7] But to return to the lady shopper, after attentively scrutinizing the fruit and vegetable section (which she finds neatly packaged, but no loose merchandise) and buying bananas, she points her trolley straight towards the dairy products and buys butter and two cheeses (a high quality Italian one and the other Danish at a special price). It is noticeable that customers inspect the produce carefully before buying it. They are probably not used to buying everything—or nearly every-thing—already wrapped and are perhaps unfamiliar with many of the brands (after all, advertising is still in its early days). Indeed, many appear to be there just to look at the display of goods rather than actually buy any. The department arousing the most wonder is proba-bly the meat one: here is the meat, already cut up, arranged on a tray and wrapped in transparent film (another plastic derivative).[8] It can be looked at, turned over, and practically handled without endangering quality or hygiene. Nothing is hidden! The lady buys two small slices before heading for a refrigerated counter. What is inside? Quick-frozen products, naturally, a real novelty for those times. There is more fish than meat and vegetables (perhaps because of the difficulty of finding it fresh), but many customers, including our lady, look at it sceptically and go straight on. This is understandable, considering the idea they have of genuine and fresh food. After all, it has a different colour and consistency, and no smell.

Immediately behind is a small counter with two smiling salesgirls offering freshly made coffee. It smells and tastes good—a product of the supermarket itself—and the lady has them grind 100 grams on the spot. It must not be forgotten that these shops are not simply retailers of goods more or less industrially packaged, but are also partly producers. Supermarkets Italiani, for example, soon discovered that in many sectors the Italian food industry was not ready to meet the needs for quality, quantity, and product control, or the punctual delivery required by a supermarket, so it started to produce its own bread, pasta, and ice cream, roast its own coffee and slice and wrap its own delicatessen goods and cheese, all at very competitive prices (the American managers were particularly proud of this, especially where the pasta was concerned: 'The stores have met with a perfect reception. [...] The products are of excellent quality and people make a 50 per cent saving. It was great to see one of the Italians' favourite foods being sold at a price they had never seen before').[9] In other cases direct agreements were made with foreign firms, skipping the long chain of middle men, and there was no shortage of early experiments with commercial brands (that is exclusively made products commissioned from outside producers with a specific label). In other words, supermarkets have had an impact on the food industry itself.

Continuing to follow the lady customer, I see she has stopped to gaze at the tins of sliced pineapple and ready-made fruit salad (exotic fruit at last to give variety to the same old dessert!). Finally, after passing through the section dedicated to personal and household hygiene, adding washing machine detergent to her trolley, she reaches the checkout desks—those modern, high-tech tills, which made such an impression on the first visitors (as did the professional young cashiers). The total bill is not at all high (in any case, the pro capita spending in Italy was a third of the American average, so that Supermarkets Italiani had their trolleys and baskets made smaller than those in the United States, to avoid embarrassing their customers). The lady is satisfied and goes off clutching her bag of goodies (in the early days the assistants often had to run after new customers to stop them leaving with their trolleys, in the belief that they had to keep them and bring them back and forth every time).

From what I witnessed, however, and from what emerges from market research and reports submitted by the managers of the first supermarkets, consumer reactions were varied. A survey by IPSOA based on 500 customers explains the reasons for their choices as follows: 133 people preferred supermarkets for the low prices, 116 for the variety, 69 for the speed of service, 62 for the freedom of choice, 47 for the quality, 34 for the hygiene, 8 for the fixed prices, and 35 for various other reasons.[10] This confirms the findings of previous Doxa surveys, which also showed how saving money tended to be greatest at the two extremes of the social scale. The least well off did so by reducing the quality of their purchases. The most affluent still went for high quality but bought in large amounts (partly because they had plenty of storage space available, together with capacious refrigerators). What characterized the middle classes, instead, was territorial mobility, so they would go in search of shops with the best prices. In this way, they all pursued the same aim, but with different strategies.[11] And there is more besides. I noticed young people inside the supermarket (as expected) but many old ones, too, like the lady I have been following. I would have expected older people to be more sceptical when faced with something new, but they turned out to be among the most faithful customers. This is because of the low prices, the chance to buy food in small quantities (avoiding any embarrassment) and the pleasure of spending some time in an enjoyable, well kept, air-conditioned environment—a new place for socializing, as it were. I also saw many immigrants, who found it easier to shop here. The very features that displeased some of the middle class where supermarkets were concerned (their sameness and lack of variety of choice, lack of human contact, and the fear that they were demeaning) were on the contrary precious in the eyes of a group struggling for social integration, and probably discriminated against in bars and shops, where everyone had known one another for years and spoke in dialect. It is significant that Supermarkets Italiani (which in 1961 had already passed completely into Italian hands, taken over by the Caprotti family, and afterward changed its name to Esselunga) was well aware of this 'democratizing' aspect of consumption and in 1966 displayed posters with a supermarket sales slip in the background and a hat in front (each time different—a lady's, a carabiniere's, and so on), accompanied by the words: 'Choice is the same for all'.[12]

What about gender, then? Women had naturally had a lot of contact with supermarkets, given that traditionally the task of doing the shopping fell on their shoulders. They found many products here, cleaned, cut, pre-cooked and ready to use. Several stages of food preparation were now accomplished industrially, which was very useful considering their family duties and increasing employment outside the home. They also played an important role as supermarket staff because, as is typical in the service sector, they represented a large part of the labour force up front and in the offices. There is a lack of studies of the lives of supermarket assistants but it is known that the internal discipline of the Italo-American supermarket was rigid. Absenteeism was combated by every available means. Married women were not employed. A clean

and tidy appearance was demanded. To compensate, pay was high for
the sector, producing continual applications for employment, and the
work environment was from many points of view pleasant and well
ordered.

But the real surprise is the number of men involved. Many of them
were to be seen fidgeting in the aisles, surrounded by packets of biscuits
and jars of tomato pur'ee (the internal reports of Supermarkets Italiani
confirm this impression: male customers accounted for 35 per cent
of the 70,000 that crowded into the store each week).[13] Why is this?
A sudden desire to help their wives with the shopping? A reversal of
roles? Nothing of the kind. It was simply that for many men, going to
the supermarket did not seem to be the same thing as burdening oneself
with the daily shopping routine. It aroused curiosity, led to the discovery of new, exotic and 'technically' interesting products (quick-frozen,
vacuum-packed, etc.). With the same budget it was possible to vary
the purchases, trying produce from far away places, for example (the
pineapple is excellent, but why not try a Chinese soup instead of pasta,
or these strange 'pizzoccheri', and as a main course, tinned Argentine
beef? Perhaps get a bit of top-quality Camembert—or would the
equally exotic Neapolitan mozzarella be better? Are *marshmallows*
good for the children?). Put simply, the time had come when choosing
food was no longer an exclusively female activity. No longer would
meals be based entirely on recipes mystically handed down from
mother to daughter. No longer would they be dictated by local tradition, but transformed into a cultural mix and indicative of a lifestyle
every member of the family wanted to take part in creating. Of course it
was not so much a question of food coming from abroad, since this was
still very limited, but dishes and produce from other Italian regions.
Large-scale distribution played an important role in overstepping local
boundaries and making typical products available at a national or at
least regional level, helping to create a cuisine that would be regarded
abroad as 'typically Italian'. Finally there was a practical motive: the
spreading habit of concentrating all the shopping into a once a week
visit to the supermarket (partly dictated by work commitments), meant
that the husband was needed (and the car if there was one). In fact the
whole family would join in the shopping ritual, given that supermarkets
were extending to the food sector the combination of entertainment
and consumption started a long time before. This is why the whole area
was so carefully looked after and every detail studied, to make the

time spent inside as pleasant and exciting as possible (including prize-winning competitions, surprise draws, free gifts, tasting samples, etc.).

Within the space of a few years many other supermarket chains appeared. Some important groups centred round regional life, such as Romana Supermarkets, which expanded within the capital and in 1966 passed into the public sphere as GS, or the Piedmontese and Ligurian supermarkets of the Garosci family, the Bennet group of Como businessman Ratti, Bastianello's and Gioel's Venetian PAM.[14] Expansion on the national level was also seen, thanks to two major department store chains, Rinascente and Standa, though they followed different strategies. The first founded an autonomous company of supermarkets, SMA which spread all over the country due to a policy of taking over smaller firms and opening new sales outlets, to the extent that by 1962 there were already 23 branches in action (it was only in a few cases that they chose to put SMA together with UPIMs). Standa instead chose to integrate food sales in their own stores (with the advertising slogan 'Standa has it all') and the choice proved a successful one, leading to great expansion. Added to these groups were many other small- to medium-sized ventures, with the result that many new inaugurations (and at times rapid closures) were seen everywhere, where supermarkets and small-sized mini-supermarkets (the 'super-ettes') were concerned. But what proved especially noteworthy were two other new forms. The first was associated sales, which blossomed during these years (the first voluntary union between wholesalers and retailers was Végé in 1959 promoted by Emilio Lombardini and the Garosci brothers, followed by Despar and A&O Selex, while buying groups among retailers were much more numerous). The second con-sisted of co-ops, which were bouncing back (by 1971 Co-op Italia already had 71 supermarkets and 700 mini-markets; in 1962 Conad was founded in Bologna).[15] According to some 1971 statistics, out of the 607 existing supermarkets, 56 per cent belonged to large-scale distribution companies, 32 to independent dealers or associates and 12 to consumer cooperatives.[16] The picture is a variegated one, there-fore (incidentally, the period was also favourable for the development of new department stores, including one which would become another outstanding presence at national level, Coin of Venice). It must also be added that the growth of large-scale distribution in Italy was not just the result of social and economic factors, but also of a complex political game, which saw as players the trade unions of the category

(Confcommercio), numerous public bodies (Chambers of Commerce, prefectures, town councils, and finally the regions), and political parties belonging to the government and opposition. In terms of politics and corporations, commerce is a major battlefield in Italy, much more so than in north European countries. Legally speaking, the 1971 settlement for the sector, strongly supported by Confcommercio and voted for by all the parties, assigned a fundamental planning role to local bodies, thus applying a definite brake on the development of large-scale distribution.[17]

Besides the practical aspects of its spread, the supermarket brought about another revolution in consumption comparable to what happened with the big department stores in the nineteenth century (and is why it is still the most widespread form of large-scale food distribution in Italy today). It helped to transform habits, made contact with merchandise direct and immediate, strengthened the role of brands (how else would it have been possible to choose between the host of products arrayed on the shelves?), presented new products, boosted the role of packaging,[18] speeded up processes in the industrial preparation of food, and became the bridgehead for various multinationals in Italy. At the same time it was not at all subservient to the industrial giants, it put its own particular sales and even production policies into action, created a price revolution thanks to expert management (in which self service was just the superficial aspect, as many would-be entrepreneurs found to their cost). And, as always, the consumers had their own personal ways of treating this novelty, thus completing the cycle.

There is, then, something else that links supermarkets with the big department stores: their cultural and social impact. As had happened eighty years before, many deemed the supermarket the archetype of a new age, representing modernity in both its positive and negative aspects: on one side, abundance of produce for all, consumer freedom, the end of penury; on the other,—with its long, goods-filled shelves— fear of uniformity, anonymity and infinite, disconcerting repetition. The supermarket as a concept quickly passed to the artistic and literary field, the most famous case surely that of Andy Warhol, who made series of consumer icons the key to his pop art. In 1964 he actually went so far as to exhibit, at the Bianchini Art Gallery in New York, a real-life supermarket with shelves, posters, fluorescent lights, stacks of tins, and huge boxes of products. The goods displayed were even on sale (creating a deliberately fuzzy boundary between art and reality: tins of

Campbell's soup signed by Warhol (18 dollars each), plastic steaks by Mary Inman (27 dollars), chromium-plated melons by Robert Watts (125 dollars) and, if short of money, at least one of Watts's eggs could be purchased for 2 dollars.[19] All to illustrate an ironic celebration of unlimited consumption.

In Italy, too, supermarkets quickly made their presence felt in the world of art, but with decidedly critical tones. In his novel *Vita agra*, the writer Luciano Bianciardi paints a cruel portrait of one of them. Just like an assembly line, the supermarket alienates and dehumanizes both customers and sales assistants:

> On entering, you are given a little trolley made of steel wire, and you have to fill it with goods and produce. They sell everything and anything. The customers go around, eyes bulging due to the bright lights and pounding music. They have forgotten how to blink. They can't see you. Now and then they crash their trolley into your back. With Macumba gestures they pull down boxes from the piles and drop them into the right compartment. Nobody says a word; with all the music and continual thump, thump, thump of the tills conversation would be drowned out anyway. [. . .]
>
> The tills are always active at the checkout. Fingers jump over the keys like crazy grasshoppers. The cashiers wear little blue berets bearing the name of the big shop. Without batting an eyelid they stare fixedly at the little numbers, and day by day their faces become paler and more worn out, with bags under their eyes a darker blue and neck more shrivelled, like so many tortoises.
>
> There are also black louts and southerners, with boxes and special luggage carriers which they will use to drag their piles of shopping back to the car: twelve bottles of gassy water, ten packets of coarse biscuits, olives with or without stones, sanitary towels for the wife, because they have been careful this month too, a plastic bone for the poodle, twenty tins of tomatoes (tomato, they say), a patented American potato peeler which can be used left-handed as well, breadsticks, and French loaves, savouries, cocktail sticks, toothpicks and serviettes with fancy designs, how delightful, how amusing!
>
> I always say, put in a stack of books and, blind as they are, they would even buy those.[20]

The searing look of an intellectual, at a world that appears distant and vulgar, partners Italo Calvino's lively description of the tragi-comic attempts by poor Marcovaldo to play his part in the consumer ritual like everyone else:

> During one of these evenings Marcovaldo was taking his family for a walk. Being without money their pastime was to watch others do their shopping [. . .]. The supermarket operated as a self-service. Those trolleys were there, like iron baskets with wheels and each customer pushed a trolley and filled it with every heaven-sent thing. Marcovaldo also got a trolley at the entrance. His wife got one, and so did each of their four children. [. . .]
>
> Well, if your trolley is empty and the others are full, it is bearable up to a certain point. Then envy takes over, heartbreak, and you can hold out no longer. So Marcovaldo, after telling his wife and children not to touch anything, went quickly around the banks of shelves, hid from his family and, taking a box of dates off a shelf, put it in his trolley. He just wanted to try the pleasure of taking it around for ten minutes, to show off what he had bought like everyone else, and then put it back where he had got it from: this box, and a bottle of fiery red sauce, a small packet of coffee and a blue pack of spaghetti. Marcovaldo was sure that, acting with discretion, he could for a quarter of an hour enjoy the pleasure of knowing how to choose a product, without even having to pay a cent. [. . .]
>
> All of a sudden the chase came to an end and there was a long empty space with fluorescent lights making the tiles shine. Marcovaldo stood there with his loaded trolley and at the end of that deserted space was the exit and check-out desk. His first instinct was to put his head down and charge at it pushing his trolley in front of him like a tank, and escape from the supermarket with his loot before the cashier could raise the alarm. [. . .]
>
> —Get back! Quickly! Get away from the check-out!—exclaimed Marcovaldo doing an about turn and hiding with all his loot behind the banks of shelves, before making a dash for it all doubled up as if under enemy fire, and disappearing down the aisle.[21]

Some intellectuals have speculated that there is an even deeper affinity between the new consumer places and modern culture. Sociologists like Moles and Dorfles maintain that one of the characteristics of societies today is *kitsch*, intended not so much in its original sense as the proliferation of objects of poor taste or paltry imitations, which could exist in any age, but as a historical expression of an abundance of goods to satisfy everyone's desire. Of course there are not rare, expensive goods, like the ones only the uppermost classes were privileged to own, but readily available cheap industrial objects. In a word, kitsch is a legacy of the industrial revolution and bourgeois society; it is modern mass society at large, which is why supermarkets and big department stores have become altars to this culture that finds fulfilment in consumption. The juxtaposition of so much merchandise we find inside them, therefore, is not coincidental or expressive of an efficiency-based logic, but the reflection of deep-seated values. An infinite number of products stretch out before our eyes, often mere substitutes for real luxuries or imitations of a style but representative of the material world that is the major system of reference for our culture. Seriality, imitation, cheapness, availability, simplicity: these are all fundamental qualities of kitsch merchandise that we may or may not like, and that may be polemically set against 'real' works of art, but they have a cultural significance that goes well beyond appearances.[22]

Whatever judgement one may wish to give, one thing is certain: supermarkets, like other consumer places, such as street markets, shops, department stores, and shopping chains, have transformed the urban landscape. They are, in fact, places to meet and congregate, and they create new geographies. Unlike the luxurious big department stores that favour central locations, supermarkets prefer to be located in highly populated zones, often in the suburbs or outskirts, which then assume new value: many of the first supermarkets were built in the new immigrant areas. And this phenomenon is something to add to the restructuring of commercial spaces that took place in the major cities between the 1950s and '70s: the number of shops remained steady or tended to diminish in historic centres (the main victims being the lower quality shops due to increased rents and fewer residents), while there was an increase in the concentration of commercial enterprises in the peripheral zones and outer hinterland.[23] Sharon Zukin has shown how, through their presence (or absence),[24] market forces have effectively modelled and transformed the physical environment over the course of time. Here can be observed how Italy's physiognomy has been characterized historically with regard not only to its factories but also to its places of commerce, which have been just as capable of structuring the landscape and creating hierarchies and new urban spaces. Consumption, too, has played its part in moulding the landscape.

To round off this discussion on supermarkets, the mind goes back to Moravia's tale of the American dream. And I realize that in almost every case, to describe the golden age of consumption and all the new things it brought in tow, I have to fall back on terms like 'American' and 'the United States'. The impact of the American model during these years was enormous, to the extent that many academics have talked about an Americanization reflected in more or less every sphere of the economy, culture, and society and which, according to the points of view, has been exalted or condemned with no half measures (partly on account of its evidently political implications).[25] It is no easy matter and has generated an enormous number of studies, in Italy as elsewhere in Europe.[26] What can be observed here is that cultural encounters are phenomena too complex to be resolved categorically, as the history of consumption well shows (I am thinking of the ways electrical appliances have spread, and of the new forms of advertising and marketing, youth consumption, many cultural products, and supermarkets themselves). As Geertz would say, a culture sees and interprets every action within a specific network of meanings that give sense to it.[27] On these lines, Italy has inevitably interpreted, used, and created its own form of 'Americanization', incorporating contents and techniques from across the ocean, but mindful of its own history and culture. The result has been a form of hybridization, or rather, as Kroes suggests, of 'Creolisation': a process whereby words and elements deriving from a foreign language are inserted into an indigenous grammar and syntax.[28]

PART IV

The Affluent Society

11

Impact of the Consumer Society

From the 1970s to the new millennium: light and shade

There was no lack of controversy at the inauguration of the famous exhibition held in New York's Guggenheim Museum in autumn 2000. For the very first time one of the world's major art institutes was dedicating a review to a very special artist who was neither painter, sculptor nor *performer* of any sort, but a fashion designer, Giorgio Armani. The Fifth Avenue rooms designed by Wright were arrayed with dazzling clothes set off against an original scenario and evocative music. Here was a room boasting precious white items, another beige, a third evening dresses, then 'destructured' jackets, suits, film star attire (first of all, Richard Gere's in *American Gigolo*). There were clothes worn by surreal mannequins looking like human figures in stylized, transcendental forms. There were clothes that to the visitors' gaze showed artistic inspiration and masterly skill in creation, but perhaps raised a few eyebrows: surely clothes are everyday things with no right to take their place beside the canonical art seen in museums? Or perhaps this was the very message the exhibition was trying to convey: perhaps some seemingly ordinary consumer goods can aspire to other social meanings, even to becoming works of art.[1]

After the extraordinary period of growth in the preceding decade, marked by the expectation of continuous development with benefits for all, the 1970s represented a rude awakening for the whole of Europe. It was the start of a period hit by economic depression (triggered by the first oil shock), rising unemployment, galloping inflation and, politically, by the eruption of terrorist violence, while—especially in Italy—there was the difficult search for a new political balance. The great age of progress really seemed to be over and Aurelio Peccei's famous book commissioned at MIT by the 'Rome Club' summed up current thought by speaking of 'limits of development'.[2]

Consumption was the first victim of the new climate, caught as it was between two fires. On one side the criticism levelled at it by radicals (always ready to condemn capitalism as degenerate, an instrument of disguised oppression and source of alienation) resounded with new vigour. For the most radical fringe there was no possible compromise, as shown spectacularly by the *Superstudio* film project presented by a group of young Florentine architects at an important New York exhibition. In one scene children and young people appear, involved in ordinary activities (eating, playing, and talking) on a technological surface looking like a sort of 'grid', with natural landscapes in the background. But there is something unusual: the complete absence of everyday objects. Walls, sofas, pictures, televisions, cars, purses, tablecloths, pans, boxes, and stamps have all vanished. In another scene a whole family is smiling down at us, suspended between bare technological flooring and a mountainous landscape, all completely naked in the most provocative of anti-consumer statements: 'a life without objects'.[3]

It must be admitted that the economic crisis and spectre of energy shortage projected a dark cloud on future development. During the golden age of progress it had seemed that, barring wars or revolutions (man-made of course), the industrialized model created by the West could go on improving almost ad infinitum. Now a dramatic question was being asked. Could there be 'natural' limits to this kind of expansion? Can our planet go on being exploited, over-populated, polluted, and consumed forever? The oil crisis, albeit motivated by international politics, was fundamentally a warning light indicating a wider problem.

So saving became the operative word. In Italy it marked the beginning of the age of austerity, as the Rumor government called it. Oil consumption had to be limited, and in the meantime the price of petrol and diesel oil rose. Cinemas and shops reduced their opening hours; heating and lighting were regulated. Most characteristic of this new climate were the carless Sundays. Films from 1973 and 1974, with a half preaching, half amused air, show us cities swarming with cyclists, regiments of men and women on horseback, tandems and far-fetched pedaled vehicles, going round and round in the deserted streets.[4] Was it the end of an age? Austerity became the keynote of a possible future, very different from the one that had been envisaged up to that moment. Meanwhile government policies moved decisively to contain public spending and the deficiency in revenue, while real wage squeezes due to soaring inflation fanned the flames of consumer distrust.

The measures struck hard at one of the major symbols of the economic miracle, the car. For the very first time the prospect of unlimited growth was put in doubt. It was no longer possible to keep on buying cars for ever, as there would not be enough petrol to go round. The apocalyptical prospects preached by some seemed to be coming true. Perhaps tomorrow there would be fewer consumer goods than today. In a world turned difficult and hostile, the collective utopias of the 1960s gave way to personal worry and private entrenchment.

Unexpectedly, however, the last twenty years of the century brought more change and during the 1980s the Italian and the international economy experienced a new spate of growth. Consumer activity resumed. For Italy there was even talk at the economic level of a 'second miracle', chiefly thanks to *made in Italy* and, at the social level, the triumph of consumerism. It was the age of the *look*, fashion, private television, and a second wave of consumer spending, no longer at a subsistence level linked to the food-home-clothes triad, but holidays, travel, cosmetics, gymnasiums, second homes, and luxury goods (often aiming at individual rather than family consumption). Advertising provides both the language and the images representing these years. Italians had never had it so good: they lived in the fifth industrial power in the world and their consumer level had finally caught up with the European average (for a comparison with the United Kingdom see Table 8). The gap that had always separated Italy from the other countries closed up during the second half of the 1980s: a historic moment indeed.

It was not all a bed of roses, however, and to put it bluntly there were many thorns on the stems. Already at the start of the 1990s the implosion of the Italian political system, the uncertainties that weighed upon the labour market and the young, the de-industrializing process, the slowing down of economic growth all over Europe, the appearance of new actors in the East, international terrorism, fears for the environment, the erosion of the welfare state, and finally globalization were all reflected in a more pondered attitude where consumption was concerned, with the emergence of new high-tech products and a strong diversification. The concept of class was put in the shade as savouring of anachronism, and to explain the growing segmentation of the market analysts and advertisers preferred to speak of differing life-styles. An ethical issue relating to consumption also came to the surface, and entering the new century was more about asking questions than giving answers. Consumption on a grand scale was now an intrinsic part of western life style, but its cultural role was undergoing change.

Table 8 Consumption in Italy and Great Britain, years 1900 and 2000

Per capita income (Geary-Khamis 1990 international dollars)	Great Britain 1900	Italy 1900[1]	Great Britain 2000	Italy 2000
(29-country western European Country average: Year 1900 = 2,892; year 2000 = 19,264)	4,492	1,785	20,159	18,786
Consumption (%)				
Food	28		11	17
Alcoholic drinks	11	64[2]	6	1
Tobacco	2	2	3	1
Shoes and clothing	9	10	6	7
House	10	8	16	22
Fuel and electrical energy	5	1	3	5
Furniture, furnishings, etc.	4	4	7	7
Transport and communications			18	18
Culture, entertainment, education			10	7
Other goods and services	31[3]	11[4]	20	15
Total	100	100	100	100

Source: A. Maddison, *Historical Statistics for the World Economy. Per Capita GDP (1990 International Geary-Khamis dollars)*; L. Michaelis, S. Lorek, *Consumption and the Environment in Europe. Trends and Futures*, Danish Environmental Protection Agency, Copenhagen (2004); ISTAT, *Sommario di statistiche storiche dell'Italia 1861–1975*, Rome (1976); Ibid., *I consumi delle famiglie. Anno 2000*, Rome (2002).

[1] Average 1901–1910.
[2] Including food and alcoholic drinks.
[3] Including transport and communications, culture, entertainment, education, other goods and services.
[4] Idem.

On the whole, this is the image remembered of the closing years of the twentieth century. Or perhaps it should be said that it is the way it is seen now, the representation of it. Once more, if the picture is turned over and look at it from the consumption angle, the focus will be on different elements and our view partly altered. Although historical studies on this last period are still rudimentary of course, there are a few suggestions that can be mooted.

The first concerns the 1970s, crisis years above all others: the 'years of lead' and, according to many, one of the most difficult periods in the whole of Italian history. Strangely enough, private consumption reveals unexpected growth, increasing throughout the decade, albeit somewhat irregularly. The only real downward plunge occurred in 1975, the worst moment of the crisis. Over the decade the average increase was 3 per cent per year (on a level with Germany and higher than the United Kingdom) so that a certain continuity of growth for the whole 1973–1993 period could be alluded to. How can such progress be explained? How can it be reconciled with a country experiencing a dramatic crisis and a regime of austerity? A physicist like Einstein would be able to explain the fact at once: it all depends on your frame of reference. The observers of the time came from a period of extraordinary economic growth when consumption had literally exploded (5.4 per cent annual growth in the 1950s and 6.6 in the 1960s), so it is obvious that a 'miserable' 3 per cent would seem to be a dramatic collapse. Add to this the political tensions (collective movements first, terrorist violence after) and it is quite understandable how a generally negative judgement was formed. Looking back from a distance and with far worse increases behind, that 3 per cent takes on a different meaning. It testifies to a vitality that does not always come out in retrospective reconstructions (except perhaps in social history studies concerning changes in family life, the new role of youth movements and, in general, the attention given to minorities and the deprived).[5]

The reasons for all this consumer activity still need to be explained. As several academics, including D'Apice and Maione, have emphasized, the numbers indicate that it was from this moment that consumer spending spread widely among the lower classes also. The mass revolution in consumption took place in Italy during the 1970–80s, lagging twenty years behind northern Europe.[6] In 1975 the annual report on durable goods by the Bank of Italy revealed that, apart from food consumption, some standard package was now widespread among the entire population. 94 per cent of families had a refrigerator and 92 per cent a television (over 78 per cent had washing machines and over 64 per cent cars). Owning such items was no longer a sign of social status, as differentiation was now indicated by new, more expensive goods (air conditioners, dishwashers), services, and entertainment.[7] Higher earnings were therefore being used to increase consumption, and this broadening of the domestic market enabled Italy to have a reasonable performance even in difficult times. For example, thinking about the trade union protests of those years, they can be imagined taking place in a square where there are posters in some corner or another urging people to spend (perhaps the famous ones by Oliviero Toscani and Emanuele Pirella for Jesus jeans, showing a curvaceous base-of-spine region with the invitation 'if you love me follow me'—shocking in its sensuous and blasphemous allusions, which Pasolini pointed out as symptomatic of the advance of a technological, secular new world, 'with a secularity that knows no religion').[8]

From a historical point of view, therefore, the 1970s were crucial years for consumption and need to be revisited. As Arvidsson observes, the prevailing rhetoric, harping on the virtues of saving and austerity, was more a self portrait than a faithful reflection of reality,[9] or as Gundle suggests, perhaps a mirror image of a political class cautiously bringing together vast sectors of Christian Democrats and Communists because they were fearful of serious social imbalances in a country undergoing rapid change.[10] An essentially political reading, however, sheds too unfavourable a light on the period, making it difficult to understand how it was possible to pass so quickly from a period of crisis and austerity to the 'second economic miracle' and consumer culture.

I now come to the 1980s and early '90s. Switching from one means of communication to another, the language of advertising took on an entirely new role and, in the political aphasia (and disillusion), symbolically aspired to represent the society of the time. Indeed, Arvidsson maintains that advertising and consumer culture would become precious symbolic resources for consumers to justify their choices and reveal their subjectivity (resources that almost count more in the symbolic and cultural sphere than in the practical one of consumer choices).[11] It is no surprise that the period is often given the advertising tag of 'Drinking Milan'. In this Ramazzotti spot we see an interesting gallery of characters chosen to represent the tireless activity of city life: young women leaping happily out of bed as the alarm clock rings, boys running in the street, people selling flowers, traffic policemen at a bar, crane operators, punks reading the financial *Sole 24 Ore*, women grabbing passing taxis, elegant customers dining in luxury restaurants, models ready for the catwalk, couples dancing together at night while streets are being cleaned, barmen threading through the traffic with their trays to bring 'the working, living person's *bitter*, the *bitter* of your life, for a day that never ends'—in a nutshell, work and well-being for all (it is easy to imagine the ridicule this 'Drinking Milan' advertisement was subjected to as a result of the *Tangentopoli* (bribery city) scandal, when it became apparent that much more than *bitter* had been drunk).

The new role of advertising was obviously strengthened by the appearance of private television channels, which adopted a skilful, pragmatic strategy to promote heavy investment in advertising (it rose from 0.3 of the GDP in 1975 to 0.5 ten years later, and 0.6 by 1990).[12] Berlusconi's Fininvest group already stood out in 1984 with the acquisition of three national channels (Canale 5, the flagship, coming from Telemilano in 1978; Italia 1, acquired from Rusconi in 1982; Retequattro, from Mondadori two years later), a production agency (Videotime), a company for managing the transmission network (Elettronica Industriale) and finally an advertising agency (Publitalia '80). Its impact on the collective imagination (combined with myriads of local radio and television channels) was enormous, not only for the advertisements themselves, but also for the kind of programmes, rich in films and successful serials (*Dallas* for example).[13] In a few words, television consumption in Italy reached spectacularly high levels (229 minutes viewing per person per day in 1999, almost a European record).[14] It is therefore understandable how the world of advertising and media-based consumption was able to take on a new social role and compete with politics for visibility in the public arena.

It is equally true that during this period consumption tended to switch from the family to the individual (that is, from refrigerators, toasters, and washing machines to bodily care, holidays, and entertainment). As seen, this actually belongs to a long-term trend whereby there was a shift towards consumer products deemed culturally more fulfilling. At the same time the importance of demographic change should not be underestimated in this respect. It has been seen that the birth rate was falling and families were getting smaller and smaller. Single-member families, which in 1977 represented less than 10 per cent of the total, doubled in twenty years to become the most widespread family structure, followed by childless couples (20 per cent) and couples with only one child (19 per cent). Instead, there was a decline in the number of families with a lot of children, as well as those extended to include relatives or outside members. The family thus changed in culture and in kind. It is also known that at the same time average life expectancy increased, producing an aging population (more than a fifth of 21st-century Italians are over 65, a record for Europe).[15] It goes without saying that consumption has punctually reflected these changes (for example, with a new attention to the age factor, meaning that it does not only concern the young, as in the 1960s, but also the old, as great consumers of medicinal products and personal services).[16]

The optimistic representation of consumption as the 20th century drew to a close, full of ever more diversified 'lifestyles' and 'linear' growth for everyone, deserves some critical attention, however. Many theorists have speculated that the analytical categories required to understand society today are different from in the past. Societies are complex, differentiated, and composed of relatively autonomous sub-systems. Individual characteristics derive not only from the social standing of the family of origin, for example, but from an infinite number of other factors (education, type of work, occupational hierarchy, place of residence, etc.) which interact with one another to create highly varied social geographies. Social fragmentation is very high. Because of this, the great divides in social structure (especially where class is concerned) have little importance today, and people are freer to create their own destiny and mould their lives as if they were a 'work of art'. At the start of the twentieth century it was possible to tell a town-dweller from a country person at a glance, whereas now it has become very hard to classify the people in the street, as they are (almost always) dressed alike. People choose their own way of being and consumer choices reflect this. These theories have in fact been adopted in many market inquiries and complex social maps have been drawn, grouping individuals in specific segments and life styles as a result of a multitude of cultural, individual, and economic factors.[17]

The consequence of this scenario, at least where consumption is concerned, would be its relative freedom from social conditioning and a greater role in self-expression. But is this really the case? Does social background not carry the same weight in today's society? And what about gender differences (which has been seen clearly at work in the past)? Some recent studies in the field have produced slightly different results (and to tell the truth, as historians, the sudden disappearance of cultural categories that had been part of society for so long is a little suspicious). Of course the background against which these data must be projected is that of a more affluent Italy, where the middle classes have become the biggest group (albeit with wide differences within them), while the geographical references must be urban and industrial.[18] The sociologist Antonio Schizzerotto has conducted a wide-ranging diachronic inquiry into people's lives over a broad statistical sample, studying factors of inequality and social mobility, which he compares with available data from previous generations.[19]

The final results are that class of origin, gender, generation, and geographical area were determining elements throughout the twentieth century, right up to the last decades, but with interesting variations. The factor that most affected people's lives in Italy at the end of the century was class. Class determined whether a higher level of education could be attained, which is illustrated by the fact that distribution of higher degrees remained incredibly constant in the long run.[20] It also influenced the time it took to find the first job, for example, through family networks or carrying on in father's footsteps. Class is related to the level of entry into the work place, which is particular important in Italy because of the relative lack of career mobility. Class is also associated with the ability to attain a secure job. Moreover, since people tend to marry partners from their own class, social climbing through marriage is less likely. Therefore people's social backgrounds still play a determining part in their social destiny. Class, or status, perpetuates social inequality.

The evolution of the gender factor seems more ambiguous. Recent generations of women have closed the education gap, right up to the highest levels. They have greatly improved their levels of income and access to work (though waiting times of entry are longer and career possibilities fewer—if not in all sectors). But they have added to their work load the same burden of family care they had in the past, a fact that is pushing them to postpone marriage and limit or avoid having children, (with consequences on their partners' lives as well). So inequality has decreased in some respects but not in others. The generation factor is equally ambiguous. Those born during the last decades of the twentieth century have enjoyed a higher level of education but are conspicuously late in joining the working world and securing a full-time job, with potentially long periods of part-time or casual work (unlike the economic miracle generation who found work immediately). In this they are curiously similar to the generations from the early years of the century. It is true that staying on with the family on a long-term basis has its advantages (high consumer rating, parental permissiveness, etc.) but it also means continuing to be dependent and, because of the late start, will have negative repercussions both on their future careers and on setting up a family of their own. In other words, compared with the opportunities for work, career, and mobility that young people growing up during the economic miracle had, in many ways those born in the later twentieth century find themselves living in more difficult conditions.[21] To conclude, the research confirms that despite substantial variations the geographical factor remains a determining element and, in particular, that living in the north of Italy follows a very different course from living in the south.[22]

All these factors are essential for a study of consumption as an integral part of social reality, since they free the field of some ambiguities. In the new millennium there remain certain divides in Italy which we saw throughout the 20th century, at times resisting with surprising tenacity. Some have lessened, others have changed (certainly, it is no longer correct to use the term 'class' in its traditional sense, because of all the cultural implications it includes historically, and we would do better to use terms like 'social background', 'status', or others suggesting more complex stratification). But the fact is that such divisions continue to structure society and, what concerns us here, culturally determine consumption patterns.[23] This is confirmed by economic pointers like the Gini index, showing increased inequality in Italy at least since the 1991–92 recession, which produced a historic inversion ('the big U-turn') after decades of social rapprochement (and revealing that Italy continues to register greater internal inequality when compared with many other European countries).[24] Therefore if it is true that two people in the street—two young men for instance—are not immediately recognizable today from the social point of view, as they would have been at the start of the twentieth century, it is not because the differences have disappeared. One protagonist has designer clothes (compared with imitations bought at the street market), a new, modern car or motorcycle (compared with an old highly polluting car or motorcycle, first victims of the driving bans), holidays in the Maldives (instead of down at grandma's), dinners and happy hours in fashionable places (instead of a pizza or the occasional happy hour in a cheap bar) and so forth. Looking alike does not mean being alike. Looks are not everything; the differences are still there, they are just less visible. As in certain paintings by Pieter Brueghel the Elder, looking from a distance can be misleading. You have to come up close to be able to detect the details and distinguish between angels and demons, animals and men, natural creatures and monsters, all entwined and caught up between heaven and earth.

That is why the idea of passing everything off merely as lifestyles and personal choices is not quite convincing, though these do have growing importance and must never be underestimated, ignoring the old and new divides along which social differences (including consumer ones) have always been articulated. Such divisions reveal different income levels and cultural choices, even within the same trends, and explain how certain segments of the population manage to prosper and enjoy luxuries while others get poorer and have to tighten their belts.

Having said this and having clarified some of the dynamics at work in complex systems like today's societies, I want now to analyse the major trends in progress, taking as the time frame the thirty years between 1973 and 2003, when family spending was on the increase (more than earnings in fact), though with different rhythms as earlier.[25] The first, amazing fact is the smaller amount spent on food, which gradually slips from 38 to 20 per cent, with a particularly sharp fall registered in the 1980s (see Table 9). The Italian family's 'new' diet is increasingly less based on meat, which in 2003 accounted for 22 per cent of food spending (and 4 per cent of overall monthly expenses, whereas it was almost three times higher in 1973).[26] This is followed by fruit and vegetables, bread and cereals, then milk and cheese, fish, drinks, sugar and coffee, fats and oils. It is a question of rebalancing where both quantity and quality are concerned: qualitatively there is a move towards a more varied and vegetarian diet, while in quantity (as Signorelli notes) Italy has partly changed from being a typical Mediterranean country with relatively high food consumption (as in Portugal, Greece, and Spain) and since the 1990s has been approaching the northen European model (Great Britain, Germany, Holland, and France) with a low percentage of food in the overall consumption pattern:[27] a significant cultural change, therefore.

The amount spent on clothing has also decreased, from 11 to 7 per cent, but is still higher than the European average, partly due to the appeal of Italian fashion.[28] The third category of traditional basic expenses, on the home and fuel, shows a sudden upsurge from 16 to 30 per cent, especially over recent years. There has therefore been a strong move to divert resources towards spending on the home, on account of the problems facing the country where the property market is concerned (certainly nothing new), a situation that has kept the amount of income reserved for spending on basic necessities fairly high.

Table 9 Average Italian monthly family expenditure by type of goods, geographical location and professional status, 1986–2005 (current lire, euro after 2001)

Italy (total)

Years	Food and drinks	Tobacco	Shoes and clothing	House	Fuel and electricity	Goods, furniture and furnishings etc.	Medical, hygiene, health	Transport and communications	Recreation and culture	Other goods and services	Total
1986–1990	525,979	27,899	192,329	318,167	98,031	162,907	46,824	348,916	135,016	287,547	2,143,616
1991–1995	653,092	35,297	214,558	532,783	145,144	192,190	81,750	494,123	195,244	403,479	2,947,660
1996–2000	764,062	39,348	259,604	853,437	186,373	266,662	156,956	679,481	255,709	448,573	3,910,205
2001–2005	439	19	153	570	109	146	86	376	139	256	2,293
Geographical location											
						North–West Italy					
1986	480,323	24,270	156,312	261,872	110,925	150,777	47,861	329,847	130,414	291,470	1,984,071
2005	470	19	156	706	126	158	115	430	158	325	2,663
						North–East Italy					
1986	449,323	23,173	180,854	254,961	112,791	148,976	41,364	309,828	121,556	273,112	1915,938
2005	432	17	152	724	139	161	118	489	157	338	2,727
						Central Italy					
1986	522,454	23,840	165,913	259,168	111,655	150,071	45,318	322,014	126,948	248,287	1,957,408
2005	467	20	153	716	124	141	75	384	136	262	2,478

South Italy

Professional status	Year											Total
	1986	491,341	28,722	135,838	222,057	62,428	121,936	21,406	221,963	81,186	167,414	1,554,291
	2005	446	23	145	410	89	129	65	309	100	168	1884
Businessmen and professionals	1986	625,264	35,588	285,868	397,207	137,659	220,730	44,464	593,898	226,902	425,821	2,993,401
	2005	531	24	331	855	153	257	99	658	230	519	3,657
Self-employed	1986	571,668	33,898	187,970	267,768	104,053	163,766	34,623	394,596	125,478	294,082	2,177,902
	2005	516	27	209	664	134	176	89	514	163	379	2,871
Employed: clerical and management	1986	530,759	30,695	210,149	313,076	98,894	174,872	39,752	374,936	164,372	326,185	2,263,690
	2005	477	22	217	701	120	195	99	513	203	386	2,933
Employed: workers	1986	534,933	33,032	150,506	219,531	89,678	139,902	35,356	303,462	107,910	230,470	1,844,780
	2005	489	29	155	519	112	138	81	445	139	254	2,361
Pensioners and unemployed	1986	386,450	15,959	98,585	210,953	82,267	96,063	32,847	151,666	65,725	153,816	1,294,331
	2005	405	17	95	558	106	109	83	265	92	170	1900

Source: elaborations on ISTAT, *I consumi delle famiglie*, years 1986–2005.

Table 10 Consumption in Europe, 1995 and 2005 (%)

Year 1995	Food, non-alcoholic drinks	Tobacco and alcohol	Shoes and clothing	House, gas, water and electricity	Furniture, furnishings, etc.	Medical, hygiene and health	Transport	Communications	Entertainment, culture	Education	Restaurants and hotels	Other goods and services	Total
EU (27 countries)	14.5	3.7	6.8	20.7	7.1	3.2	13.2	1.9	9.0	0.9	8.2	10.8	100
Belgium	14.0	3.8	6.2	22.7	6.0	3.4	13.0	1.5	9.1	0.4	5.5	14.4	100
Denmark	13.2	4.8	5.1	26.3	5.8	2.4	13.2	1.8	10.2	0.7	5.0	11.5	100
Germany	12.3	3.8	6.6	22.5	8.3	3.8	13.5	2.0	9.3	0.6	5.7	11.7	100
Ireland	15.3	6.8	7.2	15.6	7.0	3.0	11.2	1.8	7.7	1.3	14.5	8.4	100
Greece	18.0	4.2	11.0	17.6	6.4	5.6	9.0	1.5	5.1	2.0	14.7	4.9	100
Spain	17.3	2.7	6.6	14.4	6.1	3.2	11.3	1.8	8.3	1.6	18.4	8.3	100
France	14.9	3.3	5.8	22.9	6.1	3.3	14.6	1.9	8.6	0.6	5.9	12.0	100
Italy	16.7	2.5	9.1	18.3	8.7	3.4	12.8	1.8	7.1	1.0	8.6	10.0	100
Luxembourg	11.1	8.4	5.7	21.8	8.3	1.7	15.3	1.3	8.2	0.3	8.9	8.9	100
Netherlands	13.0	3.3	6.5	21.4	7.1	4.1	11.5	2.2	10.8	0.6	5.6	13.9	100
Austria	12.7	2.8	7.8	18.5	9.2	3.3	11.8	1.9	11.2	0.4	11.1	9.1	100
Poland	27.5	8.3	5.7	20.7	4.6	3.1	7.6	2.3	8.0	1.0	3.2	8.0	100
Portugal	18.4	3.9	8.5	13.5	7.1	4.9	14.2	2.0	5.5	1.2	10.6	10.4	100
Finland	15.4	6.1	4.6	24.7	4.4	3.4	12.3	1.6	10.6	0.5	7.0	9.4	100
Sweden	14.0	4.4	5.2	31.2	4.5	2.1	12.3	2.2	10.4	0.1	4.5	8.9	100
United Kingdom	11.3	4.3	6.4	18.9	6.0	1.6	14.5	2.1	11.2	1.4	11.4	11.1	100
Norway	15.9	4.7	6.1	21.8	6.1	2.5	14.1	1.8	11.4	0.4	6.3	8.8	100

Year 2005	Food, non-alcoholic drinks	Tobacco and alcohol	Shoes and clothing	House, gas, water and electricity	Furniture, furnishings, etc.	Medical, hygiene and health	Transport	Communications	Entertainment, culture	Education	Restaurants and hotels	Other goods and services	Total
EU (27 countries)	12.8	3.6	5.8	21.6	6.3	3.5	13.5	2.8	9.5	1.0	9.0	10.7	100
Belgium	13.3	3.6	5.4	23.0	5.5	4.3	14.7	2.3	9.3	0.6	5.2	12.9	100
Denmark	–	–	–	–	–	–	–	–	–	–	–	–	–
Germany	11.2	3.5	5.3	24.2	6.9	4.7	13.8	2.8	9.4	0.7	5.4	12.2	100
Ireland	5.9	5.2	5.2	19.9	6.9	3.5	12.6	3.5	7.9	1.2	15.8	12.5	100
Greece	–	–	–	–	–	–	–	–	–	–	–	–	–
Spain	14.1	2.9	5.5	16.2	5.2	3.5	11.6	2.6	9.1	1.5	18.9	8.9	100
France	13.7	3.1	4.8	24.4	6.0	3.4	14.8	2.8	9.3	0.7	6.2	10.9	100
Italy	14.8	2.6	8.0	20.6	7.7	3.2	13.4	2.8	6.9	0.9	9.8	9.4	100
Luxembourg	9.5	10.5	3.9	21.3	7.4	2.0	18.8	1.3	7.9	0.3	7.4	9.7	100
Netherlands	10.6	2.8	5.3	22.2	6.3	5.3	11.5	4.5	10.0	0.5	5.1	15.8	100
Austria	10.7	2.9	6.4	20.5	7.4	3.2	13.2	2.7	11.6	0.6	12.0	8.7	100
Poland	21.1	6.6	4.6	23.8	4.4	4.0	8.7	3.4	7.6	1.3	2.9	11.8	100
Portugal	–	–	–	–	–	–	–	–	–	–	–	–	–
Finland	12.5	5.0	4.8	25.3	5.5	4.2	12.9	2.8	11.4	0.4	6.5	8.7	100
Sweden	12.0	3.7	5.3	28.3	5.2	2.7	13.2	3.1	11.8	0.3	5.1	9.3	100
United Kingdom	9.0	3.7	5.9	19.6	5.8	1.6	15.1	2.2	12.6	1.4	11.9	11.1	100
Norway	–	–	–	–	–	–	–	–	–	–	–	–	–

Source: Eurostat (*Population and social conditions*).

It is not surprising to see that transport and communication have continued to rise steadily (from 10 to 16 per cent during the thirty-year period), while other spending has risen to a much lesser degree, from 24 to 27 per cent, subdivided in 2003 between durable goods (6 per cent), education and leisure (6 per cent), health (4 per cent), other goods and services (11 per cent).[29] What stands out here is the new consumer interest in technological goods and communication, especially during the 1980s, but on the whole there has not been such a massive shift towards 'high quality' goods and services as might have been expected. On the contrary some spending—on transport for example, and the car in particular, considering today's social arrangements—has changed its cultural significance. A car is no longer a status symbol or means of escape for a weekend or holiday, but an absolute necessity for work and travel, and should therefore be added to the list of basic needs.

The reason for these changes lies in the complex social geography we have previously outlined, which to a certain extent sees contradictory dynamics at work. Although there has been some degree of merging among social groups, consumption continues to be strongly affected by socioeconomic variables. These depend on professional status and academic qualifications (people with degrees standing out as buyers of durable goods), on age bracket (young people under the age of thirty progressively losing buying power), on gender (males spending more as a whole, particularly on durable goods). The last great variable is geography. The differences in consumption between the great geographical areas of north, centre, south, and islands (the last mentioned having undergone a slight downturn since 2000) have remained constant, confirming the traditional hierarchy. Progress has made no difference to the territorial distribution of consumer spending[30] (See Table 9).

The last element in the analysis concerns immigration. Notwithstanding transnational connotations in consumer habits due to the circulation of goods, international nature of various selling venues, and interaction between culture and consumption, there is no doubt that the massive numbers of foreign immigrants arriving in Italy over the last thirty years or so have influenced the look of the urban landscape and even the collective imagination where consumption is concerned. Specialized food shops and ethnic restaurants have sprung up in the cities, as have a variety of boutiques and other business enterprises representative of far-off cultures. Together with tourism and the media, they have also been responsible for the discovery of international cuisine and 'ethnic' tastes by present-day Italians, contributing to the inclusion on the consumer's shopping list of things that were once simply seen as different or exotic. Nor should it be forgotten that immigrants are consumers too. Their spending is not simply a poorer version of what Italians buy, but displays great internal differences and specific choices, innovatively bringing together different kinds of consumption. If on average almost half their income goes on board and lodging, a quarter is taken up by clothing and transport, while 14 per cent is sent back to their country of origin and 15 per cent goes on savings. The item owned by practically all is a mobile telephone (over 94 per cent), followed by a television set, domestic furniture and, further behind, a washing machine. Hi-fi sets and video recorders are more common than second-hand cars (a new car being a luxury that only 16 per cent can afford). Instead, 22 per cent have a PC (fewer have a dishwasher, motor scooter, or second television set). To sum up, the immigrant picture reveals close attention to costs, savings, and goods needed for communicating and socializing (mobile phone, music, television).[31] It is also a picture that confirms the widely varying social origins and cosmopolitan nature of many new immigrants. I will not make the same mistake as the ethnographer described by James Clifford who arrives at a remote Egyptian village to study ancient customs, only to find people responding with irritation because they are all busy travelling to and from Yemen, the Gulf Emirates, Saudi Arabia, Europe or wherever their jobs, military duties, and religious pilgrimages take them.[32]

To sum up, returning to the overall theme and period in question it is true that consumption has increased and diversified where content is concerned. Everyone has more things and different things, albeit not to the same extent. In certain cases a chain effect is created where consumers are pushed to buy one thing after another (the 'Diderot effect').[33] But with time their cultural meanings change. Thanks to becoming part of daily life some commodities that once seemed so exceptional and luxurious have turned out to be very ordinary things or essential comforts (car, telephone—even food has taken on a different value). After all, buying an umpteenth pair of shoes to throw in with the rest is not like buying the first pair.[34] Perhaps Gronow and Warde are right: the fundamental change at the beginning of this century was the transforming of consumption itself into routine.[35]

Politics and consumerism

What can be said about the effects of consumption on the political arena at the turn of the century? Is it possible to identify any basic trends? I can certainly make some conjectures (although a historian venturing into a period as close as this is like an explorer walking on thin ice).

On one side the first aspect that registers is the continuity of government policies. The pattern that took shape during the 1960s and '70s, with consumption as an important element for political consensus, remained undisturbed by later developments. More and more, the system seems to have owed its credibility to a knack of guaranteeing ever-improving living standards and with less need for ideological glue to keep it intact. Naturally, as reminded by Paolo Pombeni, the legitimization of a political system does not depend merely on its ability to promote the common good, but also on matters of form (guaranteed representation, proper decision-making processes).[36] Be that as it may, consumption and welfare management policies seem to have played a central role, especially as there were moves towards a certain liberalization and repeated attempts were being made to reduce welfare costs (which were leaning in favour of national insurance and away from the social services), in some cases with the involvement of private and non-profit agencies (*welfare mix*).[37] The difficulty of being able to modify a structure so glaringly tilted in favour of certain subjects and categories testifies to the delicacy of the question. The political debate on consumption thus continues to be relevant in matters concerning social integration and citizenship (in the sense indicated by Marshall).

In a country where, as noted earlier, the national integration of some sectors of the population has come about on an economic rather than political basis, and where social mobility has actually materialized in wider access to consumer goods, these 'consumption policies' were crucial in ensuring governability for several decades. However, in the early years of the new millennium such party-transcending policies seem to be suffering on account of increasing economic and social difficulties for wide swathes of the middle and working classes, limited social mobility, and employment problems for young people. If the 'pact' guaranteeing consumer access for all were to be broken, it would open up disturbing scenarios of social instability and the discrediting of the entire political class.

On the other side, there are some important new developments on the political scene: consumer movements. More precisely, I am referring to 'consumerism' in the meaning of consumer organizations. The first ones took shape in Italy during the 1950s, as they did more or less throughout Europe (though much later than in the USA), in the wake of the first food scandals. They work as private associations often with the support of magazines, to inform consumers and defend them against fraudulent practice, to call for more protective legislation and more transparency, and to compare similar products. However, an all-pervasive party politics system has left little room for these private initiatives. On the contrary one could say that only pressure from European Community agencies from the 1970s onwards has forced the political world to show any interest in regulations in the consumption area or act on community directives, and usually after long delays. Nevertheless, these movements have recently gained much greater prominence in the media, confirming a change of approach to them.[38]

The question is much more complicated, however. Apparently what is being experienced to a certain extent in the entire western world is a growing intensification of individual and collective consumer actions, with 'political' overtones. I am not talking about new kinds of behaviour, but in today's climate they take on particular significance.[39] No-buy strikes have been staged to protest against the government's fiscal policies (against increases in food or petrol prices, for example—the extreme case being the 'buy nothing day' campaign: a day when consumers were asked not to buy anything).[40] There are boycotts for ethical reasons, against products from firms accused of having scant respect for the environment, or exploiting workers in less developed countries (think of Nike or Coca-Cola). There are politically motivated boycotts against goods coming from specific countries (like USA or Israel). On the other hand there can be selective buying in favour of products that guarantee workers' rights ('fair trade'), protect the environment (organic products), or are simply linked to humanitarian campaigns. There are frequent cases when organized groups stage anti-consumerist demonstrations, maybe harking back to 'civil disobedience' methods (hanging posters in inconceivable places, staging 'die ins' when they pretend to be dead in shops, going around masked with placards or using 'culture jamming' techniques). There have even been acts of violence against chain stores and multinational firms, or for animal rights, actions prosecuted today as examples of 'eco-terrorism'.[41]

As observed by a group of researchers (Stolle, Hooghe, and Micheletti),[42] in all these cases the anti-consumerists have identified the material goods with a precise social context and performed an act of 'political consumerism'.[43] So the question is this: is behaviour like this, a form of political participation, where consumers use the market to get their message home? There are two sides to this. In the first place, the chief protagonists in these actions are people who are under-represented in the 'official' world of politics: women, young people, and socially marginalized groups.[44] Moreover, the actions take place in different locations: shops and shopping centres, but Internet too, where they circulate appeals, manifestos, and calls to action. It may be concluded that political consumerism is the means found by voices absent or far removed from the halls of power, not only to express their ethical or political position, but also to alter the existing situation with a well-aimed action (often achieving significant results). Should political consumption be recognized, then, as a new form of political participation, just as is happening on the net, where transverse collective movements are forming? They even have in common their reference to a transnational reality that outweighs national interests. Finally, as noted again in the research quoted, if this hypothesis is accepted, it may be said that it is not political participation as such that is in crisis, but the traditional forms and places associated with it.[45] Consumerism and virtual communities may be the new frontiers of politics.

New products

Production has its role to play in these changes, of course. Public attention has now been drawn to the so-called 'industrial districts': conglomerations of factories all in the same sector, where production is grafted on to a long-standing social, community-based fabric, and family and firm come together. Similar realities, sometimes with century-old traditions, now appear as an 'Italian way' of development, an alternative to the declining Ford-style giants, providing an explanation for the country's good economic progress. There are almost two hundred districts registered, starting from the north-east and branching down along the Adriatic coastline to the south of Italy, so many as to change the picture of the industrial landscape. There is no longer just the industrial triangle, or a clear-cut north-south divide, but an articulated geography that is witnessing new protagonists (the north-east and then NEC, north-east-centre) and discovering interesting clusters in southern regions too.[46]

The industrial districts are major actors in the 'Made in Italy' phenomenon, considering their success in combining craftsmanlike quality with mass production together with affordable prices (obtained thanks to favourable legislation and public incentives, though often, on the reverse side of the coin, to underpaid or undeclared labour and tax evasion). They often concern sectors for end products: textiles/clothing, machinery, household goods, food, leather/footwear, paper, plastics/rubber, and jewellery. Even if a significant part of their output is for export, a good share is also destined for the domestic market. It is difficult to overestimate how effective the promotion of these goods is in Italy, both for the quality, marketing ability, and because they are goods traditionally appreciated by Italian consumers. In other words the particular company structures have influenced consumer choice, highlighting sectors like fashion, furnishings, and food through the media (not forgetting that these were mainly the very commodities that the massive increase in advertising during the 1980s was promoting). There may have been over-exposure in Italy where some sectors were concerned but, if so, it was part of a more general culture that appreciates beauty and quality (even German consumers, once famous for buying their cars purely on the grounds of efficiency, performance, and low consumption, now consider the aesthetics and comfort side just as important). I will come back later to the 'Made in Italy' phenomenon; for now it is enough to highlight two sectors at least where the producers' 'suggestions' have had a striking impact.

The first concerns technological goods, in particular those relating to information and communication, which started to spread during the 1980s and '90s. It has been shown how technology has been a pivotal factor throughout the history of consumption, from transport to domestic appliances, to audiovisual equipment (radio, record players, TV, hi-fi, and so on). The question is this: does the latest generation of high-tech goods linked to information—computers and cell phones, for example—exert its own specific impact? Is it a new revolution? Of course it is, but at the same time it is too early to appreciate all the long-term implications. Science historians, the first to show an interest in the phenomenon, have put forward some theories. To begin with, as regards use, they agree that the concept of technology appropriation is fundamental, so that uses and meanings of an object are linked to the cultural context and the social, gender, and generational differences that are known well. Take the computer, for example. Parents (supported by schools) appreciate it for its teaching potential, but their offspring think differently and insist on using it for video games (supported by software producers). Husbands use it for work and information. Boys use it as extensions of games they have tried out in amusement arcades (on the lines of Ninterdo DS and Play Station) and see it as a chance to show off to their friends. Girls and women experiment less, using the computer more as a means of socializing; moreover, they often experience restricted access when competing with male members. In general, computers are used more in professional families, or merely in areas where these are in the majority.[47] More confirmation of the complex relationship that exists between producer and consumer can be seen in the fact that although Intel, HP, Apple, and Microsoft create products with particular characteristics, consumers do not necessarily use them in the way intended but adapt them to their own needs, albeit within a predetermined range of choices.[48] It is what De Certeau has called a 'silent overturn', taking as an extreme example what the Indios colonized by the Spaniards did: they accepted the laws and practices of the *conquistadores*, but subverted them, changing them from within and interpreting them in ways that preserved their own identity.[49]

As regards long-term effects, it is said that computers will help everyone move through multiple time and space dimensions, create as yet untried continuities between work and play, make speed more and more important, and above all put at risk the separation between public and private space as theorized by traditional sociology. By surfing the web I can enter virtual museums, observe a live conference, make purchases in a department store at any time or on any day (the implosion of time and space theorized by Ritzer!)[50] and work from home (or play in the office). The new domesticity virtually opens up to the outside world.

As elsewhere, the spread of the computer in Italy—found in 40 per cent of families in 2005—strongly reflects gender and age differences.[51] The percentage of people regularly using the Internet is 28 per cent. From this point of view Italy is experiencing a constant but gradual spread of the new technology, at least when compared to the European average of 43 per cent, with Germany and Great Britain at more than 50 per cent. The obstacles of the initial purchase cost and lack of IT literacy have slowed down its spread.[52] It could be said that the computer, IT's major instrument and symbol of a new era, has had a diffusion pattern similar to that which the car had in its time. Though symbolic of the economic miracle and desired by everyone, car ownership spread quite slowly through Italian society, taking several decades.[53]

The greatest hit belongs to the mobile—or cell-phone, however. Spreading like wildfire in very few years and at almost all social levels, it broke records in Europe (introduced by SIP on an experimental basis in 1973 and with RTMS coverage from 1985, while 78 per cent of families already owned one by 2005).Thanks to the low cost and easiness of use, it has caused a real revolution in communications, taking the place of the land-line telephone, which by European standards struggled to establish itself. On the contrary, the cell phone's lightning success recalls that of the fridge and washing machine success (which completely transformed domestic life, linking up with women's new role in and outside the home) as well as television (which for Italians opened wide the world of home entertainment and information). The cell phone was the gateway to the world of global communication.[54] Studies already exist testifying to its affective role: the ability to dispel fear or anxiety through a simple call ('Where are you? How are you doing?') or analysing its contribution to a new telegraphic, functional Italian language in use for chat purposes, a hybrid between spoken and written ('rotfl bbl') ('Rolling on the floor laughing, Be back later').[55] But the effects produced by a consumer tool that is forever being enriched with new functions and interfaces, shifting our attention from the object to the communication system itself, are still to be understood in terms of how we organize our social lives, mix moments of work and play, and identify with a group.[56]

New products have appeared not just in the technological sector alone, but in more or less all areas of consumption. Just think of the new plastic derivatives used in furniture, buildings, and transport, textile fibres, and so on. I will pause for a moment to inspect one particular sector—food—and try to remember that the food served at my table comes from a long chain starting with agriculture, passing through industry and technology, thence transported to warehouses and on to sales points (strongly influenced by politics, culture, and local history).[57]

Two thirds of the products offered to the consumer are traditional (pasta, oil, wine, and bread); a further slice (17 per cent) is made up of food that has been processed and treated for time-saving purposes (ready-made pasta sauces, prepared meals, quick-frozen food, sweets and snacks, biscuits etc.). The remaining 18 per cent is subdivided into different types of 'new' products. A first group fully deserves this definition; they are foods which for dietary, health, or convenience motives have been industrially transformed or pre-treated, such as low-calorie food, no-fat yoghurt, energy-rich drinks, nutrition sticks, dietary integrators, and ready-to-eat dishes. The second group is that of typical products (bearing the symbol DOP or IGP), which are traditional products of Italian gastronomy. So why put them here? The question of 'authenticity' is one of the most hotly debated topics in cultural history, and has revealed that many 'traditions' (including culinary ones) are inventions, not necessarily in the sense that they did not exist before, but that they did not exist with those meanings.[58] A certain local product used to be just oil, a kind of bean, a chestnut, or cheese. Now, thanks to careful codifying of the characteristics and to marketing skills it has become symbolic of an entire regional tradition: a Pretuzian Oil from the Teramo Hills, a Sarconi Bean, a Mugello Chestnut, and a Spressa of the Giudicarie Valleys Cheese. Colonnata Lard has become an internationally recognized speciality, a preciously rare product symbolizing ancient Tuscany and Italian eating—with a very different meaning to the one Carrara peasants would have given it a century ago. The third group, made up of organic products, is definitely in a niche of its own (1 per cent), also because it entails particularly high added costs (more than a fifth extra for the producer, that is double or treble the cost of the DOP stamp, traceability, or absence of GMP).[59]

Changes in the food sector do not stop here. By what miracle have eggs all become big, brown, and beautiful (what became of the small, white, and probably slightly dirty eggs we used to see in farmhouses of old)? How is it that cuts of meat are so perfect, always fresh, and all the same? Here seen at work is one of the most dramatic and spectacular examples of the manipulation of nature. As Roger Horowitz records, the effort to adapt natural foods to our social needs has a long history.[60] Partially mechanized equipment to process and pack meat was already in use in 19th-century America, while scientists were applying their knowledge to improving the health, weight, and quality of the cattle. The history of modern agriculture has been largely a tale of the appliance of science and technology (GMP being no more than the latest stage). It was during the 20th century, however, that this process accelerated, mainly through the joint intervention of biology (capable of influencing genetic characteristics and natural growth times) and chemistry (penetrating food with medicines and various concoctions, to make eggs turn brown for example). Even animals have to adapt to production cycles and human needs. They must not only be fat and healthy so that nothing will be wasted, they must also be standardized to reduce packaging and transport costs, and permit the use of mechanized equipment (why does one animal go on being large and another one small, one lean and another fat? Why are all fish not already the right size for one or two servings?).[61] The product they provide must be aesthetically correct (brown for eggshells, bright red for meat, pure white for raw fish and is pink when tinned, given that consumers trust their eyes to judge quality). So, every day in the shops can be found all the cuts of meat, types of fish, and colour of eggs we wanted, always fresh, always the right size, shade, and consistency. Also favourite fruit and vegetables can be bought at any time of the year (being seasonal is no good for the market).

But there is the other side of the coin for this level of manipulation, and it came at the end of the twentieth century with a new wave of anxiety related to food, fears of adulteration, fraud, poisoning, or even that some foods were unnatural and unhealthy. Outbreaks of sickness and scandals did the rest, giving their contribution to an increasingly widespread desire to 'return to nature' and a renewed appreciation of simple, unsophisticated food (see the success of the Slow Food movement with its food as 'culture' approach and a new way of eating revolving around local traditions).[62] Producers tried to react with advertising campaigns conjuring up white flour mills, country folk transporting cheese on horse-drawn carts, and contented cows in Alpine pastures with flowers in their ears or, more to the point, with tracking systems showing the chain of delivery and new quality standards (but carrying higher prices of course). There is no simple solution. It is not just a case of ensuring quality and genuineness at all costs. There have always been niches of excellent producers (perhaps once 'suppliers to the Royal House'). Now the challenge is to get good food to as many consumers as possible, overcoming distribution problems which have always made life hard for small-time producers, and at

competitive prices (the role of the food industry and large-scale distribution network should not be under estimated in making available to
everybody—thanks to low prices and easy availability—food once
reserved for the élite). In the end it will be up to consumers to work
out a personal mix of choices to satisfy their needs from among the
many different types of products and prices.

At the same time there still remain doubts about new kinds of foods
or food-producing methods and more generally about those seen as
excessively industrial, though there are also moves in another direction.
Since the 1990s, at least more attention has been paid to safeguarding
the natural quality of food and the environment by an increasing
number of small producers as well as big concerns, with the result
that a lot of investment has been poured into improving the quality of
goods and efficiency of the production system, saving energy, and
enhancing their image in the eyes of consumers (the dollar is also
'green', a General Electric campaign reminds us). A case of eco-mar-
keting? Perhaps, but it could lead to a turning point where companies
see respect for nature as a benefit rather than an expense.

The limits and costs of consumption

The city of Leonia starts each day anew. Every morning the citizens wake
up between fresh sheets, break open new bars of soap to wash themselves
with, put on brand new dressing gowns, take unopened cartons of milk
out of state-of-the-art fridges, all while listening to the latest jingle on the
latest hi-fi. On the pavement, wrapped in stiff plastic sacks, are the
remains of yesterday's Leonia waiting for the dust cart to pass. Not just
squashed toothpaste tubes, burnt-out light bulbs, newspapers, containers
and wrapping material, but also water heaters, encyclopedias, pianos and
china dinner sets. More than by the things that are made, sold and
bought each day, Leonia's wealth is measured by the things that get
thrown away to make space for the new. [. . .]

Nobody wonders where the daily load of rubbish is taken: certainly
outside the city, but each year the city expands, and the garbage has to be
taken further off. It turns into a mountain as the piles get higher and
higher, form layers and spread out around a wider perimeter. Add to this
the fact that the better Leonia gets at making new materials, the better
will be the rubbish to be thrown away, longer-lasting, more fireproof and

resistant to the weather, a veritable fortress of indestructible remains encircling the city, looming over it on all sides like an enormous mountain plateau. [...]

Leonia's sprawling rubbish tip would invade the world if it were not blocked by the rubbish tips from other cities, which like Leonia dump their mountains of garbage as far away as possible. Perhaps the whole world beyond the boundaries of Leonia is covered with craters of rubbish, each with a metropolis in the centre spewing out a continuous eruption.[63]

Italo Calvino's imaginary Marco Polo not only tells the emperor Kublai Khan about his surreal travels in the Far East; he effectively presents the cost to the environment of consumption (abundance creates just as many problems as poverty, it is simply that the problems are different, as Schleifer reminds us).[64] Obviously deterioration of the environment has to be seen in relation to much wider processes, to do with industrialization, urbanization, demographic growth, agricultural activities, and so forth. Thus, even by limiting research to rubbish, technically there exists many different types, depending on the raw materials, manufacturing output and finally, specifically linked to the cycle of consumption: urban waste in fact.

All I am interested in noting here is how the consumption process is increasingly linked to the environment in public debate. In fact it is placed in a systemic framework, so to say, inside the biosphere. Production uses shares of 'natural capital' that are not always replaceable; consumption, for its part, does not stop with the buying and using of the product, but is carried on into the discarding of what is left over, with equally serious consequences for the physical surroundings. Leonia's mountains of garbage are part of reality, just as urban pollution and the dwindling of some natural resources are. With the passing of time economic growth could actually prove uneconomical, as the disadvantages could on the whole outnumber the benefits, which again raises the question: are there physical limits to consumption? Is the environment—or even the entire planet—capable of supporting the consequences of endless production and consumption? And if up to now it is western economies that have been the chief protagonists of development, what will happen when other areas of the world start to grow economically?

It is known full well that the environment issue is one of the major challenges facing the twenty-first century and that there are no easy answers. Academics have put forward various theories and new areas of study have arisen, such as ecological economics.[65] They range from the most radical anti-consumption proposals to more moderate ones of 'sustainable consumption', relying on virtuous behaviour by consumers, improvements in production techniques (which at present waste more than 30 per cent of the resources fed into the production cycle), and policies that aim at a lower environmental impact.

The consumerist behaviours just seen are certainly linked to such problems and cut across the whole of society, influenced by such factors as ideological stance, local situation, socioeconomic condition and what Inglehart has defined as post-material values.[66] In fact, according to his theory, during the 1960s and '70s a 'silent revolution' took place: some sections of the population abandoned materialistic values linked to physical consumption and the search for security (always given priority because of their connection with survival) for post-material values (affection, belonging, respect, aesthetic and intellectual pleasures, environmental concerns). Members of generations that have never suffered poverty or privation, post-materialists (the young, minorities, middle to upper-middle urban classes) are often most critical and dissatisfied with contemporary politics, which they see as far from addressing their needs (unlike low-income groups, which are more materialistic). Here there is the tension that Weber noted between 'substantial rationality' (oriented to ultimate values), and 'functional rationality' (more sensitive to the means of reaching them): two forms that are equally valid and necessary but which lead to different ways of looking at society.[67] Post-materialists embody the first form, materialists the second. This explains why, in today's western societies with their amazing growth in wealth and super-abundance of material goods, enormous improvements in living standards and a substantial elimination of hunger, there is however a high degree of dissatisfaction. Priorities have changed for many people.

This phenomenon has certainly revealed itself in Italy, following the same time frames. Consider the birth of environmentalism, a typical expression of 'post-materialism'; it developed from the 1970s in the collective movements of the time, although a feeling for nature obviously went back a long way, at least to the late nineteenth, and early twentieth century with the creation of clubs and associations to protect the countryside. Neri Serneri has traced a historic profile of the movement, reconstructing its ambivalent relations with politics initially and ensuing search for a specific role in the anti-nuclear movement, to start up again in the 1980s with a much greater cultural content and widespread support. Since then it has developed both on the level of protectionist associations and at a specifically political level, choosing to enter the arena of party politics (political ecology).[68] At the end of the century the *no global* movements and books such as Naomi Klein's *No logo* drew public attention to the ethical-transnational implications of globalized production and consumption.[69]

The spontaneous adoption of behaviours to limit the impact of our daily activities on the environment (less squandering of energy and products, using bicycles instead of cars, differentiated recycling of waste, etc.) is beginning to have an effect on the urban landscape. Added to this are those organized by associations or local authorities (for example driving bans), though these often take on only symbolic value in the absence of any change in living and working conditions, which call for an intense use of transport—to get to work or school, do the shopping, deal with bureaucratic procedures—a use of communications (cell phones and computers), or household items (electrical appliances, TVs, and DVD readers), as well as a profusion of tin openers, grills, beaters, crumb gatherers, microwave ovens, coffee makers, vaporizers, slicers, razors, toothbrushes, aerosols, vacuum cleaners, and electric brooms.[70] The impression remains of finding ourselves in the typical 'prisoner's dilemma' of the Game Theory: the individual's selfish interest clashing with collective interest. The only winning strategy is to cooperate.

Among the various experiments to adapt to sustainable consumption (such as the 2005 one when the Venice city council asked a thousand families to limit their buying to what was environmentally friendly and ethically correct for ten months),[71] there has been no lack of extreme measures. A particularly interesting one reported by the Italian media is this: an American press reporter, Judith Levine, bought nothing at all for a year, with the exception of the bare necessities for survival (no ready-made food, no restaurants, cinema, books, clothing, or things for the home). She later explained that this had heightened her awareness of responsible consumption but had at the same time sidetracked her into a kind of parallel universe, cutting her off from a social life always based on consumption.[72]

Are these new behaviours related to consumption the reflections of new values in the sense indicated by Inglehart, or do they reflect a real or perceived change in the Italian situation? To reply, I turn to a special measuring index. It is known that the GDP, which only concerns economic size, is clearly insufficient in this sense, as is the later Human Development Index (HDI), which also considers sociocultural factors such as life expectancy and education level but does not take environmental variables into account.[73] On the contrary, 'sustainability' measures have recently been developed, including the Index of Sustainable Economic Wealth (ISEW), proposed by Herman Daly and John Cobb in 1989. This is based on many different economic measurements, including income, consumption, and possession of durable goods, integrated with environmental factors (such as urban expenses, commuting, pollution, road accidents, and resource depletion).[74] Well, it turns out that for a long time in Italy the ISEW grew at the same pace as the GDP, albeit at a lower level, but began to decline during the 1970s, because the negative factors increased faster than the positive ones (unlike the GDP). In other words, this means that the cost of environmental impact for a certain production and consumption model makes its negative effects felt.[75] The impression that many have of a declining quality of life, even if they are on a steady or increasing income seems to find confirmation here.

In the meantime, some consolation comes from the world of art, which has learned to use the rubbish cluttering up Leonia for a new artistic language. Following early avant-garde movements, and the protest art of contestation, much of contemporary art has always been inspired by removal and rejection: partly to denounce, partly to provoke, or perhaps to show (as if in a mirror) lives, habits, and identities through what is consumed, and thought forgotten. Bags of waste, plastic bottles, broken equipment, bits of chairs, empty frames, piles of newspapers, used batteries, burnt-out light bulbs: all enter into the repertory of trash art.[76] The objection could be raised that taking objects out of context makes a difference. Take rubbish out of its usual peace and present it in the refined, ascetic, well-lit rooms of a museum with bilingual explanation tags, and it will change mental attitudes to it. The rubbish is no longer rubbish, but consigned to art to last for ever. Some have gone further than that. Daniel Spoerri, noted for his sculpture garden in Tuscany on the banks of the Amiata, made a habit of organizing show-banquets. During the performance guests would be served with works by Arman, César, and himself made of edible material ('eat art').[77] Afterwards nothing would remain: in a single moment art and consumption literally merged.

12

Contemporary Everyday Life

Fashion and the body

The strongest consumption taboo is the body. It cannot be eaten or consumed. In contemporary societies this is perhaps the worst sin and a symptom of aberration and madness. Yet it can be said that anthropophagy is a feature much present in our culture. This is not a reference to ancient episodes of cannibalism (even if documented), but to symbolic practices where the body of a human or a god is eaten. More or less all over Europe a ritual at the end of harvesting used to take place during which the last grain gathered was baked into bread or pastry with a human shape, given thanks to and venerated, then torn to pieces and eaten by the whole community, as Frazer testifies. And there are numerous ceremonies that metaphorically call for the ritual sacrifice of a god and the consumption of his flesh and blood by the faithful.[1]

There was no gainsaying the sacred nature of the body, as the twentieth century drew to a close. Its importance and distinction are characteristic traits of this phase in history. Nevertheless, the evolution of science and a new cultural sensitivity are tending to redefine its boundaries, and it is from these that reflections concerning present-day consumption may start. If the body is sacred, it cannot be reduced to merchandise, to be bought or sold; neither can parts of it, they can only be donated (although the actual commerce in organs and bodies (slaves), is so widespread in the world that it is, like drugs, one of the main sources of illegal income).[2] But science is pushing us to redefine the limits of the body's inviolability: can we use the body or its parts for scientific purposes? Is genetic modification legal? Can cloned organs be used, and in the future whole bodies?

The use and manipulation of the body is not limited to the field of science. Physical transformation such as tattooing, piercing, scarification (cuts to create visible scars), branding ('the kiss of fire'), implantation (subcutaneous insertion of pearls or small jewels) and (even severe) mutilation, to communicate an identity, are cultural practices of long-standing tradition, but in today's context they can at times take on the actual form of 'body consumption'. Also to be included are interventions by modern medicine, which make it possible to have even extreme external and internal cosmetic surgery (lifting, liposuction, permanent tanning or complexion lightening, plastic surgery, revirgination, facial grafts, etc.), all signs of total morphing.[3] I well understand here what Marshall Sahlins means when he talks about consumption as if it were a performance:[4] making the body our work of art. Much could also be written about media and digital manipulation of the body, putting it on display and making a spectacle of its anatomy,[5] and already there opens up a whole horizon of new links with the artificial. More and more internal devices exist for the body to take inside in order to improve its functioning or change its form, from pacemakers to hearing aids, from prosthetics to artificial retinas, while nanotechnology and bio-engineering present unimagined scenarios of man-machine interfaces, if not of hybrid creatures.[6]

To get back to a more everyday world, let us think about body shapes. Certain paintings by Botero come to mind. Here is a voluptuous woman languidly stretched out on a double bed (completely filling it), another looks at herself in the mirror of a small bathroom she barely fits into; yet another is an odalisque enthroned in all her monumental nakedness.[7] The question is this: in an age characterized by abundance and often unrestrained consumption, when most people can afford to accumulate as much as they want, eat as much as they can and indulge in anything to excess, why are thin bodies appreciated, leading to cases of anorexia? Why does floridness and physical opulence not triumph? Many have been struck by this contradiction, seeing it as a removal of the body, a rejection of what is material, a kind of historical nemesis, or more simply the excessive power of the media to spread their message (possibly linked to the needs of fashion). Yet it should be said that extremely thin models—especially female ones—have a long history in the West.[8] Think of anorexic saints, who fast to triumph over the will of the flesh, reach a superior spiritual level and, according to studies like Bynum's, to display a criticism of authority as well: a thin body is a holy body.[9] Think of the aesthetic canons frequently in vogue among the upper classes, and testified by many artistic portraits, so different from those pictures of peasants (for whom 'fat is beautiful'): a thin body is a beautiful body. Remember too the importance of how well the body functions: it must be agile and well trained, for military needs, and able to work and produce its best (probably aided by a gymnasium today):[10] a thin body is an efficient body. There is also the growing pressure of medical opinion which links fatness (or at least obesity) to diseases and other health risks, goes on about 'normal weight' and recommends balanced diets: a thin body is a healthy body. Finally, as Schleifer observes, if abundance really is the pervasive mark of modernity, then distinction can only be found in abstinence and austerity. It is the same mechanism whereby art chooses the path of abstract formalism and minimalism.[11] Our quest for thinness is not deprivation but an investment we make in our body.

If the shape of our body is communicative, then the clothes covering it are even more so. Clothes and their accessories (or lack of them) have always gone beyond their protective functions to transmit culture and identity: social group, class, gender, age, kind of job, etc. Body and dress are closely connected and since both are products of our culture, it is not a one-sided connection (there is still the tendency to think fine feathers make fine birds). Speaking of 'dressing up' we cannot avoid turning to fashion and its role today, mindful of how different kinds of clothing can epitomize social and political movements. How can unisex clothes consisting of jeans, t-shirts, and gym shoes be separated from changes in gender and generation, or power dressing (a woman's suit of jacket and skirt/trousers cut to masculine lines, dark and sober— probably combined with some carefully-chosen feminine touches such as high heels, discreet jewellery or long hair) from women's entry into the managerial world?[12]

So, what is the meaning of fashion today? Many academics have addressed this question, starting with pioneers like Georg Simmel, who sees in the imitation/differentiation dichotomy the key to understanding a phenomenon typical of all social behaviours: in continuous tension between the two attitudes we all like to conform, belong to a group so as to feel secure and protected but at the same time stand out, assert our individuality, and break free. In a mass society fashion draws its meaning along class lines and tends to spread from the top downwards—an anticipation of Veblen's trickle down effect, as it were.[13] Then there is Walter Benjamin who, seeing in fashion's drive for rapid, continuous change an essential component of urban life, speaks of fascination with the almost dreamlike spectacle of goods on display, a dream alluding to values set deep in modern society, and defines fashion as the 'sex appeal of the inorganic'.[14] To tell the truth, such reflections came to be forgotten somewhat and, as noted before, Frankfurt School interpretations dominated for a long time, with fashion branded as something utterly commercial, alienating, and dictatorial.

The first cultural turn came from the socio-semiological interpretation of Roland Barthes, according to which fashion is a language: everything bought has hidden 'levels of meaning', which go back to far greater myths (a uniform stand for homeland, honour, loyalty; a miniskirt stands for sexual freedom for women, etc.). Goods are language signs through which hyman beings communicate identity, relate to others, and confront deep cultural meanings—myths in fact—all contained in an object. Following fashion means communicating, yet to understand the message it doesn't help to look at the individual items (lexis) but at their combination (syntax), which is made explicit in the descriptions found in specialist magazines for example.[15] The communication side of fashion is again stressed by the second cultural turn, the anthropological one. If it is the objects of material culture that give meaning to our actions and environment, if they are almost an 'extension' of the body, then even the clothes worn are a means of constructing our identity and fashion is a moving stage on which to display ourselves socially. For Mary Douglas first and Arjun Appadurai later, our clothes, just like all the things chosen as surroundings, speak about individual identity.[16]

It is mainly these two reading keys (fashion as language, fashion as identity builder) that have influenced following interpretations. So it is that emphasis is laid on how it is better to use the plural form today, talking about fashions rather than fashion, and about the proliferation of parallel styles, which consumers draw from and adapt for creative reuse (*détournement*).[17] Studies are made of the growing overlap between the fashion system and media world[18] and of the role of subcultures in setting up aesthetic styles to help create shared identities (or recognize oneself as part of the 'tribe', to use a Maffesoli term).[19] It is interesting to note how fashion often goes from the base upwards, from the street to the catwalk, partly thanks to so-called 'cool hunters' who study the spontaneous creativity of people, especially the young, mingling with them and working online, as they look for signs of future trends.[20] Or it is noted how the fashion phenomenon is no longer limited to clothes and accessories but also includes household furnishings, holiday destinations, and everything that helps to 'represent us' (*total living*). Indeed authors such as Landowski maintain that mechanisms typical of fashion are at work in many other social sectors as well.[21]

It goes without saying that in Italy the weight of the fashion sector (supreme expression of *visual consumption*) is particularly significant, not just from an economic perspective, but also culturally. The fashion system revolving around the stylist who proposes his lines, or even a total look, supported by a high quality production chain through a complex system of sub-suppliers, and giving equal attention to the manufacturing and the marketing, reached full maturity in the 1980s.[22] To the 'classic' designers, like Armani (with his androgynous style and destructured jackets), Versace (provocative and aggressive), Missoni (who reinvented Italian knitware) and then Krizia, Valentino, Fendi, and Ferrè, were added names like Moschino, Gigli, and Dolce & Gabbana. At the same time, increasing international competition caused the fashion houses to study new strategies. On one side resources were marshalled to enhance the value of the brand even more than the product, which meant following each and every stage of production, distribution, and promotion, paying particular attention to the final selling places, where images of the brand would be put on show (I will come back to this later). On the other side big agglomerations were created in order to compete on the global market, taking over other brands (as Gucci and Prada did, for example).

But fashion did not stop here. As design had started to do before and food was to do after, it gave Italy a new identity,[23] sweeping away some of the old stereotypes that existed in other countries and launching a different image of the country: the 'Italian way of life'.

Private and public space

A new domestic landscape. These are my thoughts as I am catapulted into a present-day kitchen, the setting that seems once more the focal point of the home, thanks to its air of conviviality.[24] But 'new' may be the wrong word; perhaps it should be 'old' domestic landscape, because I am actually in a restructured farmhouse somewhere in the Italian countryside. Inside a great white space with ceiling supported by wooden beams stands an enormous brickwork kitchen unit with steel sink, work surface, and large *La Cornue* enamelled cooker. Facing, is a fireplace with two armchairs and a rocking chair in front of it. In the middle of the room is a large antique table with chairs and precious monastery-style top, flanked by two tall wooden cupboards, with flow-ery curtains at the windows, and copper pans and various utensils hanging from the walls. The floor is made of light-coloured fir wood. At the far end are wooden stairs leading to the floor above. The atmosphere is decidedly warm and welcoming.

I have been taken back in time . . . or perhaps not. The professional couple that left the town and restructured this farmhouse have made a definite choice. They wanted to live in a more natural environment in keeping with authentic country traditions. Already noted is the mis-leading nature of this so-called 'authenticity'. This same farmhouse contains (expensive) antique furniture and modern resurfacing. It is clean, well-heated, and brightly lit (remember how farmhouses were up to a few decades ago: poor, dirty, dilapidated, without heating, stuffy, and with a smell of damp lingering everywhere). Living in this 'modern' farmhouse therefore takes on an unequivocal cultural meaning. Apart from this, what is striking us is the size of this kitchen space. To construct it they must surely have knocked down dividing walls, and now the kitchen is merged with the old parlour, to create the living room, which has become the focal point of the home. How did it happen?

There is no time to answer before being whisked away into a completely different space (better than many a teleport). It is still a kitchen—I think, even though in this immense minimalist space there is practically nothing else. This Bulthaup b3 is in effect a functioning wall right in the middle of the room, to which are attached shelves, multi-use boxes, electrical appliances, and a kind of 'floating' cooker. The domi-nant colours are white, grey, and delicate wood tones; the materials are natural or high-tech. There is hardly any other furniture in this sophis-ticated living room. All is a play of light and transparency, no pictures or ornaments, and an aristocratic emptiness reigns supreme (how different from the homes overflowing with bourgeois objects at the start of the 20th century!). Comfort and functionality merge with aesthetic refinement, which is the true mark of this space. I am, in fact, in a fashion designer's city pad which displays an extreme case of open-plan living. The old internal partitions of domestic space have been ripped away. There are no more male or female spaces, the physical space becomes one; no more public or private because the entire home is private and there is no need to hide or conceal secrets from the indiscreet eyes of outsiders. All is exposed; all is on display and communicates with the exterior. The space has become multifunctional (kitchen, study, leisure, and rest room all at the same time); it is less conventional, less rigid.[25]

Now what is happening? I have been flown to yet another place. It seems to be a kitchen, but this time the arrangement is more familiar. The room is not very big (neither is the rest of the flat) but it is self-contained and functional. Against the wall is a fitted kitchen in red laminate, with matching cupboards hanging above, and a capacious white fridge alongside. Against another wall there is a little plastic table with folding chairs and above it open shelves with plates and glasses, ornaments, plants, pepper mills, and brightly coloured cooking utensils. Instantly recognizable, it is an IKEA kitchen that a young couple of office workers, with a small child, have just purchased. The arrangement and separation of the domestic spaces is more traditional, but even here the kitchen has become the living room, the place where they spend most of their time, and the area for the little one's toys (which are scattered all around). The main entrance opens straight into it.

In their different ways, all three of these spaces represent the cultural transformations that have taken place in the last hundred years. All three show how consumer objects can define social identity and the parameters of the new domestic landscape.

As is already recognized, consumer culture has just as strong an effect on external spaces outside of the home, and here, I am not referring so much to entertainment—which has changed anyway; traditional forms of entertainment now enter the home via TV, satellite, and DVDs, causing a relative decline in the fortunes of theatres and cinemas—but of other trends. Socialising venues connected with food consumption are strongly making their presence felt across the whole of society. A good three quarters of Italians now eat meals outside the home—lunch (divided equally between convivial meals and snacks), and increasingly dinners (with a clear preference for pizzas or 'de-structured' meals, that is without the complete, three course menu), breakfast (the classic one in a bar with coffee or cappuccino) and finally appetisers or after-dinner drinks (typical of the 25–34 age bracket), not to mention canteen and collective meals. For practical reasons (increased mobility, more female employment, work timetables) and cultural ones (appreciation of food and the conviviality associated with it), eating out now accounts for a third of the total of food consumption.[26]

Where external spaces are concerned one of the most characteristic forms of consumption is probably represented by tourism. It is certainly nothing new, it was increasingly developing throughout the twentieth century, but it has now become a mass phenomenon and seems to be symbolic of this post-modern era. Witness the almost archetypal tourists, in Hanson's statues. He has a Hawaiian t-shirt and Bermudas, camera fixed round his neck, accessory case, baseball cap, and ruddy face. She is slightly overweight, with flip-flops, striped slacks and sweater, (less expensive) camera, tote bag, and handbag. They are both standing, somewhat wearily, staring straight ahead into the distance.[27]

According to academics like Urry, this stare turns everything into consumption: the landscape becomes a picture postcard, local product a souvenir, local food becomes exotic fast food, and local culture becomes typical folklore. It forces the local economy to change, abandon survival activities and rustic homes to build hotels, roads, restaurants, chalets, cable cars, tourist shops, and postcard kiosks. It encourages the inhabitants to behave in a certain way, as dictated by tradition, or better, how the tourists themselves expect them to behave; it transforms nature into a consumer spectacle (and if nature is not up to it, *ad hoc* scenery is brought in). Thanks to our fascination with the past, the mere fact of being 'historical' can create a tourist attraction. In his attempt to get away from everyday routine, even the modern 'post-tourist' of the 'new bourgeoisie' (the famous traveller rather than tourist), careful of his image, ironic and detached, fails to avoid the trap that turns culture into consumption and society into spectacle.[28] It was only during the 1970s and '80s that an alternative was developed. It is what environmental historians, anthropologists, and activists have defined as 'eco-tourism' or ecological tourism: sustainable, well-informed, in small groups, respecting culture and the environment. It is hard to say whether this kind of tourism could be practised on a large scale (or whether it is more likely to see environmental historians, anthropologists, activists, and other select categories as the main protagonists). What is certain is that today many emphasize the ambivalent nature of tourism: it is not only a phenomenon where tourists are almost seen as 'new colonialists' while the local inhabitants passively submit to their inquisitive stare, but also a moment when two equally active cultures meet (so that it is important to listen to what the 'locals' have to say as well). As a process it may affect the territory in different ways, causing either warm appreciation or hostile resistance: a kind of economic flywheel effect that can benefit the infrastructures or just as easily rebound on the traditional economy and ruin it, a cultural contact that can either make or break a country's traditions.[29] Like all forms of consumption, tourism contains unresolved ambiguity.

But if there is an area where differentiation has expressed itself in the best possible way, it is in the commercial spaces, our privileged point of observation.

The new commercial places

Disneyland or Las Vegas? Disneyland with its fantastic self-contained worlds: old-style cottages along Main Street, medieval castle in the background, swamps and jungles, wild animals, world of the future, Fantasyland (all perfectly clean, pleasant, and organized: magic in fact); Las Vegas with its casinos and gigantic hotels, pyramid and sphinx, its volcano erupting every quarter of an hour, pirate attack, reproductions of Manhattan, Bellagio, and Venice, complete with navigable canals for gondolas and starry sky (a city in continuous motion, all light and colour, both inside and outside the Strip). Which of the models is the best demonstration of consumer culture today? Perhaps both of them because they are two variations of the consumer-entertainment, and consumer-spectacle binomials, which have been around since the first nineteenth-century department stores and have reached their zenith here. According to Ritzer, this is the unavoidable direction to take if you wish to 're-enchant' a jaded consumer used to over-rationalized consumer products, i.e. homogeneous, calculable, predictable, and efficient, the perfect example being a McDonald's hamburger: always the same in every shop, competently and identically prepared, the same ingredients served the same way in similar surroundings. This is why they have to keep on inventing new ways of captivating customers.[30]

What is sure is that the latest developments in commercial places seem to be heading towards the gigantic and spectacular. Think of commercial centres—those complexes of shops and services that in the US had already made their appearance in the early decades of the twentieth century, but only took on a definitive shape after the Second World War, when the exodus of motorized affluent middle classes into the suburbs gave impetus to the creation of commercial structures in empty spaces well outside the cities. In 1956, the architect Victor

Gruen built a single structure capable of containing a whole set of shops, completely covered over, with air conditioning and plenty of greenery, on the outskirts of Minneapolis. It was the Edina Southdale Center, the first 'mall', and would set the pattern for all the others.[31] Gruen's intuition told him that creating a collection of selling places is not enough, no matter how easy they are to reach: there has to be a city atmosphere as well. This is why his malls seem to reproduce a city centre, with shops of course, but also walkways, small squares with bars and restaurants, flower beds, fountains playing, and lots of cultural and recreational initiatives: a perfect city where the streets are never dirty, surveillance guarantees safety, thieves and poor minorities are kept away, there is plenty of parking space, it never rains and is never too hot or too cold. A city outside the city in fact, a new place to meet socially (Baudrillard, on the contrary, would consider it a 'simulacrum' capable of killing the real one).

Commercial centres arrived later in Europe, and not until the 1970s in Italy (one of the first was at Pratilia, near Prato), amid much scepticism, partly because they had small shops as well as big stores or supermarkets in the same area, that is enterprises usually in competition with one another (whereas they are actually examples of 'coopetition', a strategy derived from Game Theory: not a knock-out elimination contest where winner takes all and the loser gets nothing, but cooperation in a competitive scenario where everyone can benefit). Some commercial centres have grown up around a new formula, the hypermarket, a megastructure (5,000 or 10,000 sq. m.) on the outskirts, selling food and non-food items at the same time, with rock-bottom prices and big discounts—based on the consideration that rich western world consumers tend to subdivide their spending into 'grocery' (ordinary stuff where it is better to save as much as possible) and 'non grocery' (valuable things like cars, electronic equipment, and communications where a great deal is spent in order to ensure quality and after-sales assistance). Hypermarkets with these characteristics had come into existence in 1963 with Carrefour in France, followed by Auchan (but hotly pursued by Meijer, the American superstore, and then the supercentre of what was to become the world's commercial leader, Wal-Mart).[32]

In the last few years there has been a return of these big centres to the cities, a phenomenon particularly obvious in Europe where old ports, disused factories, and warehouses are being taken over, as are entire areas of the city centre, to be restructured and revitalized, although some maintain that such operations often alter the nature and character of the places, for example their civic, religious, or artistic value, transforming them into artificial, consumer cities ('inventing' historic centres?).[33] In any case, the presence of commercial centres makes a big difference to the urban landscape, changing look and landmark since, as Zukin reminds us, the landscape is a physical space, a merging of material and social practices, as well as a symbolic representation of them.[34]

Many of these new spaces are characterized by two aspects in particular. The first is the insistence on nature: flowers and plants (even large ones), lakes and fountains, natural light that filters through the transparent canopy, the use of natural materials like wood or, if it is an open-air structure, reminders of local styles and materials; all with a particular attention to their impact on the environment. In other words, sustainable, eco-orientated architecture, not to be associated with all the cement and artificiality that only reminds one of a factory.[35] The second aspect is the highlighting of the spectacular, entertaining moment that is so much part of shopping today. The herald of this trend is Jon Jerde, creator of the Mall of America, the biggest commercial centre in the United States, which contains a whole amusement park inside it; the Universal Citywalk, a kind of walkway full of attractions and shops linking the Los Angeles studios; the Bellagio casino at Las Vegas; and Canal City Hakata, a spectacular commercial centre (*depato*) based on the water theme at Fukuoka in Japan.[36]

In Italy, large-scale distribution took off in grand style from the middle of the 1980s, in conjunction with the economic recovery and the spreading of consumer products to all social classes. It was the time the doors of liberalization opened wide and certain political barriers that had been slowing down its development collapsed.[37] It could in fact be said that, as with the department stores in the Liberal age and supermarkets during the economic miracle, the new consumer places are both cause and effect of the transformations: cause in that they stimulate buying by arousing interest and curiosity (as well as making use of technological innovation), effect because they depend on the cultural and economic changes that have issued from society itself. The large-scale distribution share of the market rapidly increased, at the expense of the small food shops in particular. It was 2005, the year of the 'overtake', when the mass retail networks seized over half the

commercial consumption, in comparison with 37 per cent for traditional shops (and 12 per cent for itinerant salesmen, direct sales, mail
orders, and other forms). But these data averages conceal a big difference between the food sector (68 per cent dominated by big firms) and
the non-food sector (static at 33 per cent) where the commercial world
seems to be more associated with small dimensions than the rest of
Europe. It comes as no surprise, therefore, that Coop-Italia, the major
Italian company, operates in the food area, nor that it is a long
way down in the international classification of large-scale retail firms:
only 49th in 2005 (in a table led at global level by Wal-Mart and, much
further down, at the European level by Carrefour).[38]

The last stage in this development is the 'factory outlet', another
American formula, which are shops directly controlled by the producer
offering the public unsold designer label goods that used to end up on
market stalls or in secondary sales channels. Developing since the
1970s, they were an answer to consumers needing to buy designer
label clothes for special occasions (often from the previous season) as
well as producers wanting to safeguard their image and market share.
Initially they were groups of simple style shops, but their success (partly
thanks to new social values acquired by the brand houses) have led
them to take on many of the characteristics typical of commercial
centres. The first Italian outlet opened in 2000 at Serravalle Scrivia,
near Alessandria, and it is among the biggest in Europe. So what does it
look like? Here I am, right in the middle of it, in Piazza Portici, a vast
paved square with a fountain in the middle and old, porticoed palaces
all around, some linked to one another by passages. Several roads
branch out from the square, some straight, others twisted, leading us
to other broadways. The pastel-coloured houses have two or three
storeys. All around I see flowers in pots, trees, benches, street lamps,
and bars with tables outside. Built by McArthurGlen as a replica of an
18th-century Ligurian historic centre, this unique town consists
completely of traditional-style shops (almost two hundred of them), as
well as bars and restaurants, and it is pedestrian only. The numerous
customers I see here are acting out a real democratization of luxury in
spaces not at all like the canonical ones (luxurious city-centre shops,
frequented by an elite clientele). A sort of staged show takes place: you
can buy designer label clothes for special occasions in a shop that looks
just like the original one, in an urban space just like its city counterpart.[39] Consumption is theatre too. What a pity I have run out of time,

otherwise I could go over to the other outlet in Castel Romano, inspired by Imperial Rome, and stroll between Piazza Augusto and Via Costantino, past walls, colonnades, arches and dozens of shops, then have a drink in the Arkadia bar.

All these places have an inclusive logic, with the idea of gathering more and more customers and extending to all social classes even the most élite consumer products; but looking closer there is also a completely opposing logic, which is exclusive and aims at differentiation and the appreciation of the lifestyles of particular segments of the public. Take the chain stores which have long been a familiar presence in urban spaces (think of Benetton, Stefanel, Prenatal, Chicco, Goldenpoint, and many others).[40] One-brand stores are trying to raise their profile as high as possible to increase their recognizability with a unique and unmistakable style, thanks to elegantly designed buildings inside which all kinds of products are offered: from bedlinen to umbrellas, from shoes to shirts (or crockery, pans, glasses, tablecloths, and all household furnishings)—as if to say a whole life could be sport in the shade of that logo. In some cases they go so far as being a 'concept store', or theme-based (in the wake of theme parks): in order to 'communicate' the company brand and philosophy, spaces are created to conjure up a certain atmosphere and lifestyle, by using a narrative. It is the triumph of 'visual merchandising' and figurative communication.[41] In Niketown everything is a reminder to you of the allure of a sporting life, where the young do everything fast, keep in trim, listen to music, draw inspiration from great champions to face the challenges of life (thanks to the use of high-tech materials, huge screens, and rhythmic music). In a Ralph Lauren shop it feels like being in an elegant drawing room, with sofas and armchairs in the centre, flowers and bookcases, and all around is clothing suitable for a sophisticated, sporting life, just the thing for someone who already has a good social standing. Disney stores plunge the consumer into a child's fairytale world, using delicate hues for the furnishings, dainty music in the background, familiar films projected along the walls, and the large quantity of brightly coloured toys all around. The eccentric arrangement of furniture from different ages in Diesel spaces, and the details picked out in lively colours against minimalist décor, are just the setting to bring out the best for a young, postmodern city dweller's wardrobe. Finally, in book and record shops like Feltrinelli, Mondadori or Virgin, there are bars and comfortable armchairs to sit and browsing through books and magazines, chat with friends, and take part in cultural events (here I definitely feel like a well-informed intellectual). In all these places elements are present that are not strictly commercial, but which serve to reinforce the sensation of following a definite lifestyle. Attention is drawn to the brand more than the single products (for the same reason, there are advertisements today that would have been unimaginable a few decades ago, presenting the brand in abstract, detached from any particular product).

The same desire to be different can be seen in fashion designers' show rooms, their first characteristic being physical separation, that is the tendency to place themselves in specific, well-defined spaces inside the city, like Milan's fashion 'quadrilateral' (between Via Montenapoleone, Via della Spiga, Corso Venezia, and Via Sant' Andrea) or the area around Via Condotti in Rome or Via Tornabuoni in Florence. Furthermore, these shops are refined in design, often the work of famous architects, with similar echoes in many international branches: New York, Paris, London, Tokyo—even if it must be said that a transnational dimension is common to more or less all new selling spaces (and this may very well be a common thread running throughout commercial history). The inside is luxurious but decidedly minimalistic, with cold colours, canny use of light and transparency and adoption of noble materials (glass, wood, metal, and marble). The goods themselves are on minimal display: four or five items of clothing hanging along the wall here, two pieces of knitware folded on a flat surface lit from behind there, a couple of shoes and boots on a metallic grating and a handbag and key holder tossed over an antique trunk. And, in this do-it-yourself age, sales assistants everywhere.

If hyper- and super markets, commercial centres, and outlets aim at accessibility and visual display of wealth, in the show rooms the dominant themes are distance and void, to bring out the preciousness of the few goods on display, so valuable as to border on art. And to tell the truth these places have certain traits that evoke them into of museums. The culmination is reached with shops like Prada in New York, designed by Rem Koolhaas: a vast empty space, almost an art installation where very few elements are reminiscent of shopping, and you are urged to 'visit' the place and observe from afar the well-dressed models ascending a broad wooden staircase as if on parade. Or even in various shops of Armani, Gucci, and others, where presentations and furnishings typical of art shows, from Italy and around the world are displayed.[42] Going around Italy, temporary 'Guerrilla Stores' might be seen before long, shops offering fashion goods in avant-garde, but very simple, surroundings seeing that they will close within six months or a year, so as to guarantee a unique buying experience, as if it were an artistic performance.[43] The clientele of these places is not kitsch as in the big selling places, but the 'camp' consumer, as defined by Susan Sontag: attentive to style and aesthetics, post-modern, ironic, sophisticated, and capable of taking silly, trivial objects and translating them to a detached or parodistic setting: in a word, capable of exorcising mass consumption, according to Gregotti.[44]

To whatever frame of reference we each belong, one thing is certain: for everyone, kitsch or camp (or perhaps both at the same time), consumer spaces are increasing all the time and are in direct contact with the wealth and culture of the country. It is calculated that in the year 2000 the entire area devoted to retail selling in the world was perhaps two billion square metres (39 per cent in the USA alone, 37 per cent in Asia, 10 per cent in Europe—of which 0.6 per cent is in Italy).[45]

But these data are partly misleading: consumer space is growing much more than they show, inside urban boundaries, in run-down areas of big cities, in the slums of half the world where more than a billion people live (the real city of the future?) and where markets, workshops, shops, and fast food outlets (McDonald's clones) are all springing up[46]—all invisible on official maps but all indicative of poverty-inflicted, marginalized consumption that is no less characteristic of our times than the rich variety. Veritable commercial centres are prospering inside airports, big railway stations, and metro systems. Selling spaces are invading 'high' culture institutes like museums (which are deriving significant returns from them—is it possible to end a visit without buying a catalogue, a small reproduction, or at least a postcard?). Goods and marketing methods are insinuating themselves into places of worship, schools, and hospitals; the entire social space is permeated with them. Then what can be said about internet buying? The net has given undreamed-of scope, not just for real buying (which in Italy only involved 15 per cent of web users in 2005),[47] but also for new forms of communication and marketing. The great virtual mall is all to be discovered.

Imagine what the boy has managed to buy for himself—a castle! It was no easy feat, and he had thought about it a long time, summed up the area and the cost of doing it up—then there were all the inside furnishings to see too. But he has managed it, whoever would have thought it possible?

There is even a swimming pool . . . imagine his friends' faces . . . he must organize a castle-warming party at once and invite everyone to it.

The boy unplugs his Nano (iPod really) from his computer, grabs his cell phone and looks up. His parents will not approve ('Why spend so much money on this? Hadn't you better save up for a new motorcycle, buy the jeans or gym shoes you wanted, put some money away? What will you do with it?')

Even his great-grandmother looking out of the yellowed photo on top of the bookcase seems to have a questioning air. She would never have understood; how could a rice weeder like her? All she could hope for was a harvest home celebration when the reaping was over; consumer spending was an impossible dream for her—as it was for the peasants waiting for the wolf in the wheat and eating salt-water soup, or the workmen huddled together in the railinged flats. For them, almost penniless as they were, what sense was there in buying, with real money, a castle in the virtual world of 'Second Life'? The old lady actually looks as if she is asking: 'I see around you so many fine things, I don't know what they are, so aren't you happier than us? Why spend money on things that don't exist? You could buy something useful and you don't. How can we be so different?'

You won't get a reply, thinks the boy punching out an sms.

But he can tell her one thing. We have changed our world with consumer goods, and consumer goods have changed us.

Notes

Chapter 1

1 '*Una grande impresa industriale*', 'L'illustrazione italiana', 17, 27th April 1879, 270. The department store Aux Villes d'Italie (or Bocconi House) was the first of its kind in Italy and was later renamed as La Rinascente.

2 A. Maddison, *Historical Statistics for the World Economy. Per Capita GDP (1990 International Geary-Kharmis dollars)*, in www.ggdc.net/maddison, 15th February 2007 (updated by A. Maddison).

3 M. Livi Bacci, *La popolazione nella storia d'Europa*, Rome-Bari: Laterza (1998), 186–8 (tables 6.3, 6.4).

4 Ibid. 247–9.

5 *I conti economici dell'Italia*, vol. I, ed. G. M. Rey, *Una sintesi delle fonti ufficiali 1890–1970*, Rome-Bari: Laterza (1991), 209. It is noted that the average calories went from 2,637 for the 1861–1880 period, to 2,158 for the 1881–1900 period and then to 2,675 between 1901–1915. Cf. V., *L'evoluzione dei consumi fra tradizione e innovazione*, in *Storia d'Italia. Annali 13. L'alimentazione*, eds. A. Capatti, A. De Bernardi, A. Varni, Turin: Einaudi (1998), 176.

6 *I conti economici dell'Italia*, vol. I, ed. G. M. Rey, *Una sintesi delle fonti ufficiali 1890–1970*, 219–26.

7 ISTAT, *Sommario di statistiche storiche dell'Italia 1861–1975*, Rome (1976), 14. In 1871 the percentage was 67.5.

8 S. Somogyi, '*Cento anni di bilanci familiari in Italia (1857–1956)*', 'Annali Feltrinelli" , II (1959), 150–1.

9 Bear in mind that the activity rate for the entire population (equalling 28,500,000 people in 1881) was equal to 56 per cent. Cf. ISTAT, *Censimenti*, various years; P. Sylos Labini, *Saggio sulle classi sociali*, Rome-Bari: Laterza (1974), 156–7 (tables 1.1, 1.2).

10 Somogyi, *Cento anni di bilanci familiari in Italia*, 134–5.

11 There is a wide expanse of literature concerning food; cf. for the different food regimes in Italian regions Capatti, De Bernardi, Varni, *Storia d'Italia. Annali 13. L'alimentazione* (particularly the first part).

12 C. Lévi-Strauss, *Il crudo e il cotto* [1964], Milan: Saggiatore (1966); cf. for Italy, among many works, M. Montanari, *La fame e l'abbondanza*, Rome-Bari: Laterza (1993).

13 R. Sarti, *Vita di casa. Abitare, mangiare, vestire nell'Europa moderna*, Rome-Bari: Laterza (1999), 213–14. About the many taboos concerning food see the 'rationalistic' explanations of M. Harris, *Good to eat: Riddles of Food and Culture*, Long Grove: Waveland Press (1998).

14 Montanari, *La fame e l'abbondanza*, 190.

15 A. Capatti, M. Montanari, *La cucina italiana. Storia di una cultura* [1999], Rome-Bari: Laterza (2005), 82–7.

16 J. G. Frazer, *Il ramo d'oro. Studio sulla magia e la religione* [1922], Turin: Bollati Boringhieri (1965), Frazer states that this personification was common in northern Europe, expecially in France, Germany, and Slavic countries. 538.

17 Concerning myth and reality in the ancient Mediterranean diet cf. V. Teti, *Il colore del cibo. Geografia, mito e realtà dell'alimentazione mediterranea*, Rome: Meltemi (1999).

18 A prime example of this is the custom of the *curmaia*: a feast to celebrate the end of rice weeding, traditionally offered by the master to the weeders (young women who left their families for long periods during the season to work in the Piedmontese and Tuscan rice fields). It is an interesting case of feminine sociability at work, giving voice to the resentment they felt against their employer and at the same time echoing themes from popular tradition. The feast was based on a rich banquet of different kinds of food and of wine consumed in abundance. Only women could take part (except for some men expressly invited) and there was singing and dancing until daybreak. On this occasion the women displayed aggressive attitudes and boldness towards any men present, some actually dressing up as men and inviting others to dance, in a significant reversal of roles (fuelled partly by their having drunk large amounts of wine, which was considered inappropriate for women). Furthermore, the songs contained clear sexual allusions (often aimed at the master). On the significance of the rice-weeding culture cf. F. Dei, *Beethoven e le mondine: ripensare la cultura popolare*, Rome: Meltemi (2002).

19 L. Gambi, *La casa contadina*, in *Storia d'Italia*, vol. 6, *Atlante*, Turin: Einaudi (1976), 481–3.

20 Ibid., 486–4.

21 On family dynamics cf. M. Barbagli, *Sotto lo stesso tetto. Mutamenti della famiglia in Italia dal XV al XX secolo*, Bologna: il Mulino (1984), 47 ff.; *Population in history: essays in historical demography*, eds. D.V. Glass and D. E. C. Eversley, London: Arnold (1969).

22 Sarti, *Vita di casa*, 243–69.

23 Collodi [C. Lorenzini], *Pinocchio, storia di un burattino*, Florence: Felice Paggi (1883), ch. 5.

24 Collodi [C. Lorenzini], *Pinocchio*, ch. 7.

25 Somogyi, *Cento anni di bilanci familiari*, 150–1.

26 Ibid., 170–4, 133.

27 Ibid., 133–5.

28 Ibid., 148–9.

29 S. Musso, *La famiglia operaia*, in *La famiglia italiana dall'Ottocento a oggi*, ed. P. Melograni, Rome-Bari: Laterza (1988), 65–6. To give an example, in Milan in 1901 the marriage rate was 37 per thousand, compared with the Italian average of 47 and the one for Lombardy of 60; the legitimate birth

rates were 169, 222, and 257 per thousand respectively. Cf. F. Della Peruta, *Milano. Lavoro e fabbrica 1815–1914*, Milan: Franco Angeli (1987), 135.

30 Della Peruta, *Milano. Lavoro e fabbrica*, 137. Even large and 'modern' companies wice pirelli used to decrease the salories of their order workers or tired them, to be replaced with younger workers.

31 H. Kaelble, *Verso una società europea. Storia sociale dell'Europa 1880–1980* [1987], Rome-Bari: Laterza (1990), 36–7.

32 The calculations include workers in the sectors of industry, building, commerce, transport, and services (excluding domestics). Cf. Sylos Labini, *Saggio sune classi sociali.* (table 1.1.).

33 G. Montemartini, '*La questione delle case operaie in Milano: indagini statistiche*', Humanitarian Society Labour Office, Milan (1903). The number of people living in one room was decidedly lower where the entire population was concerned: in 1911 in Rome it was 1.4 inhabitants and around 1.2 in many other big cities (V. Zamagni, *Il valore aggiunto del settore terziario italiano nel 1911*, in *I conti economici dell'Italia*, vol. 2, *Una stima del valore aggiunto per il 1911*, 235.

34 Musso, *La famiglia operaia*, 70–1.

35 A. Castagnoli, E. Scarpellini, *Storia degli imprenditori italiani*, Turin: Einaudi (2003), 18, 107–8.

36 E. P. Thompson, *Rivoluzione industriale e classe operaia in Inghilterra* (1963), Milano: il Saggiatore (1969).

37 Somogyi, *Cento anni di bilanci familiari*, 150–1. Few studies have researched the places and consumed goods connected with worker sociability, even if several indications maintain the existence of female forms of sociability, especially in textile and clothing factories, as testified by the presence of women in the leagues (albeit for a short time) and by professional pride (textile workers passed round the proverb: 'El mestee l'è in bottia, chi lo veeur lo porta via' [The trade is in the shop, whoever wants to carries it away]). Cf. Della Peruta, *Milano. Lavoro e fabbrica* (Milan. Work and Factory), 129–30.

38 Cf. M. Ridolfi, *Il circolo virtuoso: sociabilità democratica, associazionismo e rappresentanza politica nell'Ottocento*, Centro editoriale toscano, Florence (1990).

39 Cf. the large amount of photographic material available in the Luce Historical Archives and Audiovisual Archives of the Democratic Workers' Movement in Rome.

40 D. L. Clifford, '*Can the Uniform Make the Citizen? Paris, 1789–1791*', '*Eighteenth-Century Studies*', vol. 34, no. 3, spring (2001), 363–82.

41 S. Anselmi, *Mezzadri e mezzadria nell'Italia centrale*, in *Storia dell'agricoltura italiana in età contemporanea*, ed. P. Bevilacqua, vol. 2, *Uomini e classi*, Venice: Marsilio (1990).

42 Cf. in this sense Musso, *La famiglia operaia*, 73–4.

43 CA. Colombo, *Il quartiere di via Solari: un modello per le abitazioni operaie di Milano*, in *Quando l'Umanitaria era in via Solari*, ed. the Historical Archives of the Humanitarian Society, Umanitaria—Raccolto Edizioni, Milan (2006), 9–48.

44   C. A. Colombo, 34.

45   C. A. Colombo, 40.

46   C. A. Colombo, 36.

47   *Il primo anno del quartiere (1906–7). Dalle relazioni del custode-esattore Salvatore Sapienza*, in *Quando l'Umanitaria era in via Solari*, 92.

48   A. Corbin, *Storia sociale degli odori* [1982], Milan: Bruno Mondatori (2005).

49   Della Peruta, *Milano. Lavoro e fabbrica*, 137–43; Musso, *La famiglia operaia*, 68, 74.

50   'Il lavoratore del libro', 10th September 1912 (in Della Peruta, *Milano. Lavoro e fabbrica*, 170).

51   J. Le Goff, *Tempo della Chiesa e tempo del mercante, e altri saggi sul lavoro e la cultura nel Medioevo*, Turin: Einaudi (1977); S. Kern, *Il tempo e lo spazio: la percezione del mondo tra Otto e Novecento* [1983], Bologna: il Mulino, (1988); G. Cross, *Tempo e denaro: la nascita della cultura del consumo* [1993], Bologna: il Mulino, (1998).

52   Concerning the whole debate about leisure time cf. S. Cavazza, *Dimensione massa. Individui, folle, consumi 1830–1945*, Bologna: il Mulino (2004), 199–244.

53   S. Pivato, A. Tonelli, *Italia vagabonda: il tempo libero degli italiani dal melodramma alla pay-tv*, Rome: Carocci (2001).

54   R. Hoggart, *Proletariato e industria culturale: aspetti di vita operaia inglese con particolare riferimento al mondo della stampa e dello spettacolo* [1957], Rome: Officina (1970).

55   G. M. Ciampelli, *Il primo lustro di vita musicale del Teatro del Popolo di Milano*, Milan: Dino Grassi (1927), 102.

56   P. Bourdieu, *La distinzione. Critica sociale del gusto* [1979], Bologna: il Mulino (1983).

57   A survey by the Milan Humanitarian Society in 1903 concerning 132,000 workers revealed that 15,500 of them earned a good wage (3–4 lire or more a day) and 100,000 earned between 1 and 2.5 lire; the bulk of women workers (91 per cent precisely) received less than 1 to 1.5 lire a day; furthermore they worked fewer days a year (wages were by the day and were paid only for days actually worked). These wage amounts increased during the Giolitti period. Cf. Della Peruta, *Milano. Lavoro e fabbrica*, 163.

58   In some categories, like printing, there were strikes against employing female typesetters (as Francesco Vallardi had done in 1886 to cut down costs), alleging hygienic and moral reasons (the typesetters could be exposed to obscene or medical publications). Cf. Della Peruta, *Milano. Lavoro e fabbrica*, 127.

59   Musso, *La famiglia operaia*, 70.

60   On the whole female work issue cf. Musso, *La famiglia operaia*, 67–78; Della Peruta, *Milano. Lavoro e fabbrica*, 127–36.

61   According to the 1901 census there were 480,000 people actively involved in domestic service in Italy CF. Sylos Labini, *Saggio sulle classi sociali* (table 1.1.).

62   Peruta, *Milano. Lavoro e fabbrica*, 127.

63   Somogyi, *Cento anni di bilanci familiari*, 135 (the reference is to the inquiry by A. Pugliese, *Il bilancio alimentare di 51 famiglie operaie milanesi*, Milano: Tipografia degli operai (1914)).

64   Peruta, *Milano. Lavoro e fabbrica*, 131–3.

65   A. M. Banti, *Storia della borghesia italiana. L'età liberale*, Rome: Donzelli (1996), esp., 213–36. Cf. also *Borghesie europee dell'Ottocento* [1987], ed. J. Kocka, Venice: Marsilio (1989).

66   In these numbers I have excluded the 'bourgeois' agrarian swathe, that is sharecroppers, farmers, and tenant farmers (7,550,000 people in all) who made up 42 per cent of the active population, because of the different (non-urban) cultural references. Cf. ISTAT, *Censimenti*, various years; P. Sylos Labini, *Saggio sulle classi sociali*, Rome-Bari: Laterza (1974), 156–7 (tables 1.1, 1.2).

67   Somogyi, *Cento anni di bilanci familiari*, 166–9. In absolute terms, family budgets varied between a minimum of 1,105 lire and a maximum of 5,706 lire.

68   Note that the official statistics register a different trend for consumption in the cities compared with the national average (largely ascribed to consumption by the middle and upper classes): a greater consumption of meat and above all of coffee and sugar. But the geographical disparities are remarkable, with high consumption in the industrial triangle and a sharp divide between north and south. Cf. Zamagni, *L'evoluzione dei consumi*, 180–1.

69   M. Halbwachs, *La classe ouvrière et les niveaux de vie: recherche sur la hiérarchie des besoins dans les sociétés industrielles contemporaines*, Paris: Alcan (1913). Cf. also the discussion of these data in Capuzzo, *Culture del consumo*, 210–15.

70   Capatti, Montanari, *La cucina italiana*, 3–40, 126–31.

71   The reference is to a painting by G. Romano, *Banchetto sull'isola di Citera* (fresco), (1527–30).

72   V. Bersezio, *Le miserie 'd monsu Travet*, Turin (1863); E. De Marchi, *Demetrio Pianelli*, Milan (1890). About the world of office workers cf. also M. Soresina, *Mezzemaniche e signorine: gli impiegati privati a Milano, 1880–1939*, Milan: F. Angeli (1992).

73   S. Schama, *Il disagio dell'abbondanza: la cultura olandese dell'epoca d'oro* [1988], Milan: Mondadori (1993); for an analysis of the characteristics of European families cf. the monographs *La vita privata* (1985–1987), directed by P. Ariès, G. Duby, Rome-Bari: Laterza (1986–1988).

74   G. Bassanini, *Tracce silenziose dell'abitare: la donna e la casa*, Milan: F. Angeli (1990).

75   P. Bourdieu, *Per una teoria della pratica: con tre studi di etnologia cabila*, Milan: Cortina (2003).

76   P. Macry, *Ottocento. Famiglia, élites e patrimoni a Napoli*, Turin: Einaudi (1988), 110–1.

77 Macry,*Ottocento. Famiglia, élites e patrimoni a Napoli*, 112–9. On the relationship of the bourgeoisie with music and more generally with art cf. T. Nipperdey, *Come la borghesia ha inventato il moderno* [1988], Roma: Donzelli (1994).

78 On the history of books as cultural objects and on the history of reading see D. F. McKenzie, *Bibliografia e sociologia dei testi* [1986], Milan: Sylvestre Bonnard (1998); *Storia della lettura nel mondo occidentale*, eds. G. Cavallo and R. Charter, Rome-Bari: Laterza (1995).

79 Macry,*Ottocento. Famiglia*, 126–7.

80 M. Schwegman, *Maria Montessori*, Bologna: il Mulino (1999), 102.

81 K. Calvert, *Children in the House: The Material Culture of Early Childhood, 1600–1900*, Boston: Northeastern University Press (1992).

82 P. N. Stearns, *American Cool: Developing a Twentieth-Century Emotional Style*, New York : New York University Press (1994). It is interesting to note how this author sets this attitude towards children in the framework typical of a Victorian 'emotional style', characterized as it was by the direct expression of feelings (albeit different according to gender). After the First World War, this gave way to a new style which despised displays of emotion (pain, anger, jealousy were seen as negative; love, especially for men, became devoid of the spiritual component and largely reduced to sex). Consumption played its part in creating this new picture, diminishing the sense of guilt.

83 It should be borne in mind that although middle-class women were largely excluded from work outside the home (partly due to the restrictive laws in force), it was during this very period that the first women teachers and office workers appeared on the scene, considered by many to be transgressive symbols; Cf. C. Covato, *Un'identità divisa: diventare maestra in Italia fra Otto e Novecento*, Rome: Archivio Guido Izzi (1996); *Operaie, serve, maestre, impiegate. Atti del Convegno internazionale di studi 'Il lavoro delle donne nell'Italia contemporanea: continuità e rotture'* eds. P. Nava, Rosenberg and Sellier, Turin (1992).

84 G. L. Mosse, *Sessualità e nazionalismo: mentalità borghese e rispettabilità* [1985], Roma: Laterza (1984).

85 It is possible to construct a hierarchy of professional work (excluding businessmen and traders) based on annual incomes. In 1911 lawyers and solicitors were firmly at the top (a good 34,500 with incomes of 6,800 lire), ahead of teachers and architects (around 6,000 with incomes of 6,000 lire), followed by the medical professions: dentists (4,500 lire), doctors (a solid group of 18,600 people with 3,500 lire annually) and vets (3,000 lire). Music composers, publicity agents, and writers earned 2,000 lire; accountants, artists (a good 10,000), private teachers (16,000) and singers 2,000 lire a year. At the base of the pyramid come private office workers (15,000) and lay churchmen (67,000) with 1,200 lire. Other professions (domestics, hairdressers, laundrywomen, barbers, etc.) were more akin to the working class and earned less than 500 lire annually. Cf. Zamagni, *Il valore aggiunto del settore terziario*, 224–5.

86 '*Autentica ricchezza*', Autarchia e Commercio, 7, 3rd January 1941, in B. Maida, *Il prezzo dello scambio. Commercianti a Torino (1940–1943)*, Turin: Scriptorium (1988), 152. Cf. also D. L. Caglioti, *Il guadagno difficile: commercianti napoletani nella seconda metà dell'Ottocento*, Bologna: il Mulino (1994), 85–112, 131–44; G. Montroni, *La famiglia borghese*, in *La famiglia italiana dall'Ottocento*, 112–18; Idem. *Scenari del mondo contemporaneo dal 1815 a oggi*, Rome-Bari: Laterza (2005). As regards the thrift concept cf. G. Aliberti, *Dalla parsimonia al consumo: cento anni di vita quotidiana in Italia, 1870–1970*, Florence: Le Monnier (2003).

87 E. Gellner, *Nazioni e nazionalismo* [1983], Rome: Editori riuniti (1985).

88 J. Habermas, *Storia e critica dell'opinione pubblica* [1962], Bari Rome: Laterza (1972).

89 A. Tonelli, *E ballando ballando. La storia d'Italia a passi di danza (1815–1996)*, Milan: F. Angeli (1999), 53–64.

90 A. Montanari, *Convivio oggi: storia e cultura dei piaceri della tavola nell'età contemporanea*, Rome-Bari: Laterza (1992).

91 D. Bardelli, *L'Italia viaggia. il Touring club, la nazione e la modernità, 1894–1927*, Rome: Bulzoni (2004); S. Pivato, *Il Touring Club Italiano*, Bologna: il Mulino (2006); P. Battilani, *Vacanze di pochi, vacanze di tutti: l'evoluzione del turismo europeo*, Bologna: il Mulino (2001); Cavazza, *Dimensione massa*, 227–40.

92 C. J. Berry, *The Idea of Luxury: A Conceptual and Historical Investigation*, New York: Cambridge University Press (1994). Cf. also Capuzzo, *Culture del consumo*, 89–121.

93 G. C. Jocteau, *Nobili e nobiltà nell'Italia unita*, Rome-Bari: Laterza (1997), 8, 22.

94 Between 1902 and 1905, the 32 noble family patrimonies were worth 3,555,175 lire compared with the 290 middle-class patrimonies of 6,549,682 lire; in 1810–1811, the 17 noble family patrimonies were worth 1,283,418 compared with 81 middle class of 1,139,422 lire. Cf. A. M. Banti, *Terra e denaro. Una borghesia padana dell'Ottocento*, Venice: Marsilio (1989), 27–30.

95 Jocteau, *Nobili e nobiltà nell'Italia unita*, 14; about the matrimonial strategies that draw a picture of geographical endogamy cf. Banti, *Storia della borghesia italiana*, 57–61.

96 Sarti, *Vita di casa*, 91–2.

97 Macry, *Ottocento. Famiglia*, 110, 112.

98 Macry, 112.

99 The quotation by R. Barbiera is drawn from M. I. Palazzolo, *I salotti di cultura nell'Italia dell'Ottocento. Scene e modelli*, Milan: F. Angeli (1985), 17. Cf. also D. Pizzagalli, *L'amica. Clara Maffei e il suo salotto nel Risorgimento italiano*, Milan: Mondatori (1997); M. T. Mori, *Salotti. La sociabilità delle élite nell'Italia dell'Ottocento*, Rome: Carocci (2000); *Salotti e ruolo femminile in Italia: tra fine Seicento e primo Novecento*, eds. M. L. Betri and E. Brambilla, Venice: (2004).

100 M. Praz, *La casa della vita*, Milan: Mondadori (1958), 19.

101 M. Praz, 279–80.

102   Sarti, *Vita di casa*, 198–205; Capatti, Montanari, *La cucina italiana*, 273–84.

103   N. Elias, *Il processo di civilizzazione* [1939], Bologna: il Mulino (1988); N. Elias, *La società di corte* [1969], Bologna: il Mulino (1980). On the formation of a new model of consumption in Italian Renaissance courts cf. R. A. Goldthwaite, *Ricchezze e domanda nel mercato dell'arte in Italia dal Trecento al Seicento. La cultura materiale e le origini del consumo* [1993], Milan: Unicopli (1995); C. Mukerji, *From Graven Images. Patterns of Modern Materialism*, New York: Columbia University Press (1983).

104   The Italian word for spoon, *cucchiaio*, comes from the ancient greek *kochliàrion* (latin *cochlearium*), derived from *chiocciola* (spiral) or *conchiglia* (shell), because of its shape.

105   Elias, *Il processo di civilizzazione; Storia dell'alimentazione*, eds. J. Flandrin and M. Montanari, Rome-Bari: Laterza (1997); Sarti, *Vita di casa*, 186–93.

106   Elias, *Il processo di civilizzazione*; S. Fontaine, '*The Civilizing Process Revisited: Interview with Norbert Elias*', Theory and Society, vol. 5, no. 2, March 1878, 243–53.

107   Continental practice was to get up early in the morning and have breakfast at once, as suggested by the French proverb: *Se lever à six, déjeuner à dix | Diner à six, se coucher à dix, | Fait vivre l'homme dix fois dix* (To rise at six, have lunch at ten | To dine at six, go to bed at ten, | Makes a man live ten times ten). Cf. P. Artusi, *La scienza in cucina e l'arte di mangiar bene* [1891], Florence: Giunti (1967), 20. As regards drinks, coffee was very common also because it was considered a stimulating drink and a symbol of sobriety and lucidity (thus the opposite of alcohol); chocolate was labelled as the 'Catholic' drink (because it was permitted during fasting) as opposed to 'Protestant' coffee, while tea was not very popular in Italy. Cf. Schivelbusch, *Storia dei generei voluttuari: spezia, caffè, cioccolato, tabacco, alcol e altre droghe*, Milan: B. Mondadori (1999).

108   *Fontanellato: corte di pianura*, eds. M. Calidoni and M. Dall'Acqua, Fontanellato (2004).

109   Besides French, English was current, given the cultural and economic weight of London; Spanish was known in the South, German in Lombardy, partly because of the massive presence of Germans in key economic positions—from this came the custom of having an English governess and a German *Schwester* in the home. Cf. G. Bezzola, *La Milano dei 'loisirs'* in *Milano nell'Italia liberale 1898–1922*, eds. G. Rumi, A. C. Buratti, and A. Cova, Milan: Cariplo (1993), 121.

110   To give an example, the kitchens of the prestigious Grand Hotel in Rome, inaugurated in 1893 by Césare Ritz, were created by the famous chef George Auguste Escoffier, who then entrusted them to his pupils. Cf. A. Capatti, *Lingua, regioni e gastronomia dall'Unità alla seconda guerra mondiale*, in *Storia d'Italia. Annali 13. L'alimentazione*, 762.

111 The author knew perfectly well the kind of public he was addressing: 'It is clear that I am speaking to the well-to-do classes here, while those on whom fortune does not smile must through their ill luck make a virtue of necessity and console themselves by contemplating that an active and frugal life helps to keep the body strong and healthy'. Cf. Artusi, *La scienza in cucina*, 14 (*Alcune norme d'igiene*).

112 Jocteau, *Nobili e nobiltà nell'Italia unita*, 231–9; P. Boutry, '*Società urbana e sociabilità delle élites nella Roma della Restaurazione: prime considerazioni*', Cheiron, year V, nn. 9–10, (1988), *Sociabilità nobiliare, sociabilità borghese*, ed. M. Malatesta, 69–85.

113 Macry,*Ottocento. Famiglia*, 127–9; D. L. Caglioti, *Associazionismo e sociabilità d'élite a Napoli nel XIX secolo*, Naples: Liguori (1996).

114 A. L. Cardoza, *Patrizi in un mondo plebeo: la nobiltà piemontese nell'Italia liberale*, Rome: Donzelli (1999); cf. also A. J. Mayer, *Il potere dell'ancien régime fino alla prima guerra mondiale* [1981], Rome-Bari: Laterza (1982).

115 M. Meriggi, *Milano borghese: circoli ed élites nell'Ottocento*, Venice: Marsilio (1992); Banti, *Storia della borghesia italiana*, 181–8.

116 C. Tallone, *Ritratto della signora Gallavresi con la figlia Maria* (oil on canvas), (1889); A. Alciati, *Ritratto di Maria Luisa Pirotta Bonacossa* (oil on canvas).

117 G. Tomasi di Lampedusa, *Il Gattopardo*, Milan: Feltrinelli (1958).

118 E. Scarpellini, *Organizzazione teatrale e politica del teatro nell'Italia fascista*, new edn., Milan: Led (2004).

119 Bezzola, *La Milano dei 'loisirs'*, 117–42.

120 G. D'Annunzio, *Il Piacere*, Milan: Treves (1899).

121 G. Benucci, *Federico Caprilli: tra storia e romanzo*, in G. Benucci, F. Venturi et al., *Federico Caprilli e i personaggi del Caprilli*, Leghorn: Tipografia Toscana (2004), 10–47. Galloping horse races were chiefly promoted by rich aristocrats, who were also the owners of prestigious stables, while trotting races were more suited to the tastes of the upper-middle class. Cf. G. Taborelli, *La vita di Milano nella Belle Epoque*, in *Il mondo nuovo. Milano 1890–1915*, Milan: Electa – Bocconi (2002), 154–77.

Chapter 2

1 G. M. Rey, *Novità e conferme nell'analisi dello sviluppo economico italiano*, in *I conti economici dell'Italia*, ed. G. M. Rey, vol. 3, *Il conto risorse e impieghi (1891, 1911, 1938, 1951)*, Rome-Bari: Laterza (2003), xxiii; A. Maddison, *Monitoring the World Economy*, Development Centre OECD, Paris (1995), 25.

2 A. Cherubini, *Storia della previdenza sociale*, Rome: Editori Riuniti (1977), 10–27, 36–70; G. Procacci, *Governare la povertà: la società liberale e la nascita della questione sociale*, Bologna: il Mulino (1998).

3 S. Jacini, *Atti della giunta per la inchiesta agraria e sulle condizioni della classe agricola*, vol. xv, fascicolo I, *Relazione finale sui risultati dell'inchiesta*, Rome (1884), 83.

4 Inside public consumption there tends to be a division between social and individual benefits (by convention: assistance, welfare, health, education) resulting from R. Musgrave's concept of merit goods. Cf. M. Coccia, G. Della Torre, P. Iafolla, '*La ricostruzione dei consumi pubblici in campo educativo nell'Italia liberale, 1861–1915*', Quaderni', Dipartimento di Economia Politica, Siena, n. 388, July 2003, 1–3.

5 Cavazza, *Dimensione massa*.

6 G. Pellizza da Volpedo, *Il quarto stato* (oil on canvas) (1901).

7 Cf. many examples in this sense in J. T. Schnapp, *L'arte del manifesto politico 1914–1989. Ondate rivoluzionarie*, Milan: Skira (2005).

8 Jacini, *Atti della giunta*, 105.

9 The same policy can be noted where health and police control were concerned when prostitution was forcibly driven off the streets and channelled into houses of tolerance from 1860 onwards. Cf. M. Gibson,*Stato e prostituzione in Italia: 1860–1915* [1986], Milan: il Saggiatore (1995). Concerning health and legislation cf. G. Cosmacini, *Storia della medicina e della sanità in Italia. Dalla peste europea alla guerra mondiale. 1348–1918*, Rome-Bari: Laterza (1987); F. Girotti, *Welfare state. Storia, modelli e critica*, Rome: Carocci (1998), 139–46; E. Bartocci, *Le politiche sociali nell'Italia liberale (1861–1919)*, Rome: Donzelli (1999).

10 Cosmacini, *Storia della medicina*, 392–419; *Storia d'Italia. Annali*, vol. 7, *Malattia e medicina*, ed. F. Della Peruta, Turin: Einaudi (1984).

11 F.M. Snowden, *The conquest of Malaria: Italy 1900–1962*, New Haven: Yale University Press (2006).

12 Cf. M. Foucault, *La volontà di sapere* [1976], Milan: Feltrinelli (1978); Ibid., *Sorvegliare e punire: nascita della prigione* [1975], Turin: Einaudi (1976). cf. also *La médicalisation de la société française, 1770–1830*, ed. J. P. Goubert, Waterloo: Historical Reflections Press (1982). As regards Italy, it can be noted how encompassing many interventions were: on one side public health and hygiene, on the other economic enhancement of urban areas and architectural decorum. Typical in this sense were the special reforms for the South of Italy ordered by Giolitti.

13 In 1912, Italy spent 0.45 per cent of its GDP on redistribution expenses (equal to 4.26 per cent of the entire State expenditure), exactly a half of what was spent for example by France. Cf. G. Brosio, C. Marchese, *Il potere di spendere. Economia e storia della spesa pubblica dall'Unificazione ad oggi*, Bologna: il Mulino (1986), 59–60. The only other interventions in the sector concerned some restricted categories of state employees. About social legislation and Italian juridical thinking cf. G. Gozzi, *Modelli politici e questione sociale in Italia e in Germania fra Ottocento e Novecento*, Bologna: il Mulino (1988).

14 V. Zamagni, *Dalla periferia al centro. La seconda rinascita economica dell'Italia 1861–1990*, Bologna: il Mulino (1990), 254. Cf. also Coccìa, Della Torre,

Iafolla, *La ricostruzione dei consumi pubblici*; E. De Fort, *La scuola elementare dall'unità alla caduta del fascismo*, Bologna: il Mulino (1996).

15 0.5 per cent of the GDF was spent on education in 1872, rising to 1.8 by 1912. Cf. Brosio and Marchese, *Il potere di spendere*, 60. The data include expenditure not only by the state but also by local bodies, which always proves higher in fact. Cf. also Coccìa, Della Torre, Iafolla, *La ricostruzione dei consumi pubblici*. It is worth noting that in 1881 the level of illiteracy was 67 per cent. Where university education for women is concerned, however, the first data start with the 1901–1910 decade and show an average of 822 enrolled out of 26,301 (cf. ISTAT, *Sommario di statistiche storiche dell'Italia 1861–1975*, ISTAT, Rome (1976), 47).

16 Concerning lotteries as a central element of popular culture in areas such as Naples, cf. P. Macry, *Giocare la vita: storia del lotto a Napoli tra Sette e Ottocento*, Roma: Donzelli (1997).

17 Brosio and Marchese, *Il potere di spendere*, 80–2, 202.

18 Brosio and Marchese have calculated that during the 1866–1914 period the real increase in taxes was greater than that of the domestic product (the elasticity of the tax revenue with respect to the GDP was equal to 1.18, while it was 0.98 between the two wars and 1.15 between 1948 and 1980) Cf. ibid., 85.

19 Jacini, *Atti della giunta*, 105.

20 For the close link between education and modern nations cf. Gellner, *Nazioni e nazionalismo*; for the industrialist vocation of Italian nationalism cf. S. Lanaro, *L'Italia nuova. Identità e sviluppo 1861–1988*, Turin: Einaudi (1988), 160–71.

Chapter 3

1 Concerning the role played by local and territorial aspects on economic processes cf. L. Cafagna, *Dualismo e sviluppo nella storia d'Italia*, Venice: Marsilio (1989); S. Pollard, *La conquista pacifica: l'industrializzazione in Europa dal 1760 al 1970* [1981], Bologna: il Mulino (1984). An interesting interpretation of the way scientific management 'narrative' penetrated all fields of society is in M. Banta, *Taylored lives: narrative productions in the age of Taylor, Veblen, and Ford*, Chicago: University of Chicago Press (1993).

2 S. Clementi, 'Il commercio estero dell'Italia nel 1891, 1911, 1938 e 1951', in *I conti economici dell'Italia*, vol. III, *Il conto risorse e impieghi*, 217–54 and the summary table in the appendix.

3 G. Federico, 'Mercantilizzazione e sviluppo economico in Italia (1860–1940)', Rivista di storia economica, 2, (1986), 149–86. Note that the quota is a relatively low one, indicating a high level of mercantilization even before the modern age.

4 The exact percentages relating to the supply of private consumption by agriculture were 32.6 per cent in 1891 and 16.1 per cent in 1951; while those by the food industry were respectively 30.9 per cent and 33.4 per cent. Cf. G. M. Rey, '*Novità e conferme nell'analisi dello sviluppo economico italiano*', in *I conti economici dell'Italia*, ed. G. M. Rey, vol. 3, *Il conto risorse e impieghi*, xliv–xlv. Cf. Table 2.

5 Rey, *Novità e conferme*, xliv–xlv.

6 S. Fenoaltea, '*Il valore aggiunto dell'industria italiana nel 1911*', in *I conti economici dell'Italia*, vol. II, *Una stima del valore aggiunto per il 1911*, ed. G.M. Rey, Rome-Bari: Laterza (1992), 107 (I use here, as elsewhere if possible, the new estimates worked out to partly correct the ISTAT historical series). The total figure of 853.6 million of value-added in agriculture is made up as follows: primary cereal processing (flour) 229.5; secondary cereal processing (bread, pasta, pastry) 237.1; milk derivatives 125.1; processing of meat and fish 88.8; conserves, sweets, coffee, sugar 99.4; oil, alcohol, drinks 47.4; tobacco processing 26.2) (cf. ibid., 119–20).

7 A. Arvidsson, *Dalla «réclame» al «brand management». Uno sguardo storico alla disciplina pubblicitaria del Novecento*, in *Il secolo dei consumi*, 197–217; Ibid., *Marketing Modernità: Italian Advertising from Fascism to Postmodernity*, London: Routledge (2003).

8 Castagnoli, Scarpellini, *Storia degli imprenditori italiani*, 116–39; M. Doria, *L'imprenditoria industriale dall'Unità al 'miracolo economico'. Capitani d'industria, padroni, innovatori*, Turin: Giappichelli (1998); F. Chiapparino, R. Covino, *Consumi e industria alimentare in Italia dall'Unità a oggi. Lineamenti per una storia*, Giada: Narni (2002).

9 F. Chiapparino, *L'industria del cioccolato in Italia, Germania e Svizzera. Consumi, mercati e imprese tra Ottocento e prima guerra mondiale*, Bologna: il Mulino (1997).

10 About the significance of this product cf. S.W. Mintz, *Storia dello zucchero: tra politica e cultura* [1985], Turin: Einaudi (1990).

11 Chiapparino, Covino, *Consumi e industria alimentare in Italia*, 61–5.

12 G. D'Amato, *Storia dell'arredamento. Dal 1750 a oggi*, Rome-Bari: Laterza (1999), 239–45.

13 N. McKendrick, J. Brewer, J. H. Plumb, *The Birth of a Consumer Society: The Commercialization of Eighteenth-Century England*, Bloomington: Indiana University Press (1982). Cf. also *Consumption and the World of Goods*, eds. J. Brewer and R. Porter, London: Routledge (1993); about this period C. Campbell, *L'etica romantica e lo spirito del consumism moderno* [1987], Rome: Lavoro (1992).

Chapter 4

1 C. Baudelaire, *Il crepuscolo della sera*, in *Les fleurs du mal (n. 95)* [1857], Milan: Mondadori (1996).

2   C. E. Schorske, *Vienna fin de siècle: politica e cultura* [1979], Milan: Bompiani (1981).

3   W. Benjamin, *I 'passages' di Parigi* (1982), vol. 1, Turin: Einaudi, (2000), 13.

4   G. Simmel, *La metropoli e la vita dello spirito* [1900], Rome: Armando (1995); Ibid. *Filosofia del denaro*[1900], Turin: Utet (1984).

5   W. Schivelbusch, *Luce. Storia dell'illuminazione artificiale nel secolo XIX* (1983), Parma: Pratiche editrice (1994). The author reminds us how, as a result of Lavoisier's discovery, gas light and then electric light was first used by the police to help control urban life (giving rise to strong opposition among the public at large), even before it was used for commercial purposes. Its widespread use is a typical case of a combination of technological and cultural elements, with sectors of the middle classes trying to hang on to the intimacy of weak traditional light and commercial spaces adopting it at once.

6   Another aspect emphasizing the spectacular nature of such places is also worthy of note: the habit of installing 'panoramas' (either inside or nearby), that is huge pictures reproducing natural landscapes in minute detail which, as Benjamin reminds us, were the precursors of photography and cinema (the 'Passage des Panoramas', created in 1800, takes its name from two big rotundas facing the entrance with these large depictions of landscapes).

7   J. Delorme, A. Dubois, M. Mouchy, *Passages couverts parisiens*, Paris: Parigramme (2002); M. P. Schofield, '*The Cleveland Arcade*', The Journal of the Society of Architectural Historians, vol. 25, n. 4, (1966), 281–91 (about experiences in the USA).

8   B. Lancaster, *The Department Store: A Social History*, London-New York: Leicester University Press (1995); *Cathedrals of Consumption: The European Department Store, 1850–1939*, eds. G. Crossick and S. Jaumain, Aldershot: Ashgate (1999); W. R. Leach, *Land of Desire: Merchants, Power and the Rise of a New American Culture*, New York: Vintage Books (1994); M. B. Miller, *The Bon Marché: Bourgeois Culture and the Department Store, 1869–1920*, Princeton: Princeton University Press (1994); H. G. Haupt, *Konsum und Handel. Europa im 19. und 20. Jahrhundert*, Göttingen: Vandenhoeck & Ruprecht (2003).

9   B. Caizzi, *Il commercio*, Turin: Utet (1975), 37.

10 R.V. Moore, *L'architettura del mercato coperto. Dal mercato all'ipermercato*, Rome: Officina (1997).

11 Caizzi, *Il commercio*, pp. 51–5, 181–3.

12 Cf. the rich photographic material in the Alinari Archives.

13 E. De Filippo, *Sabato, domenica e lunedì*, Turin: Einaudi (1959) (act I, in R. Minore, U. Silva, *Il commercio nella letteratura italiana. il Novecento*, Rome: Newton Compton (1986), 78–9).

14 To quote a few examples, in a city like Milan in 1880 there were: 58 manufacturers of alcohol and liqueurs, 97 chocolate factories, 31 cheesemakers, 84 economic advisors (all dealing with retail), 798 fruiterers and herb

sellers, 422 market gardeners and botanists, 294 colonial produce shops, 218 butchers, 170 poulterers, 400 bread and pasta shops, 321 delicatessens, 185 cheese sellers, 344 firewood shops, as well as numerous bazaars (B. Caizzi, *Milano e l'Italia. La vocazione economica di una città*, Unione del Commercio e del Turismo della Provincia di Milano, Milan (1976), 96). During the same period, in the clothing sector alone, in Rome there were 40 bedlinen shops, 253 men's and 85 women's tailors, 201 haberdashers, fashion shops and novelties, 7 milliners, 9 furriers (S. Martini, *I negozi d'epoca a Roma*, Rome: Newton Compton (1995), 31). Concerning shopkeepers and their political and social placing, cf. J. Morris, *The political economy of shopkeeping in Milan, 1886–1922*, Cambridge: Cambridge University Press (1993).

15 M. Bontempelli, *Quello spaccio di sale e tabacchi*, in *Racconti e romanzi*, Milan: Mondadori (1961) (in Minore, Silva, *Il commercio*, 33–4).

16 L. Pirandello, *Un po' di vino*, in *Novelle per un anno*, Milan: Mondatori (1921) (in Minore, Silva, *Il commercio*, 14).

17 Besides the books of photographs on the history of the various cities, it is worth noting the recent interest in period shops, partly thanks to public initiatives (by city councils, regions, associations and representations), which have stressed the value of this patrimony, with related publications and specific books.

18 For this research, both concerning shops and other consumer aspects, I have made ample use of Alinari photographic material, which includes many archives.

19 About the photographs cf. G. Autilia, *L' indizio e la prova. La storia nella fotografia*, Milan: B. Mondadori (2005); G. De Luna, *La passione e la ragione. il mestiere dello storico contemporaneo*, Milan: B. Mondadori (2004); as well as the provocative work of D. Freedberg, *The Power of Images: Studies in the History and Theory of Response*, Chicago: University of Chicago Press (1989), according to which pictures have an evocative power over us much stronger than formal accounts and theoretical schemes of historians and art historians would lead us to suppose.

20 Alinari Archives, Brogi Florence Archives, Brogi photograph, inventory number BGA–F–005624–0000, Naples *c.* 1879–1910.

21 Alinari Archives, Fratelli Alinari Photographic History Museum of Florence, M. Gabinio photograph, no. FVQ–F–029895–0000, Turin *c.* 1925–1935.

22 Alinari Archives, Alinari Archives—Chauffourier archive, Florence, G. E. Chauffourier photograph, no. CGA–F–005424–0000, Naples *c.* 1900.

23 About La Rinascente cf. F. Amatori, *Proprietà e direzione. La Rinascente 1917–1969*, Milan: Franco Angeli (1989); E. Papadia, *La Rinascente*, Bologna: il Mulino (2005), 21–36. For a description cf. the catalogues published by the Rinascente and the photographic material of the Touring Club Italiano Archives, Gestione Archivi Alinari, Milan (many references concern the building reconstructed after the 1918 fire—when it became 'La Rinascente'

(The rebirth) as suggested by D'Annunzio—and the takeover by the financial group headed by Senatore Borletti).

24 *I manifesti Mele: immagini aristocratiche della belle époque per un pubblico di grandi magazzini*, ed. M. Picone Petrusa, Milan: Mondadori (1988). The Mele department stores also set up branches in Palermo, Catania, and Tripoli.

25 V. Zamagni, P. Battilani, A. Casali, *La cooperazione di consumo in Italia. Centocinquant'anni della Coop consumatori: dal primo spaccio a leader della moderna distribuzione*, Bologna: il Mulino (2004).

26 A. D. Chandler jr., *La mano visibile. La rivoluzione manageriale nell'economia americana* [1977], Milan: F. Angeli (1981).

27 S. Salvatici, *Al servizio dei consumatori. I lavoratori e le lavoratrici dei grandi magazzini* in *Il secolo dei consumi. Dinamiche sociali nell'Europa del Novecento*, eds. S. Cavazza and E. Scarpellini, Rome: Carocci, (2006), 117–39.

28 Miller, *The Bon Marché*, 166.

29 L.V. Bertarelli, 'Note intorno a un 'grande magazzino'', Le vie d'Italia, 7, July 1922, 706–7.

30 Mauzan's poster for the reopening of the Rinascente (in Papadia, *La Rinascente*, 27).

31 Notice also that department stores have often been compared to Universal Exhibitions, like the Great Exhibition in London in 1851 with its Crystal Palace, and the one in Paris in 1889 with the Eiffel Tower, as well as the Italian ones such as the Exhibition of modern decorative art in Turin in 1902 (with the fantastic and exotic pavilions designed by D'Aronco) and the one in Milan to celebrate the Simplon Tunnel (with many technological and monumental constructions). In line with the ideas expressed above, the stylistic similarity is no coincidence: the exhibitions, too, seem to have been created on the same theatrical model (spectacular, innovative, grandiose, rich in content, ephemeral); concerning their significance cf. *L'Italia industriale nel 1881: conferenza sulla Esposizione nazionale di Milano*, ed. and introd. E. Decleva, Milan: Banca del Monte (1984); L. Aimone, C. Olmo, *Le esposizioni universali 1851–1900: il progresso in scena*, Turin: Allemandi & Co. (1990).

32 About this point, much stressed by recent historiography, cf.*Getting and Spending: European and American Consumer Societies in the Twentieth Century*, eds. S. Strasser, C. McGovern, and M. Judt, Cambridge: Cambridge University Press, (1998); E. D. Rappaport, *Shopping for Pleasure: Gender and Public Life in London's West End, 1860–1914*, Princeton: Princeton. University Press (2000); *The Sex of Things: Gender and Consumption in Historical Perspective*, eds. V. De Grazia, and E. Furlough, Berkeley: University of California Press (1996).

33 M. R. Roberts, 'Gender, Consumption, and Commodity Culture', The American Historical Review, vol. 103, no. 3, June 1998, 817–44; *The Invention of Pornography: Obscenity and the Origins of Modernity, 1500–1800*, ed. H. Lynn, New York: Zone Books (1993).

Chapter 5

1   The scene is from 'Grand Hotel' directed by E. Goulding, USA (1932).

2   S. Kuznets, *Modern Economic Growth: Rate, Structure, and Spread*, New Haven-London: Yale University Press (1966).

3   Following Kuznets's analysis, ibid., 262–84.

4   '*Novità e conferme nell'analisi dello sviluppo economico italiano*', in *I conti economici dell'Italia*, vol. 3, *Il conto risorse e impieghi* [1891, 1911, 1958, 1951], ed. G. M. Rey, Rome-Bari: Laterza (2003), p. lii.

5   Ibid. xxiii. The complete data relative to private consumption in 1938 are (in millions of Lire): food, drink and tobacco 57,862 (51 per cent); house expenses 14,540 (13 per cent); footwear and clothing 10,813 (9 per cent); health, hygiene, other benefits and services 18,767 (16 per cent); non-perishables, transport and communication 12,373 (11 per cent).

6   ISTAT, *Sommario di statistiche storiche dell'Italia 1861–1975*, ISTAT, Rome (1976) 157–161. The daily calories for the 1931–40 decade average 2,641 as opposed to 2,834 for the preceding decade, and 2,694 for 1911–20 (and down to 2,171 for 1941–50); C.F. Helstosky, *Garlic and Oil: Food and Politics in Italy*, Oxford: Berg (2006).

7   Cf. in particular the inquiry by INEA (The National Institute for Agrarian Economics) of 1928–1937 concerning farming families and by the Confederation of Industrial Workers of 1937 concerning working men's families, in S. Somogyi, '*Cento anni di bilanci familiari in Italia (1857–1956*', Annali Feltrinelli, 2 (1959), 181–200. Also interesting is the research on food consumption by rice weeders in 1942 because it examines the food intake of five working gangs on different farms, all women (except for 58 men who worked on ancillary jobs), one of the very few surveys of this type. It turns out that there were significant differences: within the farms and for the same kind of work they consumed meals varying from a minimum of 2,494 daily calories to a maximum of 3,535 (on average 3,051 calories for 344 working women); while the men's diet was decidedly richer, with 4,060 daily calories (cf. ibid, 202–3).

8   A. Madison, *Historical Statistics for the World Economy. Per Capita GDP* (1990 International Geary-Kharnis dollars), in www.ggdc.net/maddison, 15 February 2007.

9   G. Toniolo, *L'economia italiana dell'Italia fascista*, Rome-Bari: Laterza (1980); *L'economia italiana nel periodo fascista*, eds. P. Ciocca and G. Toniolo, Bologna: il Mulino (1976).

10 The use of substitutes, in particular, provoked a continual flow of underground protests (duly recorded by the police authorities) that frequently took the form of irreverent jokes. Another widespread habit was to put ironic emphasis on the original product by doubling the terms (for example, on important occasions one offers 'coffee-coffee', not a substitute).

11   The references which follow come from research | carried out on illustrated magazines from the 1930s, *L'illustrazione italiana* and *La Domenica del Corriere* in particular.

12   Cf. for example the advertisement in *L'illustrazione italiana* of 18th February 1934 (Radiomarelli), 22nd September 1935 (Sniafiocco), 22nd December 1935 (Ala Littoria, Stenogenol), 1st January 1939 (Lloyd, Etrusca), 15th January 1939 (Impero), 23rd April 1939 (Caesar). About advertising (and the related debate) during Fascism cf. A. Arvidsson, *Marketing Modernity. Italian Advertising from Fascism to Postmodernity*, London: Routledge (2003), 36–64; and concerning the field of fashion, E. Paulicelli, *Fashion under Fascism: Beyond the Black Shirt*, Oxford-New York: Berg (2004). It must be remembered that it was actually during the 1930s that early modern advertising agencies first spread into Italy, on the American model. (Acme Dalmonte, since 1922, Balza-Ricc of Balzaretti and Ricciardi, Enneci of Caimi, Ima of Domenghini).

13   In this sense cf. also E. Papadia, *La Rinascente*, Bologna: il Mulino (2005), 62–5. Autarchic strategies could be read alongside campaigns like the anti-bourgeois one: both aimed at creating a new kind of Italian—warlike, resolute, thrifty, immune to the temptations of consumer pleasures—and both fell well short of their objectives.

14   I. Ghersi, *Ricettario domestico. Enciclopedia moderna per la casa*, 7th edn. Milan: Hoepli (1920)—successive editions by L. Morelli.

15   V. de Grazia, *Le donne nel regime fascista*, Venice: Marsilio (1993), esp. 17–38, 70–111. The policy of the regime towards 'deviant' consumption such as prostitution fits in this picture perfectly. Prostitution was not made illegal but controlled from above through the establishment of 'closed houses', with the combined aims of providing social, policing and sanitary control (against syphilis).

16   It must however be remembered that in the official iconography of the regime the sphere of production (male) and that of consumption (female) were well separated. In the enormous amount of pictures there are of Mussolini, for example, the leader is presented in many guises: politician and warrior (in uniform, on horseback, on a motorcycle, in an aircraft), in a producer's garb (bare-chested farmer on a tractor, miner, cinema projectionist), but never as a consumer. Cf. S. Luzzatto, *L'immagine del duce: Mussolini nelle fotografie dell'Istituto Luce*, Roma: Editori Riuniti (2001); M. Franzinelli, E.V. Marino, *Il duce proibito: le fotografie di Mussolini che gli italiani non hanno mai visto*, Milan: Mondadori (2003).

17   A. Capatti and M. Montanari, *La cucina italiana. Storia di una cultura*, Rome-Bari: Laterza (2005) [1999], 36–7. The same goes for the revival of popular folklore festivals from the past, 're-invented' to boost a local sense of identity and promote tourism. Cf. S. Cavazza, *Piccole Patrie*, il Bologna: Mulino (1997).

18   Capatti and Montanari, *La cucina italiana*, 38.

19   L'illustrazione italiana, 6th May 1934.

20   Ibid. 10th June 1934.

21   Ibid. 19th January 1936 (Moretti, Fatma).

22   Obviously the creation of a set of images linked to the colonies had already started during the preceding Liberal regime, but new life was instilled into it by Fascism. Cf. N. Labanca, *Oltremare. Storia dell'espansione coloniale italiana*, Bologna: il Mulino (2002), 269–307; «'Modern Italy'», VIII, (2003), 1; *Italian Colonialism*, eds. R. Ben-Ghiat and M. Fuller, New York: Palgrave Macmillan (2005); *Italian Colonialism. Legacy and Memory*, eds. J. Andall, D. Duncan, and Peter Lang, Oxford (2005); R. Pergher, *Impero immaginato, impero vissuto. Recenti sviluppi nella storiografia del colonialismo italiano*, Ricerche di storia politica, 10, (2007), 1, 53–66. Naturally gender and racial identities continually intersected: cf. for example G. Stefani, *Colonia per maschi. Italiani in Africa Orientale: una storia di genere*, Verona: Ombre corte (2007). In numerical terms, interaction with the colonies remained limited as regards imports (2.6 per cent out of the total for 1936 and 1.9 per cent for 1938), concentrating on exotic fruit, unworked furs, and cotton: instead, it was significant as regards exports (31 per cent for 1936 and 23 per cent for 1938), chiefly for machines and manufactured products (cf. M. Paradisi, *Il commercio estero e la struttura industriale*, in *L'economia italiana nel periodo fascista*, 308–10). An interesting study in advertising and publicizing the body during Fascism (including black people, to reinforce national identity) is that by K. Pinkus, *Bodily Regimes: Italian Advertising Under Fascism*, Minneapolis: University of Minnesota Press (1995). About the problem of constructing a culture for a geography of colonial domains, refer to the classic study by E. W. Said, *Orientalismo* [1978], Turin: Bollati Boringhieri (1991); in more general terms, for the role of consumption and cultural products in creating a sense of belonging cf. B. Anderson, *Comunità immaginate: origini e fortuna dei nazionalism* [1983], Rome: Manifestolibri (1996).

23   S. Luconi, *'Buy Italian'. Commercio, consumi e identità italo-americana tra le due guerre*, Contemporanea. Rivista di storia dell800 e del '900, July 2002, no. 3, 455–74; V. Teti, *Emigrazione, alimentazione, culture popolari*, in *Storia dell'emigrazione italiana. Partenze*, eds. P. Bevilacqua, A. De Clementi and E. Franzina, Rome Donzelli, (2001) pp. 575–97.

24   D.R. Gabaccia, *We Are What We Eat: Ethnic Food and the Making of Americans*, Cambridge: Harvard University Press (1998). The reference to food as a sign of a specific culture, different from the Anglo-Saxon one has persisted even to the present day. L. DeSalvo, Italo-American writer, in *Vertigo. A Memoir* New York: The Feminist Press (2002) writes meaningful, at times even provocative words—in the United States context—such as: 'Life, I have always believed, is too short to have even one bad meal' (cf. C. Romeo, *Narrative tra due sponde. Memoir di italiane d'America*, Rome: Carocci (2005), 120).

25 Hasia R. Diner, *Hungering for America: Italian, Irish, and Jewish Foodways in the Age of Migration*, Cambridge: Harvard University Press (2001).

26 S. Cinotto, *Una famiglia che mangia insieme: cibo ed etnicità nella comunità italoamericana di New York*, 1920–1940, Turin: Otto (2001).

27 K. Polanyi, *La grande trasformazione* [1944], Turin: Einaudi (1974), 143–7.

28 In 1938, domestic demand was made up as follows: 68 per cent private consumption (which was on a downward spiral); 18 per cent public spending; 14 per cent investments (slightly down compared with 1911); in general the trend in overall public spending took on a greater proportion with respect to the GDP (see also Table 3). Cf. Rey, *Novità e conferme*, xxiii.

29 A.T. Peacock, J. Wiseman, *The Growth of Public Expenditure in the United Kingdom*, Princeton: Princeton University Press (1961); A. Wagner, *Finanzwissenschaft*, Leipzig: Winter'sche Verlagshandlung (1883); For an overview see G. Brosio, and C. Marchese, *Il potere di spendere. Economia e storia della spesa pubblica dall'Unificazione ad oggi*, Bologna: il Mulino (1986), 24–45.

30 In 1938, for example, there were 751,000 pupils in nursery schools (of whom 378,000 were female), 5,095,000 in elementary schools (of whom 2,450,000 were female), 821,000 in secondary schools (of whom 306,000 were female), 77,429 at university (of whom 15,084 were female). Cf. ISTAT, *Sommario di statistiche storiche*, 47. About teaching: M. Ostenc, *La scuola italiana durante il fascismo* [1980], Rome-Bari: Laterza (1981); E. De Fort, *La scuola elementare dall'unità alla caduta del fascism*, Bologna: il Mulino (1996); and on the position of women, V. de Grazia, *Le donne nel regime fascista*, Venice: Marsilio (1993).

31 G. Cosmacini, *Medicina e sanità in Italia nel ventesimo secolo. Dalla «spagnola» alla II guerra mondiale*, Rome-Bari: Laterza (1989).

32 For the part relating to welfare assistance and social service regulations cf. F. Girotti, *Welfare State. Storia, modelli e critica*, Rome: Carocci, (1998), 178–200. Note also the creation of a redundancy fund in 1941, against unemployment during the war years.

33 F. Girotti, 196–7; C. Giorgi, *La previdenza del regime. Storia dell'Inps durante il fascismo*, Bologna: il Mulino (2004).

34 de Grazia, *Le donne nel regime fascista*, 70–111.

35 *Stato e infanzia nell'Italia contemporanea. Origini, sviluppo e fine dell'Onmi 1925–1975*, ed. M. Minesso, Bologna: il Mulino (2007).

36 Brosio, Marchese, *Il potere di spendere*, 62 (see also statistics, 188–190). In 1938, for example, its value was 32 per cent of domestic demand (18 per cent public consumption with 14 per cent more for investments). Cf. Rey, *Novità e conferme*, p. xxiii.

37 G. Roth, *I socialdemocratici nella Germania imperiale* [1963], Bologna: il Mulino (1971).

38 S. Cavazza, *Dimensione massa. Individui, folle, consumi 1830–1945*, Bologna: il Mulino (2004), 227–37; V. de Grazia, *Consenso e cultura di massa nell'Italia fascista*, Rome-Bari: Laterza (1981), 29–69; R. Ben-Ghiat, *La cultura fascista*, Bologna: il Mulino (2000).

39 Cavazza, *Dimensione massa*, 254.

40 S. Kern, *Il tempo e lo spazio: la percezione del mondo tra Otto e Novecento* [1983], Bologna: il Mulino (1995); *L'invenzione del tempo libero 1850–1960*, ed. A. Corbin, Rome-Bari: Laterza (1996).

41 A. Corbin, *L'invenzione del tempo libero*, in *L'invenzione del tempo libero 1850–1960*, 3–7.

42 Cavazza, *Dimensione massa*, 252–4.

43 E. Scarpellini, *Organizzazione teatrale e politica del teatro nell'Italia fascista*, new edn., Milan: Led (2004), 113.

44 M. Corsi, *Il teatro all'aperto in Italia*, Milan-Rome: Rizzoli1 (1939), 268.

45 P. Lazarsfeld, *Metodologia e ricerca sociologica*, Bologna: il Mulino (1967), 825. The dome, patented by the Spanish artist Mariano Fortuny in 1902, was particularly evocative because instead of a painted background it made use of indirect lighting which projected cloudy or starry skies.

46 Scarpellini, *Organizzazione teatrale*, 246–54.

47 de Grazia, *Le donne nel regime fascista*, 291–5.

48 A. Panebianco, *Modelli di partito. Organizzazione e potere nei partiti politici*, Bologna: il Mulino (1982), 60–5.

49 Historical Luce Archives, *Giornale Luce* B0309 of 1933 (The Prince and Princess open the Museum of Campania at Capua); *Cine Gil* CG001 of 1940 (Maria José watches the gymnastics and dancing exhibitions in the Boboli gardens) and several others.

50 Historical Luce Archives, *Giornale Luce* B0925, 22nd July 1938; or B1036 of 3rd February 1937 (At Cortina d'Ampezzo for the World Bobsleigh Competition); B0998 of November 1936 (The Ciano couple at a fox hunt with Horthy, Regent of Hungary); B1023 of January 1937 (Edda Ciano takes part in the Fascist Epiphany gift distribution to children), and many others.

51 de Grazia, *Le donne nel regime fascista*, 147–58. It is during the late Fascist period that Gundle and Forgacs also place the birth of a commercial culture, which would come into its own fully after the war: cf. D. Forgacs, S. Gundle, *Cultura di massa e società italiana 1936–1954*, Bologna: il Mulino (2007).

The predominance of American films was a constant feature during the whole regime, with the exception of the war years. In 1926, for example, the censors reviewed 733 foreign films (nearly all from the US) and 153 Italian films. In 1927 they were 630 and 108 respectively, and 624 and 62 in 1928. (cf. *I cinematografi in Italia*, in il Popolo d'Italia, 6th August 1930). It is worth noting that there was no shortage of similar references in advertising: for example *Macedonia extra* cigarettes show a short-haired, carefully made-up woman, with a dazzling smile and holding a cigarette in her hand (Il Secolo illustrato, 23rd December 1933), while *Diadermina* cream is advertised by the painter Tamara de Lempicka (Il Secolo illustrato, 30th December 1933). Both advertisements portray women with very different images from the ones shown by official propaganda.

52   H. Berghoff, *Enticement and Deprivation: The Regulation of Consumption in Pre-War Nazi Germany*, in *The Politics of Consumption. Material Culture and Citizenship in Europe and America*, eds. M. Daunton and M. Hilton, Oxford-New York: Berg (2001), 165–84. In a certain sense Götz also follows this line, when he maintains that the Nazis always tried to achieve consensus through social support policies and high standards of living for the German people and that, when economic reserves to support these ran out they launched into a policy of expansion and aggression so as to go on guaranteeing them at the expense of other peoples (cf. A. Götz, *Lo stato sociale di Hitler. Rapina, guerra razziale e nazionalsocialismo*, [2005], Turin: Einaudi (2007)).

53   Berghoff, *Enticement and Deprivation*, 184.

Chapter 6

1   W. Bright, G. Sanga, '*Le virtù dell'analfabetismo*', La Ricerca Folklorica, no. 5, April 1982, 15–19.

2   J. Baudrillard, *Il sistema degli oggetti* [1968], Milan: Bompiani, (1972).

3   N. Rosenberg, *Esplorando la scatola nera: tecnologia, economia e storia* (1994), Milan: Giuffrè, (1999).

4   I. Gagliardone, M. Geraci, *La scatola nera e il mantello di Arlecchino. Autonomie culturali nelle reti globali*, Studi culturali, 2nd December 2004, 393–414; F. De Ruggieri, A. C. Pugliese, *Futura. Genere e tecnologia*, Rome: Meltemi (2006); *How Users Matter: The Co-Construction of Users and Technology*, eds. N. Oudshoorn and T. Pinch, Cambridge: MIT Press (2003) (in particular J. Schot and A. Albert de la Bruhèze, '*The Mediated Design of Products, Consumption and Consumers in the Twentieth Century*', 229–46, for their concept of 'mediation junction' where producers, mediators, and consumers co-design products).

5   H. Kaelble, *Verso una società europea. Storia sociale dell'Europa 1880–1980* [1987], Rome-Bari: Laterza (1990), 43–65.

6   I. Paris, *Oggetti cuciti. L'abbigliamento pronto in Italia dal primo dopoguerra agli anni Settanta*, Milan: Franco Angeli (2006), 59–63; E. Merlo, *Moda italiana. Storia di un'industria dall'Ottocento a oggi*, Venice: Marsilio (2003).

7   Paris, *Oggetti cuciti*, 65–72.

8   A. Colli, *Fibre chimiche*, in *Storia d'Italia. Annali 19. La moda*, eds. C.M. Belfanti, and F. Giusberti, Turin: Einaudi (2003), 483–522.

9   To give some examples of prices, midway through the 1930s a pair of men's or women's shoes of low-medium quality could cost 30–40 lire, a man's suit 150 lire (a metre of worsted cost 42 lire, twice that of a woman's). By comparison, in 1935 10 cigarettes cost 1.70 lire; a letter postage stamp 0.50, the same as an urban bus ticket; a kilo of bread 1.80, of sugar 6, of beef 9, of coffee 29; a litre of milk 1, of wine 1.7, of oil 6 (See Table 4). It is calculated that prices went down during the first half of the 1930s then swung around to rise rapidly during the second half. Cf. ISTAT, *Sommario di statistiche storiche*, 134–8. To get an idea of prices in today's terms, multiply the 1935 figures by a factor of 1938.89 (and then change it into Euro): by a curious coincidence the given figures are similar to the Euro value in 2006.

10 R. Carrarini, *La stampa di moda dall'Unità a oggi*, in *Storia d'Italia. Annali 19. La moda*, 810–22. About the regime's policy towards fashion and its impact on the following period cf. Paulicelli, *Fashion under Fascism: Beyond the Block Shirt*, Oxford-NewYork: Berg (2004).

11 International Footwear Museum of Vigevano, *Lusso & Autarchia 1935–1945. Salvatore Ferragamo e gli altri calzolai italiani*, Città di Castello: Sillabe (2005).

12 Gazzoni was an advertising pioneer who also wrote books on the art of selling. The funny rhyme to advertise his product (written on the packet as well) is famous: 'The host said to the wine | I find you are getting old | I want to marry you off | to the water in my pail. | The wine said to the host | go ahead and publish the banns. | I shall marry Idrolitina| from the house of Cavalier Gazzoni'.

13 ISTAT, *Sommario di statistiche storiche*, 148.

14 Advertisements, such as that of the Narni Linoleum Society explained that it was a national product, suggesting an improbable Italian origin since the name comes from 'linen-oleum'.

15 G. Bigatti et al., *L'acqua e il gas* in *Italia: la storia dei servizi a rete, delle aziende pubbliche e della Federgasacqua*, Milan: Franco Angeli (1997).

16 G. L. Lapini, *Milano tecnica*, in www.storiadimilano.it, 18th May 2007.

17 M. Sironi, *Il gasometro* (oil on canvas), (1943).

18 S. Musso, *La famiglia operaia*, in *La famiglia italiana dall'Ottocento a oggi*, ed. P. Melograni, Rome-Bari: Laterza (1988), 80–1.

19 'Though recognizing that hungry or ill-fed men have achieved great things in the past, we affirm this truth: one thinks, dreams and acts according to what one has eaten or drunk. [...] We believe that above all else it is necessary to do the following: a) Abolish pasta, Italy's absurd gastronomic religion. Perhaps stockfish, roast beef and puddings do the English good. Meat cooked with cheese does the Dutch good. Sauerkraut, smoked fatty bacon and sausage do the Germans good. But pasta does not do the Italians good. For example, it goes against the lively spirit and passionate, intuitive and generous soul of the Neapolitans. [...]

The perfect lunch needs:

> A table setting (decorated glass, china and pottery) in genuine harmony with the colour and taste of the food.

Absolutely genuine food. [. . .]'

F. T. Marinetti, *Il Manifesto della cucina futurista*, Gazzetta del Popolo, Turin, 28th December 1930, in F. T. Marinetti e Fillìa, *La cucina futurista* [1932], Milan: Viennepierre (2007), 27–30.

20 ISTAT, *Sommario di statistiche storiche*, 15.

21 G. D'Amato, *Storia dell'arredamento*, Rome-Bari: Laterza (1999), 299–358; M. Salvati, *L'inutile salotto: l'abitazione piccolo-borghese nell'Italia fascista*, Turin: Bollati Boringhieri (1993).

22 F. Monteleone, *Storia della radio e della televisione in Italia*, Venice: Marsilio (1992), 81–108.

23 A. Briggs, P. Burke, *Storia sociale dei media. Da Gutenberg a Internet* [2005], Bologna: il Mulino (2007), 213–16; D. Forgacs, *L'industrializzazione della cultura italiana (1880–2000)*, Bologna: il Mulino (2000).

24 As regards the telephone, during 1933 IRI founded STET to manage the telephone service, creating a semi-monopoly regime. Subscribers exceeded 600,000 in 1942 (cf. SIP, *Il telefono 1881–1981: cento anni al servizio del paese. Appunti di storia e note di cronaca sulla telefonia in concessione*, Rome: Sat (1984)). In 1938 entertainment spending was divided into millions as follows: 102 for theatre, 587 cinema, 105 various entertainments, 37 sports events, for an overall total of 831 million. There were 965,577 radio licenses. 10,838 books were printed, of which 802 were for school use—to this must be added the fact that magazines of all levels were very popular, starting with '*Topolino*' ('Mickey Mouse'), first published by Nerbini and then Mondadori (cf. ISTAT, *Sommario di statistiche storiche*, 58–9).

25 B.R. Mitchell, *European Historical Statistics 1750–1970*, New York: Columbia University Press (1975), 659–67 (in 1838 there were 4.7 million radio licenses in France and 9.6 million in Germany).

26 Advertisements appeared during the 1930s in magazines such as L'illustrazione italiana and La Domenica del Corriere.

27 F.T. Marinetti, '*Manifesto del Futurismo*', Le Figaro, 20th Februay 1909.

28 Also interesting from this point of view is *Il motociclista. Solido in velocità* (oil on canvas), (1923), by F. Depero. With its well-defined strokes it represents the man–machine pair becoming one, clearing its way through solid and mobile space like the subject in the foreground.

29 Mitchell, *European Historical Statistics*, 640–1.

30 F. Paolini, *Storia sociale dell'automobile in Italia*, Rome: Carocci (2007), 25. Despite the low traffic levels, there were more than 31,000 accidents during 1938, including 2,500 fatal ones. The prime causes were pedestrians being run over, followed by collisions with other vehicles. (cf. ISTAT, *Sommario di*

statistiche storiche, 107). Cf. also D. Marchesini, *Cuori e motori. Storia della Mille Miglia (1927–1957)*, Bologna: il Mulino (2001).

31 It is interesting to note the transposition of sport from real space to 'mythical' space, as defined by Georges Vigarello: popular passion finds more release through events covered by the media, capable of bringing together huge numbers of people spread out in space, than through sport actually performed (cf. G. Vigarello, *Il tempo dello sport*, in *L'invenzione del tempo libero 1850–1960*, 236). This is particularly true for sport available to all, like football (with the victories of Vittorio Pozzo's national team), boxing (where the everlasting myth of Primo Carnera was created: the poor emigrant who redeems himself with his strength), cycling (with competiveness between popular champions like Girardengo, Binda, Bartali, and Coppi). Cf. A. Papa, G. Panico, *Storia sociale del calcio in Italia*, Bologna: il Mulino (2002); D. Marchesini, *Carnera*, Bologna: il Mulino (2006); Idem., *L'Italia del Giro d'Italia*, Bologna: il Mulino (2003).

32 A. Corbin, *Dall'ozio coltivato alla classe oziosa*, in *L'invenzione del tempo libero 1850–1960*, 61–71. The overall 1938 total, of passengers going through Italian ports was 4,700,000, but it is difficult to tell how many of these were clients for luxury cruises (cf. ISTAT, *Sommario di statistiche storiche*, 109).

33 *Amarcord*, directed by Federico Fellini, Italy-France (1974).

34 ISTAT, *Sommario di statistiche storiche*, 111.

35 Ibid., 104; S. Maggi, *Storia dei trasporti in Italia*, Bologna: il Mulino (2005).

36 A. Rauch, *Le vacanze e la rivisitazione della natura (1830–1939)*, in *L'invenzione del tempo libero 1850–1960*, 85–117.

37 The excursion train initiative, launched in August 1931, was a great success. These were special trains organized on public holidays which transported thousands of people (in short, more than a million for about a thousand round trips) to various tourist centres. Tickets were sold from Mondays for a day trip from 5–7 in the morning up to midnight. Cf. S. Maggi, *Politica ed economia dei trasporti (secoli XIX–XX). Una storia della modernizzazione italiana*, Bologna: il Mulino (2001), 268–9.

38 S. Maggi, 270.

39 V. Zamagni, *La distribuzione commerciale in Italia fra le due guerre*, Milan: Franco Angeli (1981), 20–1.

40 V. Zamagni, 78.

41 V. Zamagni, 23, 126.

42 R. D. L. 16th December 1926, n. 2174. Cf. Zamagni, *La distribuzione commerciale*, 89 ff.; B. Maida, *Il prezzo dello scambio. Commercianti a Torino (1940–1943)*, Turin: Scriptorium (1998), 41 ff.; J. Morris, '*Retailers, Fascism and the origins of the social protection of shopkeepers in Italy*', Contemporary European History, vol. 5, no. 3, (1996), 285–318.

43 The images referred to are available on the company website http://www.upim.it/box.html, 20th March 2007. Naturally this did not prevent the idea

of a popular fixed-price store entering into common usage together with the term itself. (cf. for example L. D'Ambra, *Il teatro «Upim»*, Scenario, November 1939, where it is used to indicate poor quality merchandize).

44 F. Amatori, *Proprietà e direzione. La Rinascente 1917–1969*, Milan: Franco Angeli (1989).

45 The pact was later denounced and not renewed by PTB in July 1944. Another recurrent aspect in the conflict between Rinascente and Standa was the continual call by the Fascist trade unions for the correct enforcement of work contracts. Up to then Borletti had even obtained an official dispensation to take on a greater number of unqualified staff than the regulations allowed. Cf. E. Scarpellini, *Comprare all'americana. Le origini della rivoluzione commerciale in Italia 1945–1971*, Bologna: il Mulino (2001), 205–10. Note that the 1929 crisis had forced the big historic Mele stores to close (cf. V. Zamagni, *Dinamica e problemi della distribuzione commerciale tra il 1880 e la II guerra mondiale*, Commercio, 20, (1985), 3 ff.).

46 Scarpellini, *Comprare all'americana*, 218–24.

47 E. De Filippo, *Napoli milionaria!* [1945], Turin: Einaudi (1971), 31–3.

Chapter 7

1 A description of the opening of the first supermarket in Milan, 27th November 1957 (cf. E. Scarpellini *La spesa è uguale per tutti. L'avventura dei supermercati in Italia*, Venice: Marsilio (2007)). The newspaper article referred to is '*Rockefeller offre pinne di Pescecane*', il Giornale, 27th November 1957; the customers' comments are recorded in Rockefeller Archive Center, Wayne G. Broehl, IV 3A 16, box 12, Italians III folder, Comments pertaining to Italian Supermarkets, R. H. Hood to W. D. Bradford, Milan, 9th November 1959 (in Scarpellini, *La spesa è uguale per tutti*, 80). Cf. also, some author's interview with people living in the neighbourhood.

2 *The Golden Age of Capitalism: Reinterpreting the Postwar Experience*, eds. S.A. Marglin, and J. B. Schor, Oxford: Clarendon Press (1990); A. Cardini, *Introduzione. La fine dell'Italia rurale e il miracolo economico*, in id., *Il miracolo economico italiano (1958–1963)*, Bologna: il Mulino (2006), 7–9. As regards the division into periods, some researchers prefer to use 1950 instead of 1945 to mark the difference between the first difficult post-war years and the economic growth which followed. As regards the final benchmark of 1973, this coincides with the first oil crisis.

3 A. Maddison, *Monitoring the World Economy*, Development Centre OECD, Paris (1995), 73–5.

4 H. W. Arndt, *Lo sviluppo economico. Storia di un'idea*, [1987], Bologna: il Mulino (1990), 71–117.

5 M. Arendt, *The Human Condition*, 2nd edn., Chicago: University of Chicago Press, [1958] (1988), 253.

6   A. Maddison, *Historical Statistics for the World Economy. Per Capita GDP (1990 International Geary-Kharmis dollars)*, in www.ggdc.net/maddison, 15th February 2007.

7   M. Livi Bacci, *La popolazione nella storia d'Europa*, Rome-Bari: Laterza, (1998), 227–31.

8   For an Italian woman the average number of children was 3.5 in 1921–1925 and went down to 2.5 during 1941–1945; to rise again later to 2.8 during 1946–1950 and settle at 2.6 during 1961–65 and 2.5 during 1965–1970. It then descended abruptly. Cf. Livi Bacci, *La popolazione nella storia d'Europa*, 233 (table. 7.3).

9   In the years 1930, 1950, and 1970 life expectancies in years were respectively: Great Britian 60.8, 69.2 and 72; France 56.7, 66.5 and 72.4; Germany 61.4, 67.5 and 71; Italy 54.9, 66 and 72.1. Cf. Livi Bacci, *La popolazione nella storia d'Europa*, 231 (table. 7.2).

10   From 1950 to 1970 the average age for Italian men rose from 64.1 to 69.3 years (+5.2); and for women from 68 to 75.3 years (+7.3). Cf. ISTAT, *Sommario di statistiche storiche dell'Italia 1861–1975*, ISTAT, Rome (1976), 25–6.

11   The 1951 census registered 8,261,000 working in agriculture, equalling 42 per cent of the active population (industry: 32 per cent; services: 26 per cent); in 1971 there were 3,243,000, equal to 17 per cent (industry: 44 per cent; services: 39 per cent). Cf. ISTAT, *Sommario di statistiche storiche*, 14.

12   Moravia, *Felicità in vetrina*, in *Racconti surrealistici e satirici*, Milan: Bompiani, (1945) (in R. Minore, U. Silva, *Il commercio nella letteratura italiana. il Novecento*, Rome: Newton Compton (1986), 128–30).

13   The average propensity to consume (private consumption/gross national income) decreased from values around 0.79 in the Giolitti period and 0.67 during Fascism, down to 0.64 during the 1960–1970 decade. Cf. *I conti economici dell'Italia*, ed. G. M. Rey, vol. I, *Una sintesi delle fonti ufficiali 1890–1970*, Rome-Bari: Laterza (1991), 42–4.

14   *I conti economici dell'Italia*, ed. G. M. Rey, vol. I, *Una sintesi delle fonti ufficiali 1890–1970*, Rome-Bari: Laterza (1991), 210, 215–16. Data are expressed in constant prices in billions (1000 millions) of lire 1963.

15   For an analysis of changes over a long period cf. B. Barbieri, *I consumi nel primo secolo dell'Unità d'Italia 1861–1960*, Milan: Giuffrè (1961).

16   C. D'Apice, *L'arcipelago dei consumi. Consumi e redditi delle famiglie in Italia dal dopoguerra ad oggi*, Bari: de Donato (1981), 53. These tendencies are confirmed by earlier researches, like that of Doxa in 1958, which revealed how the first spread of refrigerators, washing machines, and televisions in Italy depended on three elements, in this order: social class (the upper class had all three in 11 per cent of homes, while this never ever happened in the lower classes); community size (4 per cent in cities with populations over 100,000 against 0.2 per cent in those below 5,000); geographical zone (1.7 per cent north, 1.1 per cent south and islands; 1 per cent centre). Cf. P. Luzzatto Fegiz, *Il volto*

sconosciuto dell'Italia. Seconda serie 1956–1965, Milan: Giuffrè (1966), 1685–9. For other data relative to 1961 and 1965 cf. ibid. 1714–19.

17   D'Apice, *L'arcipelago dei consumi*, 96, 144. The data refer to an inquiry by the Bank of Italy relative to 1975 (in that year washing machines were present in 76 per cent of families and cars in 65 per cent).

18   D'Apice, 35, 41–2; B. R. Mitchell, *European Historical Statistics, 1750–1970*, New York: Columbia University Press (1975), 643–4.

19   Cf. for example G. Bocca, *Miracolo all'Italiana*, Milan: Edizioni Avanti! (1962).

20   Cf. In this sense S. Carrubba, *Post-Milano. Riflessioni senza pregiudizi su una città che vuole rimanere grande*, Milan: Mondadori (2005).

21   E. Scarpellini, *Consumi e commercio*, in *L'età della speranza. Milano dalla ricostruzione al boom*, ed. A. Gigli Marchetti, Milan: Skira (2007), 51–7.

22   D'Apice, *L'arcipelago dei consumi*, 42.

23   G. Maione, '*Spesa pubblica o consumi privati? Verso una reinterpretazione dell'economia italiana postbellica*', Italia contemporanea, 231, June 2003.

24   In 1973 for example, the northwest regions consumed 21 per cent more than the national average (17 for food, 24 for other items); the northeast was +11 per cent (3 food, 16 other); the centre +5 per cent (10 food, 2 other); the south and the islands −25 per cent (−20 food, −28 other). Cf. D'Apice, *L'arcipelago dei consumi*, 111, 175.

25   Cf. for example Luce Historical Archives, La Settimana Incom, no. 02497, 31st July 1964.

26   D. Roche, *Storie delle cose banali. La nascita del consumo in Occidente* [1997], Rome: Editori Riuniti (2002), 15.

27   C. Lévi-Strauss, *Il pensiero selvaggio* [1962], Milan: il Saggiatore (1964).

28   M. Douglas, *Antropologia e simbolismo. Religione, cibo e denaro nella vita sociale* [1975 and 1982], Bologna: il Mulino (1985), 165–230.

29   F. Casorati, *Fiat 600* (picture and poster) (1956).

30   A. Sannia, *Fiat 500: piccolo grande mito*, Savigliano: Gribaudo (2005). About car culture cf. *Car Cultures (Materializing Culture)*, ed. D. Miller, Oxford: Berg (2001).

31   ISTAT, *Sommario di statistiche storiche*, 106: A. Maddison, *Monitoring the World Economy*, Development Centre OECD, Paris (1995), 72. Note that the figures were very different before; in Great Britain passenger-carrying cars were, during 1913, 1950, 1973 (in thousands): 106; 2,258; 13,497: in France: 91; 1,500; 14,500; in Germany: 61; 516; 17,023; in Italy: 22; 342; 13,424, confirming the noticeable increase observed in Italy—beaten, however, by Japan, which registered during the same years: 0; 48; 14,473, while the United States recorded respectively : 1,190; 40,339; 101,986 (ibid).

32   F. Paolini, *Storia sociale dell'automobile in Italia*, Rome: Carocci (2007), 48–53.

33   S. Maggi, *Politica ed economia dei trasporti (secoli XIX–XX). Una storia della modernizzazione italiana*, Bologna: il Mulino (2001); E. Menduni, *L'autostrada del Sole*, Bologna: il Mulino (1999).

34 Bocca, *Miracolo all'Italiana*, 76.

35 S. Bellassai, *La mascolinità contemporanea*, Rome: Carocci (2004); R.W. Connel, *Masculinities*, Berkeley: Polity Press (2005): R. A. Nye, '*Western Masculinities in War and Peace*', American Historical Review, 112, 2nd April 2007, 417–38; *Mascolinità*, Genesis, 2, 2, 2003; F. Mort, *Cultures of Consumption. Masculinity and Social Space in Late Twentieth-Century Britain*, London: Routledge (1996).

36 J. Gilbert, *Men in the Middle: Searching for Masculinity in the 1950s*, Chicago: University of Chicago Press (2005); P. Vettel-Becker, *Shooting from the Hip: Photography, Masculinity, and Postwar America*, Minneapolis: University of Minnesota Press (2005); *Mascolinità all'italiana. Costruzioni, narrazioni, mutamenti*, eds. E. Dell'Agnese, and E. Ruspini, Turin: Utet (2007).

37 *Il sorpasso*, directed by Dino Risi, Italy (1962). For masculine identity changes in Italy and fears linked to a perceived 'feminization' of consumer society, as well as strategies of adaptation and negation in particular see S. Bellassai, *Mascolinità, mutamento, merce. Crisi dell'identità maschile nell'Italia del boom*, in *Genere, generazione e consumi. L'Italia degli'anni Sessanta*, ed. P. Capuzzo, Rome: Carocci (2003), 105–37.

38 G. Lindauer, *Tohunga under Tapu* (oil on canvas) (1902).

39 M. Douglas, B. Isherwood, *Il mondo delle cose: oggetti, valori, consumo* [1979], Bologna: il Mulino (1984), 143–155 (analysing the separate economic spheres in the culture of the Yurok Californian Indians, Tiv Nigerians, and Hausa tradesmen of Ibadan).

40 Super-luxury goods can sometimes be included in this category too, that is goods intended for such a restricted élite who have a very high and reliable income.

41 Paolini, *Storia sociale dell'automobile in Italia*, 63–8; D'Apice, *L'arcipelago dei consumi*, 42.

42 A newspaper survey in 1963 revealed that the most coveted goods for Italians were a car (21.2 per cent), house (20.8 per cent), new furniture (14.2 per cent), and new technological goods (6.6 per cent). Cf. Paolini, *Storia sociale dell'automobile in Italia*, 64.

43 A. Signorelli, M. C. Tiriticco, and S. Rossi, *Scelte senza potere: il ritorno degli emigranti nelle zone dell'esodo*, Rome: Officina (1977), 172–3. Cf. also G. Fofi, *L'immigrazione meridionale a Torino*, Milan: Feltrinelli (1975).

44 *Miracolo a Milano*, directed by V. De Sica, Italy (1951) (adapted from a novel by C. Zavattini).

45 V. Castronovo, *Torino*, Rome-Bari: Laterza (1987), 382–97; M. Boriani, *La città contemporanea*, in *Milano*, Touring Club Italiano-Mondadori, Milan (2007), 83–6; F. Alasia, D. Montaldi *Milano, Corea. Inchiesta sugli immigrati*, Milan: Feltrinelli (1960); L. Diena *Borgata Milanese*, Milan: Franco Angeli (1963); J. Foot, *Milano dopo il miracolo: biografia di una città* (2001), Milan: Feltrinelli (2003); G. Piccinato, *Roma contemporanea*, in *Roma*, Touring Club

Italiano-Mondadori, Milan (2007), 91–101. All this is also due to a lack of public housing, which in Italy never exceeded 10 per cent of the total during the thirty years after the war, and was around 5 per cent on average, whereas it represented 20–25 per cent in Germany, France, and Great Britain. Cf. A. Signorelli, *Movimenti di popolazione e trasformazioni culturali* in *Storia dell'Italia repubblicana*, vol. II, *La trasformazione dell'Italia: sviluppo e squilibri*, book 1, 617.

46 F. Alberoni, *Consumi e società*, Bologna: il Mulino (1964). Surveys on housing conditions in fairly rich areas around Milan, like the classic sociological research by A. Pizzorno, *Comunità e razionalizzazione*, Turin: Einaudi (1960), also conclude that a one-family house is central to expectations and synonymous with security (the second basic element is a desire to climb socially, which is, however, projected onto the children by means of a good education). Worth noting, also, is how studies on groups of English workers newly migrated to Luton show interesting analogies: private life styles revolving around the domestic environment, aspirations of acquiring higher standards of living, etc. Cf. Douglas, Douglas, *Antropologia e simbolismo*, 180–1.

47 T. Faravelli Giacobone, P. Guidi, A. Pansera, *Dalla casa elettrica alla casa elettronica. Storia e significato degli elettrodomestici*, Milan: Arcadia (1989), 65. Cf. also *Oggetti di uso quotidiano: rivoluzioni tecnologiche nella vita d'oggi*, ed. M. Nacci, Venice: Marsilio (1998). Unless indicated otherwise, the references for the descriptions that follow come from the author's analysis of the following sources: women's magazines (Gioia and Annabella in particular), periodicals (Oggi, Epoca), TV advertising programmes (chiefly Carosello, on Teche Rai), films from Luce Historical Archives, surveys and opinion polls (especially by Doxa) to collect and record consumers' points of view.

48 S. Bowden, A. Offer, '*Household appliances and the use of time: the United States and Britain since the 1920s*', Economic Historical Review, 47, 1994, 725–48; G. S. Becker, '*A Theory of the allocation of time*', Economic Journal, 75, 1965, 493–517; L. Pellegrini, L. Zanderighi, *Le famiglie come imprese e I consumi in Italia*, Milan: Egea (2005).

49 R. Sassatelli, *Genere e consumi*, in *Il secolo dei consumi. Dinamiche sociali nell'Europa del Novecento*, eds. S. Cavazza, and E. Scarpellini, Rome: Carocci (2006), 141–73; *The Sex of Things: Gender and Consumption in Historical Perspective*, eds. V. de Grazia, and E. Furlough, Berkeley: University of California Press (1996) (it also contains another sample of Bowden and Offer); *I consumi. Una questione di genere*, eds. A. Arru, and M. Stella, Rome: Carocci (2003).

50 *The Jetsons*, Hanna-Barbera cartoons, 1962. In the world of animated cartoons the Jetsons are ideally contrasted with the cave-dwelling Flintstones, another family of a distant time. Using different technological levels, both of them however exactly reproduce the lifestyles and same social roles as the average American family of the 1950s–1960s (that will come to be labelled 'the Joneses').

51   B. Fine, '*Household appliances and the use of time: The United States and Britain since the 1920s. A Comment*', The Economic History Review, vol. 52, no. 3, (1999), 558.

52   P. Ginsborg, *Storia dell'Italia dal dopoguerra ad oggi. Società e politica 1943–1988*, Turin: Einaudi (1989), 283–343; E. Asquer, *La «Signora Candy» e la sua lavatrice. Storia di un'intesa perfetta nell'Italia degli anni Sessanta*, Genesis, vol. 5, no. 1, (2006), 97–118; Ibid. *La rivoluzione candida. Storia della lavatrice in Italia (1945–1970)*, Rome: Carocci (2007).

53   V. de Grazia, *L'impero irresistibile. La società dei consumi Americana alla conquista del mondo* [2005], Turin: Einaudi (2006), 445–84. About the American influence on post-war ideas of home and domesticity cf. R. Oldenziel and K. Zachmann, *Cold War Kitchen: Americanization, Technology, and European Users*, Cambridge: MIT Press (2009); P. Scrivano, '*Signs of Americanization in Italian domestic life: Italy's postwar conversion to consumerism*', Journal of Contemporary History, 40, 2005, 317–40.

54   Social classes in 1961 can be measured as follows: 1) a restricted upper class which remains relatively stable (property owners, businessmen, directors, professionals) of 400,000 people, equal to 2 per cent of the working population; 2) a broad sector of middle classes (32 per cent), consisting of the self-employed (craftsmen, shopkeepers, service sector personnel: 3,165,000 on the increase), white-collar employees (private sector, civil service, teachers: 2,650,000 the group with the biggest increase), special categories (military, clerics and others: 630,000 increasing slowly); 3) working class (industry: 4,190,000, building trade: 1,700,000, commerce: 500,000, transport and services: 600,000, domestic service: 370,000) equal to 36 per cent; 4) finally there are farmers (4,400,000 much decreased) and paid farm workers (1,700,000, the group which lost the most). Cf. P. Sylos Labini, *Saggio sulle classi sociali*, Rome-Bari: Laterza (1974), 155–6 (in this case also we have separated data referring to the farming world).

55   Reported in Faravelli Giacobone, Guidi, Pansera, *Dalla casa elettrica alla casa elettronica*, 65.

56   Schwartz Cowan for example maintains that domestic technology has eliminated hard work, but created new tasks in exchange. The first domestic appliance, the stove/oven, reduced the men's labour of keeping the fire lit, but increased the women's work by burdening them with more culinary tasks. After that, domestic appliances cut out the heaviest work for the housewife but she was then expected to be more productive in general and take on new tasks (taking the children to school, for example). To sum up, there was still a lot of work to be done, perhaps the only change being that there was some division between the roles. Cf. R. Schwartz Cowan, *More Work for Mother: The Ironies of Household Technology from the Open Hearth to the Microwave*, New York: Basic Books (1983).

57 Along the same lines as Candy can be placed an advertisements by Philco electrical appliances, set on planet Papalla, where strange ball-shaped creatures enjoy life-improving technology.

58 One of the commonplaces in contemporary advertising was the idea that electric appliances, reducing household work, had eliminated the domestic maid. In many advertisements we see an elegantly dressed housewife using the Electrolux floor-polisher (while the maid hides behind the door), or the CGE vacuum cleaner, or doing the washing with such and such detergent (which washes everything miraculously). Statistical data say that domestic work suffered an abrupt decline immediately after the war (in 1951 380,000 people were employed, against 630,000 in 1936), and continually declined after that (staying constant only for the highest social classes), first because of other work possibilities and later through increases in their wages. Nevertheless the idea that light household work is pleasant reinforced the creation of several stereotypes regarding the housewife. Cf. also A. Arvidsson, '*The therapy of consumption. Motivation research and the new Italian housewife,*' Journal of Material Culture, vol. 5, no. 3, 2000, 251–74.

59 Alberoni, *Consumi e società*, 169–84.

60 A. Appadurai, *The Social Life of Things. Commodities in Cultural Perspective*, Cambridge: Cambridge University Press (1986), 4–5.

61 M. Mauss, *Saggio sul dono: forma e motivo dello scambio nelle società arcaiche*, Turin: Einaudi (2002).

62 About historical processes bringing the incorporation of technology into a culture whose reference was almost exclusively masculine cf. R. Oldenziel, *Making Technology Masculine: Men, Women, and Modern Machines in America, 1870–1945*, Amsterdam: Amsterdam University Press (1999).

63 The personalization of electrical appliances is present in many advertisements, as in San Giorgio's Proteus showing '12 servants at your call', which are 12 stylized men and women figurines that end up inside the apparatus (in Faravelli Giacobone, Guidi, Pansera, *Dalla casa elettrica alla casa elettronica*, 49). Another common element in publicity campaigns, concerning the different gender relationships with technology, is the enterprising husband who brings home the equipment that will solve every problem for his scatter-brained housewife. In general, about images of the home in advertising cf. L. Minestroni, *Casa dolce casa: storia dello spazio domestico tra pubblicità a società*, Milan: Franco Angeli (1996).

64 A Doxa poll in 1965 showed that the percentage of men's clothing bought ready-made (21 per cent) was practically the equivalent of clothes made to measure (22 per cent) but most of those interviewed (52 per cent) had not bought a single suit in the previous twelve months. Cf. Luzzatto Fegiz, *Il volto sconosciuto dell'Italia. Seconda serie*, 300–2. In 1963, clothing items made for men consisted of 770,000 jackets, and, in millions: 1 coats and overcoats, 2.3 raincoats, 2.9 complete suits, 4 trousers, 10.3 shirts. Cf. I. Paris, *Oggetti cuciti*.

L'abbigliamento pronto in Italia dal primo dopoguerra agli anni Settanta, Milan: Franco Angeli (2006), 324–5.

65 Again in 1963, clothing items made for women consisted of 138,000 jackets, 450,000 slacks, 870,000 skirts, and, in millions: 1 of coats and overcoats, 1.4 raincoats, 1.5 blouses, 2.8 dresses and suits. Cf. Paris, *Oggetti cuciti*, 325.

66 It was a period of great change for underwear. While slips and panties boomed, there was the disappearance of a typical item like the undervest and with it bodices and corsets in favour of brassieres, which knew a real surge (from 2 million sold in 1960 to 5 in 1965 and 10 in 1968, except when it was contested as a negative symbol during the 1970s). The sector now is worth a tenth of the total spending on clothes, showing bodily care, which does not just concern social and external appearance. Cf. Paris, *Oggetti cuciti*, 371–2; 383–4.

67 K. Peiss, *Hope in a Jar: The Making of America's Beauty Culture*, New York: Metropolitan Books (1998); N. Koehn, *Estée Lauder: Self-Definition and the Modern Cosmetics Market*, in *Beauty and Business*, ed. P. Scranton, New York: Routledge, (2001), 217–51; Id. *Brand New: How Entepreneurs Earned Consumers' Trust from Wedgwood to Dell*, Boston: Harvard Business School Press (2001).

68 Alberoni, *Consumi e società*, 43; S. Musso, *La famiglia operaia*, in *La famiglia italiana dall'Ottocento a oggi*, ed. P. Melograni, Rome-Bari: Laterza (1988), 98–101.

69 E. Danese, '*Costumi sessuali e genere femminile nell'Italia degli anni Sessanta. Inchieste cinematografiche e televisivi*', Storia e Futuro, 13, February 2007, 4, www.storiaefuturo.com.

70 A reader wrote to Gioia: 'Cosmetics [...] are no longer considered a temptation from the Devil, and every girl can make use of them to enhance her facial features. Using them or not using them makes a big difference. All women know this. If you go out without make-up and they look at you, it will be one way. Wear make-up and they will look at you in another way. Here is my problem: my boyfriend tells me off if I use certain types of make-up, such as eye-shadow. Whose side are you on?' And here is the reply: 'On your boyfriend's side, [...], what sort of looks do you get [...]? I will answer for you: it's the kind of looks that men give. Even when you are not made up, you object, men look at you just the same? Yes, but in a different way, and that, dear Vicky, does not bother or offend your boyfriend. But the other way does bother him quite a lot, and let me say that the first to be offended should be you. Instead it is all the other way round. You like it and defend the use of make-up for this very reason. Think it over and don't try to make any more excuses'. Cf. *Lettere a*, Gioia, 30, 24th July 1960, 3. About the role of female body care (which media-wise materializes in the Miss Italia contests) cf. L. Passerini, *Storia di donne e femministe*, Turin: Rosenberg & Sellier (1991).

71 All references are from the Rai Carosello advertisements (1957–1977).

72 B. Munier, *Storia dei profumi. Dagli dèi dell'olimpo al cyber-profumo* [2003], Bari: Dedalo (2006), esp. 136–42.

73 B. Munier, 143–4.

74 L. Carcano, C. Ceppi, *L'alta orologeria in Italia. Strategie competitive nei beni di prestigio*, Milan: Egea (2006), 1–16.

75 In 1960, 54 per cent of Italian adults owned a wrist watch, that is 19 million (10.6 million men and 8.4 million women), while 16 million did not. Three quarters of these watches had been sold after 1945 and chiefly during the 1950s (confirming that for many they were new products). The major variable, besides earnings, was how young their purchasers were. The price of a good watch averaged around 25,000 lire. Cf. Luzzatto Fegiz, *Il volto sconosciuto dell'Italia. Seconda serie*, 1706–12.

76 C. Cecchini, *Mo…Moplen. il design delle plastiche degli anni del boom*, Rome: R Design Press (2006).

77 J. L. Meikle, *American Plastics: A Cultural History*, New Brunswick: Rutgers University Press (1993); A. J. Clarke, *Tupperware: The Promise of Plastic in 1950s' America*, Washington: Smithsonian Institution Press (1999).

78 R. Barthes, *Miti d'oggi* [1957], Milan: Lerici (1966), 160–1.

79 It is not by chance that when advertising synthetic fabrics there was a particular insistence on the quality aspect, as can be seen in a TV spot for Rhodiatoce nylon (1963), where Caio Gregorio, 'as a Praetorian guard', talks in rhyme, shows his physique ('two yards around the chest') and mounts guard over the good quality.

80 J. Baudrillard, *Il sistema degli oggetti* [1968], Milan: Bompiani (2003), 48–9.

81 Among the most famous advertisements for these products, there was Armando Testa's poster for Punt e Mes, which gave rise to the slogan 'a shot of bitter and a half a shot of sweet'; the Gino Cervi sketches with the cartoon character Sorboli for Vecchia Romagna; and Ernesto Calindri and Franco Volpi's twosome (1962) remembering good times past: 'Life today is all a bluff, nothing lasts, nothing at all. | The only way out is to shrug it off | or go and sing a song | Right from the time of Garibaldi | China Martini, China Martini | no drinks but in little glasses | China Martini, the same as today'.

82 D'Apice, *L'arcipelago dei consumi*, 42. Cf. also Table. 6.

83 D. Forgacs, *L'industrializzazione della cultura Italiana (1880–2000)*, Bologna: il Mulino (2000), 191–8; S. Grundle, *Spettacolo e merce. Consumi, industria culturale e mass media*, in *Il secolo dei consumi. Dinamica sociali nell'Europa del Novecento*, Rome: Carocci (2006); D. Forgacs, S. Grundle, *Cultura di massa e società italiana 1936–1954*, Bologna: il Mulino (2007). Economists explain the spread of each new means with a sort of S-shaped curve: there is a slow beginning, followed by a rapid spread until the market becomes saturated (which can happen when the goods have topped 90 per cent or even at much lower levels), then a period of adjustment, and finally a more or less strong decline. The speed and scope of this phenomenon varies greatly according to the

means themselves and the historical and economic circumstances (for example the appearance of a technologically more advanced means of competition). On a short-term basis, the price of the goods and people's incomes are important, over the long term, the cultural aspects are.

84 E. Ercole, *I consumi culturali: da 'pubblico" agli stili di consumo multimediale*, in M. Livolsi, *L'Italia che cambia*, Florence: La Nuova Italia (1993), 214. The data have come from several sources because of the difficulty of making an exact estimate of cultural consumption which, as noted, is not automatically reflected in the sale of a newspaper or, even less, in that of a television or radio—especially if an estimation of the frequency of this consumption is required. Also note that entertainment consumption, sports events or live shows is too low to come into Table 6. For example from 1966 to 1970 SIAE recorded the following per capita spending: cinema 12,950 lire, various entertainments 4,900, sports events 2,200, live shows 1,100 (ibid. 212).

85 The first pocket editions, modelled on the English 'paperback', appeared in the Rizzoli BUR collection in 1949, to be followed by Oscar Mondadori in 1965. Cf. A. Cadioli, G. Vigini, *Storia dell'editoria italiana dall'Unità ad oggi: un profilo introduttivo*, Milan: Editrice Bibliografica (2004); *Storia dell'editoria nell'Italia contemporanea*, ed. G. Turi, Florence: Giunti (1997); G. C. Ferretti, *Storia dell'editoria letteraria in Italia, 1945–2003*, Turin: Einaudi (2004); G. Ragone, *Un secolo di libri: storia dell'editoria in Italia dall'Unità al post-modern*, Turin: Einaudi (1999); E. Decleva, *Arnoldo Mondadori*, Turin: Utet (1993).

86 About the transmission and its American echoes cf. S. Cassamagnaghi, *Immagini dall'America. Mass media e modelli femminili nell'Italia del secondo dopoguerra 1945–1960*, Milan: Franco Angeli (2007), 251–83. The polls declared that the programme was watched with almost equal interest by male and females; an inquiry later on comparing the entertaining *Campanile sera* with the new programme *Tribuna politica* (party political broadcast) showed a net difference of public only for the second (watched mostly by men, as imagined). Cf. Luzzatto Fegiz, *Il volto sconosciuto dell'Italia. Seconda serie*, 1402–4.

87 F. Monteleone, *Storia della radio e della televisione. Un secolo di costume, società e politica*, Venice: Marsilio (2003); F. Anania, *Breve storia della radio e della televisione italiana*, Turin: Utet (2007); Ibid. *Davanti allo schermo. Storia del pubblico televisivo*, Rome: Carocci (1997); D. Pittèri, *La pubblicità in Italia. Dal dopoguerra a oggi*, Rome-Bari: Laterza (2002); P. Dorfles, *Carosello*, Bologna: il Mulino (1998).

88 *A tavola con la TV*, Gioia, 19, 7th May 1960, 74.

89 Gioia, 30, 24th July 1960, 2.

90 Gioia, 26, 29th June 1958, 2.

91 *Per I mariti in città*, Gioia, 30, 29th July 1962, 79.

92 Cassamagnaghi, *Immagini dall'America*; A. Bravo, *Fotoromanzo*, Bologna: il Mulino (2003).

93 Signorelli, *Movimenti di popolazione*, 636–40. As regards female work, ISTAT data show that in 1970 the percentage of women working in industry was 22 per cent, in agriculture 32 per cent, in service 30 per cent (the overall share of the total of all workers was 27.5 per cent). An interesting novel depicting the problems and expectations of a Neapolitan female writer who had emigrated to Milan is the book by A. M. Ortese, *Poveri e belli*, Florence: Vallecchi (1967).

94 S. Piccone Stella, *La Prima Generazione: ragazze e ragazzi nel miracolo economico italiano*, Milan: Franco Angeli (1993).

95 Cf. also M. Degl'Innocenti, *L'epoca giovane: generazioni, fascismo e antifascism*, Manduria: Lacaita (2002).

96 On the characteristics of political commitment by the young and 1968 cf. P. Echaurren, and C. Salaris, *Controcultura in Italia 1967–1977. Viaggio nell'underground*, Turin: Bollari Boringhieri (1999); N. Balestrini, and P. Moroni, *L'orda d'oro 1968–1977. La grande ondate rivoluzionaria e creative, politica ed esistenziale*, Milan: Feltrinelli (1997); R. Lumley, *Dal '68 agli anni di piombo: studenti e operai nella crisi italiana* [1989], Florence: Giunti (1998).

97 There was a great rise in the number of students, especially at the highest levels, where there was the biggest difference. From 1950 to 1970 the number of students aged 20 to 24 rose from 3.5 per cent to 17 per cent (of whom 38 per cent were female), overtaking the levels in Germany, France, and Great Britain (the western Europe average in 1970 was 14.5 per cent). Cf. H. Kaeble, *Verso una società europea. Storia sociale dell'Europa 1880–1980*, Rome-Bari: Laterza (1990), 42; ISTAT, *Sommario di statistiche storiche*, 47–57.

98 D. Giochetti, '*Tre riviste per i «ragazzi tristi» degli anni sessanta*', Impegno, vol. 12, no. 2, December 2002.

99 Cf. a differentiated reading of Italian youth in P. Capuzzo, *Gli spazi della nuova generazione*, in *Genere, generazione e consumi*, 217–47.

100 Cf. concerning this episode, the drawing by W. Molino in '*L'incredibile drama nella scuola di Terrazzano*', La Domenica del Corriere, 43, 21st October 1956; D. Buzzati, *La «nera» di Dino Buzzati, Crimini e misteri. Incubi*, Milan: Mondadori (2002).

101 Luzzatto Fegiz, *Il volto sconosciuto dell'Italia. Seconda serie*, 377, 375.

102 Luzzatto Fegiz, 386.

103 Cf. the abundant polls on juvenile delinquency ibid. 397–421.

104 ISTAT, *Sommario di statistiche storiche*, 68–70 (in 1970 for every 100,000 inhabitants the following crimes were recorded: 2.5 murders; 10.3 manslaughters; 220 cases of bodily injury, 44 abuse; 30 crimes against the family and 18 against morality; 1015 thefts; 6 robberies and kidnappings; 54 frauds; 486 miscellaneous crimes); J. C. Chesnais, *La rivoluzione criminale: dalla violenza al furto*, in *Le rivoluzioni del benessere*, eds. P. Melograni, and R. Ricossa, Rome-Bari: Laterza (1988), 199–212; about 19th Century

perceptions of criminality cf. S. Cavazza, *Dimensione massa. Individui, folle, consumi 1830-1945*, Bologna: il Mulino (2004), 71–160.

105   M. Foucault, *Sorvegliare e punire: nascita della prigione* [1975], Turin: Einaudi (1976).

106   G. Crainz, *Storia del miracolo economico. Culture, identità, trasformazioni fra anni cinquanta e sessanta*, Rome: Donzelli (1996), 79–81.

107   E. Capussotti, *Tra storie e pratiche: soggettività giovanile, consumo e cinema in Italia durante gli anni Cinquanta* in*Genere, generazione e consumi*, 17–84; Ibid. *Gioventù perduta: gli anni Cinquanta dei giovani e del cinema in Italia*, Florence: Giunti (2004); V. M. De Angelis, *Super-Ambassadors: How Comic-Book Heroes Export American Values (Or, Do They?)*, in *Ambassadors. American Studies in a Changing World*, eds. M. Bacigalupo, and G. Bowling, Busco Rapallo: Edizioni (2006), 353–64.

108   P. Capuzzo, 'Youth Cultures and Consumption in Contemporary Europe', Contemporary European History, 1, (2001), 155–70.

109   S. Cohen, *Folk Devils and Moral Panic*, London: Routledge (1972); *Resistance through Rituals: Youth Subcultures in Post-war Britain*, eds. S. Hall, and T. Jefferson, London: Hutchinson (1976); J. Procter, *Stuart Hall e gli studi culturali* (2004), Milan: Cortina (2007), 81–126.

110   Capuzzo, *Gli spazi della nuova generazione*, 221.

111   The frequency of going to the cinema at least once a week in 1953 was 63 per cent of 16–19 year-olds, 68 per cent of 20–29, 45 per cent of 30–39, 48 per cent of 40–49, 18 per cent of the over-50s (the audiences were predominantly male: in 1960, 52 per cent males and 33 per cent females went to the cinema—15 per cent unknown). Cf. Luzzatto Fegiz, *Il volto sconosciuto dell'Italia. Seconda serie*, 223, 240. The data were substantially confirmed by a second sampling in 1957, cf. ibid. 393–6.

112   A. Arvidsson, 'From Counterculture to Consumer Culture. Vespa and the Italian Youth Market 1958–78', Journal of Consumer Culture, vol. 1, no. 1, 2001, 47–72. During this year the Vespa was still markedly a male consumption. Things changed during the 1970s when girls also used Vespas and mostly the new little motorcycle by Piaggio: the Ciao, which was lighter, more manageable and without gears (a famous advertisement of 1969 showed it with a hippy girl and the cryptic slogan: 'The mobile Sardinians eat asphalt | strawberries with Ciao').

113   Surveys confirm that record players soon appeared as typical consumer products of the young, especially among middle-class families, with little gender difference (Cf. Luzzatto Fegiz, *Il volto sconosciuto dell'Italia. Seconda serie*, 1690–4). The appearance of portable record players just a few years later would increase opportunities for meeting outside their homes.

114   S. Frith, *Sociologia del rock* [1978], Milan: Feltrinelli (1982); E. Berselli, *Canzoni. Storia dell'Italia leggera*, Bologna: il Mulino (1999).

115   The newspapers of the time were full of articles about the youth phenomenon, for the most part with a critical or ironic tone. The pictures are more interesting; cf. for example the films in Luce Historical Archives, Caleidoscopio Ciak C1767, 31st August 1966 (Inquiry into the hippies); and Radar R0156, 25th October 1967 (Hippies on the Spanish Steps). Photographs of the Beatles' Milan concert can be found in the archives of the Corriere della Sera (also on line). During the same tour they also performed at Genoa (27th June 1965) and in Rome's Adriano theatre (28th June). It is interesting to note the specific language created for youth communication, which became an in-group language, more or less unintelligible for those outside (1960s' adults understood little more than the term it reserved for them: '*matusa*' ('old fogey')).

116   Cf. the pictures of a hippy party at Rome in Luce Historical Archives, Radar R0155, 25th October 1967.

117   C. Lévi-Strauss, *Il pensiero selvaggio* [1962], Milan: il Saggiatore (1964). In his description, mythical thinking, embodied by the *bricoleur*, is contrasted with scientific thinking, as represented by the engineer, who on the contrary constructs everything by himself and with a precise intention.

118   D. Hebdige, *Sottocultura: il fascino di uno stile innaturale* [1979], Genoa: Costa & Nolan (1983); Ibid. *La lambretta e il videoclip: cose & consumi dell'immaginario contemporaneo* [1988], Edt, Turin: (1991); J. Proctor, *Stuart Hall e gli studi culturali*.

119   Based on the careers of generations of men, for lack of sufficient data for women, the research classifies as a form of social ascent the percentage of non-manual workers having workmen fathers. However, it turns out from this that during those same 1960s there were also forms of social retrogression which in some cases, as in Italy, were even more noticeable (27 per cent). Cf. H. Kaeble, *Verso una società europea*, 39. A certain tendency to remain in the same professional class as one's father and grandfather is also found in a Doxa inquiry of 1949 (cf. P. Luzzatto Fegiz, *Il volto sconosciuto dell'Italia. Dieci anni di sondaggi Doxa*, Milan: Giuffrè (1956), 1011–14).

120   For example, the age level of elected politicians was fairly low compared with what would happen later on. The case of Giulio Andreotti springs to mind, elected and joining the government as Cabinet Undersecretary at the age of 28.

121   R. Sassatelli, *Consumo, cultura e società*, Bologna: il Mulino (2004), 148–9, 189–97; ibid. *Tamed Hedonism: Choice, Desires and Deviant Pleasures*, in *Ordinary Consumption*, eds. J. Gronow, and A. Warde, London: Routledge (2001), 93–106.

122   A precise social placing of wine consumption in Italy can still be seen in 1951, so that the consumption was clearly much greater (12 litres per week) among farmers. This was followed by property owners and employers (8 litres), specialized workers and craftsmen (6.6 litres), and then unskilled workers, farmhands and managers. Cf. Luzzatto Fegiz, *Il volto sconosciuto*

dell'Italia. Dieci anni di sondaggi Doxa, 119. The most sensational case of alcohol prohibition was in America, of course, during the 1920s.

123 J. Hughes, *Learning to Smoke: Tobacco Use in the West*, Chicago: University of Chicago Press (2003); J. Goodman, *Tobacco in History. The Cultures of Dependence*, London: Routledge (1993).

124 The paid sex issue is much more complex, of course, and is subject to different limitations and prohibitions according to the form it takes, for example if it is done with children, or between homosexuals, etc. There is furthermore the sector of pornographic material which, like all the media industry, has grown enormously since the mid-twentieth century, proving to be a most profitable sector (a 2002–2004 survey estimated the business volume in Italy to be around a thousand million Euros, cf. Eurispes, *Quarto rapporto sulla pornografia*, Rome (2005)).

125 V. Berridge, G. Edwards, *Opium and the People: Opiate Use in Nineteenth Century England*, London: Allen Lane (1981); M. Booth, *Opium: A History*, London: Simon and Schuster (1996).

Chapter 8

1 R. Benedict, *Modelli di cultura* [1934], Milan: Feltrinelli (1974), p. 8.

2 Bocca, *Miracolo all-Italiana*, 5–6.

3 This is what the Budget Minister, Ugo La Malfa had to say to Parliament in 1962: 'The rapid spread of luxury goods, a symptom of imbalance in the distribution of wage increases, provokes disturbing consequences on its own accord. By a kind of imitation effect, even those on low incomes are tempted to pass over the most essential products just to possess goods, especially of a durable kind, which the example of the more affluent classes and the persuasive skills of the advertising media make them favour. The consequences cannot be measured but it would seem that they should somehow be contained' (Budget Ministry, *Problemi e prospettive dello sviluppo economic italiano*, Roma (1962), 42). Cf. also *L'economia italiana*, ed. A. Graziani, Bologna: il Mulino (1972), 31–5; 46–9. For an overall picture of the economic positions, which were obviously tied up with the political ones, cf. G. Maione, *Spese pubblica o consumi privati?*; F. Barca, *Compromesso senza riforme nel capitalismo italiano* in *Storia del capitalismo italiano dal dopoguerra a oggi*, ed. F. Barca, Rome: Donzelli (1997), 3–115.

4 H. W. Arndt, *Lo sviluppo economico. Storia di un'idea* [1987], il Bologna: Mulino (1990), 71–117.

5 S. Colarizi, *I partiti politici di fronte al cambiamento del costume* in *Il miracolo economico italiano*, 225–47; P. Scoppola, *Le trasformazioni culturali e l'irrompere dell'«American way of life»*, in *Chiesa e progetto educativo nell'Italia del secondo dopoguerra, 1945–1958*, Brescia: La Scuola (1988), 476–93.

6 S. Gundle, *I comunisti italiani tra Hollywood e Mosca: la sfida della cultura di massa, 1943–1991*, Florence: Giunti (1995). Concerning the dynamics of parties in general cf. S. Colarizi, *Storia politica della Repubblica. 1943–2006*, Rome-Bari: Laterza (2007); P. Craveri, *La Repubblica dal 1958 al 1992*, Turin: Utet (1995).

7 T. W. Adorno, M. Horkheimer, *Dialettica dell'illuminismo*[1947], Turin: Einaudi (1966); H. Marcuse, *L'uomo a una dimensione. L'ideolologia della società industriale avanzate* [1964], Turin: Einaudi (1967); G. Debord, *La società dello spettacolo* (1967), Milan: Baldini & Castoldi (2001); J. K. Galbraith, *La società opulenta* [1958], Milan: Edizioni di Comunità (1963); V. Packard, *I persuasori occulti* [1957], Turin: Einaudi (1958). For an overview cf. P. Capuzzo, *Le teorie del consumo*, in *Il secolo dei consumi*, 51–83.

8 P. P. Pasolini, '*Il vuoto del potere in Italia*', Corriere della Sera, 1st February 1975 (in P. P. Pasolini, *Saggi sulla politica e sulla società*, Milan: Mondadori (2001), 404–11).

9 P. P. Pasolini, *Gli italiani non sono più quelli*, '*Corriere della Sera*', 10th June 1974 (in P. P. Pasolini, *Saggi sulla politica e sulla società*, 308).

10 P. P. Pasolini, *Lettere luterane* (1976), in *Saggi sulla politica e sulla società*, 572.

11 Pasolini, *Lettere luterane*, 578–80.

12 Pasolini, 573.

13 Cf. G. Sapelli, *Modernizzazione senza sviluppo: il capitalismo secondo Pasolini*, ed. V. Ronchi, Milano: B. Mondadori (2005).

14 L. De Rita, *I contadini e la televisione*, Bologna: il Mulino (1964) (the quotations, in order, are on 97, 248, 287).

15 Ibid. (the quotations are on 254, 85).

16 Ibid., 294.

17 It is useful to note that the opinions expressed here equate very well with the classic studies of sociologists like Lasswell, Lazarsfeld, and Merton, who maintain that the media perform the following fundamental social functions: 1) environmental control; 2) correlation of society members; 3) transmission of social-cultural heritage; 4) entertainment.

18 G. Andreotti, '*Chiedo scusa a Pasolini*', Lettere romane: attualità di politica, scienza e arte, vol. 2, (1993).

19 W. Beveridge, *Social Insurance and Allied Services* (Parliamentary report), November 1942. See also P. Pombeni, *Crisi, consenso, legittimazione: le categorie della transizione politica nel secolo delle ideologie*, in *Crisi, legittimazione, consenso*, ed. P. Pombeni, Bologna: il Mulino (2003).

20 T. H. Marshall, *Cittadinanza e classe sociale* [1963], Rome-Bari: Laterza (2002).

21 Recent criticism has also included the fact that elements like race and gender, internal power struggles within the state, and differences between democratic and authoritarian regimes were not taken into consideration. Additionally, the Marshall theory is seen as envisaging a homogeneous community, which gradually assimilates new social components and puts

more stress on homogeneity than on identity. Cf. G. Zincone, *Da sudditi a cittadini. Le vie dello Stato e le vie della società civile*, Bologna: il Mulino (1992).

22   According to V. de Grazia, there was conflict between traditional European solidarity (social citizenship) and the American model, with its trust in the market and the proliferation of material goods (consumer sovereignty). American involvement in post-war Europe brought with it the hybrid figure of the 'citizen-consumer', as Jean-Luc Godard maintains: 'children of Marx and Coca-Cola'. Cf. V. de Grazia, *Irresistible Empire. America's Advance through Twentieth-Century Europe*, Harvard: Belknap (2005), 343.

23   Kaelble, *Verso una società europea*, 170–1.

24   Public spending on education (in 1980 billions of lire) equalled 1,471,000 for 1950, 4,631,000 for 1960 and 13,371,000 for 1971 (while spending on public works during the same period rose from 2,852,000 to 9,781,000). Cf. G. Brosio, C. Marchese, *Il potere di spendere. Economia e storia della spesa pubblica dall'Unificazione ad oggi*, Bologna: il Mulino (1986), table 4A in the appendix.

25   Arndt, *Lo sviluppo economico*, 84–98. Illiteracy levels were: 12.9 per cent in 1951 (10.5 per cent male, 15.2 per cent female), dropping to 5.2 per cent in 1971 (4 per cent male, 6.3 per cent female). Cf. ISTAT, *Sommario di statistiche storiche*, 14.

26   In 1970, enrolments in upper-secondary schools were distributed as follows: 676,000 technical institutes, 260,000 professional institutes, 221,000 teacher-training institutes, 253,000 scientific high schools, 205,000 classical high schools, 39,000 artistic high schools and art institutes. Out of a total of 1.6 million pupils 689,000 were female; 181,000 pupils of the total went to private schools. ISTAT, *Sommario di statistiche storiche*, 47, 51–3.

27   E. De Fort, *Scuola e analfabetismo nell'Italia del '900*, Bologna: il Mulino (1995); L. Ambrosoli, *La scuola italiana dal dopoguerra ad oggi*, Bologna: il Mulino (1982).

28   Students enrolled at university increased from 145,000 in 1950 to 561,000 in 1970 (of which 211,000 were female), spread over 42 sites and 271 faculties. In 1970 enrolments were divided into the following groups: 225,000 literary studies, 116,000 economics, 96,000 science, 96,000 engineering, 79,000 medicine, 59,000 law, 11,000 agriculture. Then there were 3,348 permanent professors, 5,418 lecturers, and 27,000 assistants. Cf. ISTAT, *Sommario di statistiche storiche*, 56–7. Concerning the difficult working and financial conditions of assistants, of whom 88 per cent said they had little or no job satisfaction, see the Doxa survey of 1954 in Luzzatto Fegiz, *Il volto sconosciuto dell'Italia. Dieci anni di sondaggi Doxa*, 939–58. In 1980, thousands of assistants and members of several other temporary categories gained tenure through a special *ope legis* with long-term consequences for the universities.

29   E. De Fort, *Istruzione*, in *Dizionario storico dell'Italia unita*, eds. B. Bongiovanni, and N. Tranfaglia, Rome-Bari: Laterza (1996), 483–6.

30   F. Girotti, *Welfare state. Storia, modelli e critica*, Rome: Carocci (1998), 294–321; G. Cosmacini, *Storia della medicina e della sanità nell'Italia contemporanea*, Rome-Bari: Laterza (1994). Starting from 1992–1993 successive reforms of the *Servizio Sanitario Nazionale* were directed at the standardization of local units (changed into ASL), streamlining the management (even for hospitals, which remained a cardinal point of the system), as well as cost-cutting, the introduction of the service ticket, and partial opening to private structures.

31   As a result of efforts in the health field the average number of in-patients per year climbed from 4 million during 1951–1960, to 6.8 million during 1961–1970 and to 9.7 million during 1971–1980. Cf. ISTAT, *Sommario di statistiche storiche 1926–1985*, ISTAT, Rome (1986), 67.

32   G. Brosio, C. Marchese, *Il potere di spendere. Economia e storia della spesa pubblica dall'Unificazione ad oggi*, Bologna: il Mulino (1986), 69–74, 97–119. During 1951 public spending (calculated in lire of the time) was subdivided as follows: collective consumption (goods and services) 47 per cent, transfers 37 per cent, investments 46 per cent, interest 7 per cent; during 1970 it became: collective consumption 40 per cent, transfers 46 per cent, investments 9 per cent, interest 5 per cent (cf. ibid. 100–1); cf. Table 3. For a complete interpretation of central-left policies regarding welfare cf. M. Degl'Innocenti, *La «grande trasformazione» e la «svolta» del centro-sinistra*, in *Il miracolo economico italiano*, 249–97.

33   Girotti, *Welfare state*, 271–93.

34   Ginsborg, *Storia dell'Italia dal dopoguerra ad oggi*, 200–49.

35   Brosio, *Il potere di spendere*, 84–95, table 7A for the data (in constant currency).

36   Ibid., 149, and on these subjects in general 77–164.

37   The low level of spending on housing is worth notice, linked as it is to the failure to launch effective regulations to control building development, which was mostly left in private hands (think of the resounding failure of the Sullo reform in the early 1960s).

38   Here are some international data comparing public spending in 1970 and 1981 (OECD sources): for France, total spending of the GDP for the two years respectively, 43 and 49 per cent (institutional services and defence 10 and 11 per cent, services 15 and 15 per cent, transfers 13 and 17 per cent, economic intervention 4 and 4 per cent, interest 1 and 2 per cent); for Germany, total spending 39 and 49 per cent (institutions and defence 10 and 10 per cent, services 10 and 14 per cent, transfers 13 and 17 per cent, economic intervention 5 and 5 per cent, interest 1 and 2 per cent); for Great Britain, total spending 43 and 43 per cent (institutions and defence 14 and 12 per cent, services 13 and 14 per cent, transfers 7 and 8 per cent, economic intervention 5 and 4 per cent, interest 4 and 5 per cent); for Italy, total spending 34 and 51 per cent (institutional and defence 7 and 9 per cent, services 10 and 14 per cent, transfers 10 and 15 per cent, economic

intervention 5 and 7 per cent, interest 2 and 7 per cent). Cf. Brosio, Marchese, *Il potere di spendere*, 112–17.

39 A 1963 Doxa inquiry, which was made after a series of scandals linked to contracts and corruption, revealed that 67 per cent of men and 59 per cent of women believed that 'you can get anything in Italy, if you pay'. Cf. Luzzatto Fegiz, *Il volto sconosciuto dell'Italia. Seconda serie*, p. 1001.

Chapter 9

1 Bocca, *Miracolo all'Italiana*, 58–9.

2 The famous theory of *marketing mix*, for example, identifies four key elements when selling, the four Ps: product, price, place, promotion (Cf. P. Kotler, *Marketing Management: Analysis, Planning, and Control*, Englewood Cliffs: Prentice-Hall (1967)); P. A. Toninelli, *Storia d'impresa*, Bologna: il Mulino (2006), 167–75.

3 R. S. Tedlow, *New and Improved. The Story of Mass Marketing in America*, Oxford: Heinemann (1990); *The Rise and Fall of Mass Marketing*, eds. R. S. Tedlow, and G. Jones, London-New York: Routledge (1993). Tedlow's theories, mainly referring to the American context, and therefore subject to criticism and close anaysis, has had a notable impact on economic research. For their adaptation to the Italian case see E. Scarpellini, *Comprare all'americana. Le origini della rivoluzione commerciale in Italia 1945–1971*, Bologna: il Mulino (2001), 18–23, 123–27.

4 A. Arvidsson, *Marketing Modernity. Italian Adverising from Fascism to Postmodernity*, London: Routledge (2003); G. P. Ceserani, *Storia della pubblicità in Italia*, Rome-Bari: Laterza (1988); D. Pittèri, *La pubblicità in Italia. Dal dopoguerra a oggi*, Rome-Bari: Laterza (2002).

5 A. Arvidsson, *Dalla «réclame» al «brand management». Uno sguardo storico alla disciplina pubblicitaria del Novecento*, in *Il secolo dei consumi*, 197–210.

6 S. Rinauro, '*Storia del sondaggio d'opinione in Italia, 1936–1994: dal lungo rifiuto alla repubblica dei sondaggi*', Istituto Veneto di scienze, lettere ed arti, Venice (2002).

7 Arvidsson, *Marketing Modernity*, 95–9.

8 *Storia d'Italia. Annali 15. L'industria*, eds. F. Amatori et al. Turin: Einaudi (1999); F. Amatori, A. Colli, *Impresa e industria in Italia: dall'Unità a oggi*, Venice: Marsilio (1999); L. Cafagna, *Dualismo e sviluppo nella storia d'Italia*, Venice: Marsilio (1989).

9 de Grazia, *L'impero irresistibile*, 445–55.

10 A. Castagnoli, E. Scarpellini, *Storia degli imprenditori italiani*, Turin: Einaudi (2003), 321.

11 Faravelli Giacobone, Guidi, Pansera, *Dalla casa elettrica alla casa elettronica*, 40–69; Castagnoli, Scarpellini, *Storia degli imprenditori italiani*, 320–6;

V. Balloni, *Origini, sviluppo e maturità dell'industria degli elettrodomestici*, Bologna: il Mulino (1978).

12   I have already mentioned the Candy advertisement on *Carosello*. Zoppas first put its trust in a duet with Madame the Marchioness and later in a married couple (at one time played by Dario Fo and Franca Rame) who disagreed about everything except the Zoppas washing machine. Ignis presented a whole family of dissatisfied customers who, against the backing of Ennio Morricone's music for a western film, never found the right product until they set eyes on an Ignis washing machine. Other companies relied greatly on printed paper advertising. Also worthy of note is Philco, which introduced the inhabitants of the planet Papalla, and Riello, with the untrustworthy Indian Unca Dunca.

13   The picture is complicated. Ignis was bought by Philips, and Zoppas by Zanussi, which in its turn was bought by Swedish Electrolux. Candy consolidated its position on the market, as did Merloni (which acquired Indesit and is today the third European group after Rex Electrolux and Bosch). Following this, the Nocivelli group in Brescia also made a name for itself (manufacturers of Ocean and buyer of San Giorgio in Genoa and a sector of Zanussi).

14   *Barilla: cento anni di pubblicità e comunicazione*, eds. A. Ivardi Ganapini, and G. Gonizzi, and Cinisello Balsamo: Silvana (1994).

15   The Simmenthal trademark later passed to Kraft, and Manzotin (together with Rio Mare) to Bolton, while Cremonini is still one of the leading Italian food groups.

16   A. Capatti, *La gastronomia del frullatore*, in Faravelli Giacobone, Guidi, Pansera, *Dalla casa elettrica alla casa elettronica*, 140.

17   'He seeks her here, he seeks her there, la, la, la.... he is looking for Lagostina, and here she is!' The figure by Osvaldo Cavandoli later became an animated cartoon in its own right.

18   In 1970 the average calories intake per person came to 3,147, of which 589 were of animal origin. It had been around 2,600 in the 1930s and also at the turn of the century, but with important differences: animal protein was now close to vegetable protein (43 against 50 grams), while in the 1930s the ratio had been less than 1 to 3 and from 1901 to 1910 less than 1 to 4. Fats had greatly increased, equalling 106 grams (against 60 and 57 during Fascism and at the beginning of the century); while carbohydrates remained fairly steady, equal to 440 grams in 1970, with a slight increase compared with the past. Cf. ISTAT, *Sommario di statistiche storiche 1861–1975*, 161.

19   In the *Carosello* spot a Sicilian pirate asks his captain what to do with a prisoner: 'Can we torture him, captain?' 'Wait a bit, I know just how to loosen his tongue!' is the Piedmontese captain's reply as he gets out a canister of black cherries. It is noteworthy how advertising in those days frequently

resorted to many different dialects to distinguish their personalities, a practice being gradually lost to television, or restricted to just one or two accents.

20 F. Baldini, *De' sorbetti*, Stamperia Raimondiana, Naples: (1775); cf. A. Capatti, M. Montanari, *La cucina italiana. Storia di una cucina*, Rome-Bari: Laterza (1999), 295–296.

21 M. Redclift, *Chewing Gum: The Fortunes of Taste*, London: Routledge (2004); Ibid., *Chewing Gum: Mass Consumption and the 'Shadowlands' of the Yucatan*, in *Consuming Cultures, Global Perspectives: Historical Trajectories, Transnational Exchanges*, eds. J. Brewer, and F. Trentmann, Oxford-New York: Berg (2006).

22 In 1970, the consumption per person was 32 kilograms of citrus fruit, 88 of other fresh fruit, 99 of vegetables, 47 of tomatoes, 45 of potatoes (the figures concerning 1921–1930 were respectively, 10 for citrus fruit, 31 other fruit, 71 vegetables, 21 tomatoes, 30 potatoes). Cf. ISTAT, *Sommario di statistiche storiche 1861–1975*, 159 and table 1.

23 Capatti, Montanari, *La cucina italiana*, 286–8; P. Sorcinelli, *Gli italiani e il cibo: dalla polenta ai cracker*, Milan: B. Mondadori (1999).

24 A series of inverstigations by *L'Espresso* weekly, and successively also by *Il Giorno* daily, brought to light the unbelievable sophistication perpetrated by certain food industries in the absence of effective laws. Consumers learned about sundry seed oil being passed off as olive oil, wine fraud, butter made of various fats, pasta made of soft grain, and toxic colourants and additives (cf. 'L'asino nella bottiglia', L'Espresso, 22nd June 1958). In the long run, the indignation that ensued led to the issuing during the 1960s of several legislative measures concerning food. From the cultural point of view, the scandal reinforced the identification of genuineness with simple, country food.

25 Capatti, Montanari, *La cucina italiana*, 36–40.

26 V. Teti, *Le culture alimentari nel Mezzogiorno continentale in età contemporanea*, in *Storia d'Italia. Annali 13. L'alimentazione*, eds. A Capatti, A. De Bernardi, and A. Varni, Turin: Einaudi (1998), 65–165.

27 V. Zamagni, *L'evoluzione dei consumi fra tradizione e innovazione*, ibid., 192–4.

28 Paris, *Oggetti cuciti*, 143.

29 Paris, 45, 102–9.

30 E. Merlo, *Moda Italiana: storia di un'industria dall'Ottocento a oggi*, Venice: Marsilio (2003); R. Marcucci, *Anibo e made in Italy: storia dei buying offices in Italia*, Florence: Vallecchi (2004).

31 Paris, *Oggetti cuciti*, 382.

32 Paris, 396–404.

33 At the 1967–1968 ready-to-wear high fashion shows in Milan and Florence the prices of single garments, as indicated by ANIBO, the buyers' association, were around 100,000 lire (the garments would later cost much more in the shops); by way of comparison just think that in 1965 a well-tailored suit

could be bought in a shop for 22–30,000 lire, a lightweight overcoat for 26,000, a heavy Marzotto overcoat for 38,000, a blouse for 4,000, and a pair of shoes for 10,000 (the prices of casual and youth wear were even cheaper). Cf. Paris, *Oggetti cuciti*, 392–3, 466.

34 S. Testa, *La specificità della filiera italiana della moda*, in *Storia d'Italia. Annali 19. La moda*, eds. C. M. Belfanti, and F. Giusberti, Turin: Einaudi (2003), 699–720; S. Gnoli, *Un secolo di moda italiana: 1900–2000*, Rome: Meltemi (2005); R. Carrarini, *La stampa di moda dall'Unità a oggi*, in *Storia d'Italia. Annali 19. La moda*, 822–34.

35 A. Branzi, *Introduzione al design italiano: una modernità incompleta*, Milan: Baldini & Castoldi (1999); C. Neumann, *Design in Italia*; P. Sparke, *A modern identity for a new nation: design in Italy since 1860,* in *The Cambridge Companion to Modern Italian Culture*, eds. Z. G. Baranski, and R. J. West, Cambridge: Cambridge University Press (2001), 265–77.

36 See Memoria e ricerca, eds. J. Morris, and C. Baldoli, 23, 2006.

37 Faravelli Giacobone, Guidi, Pansera, *Dalla casa elettrica alla casa elettronica*, 70–98.

Chapter 10

1 Scarpellini, *Comprare all'americana*, 86–7; F. Antonioni, '*Anche il nostro pane quotidiano surgelato*', Il Messaggero, 22nd June 1956. The pictures of the EUR exhibition can be seen in Luce Historical Archives, La Settimana Incom n°. 01419, 21st June 1956; and also ibid. L'Europeo Ciac, n°. E1010, 21st June 1956. Notice that the comments are not without a hint of irony, affirming as they do that purchases should be made in good faith and that the only inconvenience of the American supermarket is that one pays Italian-style.

2 About the role that market economy successes played during the cold war cf. J. L. Gaddis, *The Cold War: A New History*, New York: Penguin Press (2005). On the exportation of the American model within the economic sphere cf. J. Zeitlin, '*L'«americanizzazione» e i suoi limiti. La rielaborazione della tecnologia a del management statunitensi in Europa e in Giappone nel secondo dopoguerra*' (2000), Annali di storia dell'impresa, vol. 11, 2000, 259–337; H. G. Schröter, *Americanization of the European Economy: A Compact Survey of American Influence in Europe since the 1980s*, Dordrecht: Sprinter (2005).

3 E. Scarpellini, *L'utopia del consumo totale. L'evoluzione dei luoghi di consumo*, in *Il secolo dei consumi*, 34–7.

4 ISTAT, *5° Censimento generale dell'industria e del commercio 25 ottobre 1971*, vol. 4, *Commercio e servizi*, Rome (1976); Scarpellini, *Comprare all'americana*, 248–54 (for a complete picture).

5 The first experiment was probably the Formica of Quirino Pedrazzoli, 'store without sales assistants—Self-Service American System', which

opened in the centre of Milan, and lasted for a couple of years. The display equipment used at EUR was instead taken up by 'Supermercato SPA' of Rome (owned by Franco Palma and Amedeo Malfatti), which opened its first outlet in Viale Libia in March 1957, but here again the success was short lived, and the enterprise, futilely offered to Supermarkets Italiani, was then taken over by the food sector of Rinascente, despite the serious losses, so as to avoid licensing problems. Alongside this there were other experiments (like the Standa food departments, at Naples and Verona) and other isolated ventures. Cf. Scarpellini, *Comprare all'americana*, 86–9.

6 Cf. the history of Supermarkets Italiani in Scarpellini, *La spesa è uguale per tutti*.

7 Rockefeller Archive Center, Wayne G. Broehl, IV 3A 16, box 12, folder 'Italiani II', R. W. Boogaart to W. D. Bradford, Milan, 9th December 1957.

8 Transparent film had its birth originally as cellulose film, which was put on the market at the beginning of the twentieth century by its inventor J. E. Brandenberger with the name of Cellophane, which would go on being used to indicate this type of product even after it started to be made of synthetic polymers (PVC and similar) in the 1960s.

9 Rockefeller Archive Center, Wayne G. Broehl, IV 3A 16, box 12, folder 'Italiani III', R. W. Boogaart to W. D. Bradford, Milan, 4th April 1959, 6th April 1959.

10 '*Aumentano I clienti dei supermercati*', Il Giorno, 15th May 1959.

11 Bollettino della Doxa, 30th December 1958, 207 ff. In 1964 the percentage of families frequenting supermarkets came out as 22 per cent in towns and 17 per cent in rural areas (ibid., 30th November 1964, 195).

12 The posters, also like several photographs inside the first supermarkets, are reproduced in Scarpellini, *La spesa è uguale per tutti*.

13 Rockefeller Archive Center, Microfilm series Ibec, 9 'Supermarkets Italiani', J. C. Moffett, *American Supermarkets in Milan or Sunflowers Grow in Italy*, 15th January 1960. Similar percentages, between a third and a quarter of the total, were also registered for the first supermarket in Rome (cf. '*First U.S.-Style Supermarket in Rome is Highly Successful*', New York Times, 18th March 1957).

14 Scarpellini, *Comprare all'americana*, 167–40.

15 Aigid, 'Notizie per la stampa', 55, 15th December 1975; ibid., 54, 20th November 1975; V. Zamagni, P. Battilani, A. Casali, *Centocinquanta anni di cooperazione di consumer*, Bologna: il Mulino (2004).

16 Aigid, 'Notizie per la stampa', 36, 3rd May 1972.

17 For the political complexities that affected trade and commerce see Scarpellini, *Comprare all'americana* (particularly for the story behind law n°. 426 of 11th June 1971, which stayed in force until 1999, cf. 297–317).

18   G. Anceschi, V. Bucchetti, *Il'packaging» alimentare'*, in *Storia d'Italia. Annali 13. L'alimentazione*, 847–86.

19   *The American Supermarket*, exhibition at the Bianchini Gallery in New York, October–November 1964 (cf. C. Grunenberg *The American Supermarket*, in *Shopping. A Century of Art and Consumer Culture*, eds. C. Grunenberg, and Ostfildern-Ruit: M. Hollein Hatje Cantz (2002), 171–5).

20   L. Bianciardi, *La vita agra* [1962], Milan: Rizzoli (1995), 160–2.

21   I. Calvino, *Marcovaldo* [1963], in *Romanzi e racconti*, eds. M. Barenghi, and B. Falcetto, Milan: Mondadori (1991), 1147–9. About the reception of supermarkets by the literary world cf. F. Ghelli, '*Supermercati di parole. Note su un tema / luogo letterario fra moderno e postmoderno*', in Studi culturali, 3, December 2007, 377–400.

22   A. Moles, *Il Kitsch, l'arte della felicità* [1971–72], Rome: Officina (1979); G. Dorfles, *Il kitsch: antologia del cattivo gusto*, Milan: Mazzotta (1968); J. Baudrillard, *La società dei consumi: I suoi miti e le sue strutture* [1970], Bologna: il Mulino (1976); on the aesthetic dimension of the phenomenon M. Mazzocut-Mis, *Il gonzo sublime: dal patetico al kitsch*, Milan: Mimesis (2005).

23   Cf. for example about Milan '*Il rapporto sulla Provincia di Milan*', commissioned by the Unione Commercianti (Dealers' Union), published in Il Commercio Lombardo, 5th June 1964; S. Ravalli, '*Sviluppo demografico e mercantile negli ultimi dieci anni a Milano*', ibid. 29th November 1963.

24   S. Zukin, *Landscapes of Power: From Detroit to Disney World*, Berkeley: University of California Press (1991).

25   M. Teodori, *Maledetti americani: destra, sinistra e cattolici. Storia del pregiudizio antiamericano*, Milan: Mondadori (2002); ibid. *Benedetti americani: dall'alleanza atlantica alla Guerra al terrorismo*, Milan: Mondadori (2003); *Nemici per la pelle: sogno Americano e miti sovietico nell'Italia contemporanea*, ed. P. P. D'Attorre, Milan: Franco Angeli (1991); *Antiamericanismo in Italia e in Europa nel secondo dopoguerra*, eds. P. Craveri, and G. Quagliarello, Soveria Mannelli: Rubbettino (2004).

26   About Americanization cf. de Grazia, *L'impero irresistibile*; R. F. Kuisel, *Seducing the French: The Dilemma of Americanization*, Berkeley: University of California Press (1993); M. van Elteren, *Americanism and Americanization: A Critical History of Domestic and Global Influence*, Jefferson: McFarland (2006); *The American Century in Europe*, eds. R. L. Moore, and M. Vaudagna, Ithaca: Cornell University Press (2003); D. W. Ellwood, *L'Europa ricostruita: politica ed economia tra Stati Uniti ed Europa occidentale, 1945–1955* [1992], Bologna: il Mulino (1994).

27   C. Geertz, *Interpretazione di culture* [1973], Bologna: il Mulino (1987).

28   R. Kroes, *If You've Seen One, You've Seen the Mall: Europeans and American Mass Culture*, Urbana: University of Illinois Press (1996).

Chapter 11

1 The exhibition went on to visit other important cities before coming home to Milan during the spring of 2007. Cf. the *Giorgio Armani* catalogue, Milan: Electa (2007).

2 *I limiti dello sviluppo: rapporto del System dynamics group Massachusetts institute of technology (MIT) per il progetto del Club di Roma sui dilemma dell'umanità* [1972], Milan: Mondadori (1972).

3 P. Lang, W. Menking, *Superstudio, Life Without Objects*, Milan: Skira (2003) (the project film presented at MoMA in 1972 entitled *Life, Supersurface*).

4 Luce Historical Archives, Radar R0619, 12th December 1973; Sette G S0370, 11th December 1973 and S0372, 4th January 1974.

5 *Culture, nuovi soggetti, identità*, eds. L. Lussana, and G. Marramao, Soveria Mannelli: Rubettino (2003); for a historiographic picture, cf. B. Armani, '*Italia anni settanta. Movimenti, violenza politica e lotta armata tra memoria e rappresentazione storiografica*', Storica, vol. 32, no. 11, 2005, 41–82; cf. also G. Crainz, *Il paese mancato: dal miracolo economico agli anni Ottanta*, Rome: Donzelli (2003).

6 C. D'Apice, *L'arcipelago dei consumi. Consumi e redditi delle famiglie in Italia dal dopoguerra ad oggi*, Bari: de Donato (1981), 57–74, 95–8; G. Maione, '*Spesa pubblica o consumi privati? Verso una reinterpretazione dell'economia italiana postbellica*', Italia contemporanea, vol. 2, 31 June 2003.

7 D'Apice, *L'arcipelago dei consumi*, 96–7.

8 P. P. Pasolini, *Il folle slogan dei jeans Jesus*, 'Corriere della Sera', 17th May 1973 (in P. P. Pasolini, *Saggi sulla politica e sulla società*, Milano: Mondadori (2001), 282). The quotation specifically refers to another slogan used by the same advertising company: 'Thou shalt have no other Jeans before me!'.

9 A. Arvidsson, *Marketing Modernity. Italian Advertising from Fascism to Postmodernity*, London: Routledge (2003), 119–37.

10 S. Gundle, *I communisti italiani tra Hollywood e Mosca: la sfida della cultura di massa, 1943–1991*, Florence: Giunti (1995), 311–407.

11 Arvidsson, *Marketing Modernity*, 8.

12 Television channels were the big beneficiaries of the advertising boom securing almost half for themselves, at the expense of newspapers and magazines (in 1985 television absorbed 49 per cent of advertising resources, against 22 per cent for newspapers and 20 per cent for periodicals; in 1970 RAI had had 12 per cent, newspapers 30 per cent and periodicals 35 per cent). Cf. Arvidsson, *Marketing Modernity*, 134.

13 I. Ang, *Watching Dallas: Soap Opera and the Melodramatic Imagination*, London: Routledge (1952).

14 Great Britain was ahead of Italy with 232 minutes; France (199) and Germany (198) came behind. The European average (15 countries) was 206 minutes a day. Cf. R. Ippolito, *Vivere in Europa. Un confronto in cifre*, Rome-Bari: Laterza (2002), 144. Ethnographic studies show how even watching

television should not necessarily be considered as passive, isolated activity bereft of cultural overtones, but belongs to 'domestic consumption', enjoyed differently according to gender, time, etc. (cf. D. Morley, *Television, Audience and Cultural Studies*, London: Routledge (1992)). Besides, successful soap operas and serials create real communities, as do literary genres, who creatively adapt the programme contents to their own emotional lives (cf. Ang, *Watching Dallas*; ibid. *Living Room Wars. Rethinking Media Audiences for a Postmodern World*, London: Routledge (1995); J. A. Radway, *Reading the Romance: Women, Patriarchy, and Popular Literature*, Chapel Hill-London: University of North Carolina Press, (1984); A. Bravo, *Il fotoromanzo*, Bologna: il Mulino (2003)). Cf. R. Sassatelli, *Consumo, cultura e società*, Bologna: il Mulino (2004), 205–8.

15 A. Signorelli, *Introduzione allo studio dei consumi*, Milan: Franco Angeli (2005), 252–3; cf. ISTAT censuses, various years.

16 To give an example, in 2005 37 per cent of Italians declared they were in the habit of taking medicines, but their use was more highly concentrated among older people: 55 per cent of the over-seventies and 84 per cent over seventy five. Cf. ISTAT, '*La vita quotidiana nel 2005*', *Informazioni*, 7, 2004, 79–80.

17 G. Fabris for example describes society as a map in which ten 'lifestyles' can be identified, understood as Weber ideal types: innovators, self-directing, affluent, radical, hetero-directed, integrated, self-sufficient, disorientated, conservative, and archaic (G. Fabris, *Consumatore & Mercato*, Milan: Sperling & Kupfer (1995)). Cf. also G. Ragone, *Consumi e stile di vita in Italia*, Naples: Guida (1985).

18 The beginning of the nineteenth century already saw the numbers in the middle classes exceed the working class (even if the latter included paid farm workers). In 1993 the upper-middle class was more or less stable, around 3 per cent; the middle class reached 52 per cent with almost all components on the increase (including: craftsmen 6 per cent, shopkeepers 11 per cent, civil servants 18 per cent, clerks 11 per cent, other categories 6 per cent); farm owners (6 per cent) and paid farm workers (3 per cent) show a further decrease; the working class only reached 36 per cent and was slowly going down, both for factory workers (25 per cent; it was 31 per cent in 1971) and among other categories (11 per cent). Cf. P. Sylos Labini, *Le classi sociali negli anni'80*, Rome-Bari: Laterza (1986), 20–1, 207; ibid. *La crisi italiana*, Rome-Bari: Laterza (1995), 23 (the percentages concerning agriculture are also shown separately here). Where individual income is concerned, however, (in Geary-Khamis dollars) it rose from 10,634 dollars in 1973 to 13,391 in 1983, 16,436 in 1993 and 19,150 in 2003, clearly nearing the average for the 29 European countries (19,912 in 2003) and slightly exceeding countries such as Germany (by comparison the average American income in 2003 equalled 29,037). Cf. A. Maddison, *Historical Satistics for the World Economy. Per Capita*

GDP (1990 International Geary-Khamis dollars), in www.ggdc.net/maddison, 15th February 2007.

19 *Vite ineguali. Disuguaglianze e corsi di vita nell'Italia contemporanea*, ed. A. Schizzerotto, Bologna: il Mulino (2002), to which reference may be made for quantitative data.

20 Statistics on Italians with degrees, who were born up to the 1970s and divided according to class of origin, actually show an increase in class differences in obtaining the diploma, from the start of the century up to the 1990s. Clearly in the lead are the young from the upper-middle classes (almost half the sample on their own), followed by the white-collar class and much further down the urban lower-middle class. Trailing behind we find the rural lower-middle class, urban-working class and rural-working class. Cf. *Vite ineguali*, 148–9.

21 However it must be pointed out that when talking about mobility regarding the 1950s–1960s, I am speaking about a selective phenomenon. The economic success of many small businessmen who had been workers, craftsmen or in farming before, and were able to set themselves up in the miracle years, only concerns categories of under-educated, male manual workers, often concentrated in specific geographical areas. Therefore it deals only with partial mobility, limited above all by strictly economic aspects, as R. Chiarini keenly observed when speaking about 'a long, uninterrupted race towards social emancipation that has given origin to a kind of alternative economic democratization compensating for incomplete' "political democratization"' (R. Chiarini, *Destra italiana: dall'Unità d'Italia a Alleanza Nazionale*, Venice: Marsilio (1995), 73). Confirmation of the limited mobility in Italy (as opposed to northern Europe, for example), both relative to class of origin and between generations, that is regarding career possibilities, can be found in ISTAT, '*La mobilità sociale*', Informazioni, 22, 2006; CENSIS, *Meno mobilità, più ceti, meno classi*, Rome (2006).

22 For a detailed analysis of socioeconomic and geographical differences during recent years look at the ISTAT publication, *I consumi delle famiglie* (various years) and the numerous studies by CENSIS, for example the CENSIS-Findomestic report about *Consumi e stili di vita* in various Italian regions, and also that by CENSIS-Confcommercio on *Valori, consumi e stili di vita degli italiani* (2004).

23 For a discussion of class and consumption from a sociological point of view cf. R. Crompton, *Consumption and class analysis*, in *Consumption Matters. The Production and Experience of Consumption*, eds. S. Edgell, K. Hetherington, and A. Warde, Oxford: Blackwell (1996), 113–32.

24 In 2005, the Gini index in Italy registered a value of 33 per cent, which was higher than the European average of 31 per cent for 25 countries, and definitely higher than northern Europe, France or Germany's 28 per cent (Eurostat sources). Since the inversion of tendencies at the start of the 1990s,

towards greater disparity, a shifting of wealth has been seen in Italy. from the medium-high classes towards the very top and later, from employed to self-employed work. This would seem to belong to a vaster phenomenon first registered in the USA in the 1960s, which shows increasing inequality first in household incomes and then between different wage levels too (cf. B. Harrison, B. Bluestone, *The Great U-Turn: Corporate Restructuring and the Polarizing of America*, New York: Basic Books (1988)); a phenomenon later confirmed in Europe as well.

25   This means that there was an increase in the average tendency to consume goods (in 2000 equal to 86 per cent), reaching levels similar to the European average at the end of the 1990s. In effect consumption changed to adjust to structural changes in the family and society. It is also worth noting that real available income was tending to diminish (and within it, capital gains and pensions were doing better than earned income), but many families enjoyed greater average wealth, mainly due to the revaluation of the property market (as Pellegrini and Zanderighi succinctly put it: smaller incomes, greater wealth). Cf. L. Pellegrini, L. Zanderighi, *Le famiglie come imprese e i consumi in Italia*, Milano: Egea (2005), 28–35, 55–89.

26   These are obviously percentage values of expenses that have grown in absolute terms, meaning that the per capita meat consumption, around 60 kg in the early 1970s, increased to about 80 kg over thirty years (ISTAT data).

27   Signorelli, *Introduzione allo studio dei consumi*, 297–8. In 2003, Italian families spent 15 per cent of the total on food and non-alcoholic drinks, compared with the European average of 13 per cent (France 14 per cent, Germany 11 per cent, Great Britain 9 per cent). Cf. Eurostat data, *Population and social conditions*.

28   The reported data come from ISTAT information (cf. ISTAT, Annuario statistico italiano Rome, various years; ibid., Contabilità nazionale. Conti economici nazionali. Anni 1970–2005, 10, 2007; and also Signorelli, *Introduzione allo studio dei consumi*, , 251–328 for summary data and tables for the period). Other international sources, like OECD, give partly discordant data (for example, higher in the case of clothing). Cf. Table 10.

29   ISTAT, *Annuario statistico italiano 2004*, Rome (2005); Ibid., '*I consumi delle famiglie. Anno 2003*', Annuario, 10, 2005. In 2003 the average family spending in Italy was equal to 2,313 euros (2,538 euros a month in the north, 2,466 in the centre and 1,892 in the south). Among the various data stands out the scant amount spent on cultural consumption compared to other countries (newspapers, books, museums, music, etc., with the exception of television watching), and could also be related to the poor educational level of Italians (in 2006 only 11 per cent of the population aged 25–64 had degrees, one of the lowest data among developed countries: cf. OECD, *Education at a Glance 2006*, Paris (2006)).

30   Signorelli, *Introduzione allo studio dei consumi*, 256–61.

31   The data are taken from the CENSIS-Estat Delta Group inquiry, *Immigrati e cittadinanza economica. Consumi e accesso al credito nell'Italia multietnica*, Rome (2005). The inquiry observes different buying behaviours within the sample (especially between Africans and Asians immigrating during the 1980s and 1990s who have become more permanent and relatively well integrated, and more recent, more mobile immigrants coming from Eastern Europe and Latin-America). An interesting fact is the remarkable homogeneity of consumer choices among groups with different incomes (from 600 to over 2,000 euros a month). On the whole, the commodities possessed were the following: mobile telephone 94 per cent, first television set 83 per cent, domestic furniture 80 per cent, washing machine 69 per cent, hi-fi set 48 per cent, video recorder 44 per cent, second-hand car 42 per cent, personal computer and dish antenna 22 per cent, dishwasher and motor scooter 21 per cent, second television set 20 per cent, new car 16 per cent, home Internet 12 per cent.

32   J. Clifford, *Strade: viaggio e traduzione alla fine del secolo 20* [1997], Turin: Bollati Boringhieri (1999), 9.

33   As McCracken reminds us, Diderot tells the story of when he received the gift of a magnificent suit. Delighted with this unexpected present, he realized that it clashed with his shabby old studio, so he began to change things. He bought a new leather chair, an elegant desk, and so on, until he had changed all the furnishings. In the end he came to hate the present that had 'enslaved' him. Today this effect can be related to 'cluster' commodities, ones with a sort of cohesion between them. Cf. G. McCracken, *Culture and Consumption*, Bloomington: Indiana University Press (1988), 118–9.

34   R. Schleifer, *Modernism and Time: The Logic of Abundance in Literature, Science, and Culture, 1880–1930*, Cambridge: Cambridge University Press (2000), 46–7.

35   *Ordinary Consumption*, eds. J. Gronow, and A. Warde, London-New York: Routledge (2001).

36   P. Pombeni, *Crisi, consenso, legittimazione: le categorie della transizione politica nel secolo delle ideologie*, in *Crisi, legittimazione, consenso*, ed. P. Pombeni, Bologna: il Mulino (2003), 10–11.

37   F. Girotti, *Welfare state. Storia, modelli e critica*, Rome: Carocci (1998), 323–61; *Citizenship and Consumption*, eds. K.Soper, and F. Trentmann, Basingstoke: Palgrave Macmillan (2007); *Governance, Consumers and Citizens. Agency and Resistance in Contemporary Politics*, eds. M. Bevir, and F. Trentmann, Basingstoke: Palgrave Macmillan (2007).

38   R. Sassatelli, *La politicizzazione del consumo. La cultura di protesta e l'emergere delle associazioni dei consumatori in Italia e in Europa*, in *Genere, generazione e consumi. L'Italia degli anni Sessanta*, ed. P. Capuzzo, Rome: Carocci (2003), 63–89; M. Hilton, *Prosperity for All: ConsumerActivism in an Era of Globalisation*, Ithaca NY: Cornell University Press (2009).

39 Famous examples were the tobacco strikes, which were called during the Risorgimento to damage Austro-Hungarian revenues.

40 This campaign was launched in 1992 in the USA to make consumers aware of what the act of buying meant. In 1997, in Great Britain ,they went so far as to prepare 'No Shop' stores. One entered, went around scrupulously empty shelves and at the end got a sales slip on which was written, 'Thank you for not buying'. Cf. Tae-Wook Cha, *Ecologically Correct*, in *Harvard Design School Guide to Shopping*, eds. C. J. Chung, J. Inaba, R. Koolhaas, and SzeTsung Leong, Köln: Taschen (2001), 314–19. When governments support consumption (with buying or demolition, incentives) the decision not to consume can be seen as political.

41 A. Gaspari, V. Pisano, *Dal popolo di Seattle all'ecoterrorismo: movimenti antiglobalizzazione e radicalismo ambientale*, Milan: 21mo Secolo (2003).

42 D. Stolle, M. Hooghe, and M. Micheletti, '*Politics in the supermarket: Political consumerism as a form of political participation*', International Political Science Review, vol. 26, no. 3, (2005), 246.

43 In this context recall *GAS* (United Buying Groups), consumerist groups that joined together spontaneously for collective buying, especially where food was concerned, not related to any organizations or institutions (in strong expansion since 2000). The peculiarity of this phenomenon is that the group shares a kind of political and ethical vision of consumption (through forms of group socialization, selection in favour of small or organic producers attentive to personal needs), which does not exclusively boil down to saving money; cf. L. Valera, *Gas. Gruppi di acquisto solidali*, Milan: Terre di Mezzo (2005); A. Saroldi, *Gruppi di Acquisto Solidali*, Bologna: Emi (2001); F. Brunetti, E. Giaretta, and C. Rossato, *Il consumo critico in azione: l'esperimento dei Gruppi di Acquisto Solidale*, in www.escp-eap.net/conferences/marketing, September 2007.

44 M. Williams, *Voice, Trust, and Memory*, Princeton: Princeton University Press (1998).

45 Stolle, Hooghe, Micheletti, *Politics in the supermarket*.

46 G. Becattini, *Dal distretto industriale allo sviluppo locale: svolgimento e difesa di un idea*, Turin: Bollati Boringhieri (2000); Istituto per le promozione industriale, *L'esperienza italiana dei distretti industriali*, Rome (2002).

47 *Consuming Technologies: Media and Information in Domestic Spaces*, eds. Silverstone, and E. Hirsch, London: Routledge (1992); *Consumption in an Age of Information*, eds. S. Cohen, and R. L. Rutsky, Oxford: Berg (2005).

48 M. Pantzar, '*Domestication of Everyday Life Technology: Dynamic Views on the Social Histories of Artifacts*', Design Issues, vol. 13, no. 3, 1997, 52–65.

49 M. De Certeau, *L'Invenzione del quotidiano* [1990], Rome: Edizioni Lavoro (2001), 66–7.

50 G. Ritzer, *La religione dei consumi: cattedrali, pellegrinaggi e riti dell'iperconsumerismo* [1999], Bologna: il Mulino (2000).

51 In 2005, computers were used by more than 50 per cent men and 40 per cent women. The highest peak was among users aged 15–17 (more than 80 per cent), and the lowest level was for the over 65-year-olds (5 per cent). Cf. ISTAT, '*La vita quotidiana nel 2005*', Informazioni, 4, 2007, 99–139.

52 The total cost of IT in Italy (Information technology: hardware, software, accessories, and services) in 2005 corresponded to 1.9 per cent of GDP against the European average of 3 per cent (data from Eurostat, *Population and social conditions*); ISTAT, '*I consumi delle famiglie. Anno 2005*', Annuario, 12, 2007, 30–2.

53 In 2005, 80 per cent of Italian families owned a car, while motorcycles came a very poor second (15 per cent had scooters, 7 per cent motorcycles), whereas being ecological and having a bicycle is significant (51 per cent). Cf. ISTAT, *I consumi delle famiglie. Anno 2005*, 32–5. Italy has reached record levels for private motorization, confirming its position as one of the major sales markets for cars: in 2004 there were 591 cars per 1000 inhabitants, compared with 546 in Germany, 481 in France, 463 in Great Britain and an average of 494 among the then 15 EU countries—though always way behind the USA's 771 (data from Eurostat, *Transport*); cf. also F. Paolini, *Storia sociale dell'automobile in Italia*, Rome: Carocci (2007), 85–109.

54 In 2005 Italian families possessed the following durable goods: fridge 99 per cent, dishwasher 37 per cent, washing machine 97 per cent, air conditioner 23 per cent, land-line telephone 78 per cent, cell phone 78 per cent, telephone answering machine 12 per cent, FAX machine 6 per cent, television 97 per cent, video recorder 69 per cent, hi-fi unit 58 per cent, personal computer 31 per cent. The overall cost of a cell phone (on average 160 euro) compared well with a PC (716 euro); most expensive of all was the air conditioner (925 euro). In 2005 spending on ITC (Information technology and communication: hardware, software, and telecommunications services) in Italy was equal to 3.4 per cent of GDP, in line with the European average, and more than France 2.6 per cent and Germany 3.2 per cent. Cf. 'ISTAT, *I consumi delle famiglie. Anno 2005*', 30–2; data from Eurostat, *Population and social conditions*.

55 V. Andreoli, *La vita digitale*, Milan: Rizzoli (2007); E. Pistolesi, *Il parlar spedito. L'Italiano di chat, e-mail e sms*, Padua: Esedra (2004); I. Bonomi, A. Masini, S. Morgana, *La lingua italiana e i mass media*, Rome: Carocci (2004).

56 P. Mäenpää, *Mobile communication as a way of urban life*, in *Ordinary Consumption*, 107–23; M. Ferraris, *Dove sei? Ontologia del telefonino*, Milan: Bompiani (2005); B. Scifo, *Culture mobile. Ricerche sull'adozione giovanile della telefonia cellulare*, Milan: Vita e Pensiero (2005).

57 *Land, Shops and Kitchens: Technology in the Food Chain in Twentieth-Century Europe*, eds. C. Sarasua, P. Schmolliers, and L. Van Molle, Turnhout: Brepols (2005). According to a study by Coldiretti, in 2006 out of the 467 euro spent monthly by an Italian family on food, 51 per cent went to marketing, 31 per cent to

the food industry and 19 per cent to the farmers (cf. *News Coldiretti*, 734, 10th October 2007).

58 V. Teti, *Le culture alimentari nel Mezzogiorno continentale in età contemporanea*, in *Storia d'Italia, Annali 13. L'alimentazione*, eds. A. Capatti, A. De Bernardi, and A. Varni, Turin: Einaudi (1998), 158–63; A. Capatti, M. Montanari, *La cucina italiana. Storia di una cultura*, Rome-Bari: Laterza (1999), 96–8.

59 Agricoltura 55, February 2005 (data from ISTAT-Federalimentare); cf. also the data of the European Commission for Food and Agriculture.

60 R. Horowitz, *Putting Meat on the American Table. Taste, Technology, Transformation*, Baltimore: John Hopkins University Press (2006).

61 Ibid. 72, 129–52.

62 In contrast with 'fast food', Slow Food was founded in 1986 as a reaction against the opening of the first Rome McDonald's in Piazza di Spagna. Today it has a publishing house and has created at Pollenzo the University of Gastronomic Science Studies, cf. C. Petrini, *Slow food. Le ragioni del gusto*, Rome-Bari: Laterza (2001).

63 I. Calvino, *Leonia*, in *Le città invisibili*, Turin: Einaudi (1972), 119–20.

64 Schleifer, *Modernism and Time*, 48.

65 H. E. Daly, *Oltre la crescita. L'economia dello sviluppo sostenibile* [1996], Turin: Einaudi (2001); N. Georgescu-Roegen, *Bioeconomia: verso un'altra economia ecologicamente e socialmente sostenibile*, ed. M. Bonaiuti, Turin: Bollati Boringhieri (2003).

66 R. Inglehart, *La rivoluzione silenziosa* [1977], Milan: Rizzoli (1983).

67 M. Weber, *Economia e società: l'economia in rapporto agli ordinamenti e alle forze sociali* [1922], Rome: Donzelli (2003).

68 S. Neri Serneri, *Culture e politiche del movimento ambientalista*, in *Culture, nuovi soggetti, identità*, 367–99.

69 N. Klein, *No logo: economia globale a nuova contestazione* [2001], Milan: Baldini & Castoldi (2001); *Questo mondo non è in vendita. Come opporsi alle strategie del super-mercato mondiale*, ed. A. Zoratti, Milan: Terre di Mezzo (2003).

70 The amount of rubbish produced in Italy is continually on the increase. In 2005, urban garbage alone was equal to 539 kilograms per inhabitant (a little below the European average), with a far greater increase than economic growth (for the 2003–2005 period, when there was a rise in GDP of 1 per cent, family spending 0.6 per cent but urban waste grew 5.5 per cent). Cf. Agenzia per la Protezione dell'Ambiente e per i Servizi Tecnici, *Rifiuti 2006*, Rome (2006), vol. I, 10–11, 32.

71 *Cambieresti? La sfida di mille famiglie alla società dei consumi*, ed. M. Correggia, Milan: Terre di Mezzo (2006). Cf. also P. Dell'Aquila, *Verso un'ecologia del consumo*, Milan: Franco Angeli (1997).

72 J. Levine, *Io non compro* [2006], Florence: Ponte alle Grazie (2006); cf. for example the book review in '*Un anno senza shopping*', Gioia, 4th July 2006, 44–5: the women's magazine evokes the topic on the cover, among the

Manuals for survival and the good life together with other useful advice ('How to find a man and hold him tight. How to become rich. Choose the right colour. Be excellent at sex.').

73   The HDI (Human Development Index) is constructed on per capita earnings, life expectancy, percentage of literacy, and spread of higher education. According to this classification, in 2006 Italy occupied 17th place, lower than its 7th place using the GDP scale—Norway held first place and the last was Niger at 177th. It is interesting to note that an HDI has also been worked out by gender, that is measuring the inequalities in this factor between men and women. According to this classification Italy is definitely further down, at 62nd place (the first place, that is with the least differences, is Luxemburg, the last is Yemen).

74   F. M. Pulselli, S. Bastianoni, N. Marchettini, E. Tizzi, *La soglia della sostenibilità ovvero quello che il Pil non dice*, Rome: Donzelli (2007), 145–60.

75   From a comparison with other European countries (the ISEW index is not available for all of them) it turns out that the environmental situation is especially delicate in Italy and Germany, which have been in 'ecological deficit' for some time and are coming close to the biophysical 'edge'. Cf. Pulselli, Bastianoni, Marchettini, Tizzi, *La soglia della sostenibilità*, 227–36.

76   L. Vergine, *Quando I rifiuti diventano arte. Trash rubbish mongo*, Milan: Skira (2006).

77   *Daniel Spoerri. La messa in scena degli oggetti*, ed. S. Parmiggiani, Milan: Skira (2004).

Chapter 12

1   J. G. Frazer, *Il ramo d'oro. Studio sulla magia e la religione* [1922], Turin: Bollati Boringhieri (1965), 572–85 in particular.

2   United Nations Office on Drugs and crime, *Trafficking in Persons: Global Patterns*, Vienna (2006). Modern slavery chiefly deals with forced labour and exploitation of sex. As regards prostitution, it can be seen that in contemporary society, despite the increasing liberalization of sex, the entire sex-linked market is growing apace (prostitution itself, sex magazines, films and DVDs, web sites, and sexual tourism). As Leonini observes, this belongs to the idea that sexuality is totally separate from affection and falls right into the category of consumption. The presence of mainly foreign prostitutes then adds to the phenomenon a social element that is a reminder to us of how unequal less developed countries are, in comparison with wealthy western nations. Cf. *Sesso in acquisto. Una ricerca sui clienti della prostituzione*, ed. L. Leonini, Milan: Unicopli (1999).

3   *Texture. Manipolazioni corporee fra chirurgia e digitale*, ed. E. Ciuffoli, Rome: Meltemi (2007); C. Benthien, *Skin. On the Cultural Border Between Self and World*, New York: Columbia University Press (2002).

4   M. Sahlins, *Isole di storia: società e mito nei mari del Sud* [1985], Turin: Einaudi (1986).

5   *Texture*, 57–90.

6   R. Marchinesi, *Post-human. Verso nuovi modelli di esistenza*, Turin: Bollati Boringhieri (2002). Concerning redefinition, the transformations that are entering into human-animal relations should also be mentioned. In modern times these relationships have often taken on characteristics of consumption and marketing of domestic pets, implying that they are animal-objects, but now calling into question relations between human beings and animal-subjects, as suggested by zoo-anthropology. Cf. R. Marchesini, S. Tonutti, *Manuale di zooantropologia*, Rome: Meltemi (2007).

7   F. Botero, *The Letter* (oil on canvas), (1976); *The Toilet* (oil on canvas), (1989); Odalisque (oil on canvas), (1998); cf. F. Botero, *Donne*, edited by P. Gribaudo, Milan: Rizzoli 2003.

8   V. Teti, *Le culture alimentari nel Mezzogiorno*, 162.

9   C. S. Bynum, *Sacro convivio, sacro digiuno: il significato religioso del cibo per le donne del Medioevo* [1987], Milan: Feltrinelli (2001); cf. also W. Vandereycken, R. van Deth, *Dalle sante ascetiche alle ragazze anoressiche: il rifiuto del cibo nella storia* [1994], Milan: Cortina (1995).

10 R. Sassatelli, *Anatomia della palestra. Cultura commerciale e disciplina del corpo*, Bologna: il Mulino (2000).

11 Schleifer, *Modernism and Time*, 26.

12 Power dressing is seen as a way for women to enter a predominantly masculine world, playing down specifically sexual attributes so as to facilitate relations with male colleagues—who would otherwise be distracted by the erotic messages emitted by a provocative dress-code. However, at the same time women do not forget their femininity, using certain symbols and accessories in a complex game of male/female cross-referencing. Cf. J. Entwistle, *The Fashioned Body: Fashion, Dress and Modern Social Theory*, Cambridge: Polity Press (2000), 181–207. For a general picture of the meaning of dress and fashion in today's society cf. E. Wilson, *Adorned in dreams: Fashion and Modernity*, London: Virago (1985).

13 G. Simmel, *La moda e altri saggi di cultura filosofica* [1895], Milan: Longanesi (1985); T. Veblen, *La teoria della classe agiata: studio economico sulle istituzioni* [1899], Turin: Einaudi (1949).

14 W. Benjamin, *Strolling in Paris*, vol. I, [1982], Turin: Einaudi (2002), 84.

15 R. Barthes, *Miti d'oggi* [1957], Turin: Einaudi (1974); Ibid., *Sistema della moda* (1967), Turin: Einaudi (1970).

16 M. Douglas, B. Isherwood, *Il mondo delle cose: oggetti, valori, consumo* [1979], Bologna: il Mulino (1984); *The Social Life of Things: Commodities in Cultural Perspective*, ed. A. Appadurai, Cambridge: Cambridge University Press (1986). About objects and material culture cf. also Leonini, *L'identità smarrita: il ruolo degli oggetti nella vita quotidiana*, Bologna: il Mulino (1988). For an overall

picture with a philosophical approach cf. L. F. H. Svendson, *Filosofia della moda* [2004], Parma: Guanda (2006).

17 S. Gnoli, *Un secolo di moda italiana: 1900–2000*, Rome: Meltemi (2005); U. Volli, *Block modes: il linguaggio del corpo e della moda*, Milan: Lupetti (1998).

18 R. Fabbri, *Ciak: si gira la moda. Cinema e moda, sistemi di senso e industrie di emozioni*, Urbino: Quattro Venti (2006); P. Calefato, *Mass moda: linguaggio e immaginario del corpo rivestito*, Genoa: Costa & Nolan (1996).

19 D. Hebdige, *Sottocultura: il fascina di uno stile innaturale* [1979], Genoa: Costa & Nolan (1983); M. Maffesoli, *Il tempo delle tribù: il declino dell'individualismo nelle società di massa* [1988], Rome: Armando (1988).

20 T. Polhemus, *Street Style: From Sidewalk to Catwalk*, New York: Thames & Hudson (1994); A. Arvidsson, *Dalla 'réclame' al 'brand management'. Uno sguardo storico alla disciplina pubblicitaria del Novecento*, in *Il secolo dei consumi. Dinamiche sociali nell'Europa del Novecento*, eds. S. Cavazza, and E. Scarpellini, Rome: Carocci (2006), 213–17.

21 E. Landowski, *La società riflessa* [1989], Rome: Meltemi (1998); *Total living*, eds. M. L. Frisa, M. Lupano, and S. Tonchi, Milan: Charta (2002).

22 E. Merlo, *Moda italiana: storia di un'industria dall'Ottocento a oggi*, Venice: Marsilio (2003); S. Testa, *La specificità della filiera italiana della moda*, in *Storia d'Italia. Annali 19. La moda*, eds. C. M. Belfanti, and F. Giusberti, Turin: Einaudi (2003), 699–734.

23 Cf. the essays of P. Sparke, *A modern identity for a new nation: design in Italy since 1860*, and E. Paulicelli, *Fashion: narration and nation*, in *The Cambridge Companion to Modern Italian Culture*, eds. Z. G. Baranski, and R. J. West, Cambridge: Cambridge University Press (2001), 265–77, 282–92, and for a look further back: *Moda e moderno. Dal Medioevo al Rinascimento*, ed. E. Paulicelli, Rome: Meltemi (2006).

24 An interesting book about the role of the kitchen in today's imagination is the first novel by B. Yoshimoto, *Kitchen* [1988], Milan: Feltrinelli (1991). It begins: 'There is nowhere in the world that I love more than the kitchen. It does not matter where it is or what it is like: as long as it is a kitchen, a place where they make things to eat, I am happy there'.

25 F. Ramondino, *Star di casa*, Milan: Garzanti (1992); G. D'Amato, *Storia dell'arredamento. Dal 1750 a oggi*, Rome-Bari: Laterza (1999), 407–12.

26 Ismea-AcNielsen, 'Extradomestici: indagine qualitative secondo semestre 2006', Consumi, 2, September 2007 (giving specific data concerning geographic and socio-professional differences); Fipe-Confcommercio, *Comportamenti di consumo al ristorante*, Rome (2004). In 2005, Italy was in line with the European average for extra-domestic consumption (25 nations) equalling 32 per cent, with Ireland at 51 per cent. The Italian figure was lower than that of other Mediterranean countries, where higher values were recorded (Spain 50 per cent, Greece 47 per cent), but it was growing rapidly. Cf. Nomisma, *Il fuori*

casa in Italia: stato dell'arte, dinamiche, nuovi trend del consumer extra-domestico,
Bologna (2007).

27 D. Hanson, *Tourists II* (glass fibre sculpture), (1988).

28 J. Urry, *Lo sguardo del turista: il tempo libero e il viaggio nelle società contemporanee*
[1990], Rome: Seam (1995).

29 A. Galvani, *Ecotourismo*, Bologna: Martina (2004); A. Stronza, '*Anthropology of
Tourism: Forging New Ground for Ecotourism and Other Alternatives*', Annual Review
of Anthropology, 30, 2001, 261–83.

30 R. Venturi, D. Scott Brown, S. Izenour, *Learning from Las Vegas: The Forgotten
Symbolism of Architectural Form*, Cambridge: MIT Press (1977); M. Augé,
Disneyland e altri nonluoghi [1997], Turin: Bollati Boringhieri (1999); G. Ritzer,
Il mondo alla McDonald's [1993], Bologna: il Mulino (1997). Cf. also *I parchi di
divertimento nella società del loisir*, eds. E. Minardi, and M. Lusetti, Milan: Franco
Angeli (1998) (on theme parks).

31 M. J. Hardwick, *Mall Maker: Victor Gruen, Architect of an American Dream*,
Philadelphia: University of Pennsylvania Press (2004); L. Cohen, '*From
Town Center to Shopping Center: The Reconfiguration of Community Marketplaces
in Postwar America*', American Historical Review, 101, 4th October 1996,
1050–1081. Although, the first example of a mall is said to have been the
Country Club Plaza in Kansas City (1939).

32 On a par with what happened with the big department stores, which
hypermarkets came first is also debatable, because it depends on the features
used to define them. In general they are called hypermarkets if they are self-
service establishments mostly for food, and covering an area of over 4,500 sq.
m. (sometimes the really big ones, that is over 8,000 sq. m. are classified
separately). Below that level they become 'superstores' (2,500–4,499 sq. m.);
yet further below are the classic supermarkets, going from 400 to 2,499 sq.
m. (smaller self-service shops are called 'superettes'). The picture is com-
pleted with the 'discount' formula: born in Germany during the 1970s with
Aldi, a pre-existing chain of shops created in Essen in 1913, it is a formula
that aims to offer very low prices, up to 50 per cent less in the 'hard discount'
version, thanks to saving on the internal furnishings and control over the
entire production-distribution chain. In Italy this appears as Lidl, which
opened its first store in Verona in 1992. As regards the share of the Italian
market, supermarkets clearly predominate with 40 per cent in 2005, followed
by hypermarkets (13 per cent), superettes (9 per cent) and hard discount (6
per cent) (cf. Table 10 for 2006 data). The rest is a mixture of traditional
shops (22 per cent), itinerant salesmen and other forms (10 per cent). To
cover everything, it should be remembered that wholesale 'cash & carry'
(started by Lombardini in 1964) and now giants like the German Metro also
belong to large-scale distribution. Cf. L. Pellegrini, *Il commercio in Italia. Dalla
bottega all'ipermercato*, Bologna: il Mulino (2001), 54–60; Federdistribuzione,
Mappa del sistema distributivo italiano, Milan (2007), 4.

33   A. Terranova, *Centro storico. Difendere il centro storico dal centro storico? Millecentri, millestorie, milleprogetti*, in *Attraversamenti. I nuovi territori dello spazio pubblico*, eds. P. Desideri, and M. Ilardi, Genoa: Costa & Nolan (1997). Cf. also *La città vetrina. I luoghi del commercio e le nuove forme del consumo*, ed. G. Amendola, Naples: Liguori (2006); *Casa e supermercato. Luoghi e comportamenti del consumo*, eds. G. Triani, Milan: Elèuthera (1996).

34   S. Zukin, *Landscapes of Power: From Detroit to Disney World*, Berkeley: University of California Press (1991), 16. Cf. for example the study about the changes made in Rome by consumer places in *Architetture dello shopping. Modelli del consumo a Roma*, ed. A. Criconia, Rome: Meltemi (2007). Naturally, these complex commercial structures are not new to our age; just thinking about urban spaces calls to mind the extraordinary architecture of the Grand bazaar of Istanbul or the bazaar of Isfahan, or the more ancient, spectacular Trajan Markets with numerous *tabernae* on the ground floor, large hall, perhaps for bargaining purposes, and an upper floor with a huge number of small shops distributed among the 150 rooms.

35   An example of this type is the 'Vulcano buono', a megacentre designed by Renzo Piano at Nola, in the form of an artificial hill surrounded by trees, with an immense empty square in the centre and a structure inspired by Vesuvius facing it. The innovative 'Etnapolis' (Catania) by the architect Fuksas, does not forego naturalistic reminders either: (artificial) lake, park with citrus fruit and olive trees, and underground parking.

36   F. Anderton, *You Are Here*, London: Phaidon, (1999).

37   The new trends, reinforced by changes in the political picture and by community pressures, found expression in the 'Bersani law' (legislative decree of 31st March 1998, no. 114), which extended to the commercial field the criteria for competition, productivity, and liberalization already in force where industry laws were concerned.

38   Federdistribuzione, *Mappa*; Deloitte classification (*2006 Global Powers of Retailing*). FAID data differ slightly from reports by other sources; for a discussion of problems relating to timing in the sector cf. P. Battilani, '*Perché il brutto anatroccolo non è diventato cigno: la mancata trasformazione dal basso del settore distributivo italiano*', Imprese e storia, 33, January–June 2006, 111–56. About the developments peculiar to the Co-op in the Italian context, as well as this article cf. V. Zamagni, P. Battilani, and A. Casali, *Centocinquanta anni di cooperazione di consumo*, Bologna: il Mulino (2004).

39   It is interesting to note that this centre, which presents a style new to Italy, was the outcome of intense negotiations between the town council and local community. It has had a significant impact, varying according to area, as witnessed by the studies carried out on it (despite aid from the investors to restore the historic centre of the nearby town, financing for cultural initiatives, the creation of jobs, increasing services in adjoining areas, at the same time there has been increased traffic, failure to integrate satisfactorily

with the territory, and an emptying of areas farther afield of resources and people). Cf. G. Brunetta, C. Salone, *Commercio e Territorio: un'alleanza possibile? Il Factory Outlet Centre di Serravalle Scrivia*, Turin: Regione Piemonte, (2002).

40 Specialized chain stores are one of the formulas of rapid growth in the Italian non-food sector, and have recently been joined by big foreign chains (H&M, Zara, Mango, and Decathlon), often resorting to franchizing. Together with the large retail facilities (household and electronics for example) in 2005 they occupied 23 per cent of the market compared with 52 per cent for traditional shops (8 per cent for hyper- and supermarkets, only 2 per cent for department stores and 14 per cent for all other forms). Cf. Federdistribuzione, *Mappa*, 5. By the way, the presence of foreign firms is most conspicuous in the early 21st century, considering their acquisition of many classic Italian brands (GS taken over by Carrefour, Sma by Auchan, Standa by Rewe, and Conad in agreement with Leclerc, etc.).

41 *Scene del consumo: dallo shopping al museo*, eds. J. Pezzini, and P. Cervelli, Rome: Meteci, (2006); V. Codeluppi, *Lo spettacolo della merce*, Milan: Bompiani, (2000), 87–93.

42 C. Béret, *Shed, cathedral or museum?*, in *Shopping. A Century of Art and Consumer Culture*, eds. C. Grunenberg, and M. Hollein, Ostfildern-Ruit: Hatje Cantz (2002), 76–79.

43 C. Marenco Mores, *Da Fiorucci ai Guerillas Stores. Moda, architettura, marketing e comunicazione*, Venice: Marsilio (2006).

44 S. Sontag, *Contro l'interpretazione* [1966], Milan: Mondadori (1967); V. Gregotti, *Kitsch e architettura*, in G. Dorfles, *Il kitsch: antologia del cattivo gusto*, Milan: Mazzotta (1968), 255–76.

45 Even when considering square metres of selling area per person, there is always a big gap between the USA (2.2 sq. m. per head) and other countries: Japan 0.8 (the average for Asia is 0.2); Europe 0.4 (with a maximum for Great Britain with 0.9, followed by France and Sweden with 0.8; Italy is below average with 0.2 sq. m. per person, together with Germany; Greece is at the bottom of the table with 0.1); the continent with the least commercial building is Africa with 0.01 sq. m. per head; the world average is 0.3. Cf. *Harvard design school*, 517.

46 M. Davis, *Il pianeta degli slum* [2006], Milan: Feltrinelli (2006); R. Neuwirth, *Città ombra. Viaggio nelle periferia del mondo* (2004), Rome: Fusi orari (2007). Concerning McDonald's, it is known to be so widespread that a special index has been created to measure buying power, based on how much a Big Mac costs in each country compared with the price in the USA, and it shows enormous disparities (much higher prices in Northern Europe, much lower ones in Asia).

47   In 2005, purchases mainly concerned trips and holidays (33 per cent), books
     and newspapers (27 per cent), cell phone recharging (20 per cent), films and
     music (19 per cent), then software/videogames, electronics, clothing/sports
     equipment, all at 17 per cent. The reasons all users indicated for not buying
     on Internet were: preferring to buy in person and lack of need; lower down,
     fear of communicating credit card details, then lack of trust in the delivery/
     return of the goods and reluctance to give personal date; the remaining 12
     per cent said they did not have a credit card. Cf. ISTAT, '*La vita quotidiana nel
     2005*', 103, 128–37.

Index

Page references in *italics* indicate a table.

accident insurance 53, 96, 97
Adorno, T. W. 178
adulteration 249, 314 n.24
advertising 62, 66, 113, 139, 146, 191, 227,
    290–1 n.51, 303 n.81
  agencies 193, 194, 287 n.12
  campaigns 104
  colonial goods 89–90
  cosmetics and toiletries 152, 153
  domestic appliances 147–8, 151, 199
  domestic hygiene products 153
  'Drinking Milan' 230
  Fascist regime 87
  female body 152
  food 198, 199, 200, 201, 249
  'Made in Italy' 66, 87, 227, 245
  motor scooters 143
  new products 196
  psychology and 193–4
  rhymes 292 n.12
  television 163, 180–1, 230–1
  washing machines 313 n.12–13
affluent society 225–70
aging population 231
Agnelli, Giovanni 115
Agnesi of Oneglia 62
air transport 87, 116–17
Alberoni, Francesco 145, 180, 193
alcohol:
  abuse 169, 173
  beer 64–5, 130, 202
  fortified wines 64, 158
  sparkling wine 64, 202
  wine 59, 64, 130, 173, 202
Alfa Romeo 115, 171
'American dream' 128, 222
Americanization 177, 209
ancient Greeks 35
Andreotti, Giulio 182
Annabella magazine 163
Appadurai, Arjun 150, 258
arcades 68–9

Arcimboldi, Giuseppe 28
Arendt, Hannah 126
Argillo, Princess 40
aristocracy 20, 35–46, 99, 103
Ariston brand 196
Armani, Giorgio 206, 225, 259
Arndt, H. W. 177
art, and consumption 28, 29, 50, 218–19,
  225, 256, 268–9
Artusi, Pellegrino 42–3
Arvidsson, A. 230
Atahualpa, Emperor of the Incas 105
austerity 226, 229, 230, 257

'baby boom' 127, 210
Bacci, Massimo Livi 8, 127
balconies 17, 19, 30
Baldini, Filippo 201
Barilla company 62, 197
Barrymore, John 83
Barthes, R. 156–7, 258
bathrooms 19, 39, 114, 155–6, 177, 256
Baudelaire, C. 67, 68, 77
Baudrillard, J. 105, 157, 178, 264
Beatles, The 171
Becker, Gary 146
bedrooms 13, 19, 31, 32, 39, 112, 151–4,
  158, 165–6, 170
beer 64–5, 130, 202
Benedict, Ruth 176
Benjamin, Walter 68, 257
Berghoff, H. 104
Berlin 68, 70, 103
Berlin Olympics (1936) 102
Berlingieri, Marquess of Naples 37, 65
Berlusconi, Silvio 231
Bertolli olive oil 198
Beveridge, William 183
Bianchi, Edoardo and Tommaselli,
  Giovanni 117
Bianciardi, Luciano 219
bicycles 117

birth rates 4, 15, 231, 296 n.8
biscuits 63, 200, 203
Bocca, Giorgio 139, 176
Bocconi brothers 3, 70, 76–7
body, and fashion 255–9
Bontempelli, Massimo 74
books 161, 162
bookshops 118, 267–8
Borghi, Giovanni 196
Borletti, Senatore 119, 120, *see also*
        Rinascente
Borletti company 120, 295 n.45
Botero, F. 256
Bottai, Giuseppe 95
Boucicault, Aristide 70
Bourdieu, Pierre 23, 28, 30, 205
bourgeois 25, 39, 45, 69, 78, 221, *see also*
        middle class
Bramieri, Gino 157
Brando, Marlon 169
brands 61–4, 197–200, 218
bread 9, 10, 11, 110, 129, 142,
        182, 200, 214, 220, 235,
        248, 255
Britain:
    car ownership 133
    consumption compared with Italy *228*
    earnings 127
    Harrods department store 70
    industrialization model 194
    Internet use 247
    motor scooters and youth
        subculture 143
    National Health Service 187
    opium use in 174
    shopping arcades 68–9
    social mobility 173
    supermarkets 210
    'Swinging London' 172
    televisions 131
    youth culture 169–70
British Empire 66
Brosio, G. and Marchese, C. 189,
        281 n.18
Buitoni 62, 63, 90, 197

Caffè, Federico 58
Calindri, Ernesto 139

Calvino, Italo 219–20, 250–1
Camerini, Paolo 17
Candy 146, 149, 151, 196, 301 n.57, 313
        n.12–13
cannibalism 255
canning sector 197–8
Cappiello, Leonetto and Depero,
        Fortunato 193
Caprilli, Federico 46
Caravaggio, Michelangelo Merisi da 28
Carnival 14
'Carolina the Cow' 191
Carosello 163, 180–1, 194, 313–14 n.19
Carrefour 264, 266
Carri di Tespi (Thespian Wagons) 100–1
cars/car industry 104, 114–16, 131, 151,
        207, 229
    'Italian dream' and 136–40
    masculine identity and 139–40
    moral doubt 138–9
    oil crisis and 226–7
    ownership 115, 133, 247, 297 n.31
    spending on 240
Caruso, Enrico 113
Casati law (1859) 53
Casorati, Felice 137
Castelnuovo, Nino 198
catering sector 117–18
Catholicism 10, 14, 51, 53, 177
Cavazza, Stefano 49, 99
chain stores 83, 211, 244, 267–8,
        331 n.40
charitable associations 48, 49, 51, 52
cheese 63–4, 64, 130, 191, 202, 214, 248,
        249
chemical industry 59, 108, 195
chewing gum 201
Chiari, Walter 198
childhood 32–3, 166–7
children:
    food products aimed at 201
    industrial workers 24
    middle class 32
    peasants 12–13
    toys 33, 76, 166, 267
chinaware 41, 42, 66, 76, 199, 250, 267
chocolate 63, 200
Christian Democrats 177, 182, 230

Ciano, Galeazzo and Edda 103
Ciao Amici magazine 165
cigarettes 87, 104, 154, 165, 173–4, 290–1
   n.51, 292 n.9
cinema 83, 98, 102, 103, 104, 113, 116,
   144, 159, 161, 162, 226
  American 290 n.51
  'Americanization' of 177
  attendance 306 n.111
  cars and masculine identity 140
  stars 153, 166
  youth and 169, 170
Cirio 63, 197
citizenship 183, 242
civil rights 183
Clifford, James 241
clothing 85, 131, 151, 204–6, 257, 314–15
   n.33
  for the aristocracy 43–5, 46
  department stores 76
  from factory outlets 266–7
  identity and 258
  immigrants and 136
  industry 211
  men 300 n.64
  middle-class 26, 106–8
  peasants 13
  prestige 28–9
  reduced spending on 235–6
  'Roman style' 87
  teenage 166, 167, 171–2
  underwear 68, 76, 118, 151, 302 n.66
  uniforms 18
  working-class 18
clubs and associations 21, 48, 49, 51, 52,
   98–9
Coop Italia 217, 266
coffee 130, 173, 198, 207, 213, 278 n.107
Cohen, Stanley 170
colonies 89, 288 n.22
comics 167, 169
commercial centres 263–70, 330 n.34
Common Market 126
communal living 19–20
communication 150, 240
  mobile phones 247–8
  telephones 112, 113, 114, 145, 158, 293
   n.24
Communist Party 177, 230

company sales outlets 119
computers 245, 246–7, 324 n.51
confectionery 118, 130, 199–201
consumer culture 15–16, 70, 78, 163,
   176–82, 230, 261, 263
consumer movements 243–4, 323 n.43
consumer revolution (1945–73) 125–34
consumption 84–5, 168, 234–5, 322 n.31,
   324 n.53–4
  aspirational 163
  behaviour models 181
  collective 98–104
  commercial centres of 263–70
  conspicuous 33, 57
  coveted goods 298 n.42
  criticism of excessive and
   hedonistic 176–82, 225–6
  cultural 90–1, 159, 161–2
  democratizing 215
  economic growth and 227–9
  European comparisons *228*, *238–9*
  Fascist policy 92–8
  geography and 240
  immigrants and 145, 240–1
  nationalism and 87–90, 92, 104
  politics and 176, 242–4
  pollution and 250–4
  private and public space 259–63
  production and 56–7
  public 47–55, 92–4, 183–90, 184
  race and 89
  research 228–35
  responsible 253
  role models for 103
  society and 173–4
  sustainable 252–4
  theories 57
  urban 275 n.68
  young people 167
cooperatives 119, 217
Coppedé, Mariano 65
Coppino law (1877) 53
Corbin, A. 20, 99, 100
cosmetic surgery 256
cosmetics 152–3, 167, 302 n.70
covered markets 72
craftsmanship 65, 66, 72, 194
crime 54, 167–9, 305 n.104
crockery 41, 42, 66, 76, 199, 250, 267

cultural consumption 90–1, 159, 161–2,
    see also cinema; music; theatre
cultural studies 21–2
cutlery 40, 41, 76, 163, 199, 278 n.104

dairy products 14, 15, 63–4, 130, 202
Daly, H. and Cobb, J. 254
Daneo-Credaro law (1911) 53
D'Apice, C. 229
De Certeau, M. 246
de-industrialization 227
De Marchi, E. 29
De Rica tomatoes 197
De Rita, L. 180–1
Dean, James 166, 169
Debord, G. 178
delicatessens 117, 214
democracy 54, 183, 210
democratization of luxury 78–9, 140–2,
    152, 266
demography 4, 8, 112, 118, 127–8, 148,
    173, 210, 231
department stores 70, 75–80
    American 205
    Bocconi brothers 3, 70, 76–7
    Fascist regime 118–21
    international exhibitions and 285 n.31
    laws on 120
    supermarkets and 218, 221
    theatrical metaphor 79–80, 212–13
designer labels 266–7
detergents 59, 150, 153, 195, 214,
    301 n.58
Diderot, Denis 322 n.33
diet 9, 15, 130, 203–4, 235, 286 n.7,
    313 n.18
Diner, Hasia 91
disease 52, 96, 187
dishwashers 131, 147, 196, 209
Disneyland 263
domestic appliances 108–9, 112, 131,
    146–51, 196, 209, 253, 296 n.16, 300
    n.56, 300 n.63, *see also under* individual
    appliances
domestic hygiene 59, 150, 153, 195, 214,
    301 n.58
Douglas, Mary 135, 258
drinking chocolate 278 n.107
drinks cabinets 158

drugs 174, 187
Ducrot, Vittorio 65
Dudovich, Marcello 76, 120, 193

earnings 4, 131, 190, 229, 275 n.57
    distribution 84–5
    industrial workers 14
    international comparison 86, 125
    middle-class 26
    peasants 8
    post-war 127
    professional work 276 n.85
economists 37, 56, 57, 58, 83, 141, 147,
    177
education 50–1, 53, 55, 161–2, 233, 289
    n.30, 305 n.97, 310 n.24–8
    Fascist policy on 95
    Montessori 32
    physical 102
    reform 184–6
    spending 281 n.15
    spread of 21
    technical 185
    university 185–6, 320 n.20
electric lighting 77
electrical appliances, *see* domestic
    appliances
Elias, Norbert 40, 41, 153
emigration 4, 90–1, 127, 128, *see also*
    immigration; migration
emotional style 276 n.82
employment legislation 24, 53, 96, 97
Engel's Law 27, 141
English goods 63, 66, 107, 117, 304 n.85
'English' Saturday 100
entertainment 21, 34–5, 159–60
    aristocracy 45
    Fascist policy on 98–104
    home 261
    spending on 113, 293 n.24, *see also*
    cinema; music; television; theatre
entrepreneurs 194–7, 218
environmentalism 252–3
Epoca magazine 163
equestrian sports 45–6, 279 n.121
Erba, Carlo 52
Escoffier, George Auguste 278 n.110
espresso coffee machines 207
Esso company 116

Ethiopia 86, 90
ethnic identity 90–1
etiquette 40–1
exports 58, 63, 90, 196

factory outlets 266–7, 330 n.39
families 12–13, 231, 233–4, *236–7*
  nuclear 12, 17, 33, 128, 148
family allowances 97
Fascism 83–121, 85, 105–21, 182, 183
  collective consumption 98–104
  consumption policy 92–8
  economic control policy 119
  'Italianization' campaign 86–90
fashion 204–6, 235, 257–8, 258–9
fashion designers 206, 225, 259, 260, 268
fashion magazines 108
Fellini, Federico, *Amarcord* 116
feminine identity 147
Ferrari, Paolo 153
Fiat company 115, 134, 136, 195
Filippo, Eduardo De 73
First World War (1914–18) 121, 154, 193
fish 5, 6, 15, 63, 117, 202, 214, 249
flaneurs 68
Florence 46, 65, 72, 76, 107, 108, 205, 268
food consumption 85–6, 130, 248–9, 282
  n.4–6
  aristocracy 41–2
  branding 58–64
  children 201
  culture and 10–11, 13, 27, 272 n.18
  eating out 34, 261, *see also* restaurants
    and cafes
  ethnic identity and 90–1
  European comparisons *5–7, 8,* 27–8
  geography 297 n.24
  health and 199
  high fragmentation 203
  innovation 197–204, 247–50
  middle class 26
  peasants 8–11
  personification of 10
  reduced spending on 235
  by rice weeders 286 n.7
  substitutes 221, 286 n.10
food shops 117, 211
footwear 85
fortified wines 64, 158

Fortuny, M. 290 n.45
Forzano, Giovacchino 101
Foucault, Michel 52, 169
France:
  car ownership 115, 133
  cuisine 42, 43
  earnings 127
  social mobility 173, *see also* Paris
Francophile culture 42, 70
Frankfurt School 178, 258
Frazer, J. G. 10, 272 n.16
French Revolution 18
Friedman, Milton 57
fruit *5*, 28, 59, 63, 75, 86, 89, 117, 202,
  203, 213, 214, 235, 249, 314 n.22
functionality 156, 157–8, 260
furniture 31–2, 37, 38, 65, 112, 157,
  158–9, 207–8, 267
Futurists 114, 171

Gabaccia, Donna 91
Galbraith, J. K. 178
Gallavresi, Lady 44
Garbo, Greta 83
Garosci family 217
gas lighting 69
gas supplies 109
Gazzoni, Arturo 108, 292 n.12
GDP (gross domestic product) 85, 95, 96,
  177, 187, 189, 231, 254, 311 n.38, 325
  n.70, 326 n.73
Geertz, C. 222
Gellner, E. 34
gender 145–65, 232, 233
  clothing 257
  computers and 246
  consumer goods and 154
  division of labour 150
  education and 53, 95–6
  employment 23–4, 164
  feminine identity 147
  'Italianization' campaign and 88
  masculine identity 139–40
  middle-class children 32
  supermarkets and 215–16
  time-saving domestic appliances
    and 147
  wrist watches and 154–5
Gentile reform (1923) 95

Gere, Richard 225
Germany 51
    advanced social legislation 50
    car ownership 115, 133
    clubs and associations 98
    Internet use 247
    Nazi 103–4, 291 n.52
    post-war boom 126, 127
    social mobility 173
    supermarkets 210
    televisions 131
Giani, Mario 99
Gini index 234, 320–1 n.24
Ginori, Richard 66
Giorgini, Giovanni Battista 205
Gioia magazine 163
Giolitti era 8, 51, 52, 53, 109, 280 n.12
Giovani magazine 165
glassware 66
gramophones 112, 113
Grand Hotel magazine 163
Grazia, Victoria de 88
Great Depression 119, 120, 210
Gregotti, V. 269
grocers 117, 211, 264
Gronow, J. and Warde, A. 241–2
Gruen, Victor 263–4
Gualino, Riccardo 118
'Guerrilla Stores' 269
Gundle, S. 177, 230

Habermas, J. 34, 80, 169
Halbwachs, Maurice 27
Hall, Stuart 145, 170
handicapped people 187
Hasuike, Makio 208
HDI (Human Development Index) 254,
    326 n.73
health foods 248
health hazards 20
healthcare 51–2, 96, 186–7, 269
holidays and travel 45, 89, 104, 116–17,
    160, 227, 262–3, 294 314 n.37
homes 145–6, 299 n. 46–7
    aristocratic 36–9
    contemporary 259–60
    Fascist regime 106–14
    increased spending on 235
    industrial workers 16–17, 19

middle-class 26–7, 29–33
    noise and 158
    peasant 11–13
hooliganism 168, 169
Horkheimer, M. 178
Horowitz, R. 248
horse racing 45–6, 279 n.121
hospitals 51, 52, 96, 187, 269
hotels 34, 42, 65, 116, 118, 238, 262, 263,
    279 n.110
human capital 48, 53, 84, 185
hygiene 15, 19, 20, 34, 38, 51, 52
    domestic 59, 150, 153, 195, 214, 301
        n.58
    food 203, 213
    personal 114, 153–4, 155, 214
hypermarkets 264, 329 n.32

ice cream 42, 201, 214
IKEA kitchens 261
immigration 136, 170, 221, 240–1
imports 58, 86
industrial districts 244–5
Industrial Revolution 4, 61, 62, 66, 221
industrial workers 14–24, 55
    female 23–4
    free time 21
    house-buying 144
    and peasants 17
    redistributive spending 98
    skilled 20–1
    sociability of 16, 18–19
    spatial mobility 15–16, *see also* working
        class
industrialization 48, 58, 86–7, 94, 128,
    194–5
inequality 8, 35, 232, 233–4, 321 n.24
Inglehart, R. 252, 253
institutions 96–7, 183, 188
Internet 246, 269–70, 332 n.47
ISEW (Index of Sustainable Economic
    Wealth) 254
Italo-Americans 90–1

Jacini, Count Stefano 49, 50, 54–5
Japan, and social mobility 173
jewellery 152, 153
José, Maria 103
Juan Fernandez archipelago 92

jukeboxes 170
juvenile crime 167–9

Kern, S. 99
Kessler twins 172
Keynes, J. M. 57
Keys, Ancel 203
Khrushchev, Nikita 209
kitchens 145–51, 197–9
 'American' 208, 209
 aristocratic 38–9
 contemporary 259–61
 industrial workers 19
 literature 328 n.24
 middle class 108–9, 112
 peasant 12
 plastic in 156
 utensils 12, 199
kitsch 220–1
Klein, N. 253
Koch, Robert 52
Kroes, R. 222
Kuznets, S. 83, 84, 105

Lambrettas 142–3, 167, 196
Lampedusa, Tomasi di, *The Leopard* 45
Lancia, Vincenzo 115
Landowski, E. 259
Lazarsfeld, P. 101
League of Nations 86
leisure time 21, 78, 98–104, 149
Lévi-Strauss, C. 10, 135, 172, 307 n.117
Levine, Judith 253
life expectancy 4, 127, 296 n.9
Life magazine 163
lifestyles 35, 36, 45, 84, 133, 159, 193, 216, 227, 232, 234, 267–8, 319 n.17
lighting 69, 77, 283 n.5
Lindauer, Gottfried 140–1
lingerie 68, 76, 118, 151, 302 n.66
lipstick 152–3
literacy 53, 163, 184
literature 13–14, 45, 169, 219–20, 250–1, 328 n.24
living standards 84, 182, 210
logos 61, 62, 63, 197, 253, 267, *see also* brands
luggage 118
luxury goods 35, 58, 117, 177, 241, 308 n.3

cars 114–15
 democratization of 78–9, 140–2, 152, 266
 shops 73
luxury liners 116
Luzzatto Fegiz, Pierpaolo 193

McCracken, G. 322 n.33
McDonald's 263, 269, 325 n.62, 332 n.46
Maddison, A. 126
Maffei, Countess 37
magazines 158, 161, 162, 163–7, 205
Maione, G. 133–4, 229
maize 5, 11, 14–15, 86, 200
Marcuse, H. 178
margarine 198–9, 202
Marinetti, F. T. 112, 114
market liberalization 125
marketing 57, 61, 71, 147, 152, 191–2, 312 n.2
markets 71–2, 330 n.34
Marshall, Alfred 194
Marshall, Thomas 183–4
Marshall theory 309 n.21
Marx, Karl 25, 56
masculine identity 139–40, 154–5, 298 n.37
Maserati, Alfieri 115
materialism 182, 252
maternity laws 23, 97
Mauss, Marcel 150
meat consumption 9, 10, 13, 14, 130, 202, 203, 213
mechanization 61, 62, 63, 112, 155–7, 157
medical insurance schemes 186–7
medicine 114, 319 n.16
Mediterranean diet 203–4
Mele, Emidio 77
Mengoni, Guiseppe 69, 72
Merlin law (1958) 174
Merloni, Aristide 196, 208
middle class 15, 25–35, 103, 133–4, 148–9, 232
 'anthropological' transformation 178–9
 clothing 28–9
 department stores 77, 78, 120
 expansion 84, 85, 319 n.18
 Fascism 88, 106–14
 homes 29–33

middle class (*cont.*)
    supermarkets 215
    time perception 100
    tourism and travel 116–17
    women 88, 276 n.83
    youth 143, 167
migrants, and consumption 4, 136–40,
        142–5, *see also* emigration;
        immigration
Milan 144, 283–4 n.14
    aristocracy 44
    Beatles in 171
    department stores 3, 70, 75–7
    fashion 206
    fashion designers 268
    illegal habitations 144
    shopping arcades 69–70
    Società Umanitaria 19–20
    traffic 139
milk 130, 202
Miller, M. B. 78
mineral waters 108, 202
mobile phones 247–8
modernity 77–8, 156–7, 179, 213, 218
Molini, Gaetano 44
Monroe, Marilyn 153
Montecatini company 156, 195
Montessori, Maria 32
Montini, Cardinal 138
Monzino brothers 120
morality 33, 80, 168
Moravia, A. 128, 222
mortality rates 4, 127
Moscow 209
Mosse, G. L. 33, 166
motor scooters 142–3, 167, 195–6, 306
        n.112
motorcycles 131, 142–3, 195–6, 207
motorways 115–16
multi-storey flats 17, 19, 144, 151
music 22
    festivals 101
    at home 146, 159, 166, 167, 171
    middle-class 31
    radio 113
    supermarkets 213
    teenage 170–1
Mussolini, Benito 94, 287 n.16
mutual assistance companies 53

Naples 31, 33–4, 43, 52, 77
national insurance 188, 189
nationalism 33, 86, 87–90, 92, 104
Natta, Giulio 156
natural monopolies 109
Nazis 103–4, 291 n.52
Neri Serneri, Simone 252
New Zealand 140
newspapers 161
Nixon, Richard 209
nuclear families 12, 17, 33, 128, 148
Nutella 200
nylon stockings 172

oil crisis 226
old-age pensions 53, 96, 97, 188, 189, 190
oligopoly 56, 64
olive oil 64, 130, 203
Olympic Games 102
OND (National After Work
        Recreation) 99, 100, 101, 104, 113
organic products 243, 248, 323 n.43
ovens 19, 34, 108, 143, 146, 147, 196, 202,
        208, 253, 260, 300 n.56

packaging 59, 62, 63, 64, 197, 201, 202,
        203, 213, 218, 249, 316 n.8
Packard, V. 178
Paris:
    Baudelaire on 67–8
    Bon Marché department store in 70
    fashion houses 204
    Halles covered market in 72
    public hygiene policy 52
    shopping arcades 68–9, *see also* France
Pasolini, Pier Paolo 178–80, 182, 230
pasta 62, 197, 203, 214
Pasteur, Louis 52
paternalism 17
patriotism 25, 33, 34, 37, 43, 44, 54, 87,
        104
Pavesi of Novara 200
Peacock, A. T. and Wiseman, J. 94
peasants:
    diet 203
    food consumption 8–11
    and industrial workers 17
    shelter 11–13
    television 180–1

time perception 100
urban migration of 136–7
Peccei, Aurelio 225
pensions 53, 96, 97, 188, 189, 190
Perfetti brothers 201
perfume 153–4
personal hygiene products 114, 153–4, 155, 214
Perugina products 63
pharmaceutical industries 52
Piedmontese aristocracy 44
'Pinocchio' 13–14
Pirandello, Luigi 74
Pizarro, Francisco 105
plastics 155–7, 195, 207, 247
Polanyi, K. 92
politics and political parties 177, 183, 218, 227, 230
pollution 156, 250–4
Pombeni, Paolo 242
Ponzi, Tom 167
post-materialism 252
posters 137, 193–4, 229–30
    Dudovich 76, 120
    supermarket 215
    youth culture 166
poverty 48–9, 51, 55, 104
power dressing 257, 327 n.12
Praz, Mario 38
preserves 61, 63
pressure cookers 199
price control 121
prices comparison (1861–1985) *110–11*
private and public space 259–63
Procter and Gamble 108, 195
production 56–66, 125, 126, 194–5, 194–7
propaganda 93, 94, 97, 101, 115, 193
prostitution 68, 69, 80, 174, 280 n.9, 287 n.15, 308 n.124, 326 n.2
psychology 193–4
PTB stores 120–1
public consumption 47–55, 92–4, 98–104, 184, 311 n.38, *see also* education; healthcare; welfare state
public opinion polls 168, 214
public sphere 34, 80, 176, 246, 259–63
Pucci, Emilio 205
Puricelli, Piero 115
Pyrex 199

Quant, Mary 172

race 89, 96, 288 n.22
radio 102, 104, 112–13, 114, 146, 159, 161, 162, 194, 231
radiograms 159
railways 116–17, 294 n.37
reading 161
record players 146, 166, 167, 171, 306 n.113
recreation 34, 98–9, 98–104, 100, 159–65, 264
redistributive spending 97–8, 187–9, 280 n.13
redundancy fund scheme 188
refrigerators 146, 147, 149, 151, 196, 202–3, 229
restaurants and cafes 34, 67, 68, 108, 118, 136, 200, 230, 240, 264
Ricardo, D. 56
Rinascente department store chain 119, 120, 193, 207, 217
Risi, Dino 140
Ritzer, G. 246, 263
roads 115–16, 144
Roche, Daniel 135
Rockefeller, Nelson A. 212
Rolex watches 155
Romana Supermarkets 217
Rome 28
    aristocracy 43
    beatniks 171
    department stores 76–7
    fashion houses 205
    illegally built 'townships' 144
    supermarket exhibition 209
Rossi, Alessandro 17

Sahlins, Marshall 256
sales assistants 73, 76, 77, 213
Santato, Arturo and Egidio 167
Sanvitale di Fontanellato, Count 42
Sapienza, Salvatore 20
Sassatelli, Roberta 173
Schama, S. 29–30
Schiapparelli, E. 52
Schivelbusch, W. 69
Schizzerotto, A. 232
Schleifer, R. 257

Schuster, Archbishop of Milan 138
Schwartz Cowan, R. 300 n.56
Second World War (1939–45) 126, 201
self-consumption 58, 61
self-sufficiency 88, 92, 112, 136
Serono, Cesare 52
servants 42, 107, 108, 301 n.58
shirt-making 106
shoemakers 108
shopping 78, 131, 147, 205, 206, 215–16,
    219–20, 265
shopping arcades 68–9
shopping malls 263–4
shops 68–80, 72, 73, *211*
    in age of austerity 226
    anti-consumerists 243–4
    colonial produce 90
    display of merchandize 75–6, 78, 119
    Fascist regime 117–18, 119
    foreign immigrants and 240–1
    interiors 73, 74–5
    license required to start up 119
    non-food 210
    photographs 74–5, 119, *see also*
        department stores; supermarkets
Simmel, G. 68, 257
Sironi, Mario 109
Slow Food movement 249, 325 n.62
SMA supermarkets 217
Smith, A. 56
sociability 16, 18–19, 31, 34, 36–8, 273
    n.37
social change 221, 229
social class 232, 233, 234, 300 n.54
    consumer habits study 27
    consumer spending 133–4
    earnings distribution and 84–5
    Fascist education system 95, 96
    television ownership 159
    time perception 99–100
social mobility 16, 173, 185, 186, 232, 242,
    320 n.21
social rights 183
social security 53, 96, 188
socialism 19, 21, 50, 53, 55, 98
socialization 181, 215, 261
Società Umanitaria 19–20
sociology 172, 220–1, 232, 246
soft drinks 108, 202

Sombart, Werner 25
Spain 92, 105, 128, 246
sparkling wine 64, 202
Spoerri, D. 254
sport 35, 45–6, 98, 102, 113, 294 n.31
sportswear 267
Standa department store chain 120, 217
status/status symbols 21–3, 136–8, 158,
    229, 240
steamship lines 87
student unrest 185
sugar 64, 130, 203
sumptuary laws 28
supermarkets 125, 209–22, 316 n.5, 329
    n.32
Supermarkets Italiani 212–14, 215, 216
sustainability 252–4
Swatch 155

tableware 40, 41, 76, 199
taboos 41, 141, 255
tape recorders 166
tattooing 140–1
taxation 54, 55, 64, 189
technological goods 240, 245–7
technology 85, 104, 105–6, 112–14, 182,
    194–7, 209
Tedlow, Richard 191
teenagers 165–73
Teflon 199
telephones 112, 113, 114, 145, 158, 247–8,
    293 n.24
television 131, 145, 146, 147, 159, 161,
    162, 229, 247
    advertising 194, 318 n.12
    'Americanization' 177
    ethnographic studies 318–19 n.14
    private channels 230–1
    programmes 157–8, 162–3, 180–1
Testi, Armando 193
textiles 87, 107, 118, 157, 172, 204, 205
theatre 45, 79–80, 98, 100–2, 159, 161
Thompson, Edward 18
Thonet, Michael 65
time perception 99–100
tobacco 173–4
tomatoes 8, 11, 61, 63, 91, 130, 197, 202,
    216, 219
Topo Gigio 200

tourism 89, 116–17, *160*, 262–3
toys 33, 76, 166, 267
trade unions 99, 100, 121, 217, 229, 295 n.45
trademarks 61, 118
traffic accidents 293 n.30
transport 109, 113, 114–17, 131, 240, 253, *see also* cars/car industry
travelling salesmen 72–3, 117

Umberto, Prince of Piedmont 103
underwear 68, 76, 118, 151, 302 n.66
unemployment 126
uni-sex clothing 257
Unica 118
Unilever 195
United States of America 200
    after-work recreation 99, 100
    aspirational influence of 148
    car ownership in 115
    chewing gum 201
    consumer revolution 126
    department stores 70
    exhibitions 209, 225
    fast food 263, 269, 325 n.62, 332 n.46
    happiness 128–9
    Italian emigrants in 90–1
    psychology and advertising 193
    shopping malls 265
    social integration through consumption 182
    social mobility 173
    supermarkets 209–10, 212
universities 185–6, 320 n.20
Upim stores 119, 120, 217
urban life 67–8, 77–8, 78, 230
urban waste 250–1, 254, 325 n.70
urbanization 84, 85, 109, 128, 152
Urry, J. 262

vacuum cleaners 131, 150, 253
Valentino 206, 259
Valle, Ondina 102
Valletta, Vittorio 115
Veblen, T. 57, 257
vegetables 86, 130, 202
Verona 119
Versace, Gianni 206, 259
Vespas 142–3, 167, 195–6, 306 n.112

Vigarello, G. 294 n.31
violence 167–8, 169
Volpedo, Pellizza da 50

Wagner, Adolf 94
Wal-Mart 264, 266
Warhol, Andy 174, 218–19
washing machines 131, 146, 147, 149, 151, 229
watches 154–5, 303 n.75
water supplies 109
Watts, R. 219
Weber, M. 25, 56, 252
welfare state 182–90
Wilsdorf, H. 155
wine 59, 64, 130, 173, 202, 307 n.122
wine shops 74
women 80
    cars 138–9
    detergents 195
    emigrants 165
    employment 23–4, 112, 274 n.58
    Fascist policy and 96, 97, 98, 112
    fashion 205–6
    First World War mobilization of 109
    magazines 152
    physical education policy 102
    supermarkets 215–16
    time-saving appliances and 147–51
Woolworth, Frank W. 119
working class 49–50, 58, 119–20, 149, 179, *see also* industrial workers
wrist watches 154–5, 303 n.75

Yoshimoto, B. 328 n.24
young people 165–73, 233–4, 307 n.115
    cars 139
    employment problems 243
    fashion 206
    identity 172
    motor scooters 143
youth movements 33, 95

Zanussi, Lino 196
Zatterin, Ugo 152
Zenith wrist watches 154
Zola, Émile 70
Zoppas, Riccardo 196
Zukin, S. 221, 265